THE OXFORD IBSEN

Volume III

BRAND

PEER GYNT

THE OXFORD
IBSEN
Volume III

BRAND
PEER GYNT

Edited by
JAMES WALTER MCFARLANE

with translations by
JAMES KIRKUP
and
CHRISTOPHER FRY

with the assistance of
JAMES WALTER MCFARLANE *and* JOHAN FILLINGER

London
OXFORD UNIVERSITY PRESS
NEW YORK   TORONTO
1972

Oxford University Press, Ely House, London W. 1

GLASGOW TORONTO MELBOURNE WELLINGTON
CAPE TOWN IBADAN NAIROBI DAR ES SALAAM LUSAKA ADDIS ABABA
DELHI BOMBAY CALCUTTA MADRAS KARACHI LAHORE DACCA
KUALA LUMPUR SINGAPORE HONG KONG TOKYO

ISBN 0 19 211360 7

This edition
© Oxford University Press 1972

Printed in Great Britain by
The Camelot Press Ltd., London and Southampton

CONTENTS

CONTENTS

PREFACE

The translations of *Brand* and *Peer Gynt* in this volume are based on the Norwegian texts as printed in the Centenary Edition (*Hundreårsutgave*, 1928–57), edited by Francis Bull, Halvdan Koht, and Diderik Arup Seip. The translation of the 'epic Brand' was made direct from the manuscript in the Royal Library, Copenhagen (Ny. kgl. Samling, no. 2869,1,4°), with the additional assistance of Karl Larsen, *Henrik Ibsens episke Brand* (Copenhagen and Christiania, 1907). The draft material for *Brand* and *Peer Gynt* was edited and translated from manuscripts at present in the University Library, Oslo (UB.Ms. 1940, 8°: fragment of a scenario of *Peer Gynt*) and in the Royal Library, Copenhagen (Collinske Saml. no. 262,4°: complete draft of *Brand*; Ny. kgl. Saml. no. 2869,2,4°: complete draft of *Peer Gynt*), and from photocopies of them. A very considerable debt of gratitude is owing to the Librarians and the staffs of these two libraries in particular for their ready and expert assistance. None of this draft material of the dramas proper has been available in English before.

The division of responsibility in this volume is as follows: James Kirkup collaborated with James McFarlane to produce a translation of *Brand* based on a literal translation by the latter; Christopher Fry based his English version of *Peer Gynt* on a literal translation by Johan Fillinger; James McFarlane translated the 'epic Brand', wrote the Introduction and the Appendices, and took overall editorial responsibility.

Sincere thanks are due to Miss Ena Sheen and the Editorial Department of the Oxford University Press in London for their expert assistance; to Miss Mary S. Hodgson and the staff of the BBC Written Archives Centre, Caversham Park, for information about BBC productions of the two works; and to Miss Enid Self who typed the final manuscript.

UNIVERSITY OF EAST ANGLIA   J. W. McF.

NORWICH

INTRODUCTION

Brand was many things before it finally received the stamp of drama: a cry of shame; an act of exorcism; an accusation of wrongful inheritance; an admission of guilt and complicity; a call to expiation; a shudder of repudiation; a spasm of disgust.

It began, improbably, as an appeal for urgent sanitary measures: 'I see a corpse,' Ibsen wrote in the very earliest stages of the work's composition, 'monstrous as Ymir's body, lying and spreading its pestilential air over field and fjord, infecting rich man and beggar alike. Wrap the corpse in all the flags of Norway: Help, youth, to sink it deep in the sea!'

It was a cathartic discharge of venom: 'While I was writing *Brand*,' Ibsen reported, 'I had standing on my desk an empty beer glass with a scorpion in it. From time to time the creature became sickly; then I used to throw a piece of soft fruit to it, which it would then furiously attack and empty its poison into; then it grew well again. Is there not something similar to that about us poets?'

It spat in the faces of his countrymen. Writing of the moment of *Brand*'s conception, of those pregnant days when the work began to grow within him 'like a foetus', he declared: 'I was in Berlin when the victory parade took place [in early May 1864 after the Prusso-Danish War], and I saw the mob spit into the mouths of the [Danish] Dybbøl cannon, and it seemed to me a sign of how history will one day spit in the faces of Sweden and Norway for their part in the affair.'

In its origins, *Brand* was above all else an act of repudiation and disavowal, a passionate denial of earlier assumptions and beliefs. Compounded of distaste, guilt, contempt, and frustration, it represented a breakaway from what was now seen as a whole world of false values and spurious ideals. It cut away from the past, away from inauthentic living and writing. For twelve months and more Ibsen strove to give shape to the inchoate amalgam of passions and recognitions and attitudes that now obsessed him. When the solution did eventually present itself, it came swiftly and with all the force of a revelation. It was a day in July 1865, by which time Ibsen had already been struggling with his material for a year. He found himself in Rome on an errand (he wrote to Bjørnson) and he walked into St.

Peter's: 'There, suddenly, the form for what I had to say came to me, forcefully and clearly.' He abandoned the narrative poem on which he had been working and which had caused him increasing torment; the new work grew under his hands as never before. In under four months, and before the end of the year, *Brand*, a dramatic poem in five Acts, was complete.

What he had struggled so long and in vain to communicate, and for which he now suddenly found the appropriate vehicle, was thus a thing of some complexity. The same letter to Bjørnson admitted that whilst the form of the work was new, the 'content and mood' of it had been hanging over him like a nightmare 'since those many unhappy events back home'. Ibsen had sailed from Christiania on 5 April 1864, and arrived in Copenhagen the following day. Some time after the middle of April he left Denmark for Italy, just about at the time of the Danish defeat at Dybbøl; he travelled via Lübeck to Berlin, where on 4 May he witnessed the Prussian victory parades. He was seized with anger and shame—shame not only at the betrayal by the Norwegians and Swedes of their Danish brothers, but also at the cowardly blow which was thereby dealt to the whole stirring notion of Scandinavian solidarity which had recently been the subject of so many reverberant speeches, so many high hopes. 'If I had stayed any longer in Berlin,' he later stated, 'where I saw the parades in April, saw the crowds surge round the trophies from Dybbøl, saw them ride on the gun carriages and spit on the cannon—those same cannon which had received no help and which nevertheless kept on firing until they burst—I don't know how I would have kept my reason.'

Closely following these (to him) shattering Berlin events came another experience that moved him almost equally deeply, though it was of a very different kind. Travelling south from Berlin, through Austria, he crossed the Alps into Italy on 9 May. This too was a revelation, an experience that remained vivid in his memory until the end of his life. He drove from the north under the great curtain of cloud and into the tunnel, and emerged at the other end into the gleaming white world of Mira Mora; many years later he recalled 'a feeling of being released from darkness into light, escaping through a tunnel from mists into sunshine'. All the beauty of the South suddenly stood revealed—something which, he himself admitted, left its mark on all his later work. In the months that followed, his letters tell repeatedly of the joy he was taking in his work, the peace of mind which he now found he could bring to his writing. The great monuments of classic and Renaissance art brought delight and insight. The whole spirit of life in this Mediterranean land was different.

The letter to Bjørnson nevertheless does not stop short at the reference to the 'many unhappy events back home'. Ibsen went on to say that he had been impelled by these events also to look deep within his own soul, to look hard and long at many things in the Norwegian way of life that he had earlier simply accepted unthinkingly, and to take stock of life anew. It was therefore only in an immediate and limited sense that *Brand* derived from the public and political events of the day. At a deeper and more significant level, the new work drew on whole areas of his earlier life and career: on his own childhood, and on his relations to parents, brothers and sister; on his earlier authorship, its aims, its purposes, and its disappointing achievements; on the frustrations and humiliations of his professional life in the theatre, 'a daily repeated abortion', he was later to call it; on the realization of his earlier unthinking acceptance of conventional beliefs and current ideas; and on his new and increasing awareness of standards and values fundamentally different from those that served his contemporaries back home. He was moved to contrast the realities of his Italian experience with the defensive fictions of the Norwegian Myth, with the 'life lies'—to use his later term—of Scandinavian national romanticism: those notions, to which he had himself shamefully given currency by his pen, of the decay and effeteness of Mediterranean culture when compared with the gale-swept, invigorating strength of the North. He began to see the crippling provincialism of that way of life which had been his lot for half a lifetime—he was now thirty-six—and which he now recognized as hollow and empty and based on cruel delusion. Now he was in a position to measure the extent of that smug self-deception which sought to sustain local morale by a kind of xenophobic denigration of others. He squirmed when he recalled the active part he had played as a writer in preserving these illusions, in promulgating these lies: notions of Nordic supremacy, of the staunch courage and clear-sighted virtue of this brave little race, of the latent poetic and artistic skills that were supposed to be slumbering in the people, waiting to be roused. He was filled with resentment at the realization that social and cultural forces had somehow manipulated him, had exploited his talents in the interests of a spurious and lying ideal.

The distaste, revulsion even, that he began to feel for much of his own earlier work—things which, with notable exceptions here and there, had in servile fashion propagated the very Myth he was now determined to repudiate—took command. His previous rather solemn dependence on folksy elements, the preoccupation with goblins and trolls and nixies and the fairy folk of mountain and stream, was something he was determined to get away from in this first work of his exile. He relived his earlier exasperation at the public's disapproval of anything that had poked fun at their sacred beliefs—especially he recalled the reception given to *Love's Comedy*, 'a forerunner to *Brand*' as he himself described it. It took little effort to persuade himself that he had left behind a country of big mouths and timid hearts; a people given in their cups to fierce Viking cries but who, when challenged, quickly changed their adopted *persona* to one of 'a little people', wholly absorbed in the daily struggle for existence, ploughing their fields and fishing their Northern seas.

Those passions which the Norwegian defection of 1864 roused in him, deeply felt though they were, were thus important less for their own sake than as a kind of fuse that set off a veritable explosion of thought and feeling in his life. Things he had suffered and proved on his own nerves, things he had himself 'lived through'—a phrase Ibsen was very explicit about to a number of correspondents, as something to be distinguished from his merely having witnessed, or experienced from the outside—now combined to impose upon him a fundamental reappraisal: the social pressures, the cultural impositions, the received ideas, the wishful thinking, the public hypocrisy, the individual self-deception, the false assumptions, the spiritual chauvinism, the empty phrases, the little-Norwegian attitudes, and all the sickening *Hurra-patriotismus* on which he could now look back across the entire length of Europe, all were now distanced, and seen for what they really were.

The immediate consequence of this turmoil of feeling was the astonishing poem 'To my fellows in guilt'. In the most forthright and uncompromising way, it announced that its author was breaking with his own past. In this poem Ibsen declared that he was turning away from earlier sentimentalities, away also from ineffectual dreams of the future, in order to face the realities of the present. It represented both an analysis and a manifesto; and as such it stands as one of the most important programmatic statements about his work and beliefs that Ibsen ever made.

In effect, the poem was a call to Ibsen's fellow countrymen to repudiate the lying pretence that had been infecting all levels of public and private life. The past, he insisted, was dead; the Viking spirit upon which the people so pathetically prided themselves, apostrophizing it at every Independence Day celebration, was no longer a living thing but a rouged and embalmed corpse, pestilential; it spread a plague that sapped the strength and drained the initiative of all men along the length and breadth of the fjords; the ancient grandeur had vanished, and the modern generation was too puny even to attempt to wear the trappings of that earlier heroic age, too feeble to be worthy of the inheritance. (One compares this with the phrases he used when writing to Bjørnson on 16 September 1864: 'We might as well cross out our ancient history; for the Norwegians of the present age obviously have no more to do with their past ages than the Greek pirates have with the race that sailed for Troy and were helped by the gods.' It was clearly a notion that had taken firm root in his mind, for he used it again almost word for word over eighteen months later when writing to John Grieg.) Geography, far from being a beneficent factor and acting—as the Myth claimed—to preserve uncontaminated the pure strain of traditional virtue, was in reality a malevolent force, an inhibition, an obstacle to movement, a barrier to free flight, blocking the sun and making narrow the spirit. The one paramount thing, the poem insists, is to be honest with oneself and to face realities, to explore the mist-ridden world of the present in all its wind and rain and discomfort, with a single mind.

Essentially what this poem bears witness to is a fundamental change in Ibsen's conception of the role of the poet. In his earlier career he had been quick to cast himself for the role of skald in the traditional mould: praising heroism, idealizing events, sustaining morale. Now, he declared, he had sung his last song in his capacity as bard. Now he saw his duty as that of the solitary observer, recognizing the realities of life, taking distant views, getting the perspectives right, showing honesty and courage in putting the truth, however unpalatable it may be. When about this time he was asked, by one who had in fact volunteered for service at the front, why he had not himself enlisted, he answered, 'We poets have other tasks.' The remark should perhaps not be regarded wholly as the defensive reply of one whose conscience on this point was uneasy, for from now on Ibsen's work took on much more clearly the character of a campaign: assaulting errors of thought and conduct, storming the citadels of prejudice, holding high the banner of truth.

'To my fellows in guilt' was eventually incorporated as the first section of that work which has come to be known as the 'epic Brand', the extended but still fragmentary narrative poem that long occupied Ibsen's attention and energies before he finally, in July 1865, threw it over in favour of dramatic form. In its role as prologue to this long narrative poem, 'To my fellows in guilt' warns the reader not to over-look the hidden meaning in what was to follow: 'My lute is tuned to play a muted song; but deeper strings lend colour to the chords. A poem is thus concealed within the poem; and he who fathoms *this* will grasp the song.' Initially, these lines were doubtless meant to alert the reader to the symbolic attack which the poem was to mount on the Norwegian Myth; but other things too came crowding in as the work progressed, and it is rewarding to try to identify the stages in the composition of the 'epic Brand', one by one, in an effort to follow the changing pattern of intent. Each of the successive stages has left a kind of deposit, not only within the poem itself but also, though less distinctly, within the drama that supervened.

Assuming that 'Over the great mountain'—ultimately the third section of the 'epic Brand'—was the part of the work that next occupied Ibsen's attention,[1] the inference seems to be that he was anxious in the early stages to set *en face* two opposing philosophies of life, to permit one spokesman for each to present a case, and for any inherent didacticism to emerge from this confrontation. The two ways of life represented were, as stanza 97 puts it, the way of the pulpit and the way of the palette.

As promised in the introductory section 'To my fellows in guilt', the whole of 'Over the great mountain' is heavily, even portentously, charged with secondary meaning. The initial encounter itself takes place in a markedly symbolic landscape, at the very watershed of Norway's east and west, 'that place on the wasteland's broad breast where, out of the marsh, the river trickles out to east and west', towards the gentle, undulating, sunlit valleys in the one direction, and to the mist-laden, precipitous, rocky steeps in the other. From the sunlit east come Agnes and Einar—actually in the earliest drafts called Dagmar and Axel—to represent the idea of *carpe diem*. Life for them is a game, the play of butterflies; they exist in the present, with no regret for the past, and no care for the future; sorrow is formally outlawed from their union, and they live for art and beauty. Not that 'beauty' was in any sense a merely decorative adornment to life; it was a guiding

[1] The bases for this assumption are argued out in their more technical detail in Appendix I.

principle, a vital force, a power that seemingly had proved itself more efficacious than even the science of medicine itself. Einar, seeking beauty as a painter among the mountains and the moor's pines and the forest rivers, discovered its real power only after he met the ailing Agnes. 'Then he painted his best masterpiece', said the doctor. 'He painted healthy roses on your cheeks; two eyes he painted radiating happiness, and then a smile that laughed its way into the soul. I soon realized that I, your old doctor, was superfluous to such a cure. His songs worked better than any medicines, better even than bathing in God's nature.' Einar and Agnes dance and sing their way towards the west, and their song is like transmuted laughter. By contrast, Brand's song resounds through the hills like a mighty organ in the church of Nature, deafening the river's roar and the thunder of the falls. It halts the happy couple in their tracks by its fearsome power, by the terror of its stern demands. Brand's song is an appeal for pain and suffering and prayer, for strength to resist the temptations of the flesh, for the enrichment of life through sorrow.

As it stands in these drafts, the confrontation is one not so much between personalities as between personifications, between the representatives of two conflicting *Weltanschauungen*: the hedonist and the puritanical, the ecstatic and the ascetic, or (to use Kierkegaardian terms much current in these years when *Brand* was being written) the aesthetic and the ethical. Striking about *this* version is how very much more evenly matched the two are as spokesmen for their ideologies than they are in the final drama. The arguments are more evenly weighted, the eloquence not nearly so one-sided as was to be the case later. In the drama, Einar is crushed and virtually silenced by the vehemence of Brand's outburst; in the narrative poem, although the two lovers are frightened and subdued by Brand's outburst, Einar is nevertheless permitted to score some shrewd points—arguments which were ultimately cut from the drama. How little Brand is capable of grasping the mystery of beauty, Einar accuses: 'Do you think a flower's right to blossom is greater if it holds medicinal properties in its sap or leaf than if it simply has scent and colour? Do you think that a bird should sit silent in the forest unless its song can ease somebody's grief?' In the narrative poem, until Brand shifts his ground and attacks what Einar is actually in no way concerned to represent, the implication is indeed that both views might well claim equal justification, that the palette can surely serve God's ways as properly as the pulpit. Not until Brand directs his strictures away from the purely aesthetic mode of life and on to the hypocrisy that grows out of it—that hypocrisy of big talk and cowardly deed which had figured as the target in 'To my fellows in guilt'—not until then are the two lovers left crushed and the victory in the battle of words goes, rather unfairly, to Brand.

Next in the genesis of the narrative poem seems to have been a decision to try to establish plausible antecedents for the two spokesmen; and things are traced back to the formative influences of their childhood. The two men had already been described as 'a pair of schoolboy friends' who met thus in later life. What Ibsen now apparently did was to develop this notion by introducing into the poem an equally dualistic encounter between the two while they were still boys, an episode in which Agnes too is allowed to appear in a subsidiary role. In the new section, entitled 'From the time of ripening', the treatment was no less heavily symbolic than before. Unexpected, however, is that, in attempting to trace back to childhood experience those attitudes and values that dominated the adult lives of the two spokesmen, the poem becomes boldly and even crudely naturalistic, Darwinian almost, in its simplistic emphasis on the role of heredity and environment.

Once again the leading figures occupy a geographical half-way stage, a ridge in the landscape that offers a vantage point for surveying two ways of life: to the South lie the houses in the sun, the gaily beflagged ships in the bay, the islands in the open fjord; while to the North lies the wilder landlocked country, the dark forests, the inland lakes. Two boys sit in the evening light: one, the Einar of the later episodes, is blond, open-featured and gay, with his gaze (literally) turned to the sunny side of things; the other, Brand, has his back to the sun, and his face turned to the North, looking and yet somehow not seeing, *committed*. He seems 'to look *beyond* what he saw, as though something unseen lay hidden beyond the view'—an oblique invitation to the reader once again to do what the opening section of the poem had enjoined him to do: to look for the hidden meaning, for the poem within the poem. And beyond the two horizons, one to the South and one to the North, lie reminiscences—symbolic reminiscences which pivot about a North–South axis in a way not wholly unexpected in an author who so recently had quit a memory-filled North for the inviting South.

The two narratives, Einar's and Brand's, again pivot about the basic dichotomy. The former's account is of Sunday mornings in summer in his childhood home to the South, an account that stresses all that is colourful, healthful, loving, companionable, and is full of the joy of life; the latter's is of the events of a winter night far to the North, where all is black and frostbound, a tale of sickness and death and bitterness. It is a tale so full of terror, indeed, that the teller of it has to pretend not only that it happened to some third person and not to himself, but also that it happened only in a dream. Mother-love in the one is terrifyingly matched by mother-hate in the other—a duality that Ibsen was eventually to work out in elaborate detail in the dramas of *Brand* and *Peer Gynt*.

Still, as yet, there was in the work no real indication that the centre of interest was eventually to become the figure of Brand; still less any hint that the poem might seek to enlist sympathy or admiration for him. He emerges from this stage of the work as a distinctly repellent figure: twisted in mind, cruel and even sadistic in his responses. The incident where he cruelly beats his dog to death in order to be able to torment his mother by his knowledge of her secret conduct is a peculiarly contrived and grotesque incident. Brand seems at this stage not merely untouched by any kind of loving or humane impulse, but positively evil. Not until the next stage was it that Brand, as a character with individual as distinct from typical characteristics, began to emerge as a central figure. In the first five stanzas of the succeeding section of the 'epic Brand', entitled 'Two on the way to church', there is a new and significant development. (There are, incidentally, also technical reasons—partly to do with the change of name from Koll to Brand, and partly relating to a change in the ink (see p. 430)—why these five stanzas draw attention to themselves.) Up to this stage, the characters in the narrative rather obviously *represented* certain philosophies of life, philosophies which themselves were somewhat crudely delineated. Now, for the first time in the poem, one detects a distinct concern for psychological light and shade.

As Brand now makes his way along the edge of the abyss after parting company from Agnes and Einar, his eye—the poem reports— was turned *inward*; and, matching this, the poem's eye now allows itself to penetrate beneath the surface of outward event to explore the complexities and paradoxes of the individual heart and soul. The poem is not content merely to remark the 'crusading zeal' transfiguring Brand's face; it also reveals his curiously mixed inner feelings, the fact that he 'revelled in the agonized delight which a soul can draw from the word "regret"—poised between embracing and condemning'.

B1

In the earlier draft version, Ibsen made no fewer than four attempts at the last line of this stanza to get it right; and in following the line of 'reported thought'—in which Brand recognized that he had deadened the song of the summer-glad singer by his own words, and had turned the man's eyes from the sun to the ground—the draft originally allowed Brand to admit 'that he had committed evil and craved remorse', before reaching the final formulation that 'he saw what he had done and writhed in his remorse'.

The access to the inner thoughts of Brand which the poem now permitted itself was not only new; it was also symptomatic of the shift of focus away from a simple clash of ideologies, aesthetic and ethical, and towards a livelier interest in the character and fate of Brand himself. Brand now becomes a more complex creature than he was earlier when cast for the role of 'scourge of the world' taking a simple pleasure in chastisement; and it marks an intermediate stage in the development of Brand towards what the next section defines him as: 'the midwife of the age'.

From now on, Brand's inner reactions to things are given more precise attention: the sight and memory of familiar scenes, the recollection of the boy who amputated his finger, the spectacle of the village congregation on its way to church, the encounter with the gypsy girl. He is assailed by memories from the past, by 'the terror of home', as a consequence of which he feels his strength shrink and his determination weaken. His thoughts, 'half spoken aloud', reveal his contempt for the hypocrisies of Independence Day oratory. The train of his thought as he observes the people making their way to church is essentially an inner monologue, though convention allows the explanation that 'compulsively, the words come in a low voice from his breast'. His anguished self-questioning is opened up to the reader. His encounter with the gypsy girl brings long-forgotten things once more to the surface of his mind, where they too are laid bare for inspection: 'A name flashed like flickering lightning through the night of his memories, coming and going, hissing and beckoning. . . . Gradually its features grew familiar. . . . He remembered a remote valley. . . .'

By stages the whole section builds up to an *argued* inner conflict (stanzas 185–189): his deeper desires, his memories, his instinctive reactions, his inner visions, his fears, all announce themselves, until finally the three things that clearly disturb him and threaten to deflect him from his high mission of redeeming the whole world are enumerated: 'What concern to him was that churchgoer up in the snows? Or those two who chose the way to church through joy? Or the crowd that crept along the deep and narrow valley? *He* was to cure the whole world's pain! *His* voice was to ring out for all.' Three menacing distractions: the Ice Church and all it stood for, its natural grandeur, its severe demands, its bleak immunity against the impious work of little men; aestheticism, with its attendant meekness and humility, its love and its charity, its search for God through joy and the pursuit of beauty; and the dumb appeal of those helplessly weak mortals creeping to church, deprived of spiritual leadership, dependent (it seemed) on somebody like himself with his strength of will and forceful personality if ever they were to be helped to salvation.

With this, the central conflicts of the work moved to a different plane. Externalized ideological clash was superseded by inner psychological and moral tension; things outgrew their earlier declamatory stage and became problematical. The focus and the grouping of figures within the composition underwent alteration: Brand was moved much nearer the forefront of things, and grew bigger—almost as though the author had heeded the words he gave to Agnes: 'But did you see how, as he spoke, he grew?' And to accommodate Brand, and to admit those new elements which, by their relationship to him, were to reveal his true dimensions, the others—Einar and Agnes—were set further back. Brand began to dominate the work as never before.

Declamation—even the murmured declamation of inner brooding —proved to be increasingly inadequate to the changed circumstances of the work as Ibsen tried vainly to make progress with the final section 'By the church'. Here at last Brand literally does mount the pulpit. But words, oratory, *declaimed* character no longer served for what the work had become. It had moved too far in the direction of drama; it required not rhetoric, but action. The sermon which Brand begins in the poem was seemingly never completed. Four stanzas were enough to persuade Ibsen that the material was beginning to burst the limitations of the epic form. He recognized that the new patterns of conflict within it craved dramatic treatment—not theatrical treatment, necessarily, but a form that would accommodate the developing range of relationships he now found himself faced with. It is possible—though the evidence is scant—that Ibsen at one point might have contemplated a more ritualized and rhetorical mode of drama than the form he eventually adopted. One surviving scrap of dialogue (see p. 433) contains lines which, as drafted, might have been meant to be spoken

by detached, even unnamed, observers, by some chorus-like figures
standing outside the drama's world of space and time. But nothing
else seems to have survived to sustain the notion that this ever got
beyond a passing idea; and no trace of this has persisted in the final
form of the drama.

The moment in the narrative poem, therefore, when Brand feels a
'crusading zeal', when a hot tear burns on his cheek, when he opens
wide his arms and calls out Einar's name as though in dread, when he
finds himself poised between embracing and condemning and discovers
the sweet anguish of remorse—this moment not only marks a new
departure in the total conception of Brand, but also anticipates the
final shattering moments of the drama that was still to be written.
'What is this?' Gerd asks him in those tense moments before the
avalanche descends. 'You are weeping . . . weeping hot tears that turn
to smoke upon your cheeks. . . . Man, why have you never wept
before?' The strict answer was that he *had*, but not as the Brand of the
drama; and the drama itself is open to definition as an exploration in
depth and in detail of those factors that eventually brought a man like
Brand to the point of tears.

These same lines in the narrative poem also contain other phrases
that find a different echo elsewhere—an echo no less significant in its
own way than the other. The parallel this time is with Ibsen's own
phrases when, in a letter to Bjørnson of 4 March 1866, he recalled the
zest he had brought to his work on *Brand*: 'Last summer, when I was
writing my work, I was so indescribably happy despite all the shortages
and difficulties; I felt within me a crusading joy, and I cannot think
what I wouldn't have had the courage to attack.' The terms he uses
here of himself—'Korstogsjubel' and 'lykkelig'—are immediately
reminiscent of the 'Korsdragerlykke' he ascribes in the narrative poem
to Brand, and betray the growing identity of purpose that began to
emerge between Brand and his creator. The tight-lipped and cruel
attitude to life of the earliest Brand, with his warped mind and dis-
believing refusal to admit warmth and love and companionship as
things with any real part in life, now for the first time showed an
unexpected vulnerability to feeling. Conscience now became a factor;
and the earlier starkly drawn and even rather grotesque figure of hate
and cruelty and vindictiveness acquired more humane dimensions.
'Brand is myself in my best moments', Ibsen later admitted. It is not
the kind of remark he would have readily made if Brand had remained

as he was in 'From the time of ripening', or even in 'Over the great mountain'.

This crusading zeal is intimately linked with what they both, creator and created, spoke of as their 'call' or 'mission'; for both Brand and Ibsen were greatly conscious of possessing one. In the narrative poem, Brand's 'call' is still uncertain, and Einar recognizes here a chink into which he drives one of his more wounding arguments; whereupon Brand is forced to admit to some degree of uncertainty in his 'call': 'Like the moon it waxes and wanes; I rise and fall like a ship at sea.' By contrast, the Brand of the drama shows inflexible confidence in his 'call' from the very first moments. This confidence, this unshakeable conviction, is matched in the phrases Ibsen himself used in his grant application to the King of 15 April 1866, not long after completing *Brand*, in which he wrote: 'I am not seeking to claim any kind of carefree existence; I am battling for the mission which I implicitly believe in and know that God has placed upon me—the mission which is for me the most important and the most necessary in Norway: that of rousing the people and getting them to think big.' Brand's mission was Ibsen's mission at one remove.

The chronology of events is nevertheless important. From Ibsen's own account, it was seemingly in July 1865 that he finally found the form that would allow him to say 'what he had to say'—fifteen months after leaving Norway, and about a year after first starting work on the narrative poem. The question that immediately obtrudes is whether 'what he had to say' had altered very much in the meantime. If one takes 'To my fellows in guilt', presumably written not later than the summer of 1864, as the programmatic statement it obviously was, one needs to ask how far it was still a valid programme for 1865. To what extent, if any, had the emotional and intellectual 'mix' of his mind undergone change? The evidence is necessarily indirect, and the arguments speculative.

In the first place, it is clear from his correspondence and from the testimony of friends who shared his company in these months that his feeling of revulsion for the life he had put behind him remained undiminished, though perhaps as time passed it lost something of its original rawness. His disgust with the more official sides of life in Norway, with state and local politics, with organized religion, with the empty public phrases; and his impatience with the supine acceptance of these conditions of life, the pusillanimity, the pretence and the hypocrisy—these things persisted, as the finished *Brand* bears witness.

Secondly, the impact of Mediterranean culture had gone even deeper in the months following those earliest impressions, had permeated the very fibres of his thought, and left an enduring mark on both his ideas and his authorship. The astounding experience of classical art and of ancient monuments, the growing familiarity with the works of the Renaissance artists, and—finally, mysteriously, overwhelmingly —the towering achievement of St. Peter's itself gave new dimensions to his work, encouraged him to a sublimer rhetoric, to contemplate the grander emotions, to venture a bolder symbolism. Along with this, and despite his very real economic worries, his life in Italy gave him new confidence in his powers as a writer, and he exulted in his new-found freedom. No longer the drudge of a bankrupt theatre, no longer the servant of a despised and dispirited society, he was a free agent under an open sky, answerable only to his artistic conscience. His vision grew clearer, his horizons wider, his powers suppler.

Thirdly, Ibsen's righteous indignation came in time to be tempered by a somewhat uneasy conscience. Though he had known anger and shame at the events of early 1864, he came to realize that he had in effect turned his back on the situation, had run away from his obligations. In Italy he found himself very much in the company of the close relatives of Christopher Bruun—his anxious mother, his sister and brother. Bruun himself was at the battlefront, having volunteered for military service. Later they were all joined in Italy by Bruun himself, a one-time theological student and an impressively dedicated and single-minded young man. Though quick to deride others' inaction, Ibsen himself was doubtless uneasily conscious of having himself *done* nothing. All he could bring himself to do—for he made no secret of the fact, either to himself or others, that when it came to physical confrontation he was not the most courageous of men—was to try his best with words. But from its initially rather obvious purpose as a vehicle of denunciation and reproach, *Brand* more and more became the means whereby its author wrote himself free of a condition of life in which not only public anger and shame were prominent, but private defensiveness and an uneasy conscience also played their parts. *Brand* 'developed in its day as the result of something lived through—not merely observed', Ibsen wrote to a correspondent some four years after the publication of the book. 'It was imperative for me to free myself in the form of literature of something which, inwardly, I was finished with; and when by this means I had rid myself of it, my book no longer had any interest for me. . . .'

Finally, and growing out of all this, there was the fascination which the whole personality of Christopher Bruun began to exert on Ibsen. One feels no sense of surprise that a dramatist like Ibsen would soon cease to find artistic nourishment in the merely symbolic clash of ideologies which the earlier forms of *Brand* represent; and that he would seize avidly on the rich potential of this model, on its human fascinations, on its psychological complexities. The emergence of Brand as the dominant figure of the work seems to have kept pace with the growth of Ibsen's admiration for the person of Christopher Bruun. That this admiration was grudging, or at least qualified, merely served to enhance the fascination. Brand began to take form as a dedicated but essentially *driven* man, a fanatic whose spirit is endlessly willing, but whose flesh—though in no sense weak—is only finitely strong, only limitedly capable of meeting the demands of his relentless will; whose determination is greater than his physical or mental powers, and who—to use the awkward but expressive literal translation of the original terse Norwegian phrase—*wills* more than he *can*.

Brand, as a character, therefore came to serve a double purpose for Ibsen. On the one hand he made a splendid instrument with which to castigate Ibsen's contemporaries and compatriots—obliquely now, and through the mouth of an invented character, rather than directly and in hortatory fashion as in the epic. But also, and more importantly, Brand offered a further and absorbing opportunity to explore that theme which had obsessed Ibsen ever since the days of his earliest drama *Catiline*: 'the clash of ability and aspiration, of will and possibility, at once the tragedy and the comedy of mankind and of the individual' (Preface to the Second Edition of *Catiline*, 1875).

Some of the targets Ibsen selected for attention in the drama— particularly the more public figures like the Dean, the Mayor, the Schoolmaster and the Sexton—were in the event so heavily and so devastatingly satirized that it really did not require the invention of a Brand for denunciation to work. They condemn themselves out of their own mouths; they act as agents for their own contemptibility. Brand's role in his relations with *them* is very largely limited to that of *agent provocateur*; though, admittedly, when these pillars of society are in the end allowed to enjoy a popular victory over Brand, the satire ceases to be merely bitter and becomes bloody. By contrast, the condemnation of society as represented by the Peasant, by Einar, and by Brand's Mother required a Brand if it was to be mounted effectively. Only when judged by the stern principles, the palpable courage, the unyielding standards, the flint-hard integrity of a Brand is their conduct judged deficient. Essentially, their culpability in Brand's eyes lies in their readiness to come to terms with life, to haggle, to adjust, to compromise. Brand's Mother, in the event, is prepared to go not half but fully nine-tenths of the way to meet Brand's demands; and the Doctor, speaking with the sturdy common sense and realism that members of the medical profession are so often ready to display in Ibsen's dramas, urges that for all practical living and in the name of common humanity this is surely sufficient. Even the Peasant is censured in Brand's terms not because of any real vice of which he might be held guilty—to be so positive would in Brand's view almost redeem him—but because he is merely partial even in his virtues, 'a vulgar fraction of evil, a fragment of good'. (In parentheses, it is noteworthy that whereas the English phrase 'the spirit of compromise' has a sufficiently obvious pejorative overtone to make it a not unnatural target for attack by a much less single-minded reformer than Brand, the Norwegian phrase 'Akkordens Aand' [lit. the spirit of accord] tends to emphasize even more the stern rigour of Brand's own criteria.)

Nature also brings her own peculiar and symbolic reinforcement to the drama's general sense of hostility. She is here almost entirely stripped of those blander and more reassuring features that character-ized the Norwegian landscape of national romanticism: the rippling streams, the nestling valleys, the protective hills, the magnificent peaks, those custodians of art and virtue and of a proud way of life which had with Nature's help remained inviolate for centuries. Even in the 'epic Brand' a sense of the sunnier, kindlier, gentler aspects of the landscape 'to the east' had been allowed to coexist on almost equal terms with the awesome landscape of the west. Now, in the drama of *Brand*, there is but a momentary glimpse of the sunlit heather that had served as the setting for the butterfly game of Agnes and Einar, and even that ends abruptly and terrifyingly on the edge of the abyss. From the opening moments, Nature in *Brand* reveals itself as a menac-ing, hostile force: storm and gale and brittle ice, and precipitous steeps. Her elements whip the fjord to a fury where few men dare venture; she severs the land routes, and cuts off men from help even in the extremities of their distress. The valleys seem to have grown narrower than they were before. 'It all seems to look greyer now,' Brand comments, 'and smaller; the mountain's suspended avalanche of snow hangs over . . . and has narrowed even more the valley's narrow sky. How it glowers, threatens, overshadows, robbing us of the light of the sun.' The sunlessness and the freezing cold bring sickness and death; the mountains and the sea fill the churchyard with the bodies of men who have died a violent death. The repudiation of Romanticism's Nature is abrupt and vehement.

What life as lived by Brandian principles is like—in terms of sacrifice, dedication, and the cost in human happiness—is movingly told by the history of Brand's marriage to Agnes: the loss of their child; her anguish, intensified as it is by Brand's harsh imperatives; and her own eventual death. After the initial sense of terror and compassion, however, the spectator is left with two rather more enduring recognitions: that no obvious positive achievements, certainly no lasting satisfactions, seem to follow this regime; and that, paradoxically, Brand's is in a most important sense an easy road to follow. There is no difficulty about knowing the path; only the *going* is hard. He stands not so much for a way of life as a code of conduct —a code, indeed, of easy three-word brevity: 'All or Nothing.' The difficulties and anxieties of this mode of life lie not in the usual anguish of deciding what to do for the best, not in resolving a series of difficult alternatives, but simply in doing as one's code requires. Life is lived by a single, portable yardstick which is offered up to all life's problems and a decision read off. The pain lies all in the doing, not in the deciding. The degree of self-discipline required is formidable, but the instructions are always clear; one commandment is universally applicable, eternally valid. It is a categorical imperative without feedback; the inner voice speaks, but with a one-track insistence. There is no dialogue within the soul, only endless reaffirmation of the sovereignty of the code. Brand's mind is shut, or it at least derives such strength as it has from being shut. (The one mind more tightly and more terrifyingly closed than Brand's is that of Einar on his last appearance, where the extremity of his bigotry and his 'holier than thou' attitude parody the denunciation he himself suffered earlier at the hands of Brand.) Those moments when Brand's mind seems open to alternative instructions are for him moments of weakness. Right and wrong are curiously matters of quantitative not qualitative concern: all or nothing.

Although the admiration Ibsen felt for his character was real, it was —as was said above—also qualified. As a scourge, as an instrument of correction, as a crusading force Brand might well be necessary in what Ibsen was at pains to demonstrate was an imperfect world; yet the drama also seems to imply that his view of life was flawed by a fatal deficiency. This aspect of Brand Ibsen explores in that other series of encounters within the work: those with Gerd—encounters which are of a very different order from, for example, those with the Dean, with Brand's Mother, with the Peasant and the rest, and which make their eloquent point in a different and almost metaphysical way. Brand meets her on a number of different occasions within the drama, in Acts I, III, and V; and the *spiritual* distance he moves, the extent of the shift of sensibility which he undergoes, is well measured by the first and last of these encounters. Initially, Gerd is in Brand's view merely mad, with her prattle of the Hawk and the Ice-Church; and he marks her down—or, at least, what she stands for—as something to be combated. As he prepares to descend into the valley, he identifies three targets, three states of mind which he feels he must vanquish if he is to fulfil his mission: one is the frivolity of mind [*lettsind*] represented by Einar; the second is the dullness of mind [*slappsind*] represented by the Peasant; and the third is the madness of mind [*vildsind*] represented by Gerd. To-gether they constitute the 'triple threat' against which he must do battle:

> I now behold the nature of my mission on earth!
> The downfall and death of those three demons
> Would cure this world of all its sickness.

At this point, Brand distinguishes no real difference in kind among these three phenomena; indeed, the terminological similarity em-phasizes the identity they share, and their comparability. They invite a common hostility.

By the end of the play, two things of deep significance have occurred. On the one hand, Gerd's utterances which Brand once thought merely mad he now recognizes as visionary; *she* recognized, long before it occurred to any of the others to comment on it, the meanness and ugliness of the man-built church, of the established and official religion; she was the first to point out, *à propos* of Alf, the element of idolatry in the worship of the Child. Like Ellida Wangel of a later play, she thinks in images; and Brand himself comes in time to see that rational discourse is not the only nor even necessarily the best path to truth. What Agnes calls 'knowing without knowledge', and what Brand acknowledges as the 'vision in the dreams people dream' sometimes lead straighter to the heart of things than the way of reason and common sense.

The other thing is that Brand, at the end of his career and without willing it or having consciousness of it, finds himself in the Ice Church —that which he had earlier dismissed as the ravings of a deranged mind. Insistently, in those final moments, Gerd asks him: 'Do you know where you are standing now?' And as the mists lift, and Brand realizes where he is, she underlines the significance of it all: 'So you came to *my* church after all.' Such is the outward index of the deeper insight that Brand finally works his way towards, and which informs the closing moments of his life: the ultimate realization that his 'All' had been a deficiently quantitative thing, a thing of common sense and commonplace dimensions. The 'All' that he had demanded of his mother was something that could be counted and assessed; even the 'All' that he demanded of his fellows—that of total self-sacrifice, of the commitment of one's very life—was something terminable and finite. It is only when Brand, after having committed his 'All'—his wife, his child, his career, his happiness, his material and spiritual well-being—to the symbolic project of rebuilding the village church, is left deeply dissatisfied, that doubts about the 'All' of his code, as he has hitherto understood it, begin to assail him. There stood the church, splendidly rebuilt; and all Brand's resources, human, spiritual, and material, had gone into the rebuilding. Yet the result was mean, the organ discordant; and it seemed to him that the Lord himself was greatly displeased. He begins dimly to see on the one hand that 'All' was not an absolute but a disturbingly relative thing; he recalls that Agnes, if she had lived, would have discovered the great in the small, for she 'could marry earth and heaven . . . as a tree roofs itself in its own leaves'; and he begins to sense that the infiniteness of this 'All' was somehow independent of scale, and realizable in both the large and the small, the familiar and the remote. Only now he sees how wrong he was to suppose that 'All' could be achieved by crying 'Double it . . . that will do! Five times greater . . . surely that will do!' He sees that man must strive for a 'greatness' that cannot be measured in conventional units, but which instead 'beckons towards the realms of dreams and wonders, and towers over us like heaven ablaze with stars'. The 'All' that he has sacrificed has been in vain; the result has been no more than one monstrous compromise with dogma and narrow faith. Now he announces:

> The church is infinite and without end.
> Its floor is the green earth—
> Mountain, meadow, sea and fjord;
> The Heavens alone are vast enough
> To span its great and vaulted roof.
> There you shall live your active faith. . . .

He urges the people up and into the high mountains, the frozen wasteland, to the cleaner air, there to set up God's image anew in *life*'s great church. Unconsciously he is echoing Gerd's words to him on their first encounter when she speaks of *her* church of ice and snow, a *real* church where the wind prays from the glacier cliff, and mass is sung by avalanche and waterfall.

So that when, stoned and abandoned by the people, torn and bleeding, tormented in spirit, Brand is brought to the realization that, without knowing it, he has made his way to the Ice Church, he knows too that his Will has driven him to the limits of endurance, to the frontiers of madness. He occupies the same territory, is a worshipper in the same church, as Gerd, the wild-eyed, visionary girl. Her vision of him is of Christ the Saviour, with the blood on his brow from the crown of thorns, the wounds in his hands from the nails. He too knows a kind of self-identification with Christ, and his vision of the Tempter in the Wilderness is transposed by his tormented mind into a very Brandian nightmare. His quest to relate the code of 'All or Nothing' to his own life has brought him in the end to breaking point, that point which must inevitably mark the end of the road for any man 'who *wills* more than he *can*'. Cumulatively, the experiences of grief, death, isolation, rejection, and failure have left him unable to go on. The full implication of Gerd's 'So you came to *my* church after all' is the final stroke. He breaks: he gives way to tears; he is brought to his knees; and he yields to the desire for 'light and sun and gentleness, for tender and serene calm, for the summer kingdoms of this life'. Hot tears melt the frozen grandeur of his will, the icy hold of his resolve; and, like an avalanche released by sudden thaw, his life crumbles and comes roaring down about him.

The essential complementarity of *Brand* and *Peer Gynt* is something which criticism, taking its cue directly from Ibsen himself, has been tirelessly concerned to assert. It has served as a starting point for commentators as far apart in time and attitude as Arne Garborg—who in 1876 called *Peer Gynt* the 'correlating caricature' of *Brand*—and W. H. Auden, who in 1963 related the two dramas through their main characters in the ratio 'apostle and genius'. As succinct a statement as any of this complementarity was given by Philip Wicksteed in his lectures of the early 1890s:

In *Brand* the hero is an embodied protest against the poverty of spirit and half heartedness that Ibsen rebelled against in his countrymen. In *Peer Gynt* the hero is himself the embodiment of that spirit. In *Brand* the fundamental antithesis, upon which, as its central theme, the drama is constructed, is the contrast between the spirit of compromise on the one hand, and the motto 'everything or nothing' on the other. And *Peer Gynt* is the very incarnation of a compromising dread of decisive committal to any one cause. In *Brand* the problem of self-realization and the relation of the individual to his surroundings is obscurely struggling for recognition, and in *Peer Gynt* it becomes the formal theme upon which all the fantastic variations of the drama are built up.

'*Brand* is *Peer Gynt*'s "modsætning",' Ibsen declared flatly in a letter to Edmund Gosse in 1872, balancing the peremptoriness of the statement with a fair measure of ambiguity in the crucial term: 'opposite', 'counterpart', 'contrary', 'antithesis' are all terms that might make claim to be the most appropriate translation in this context.

Clearly, circumstances imposed on the two works a relationship of special intimacy. They belong to the same brief and critical period of residence in Italy, and were published in successive years. They grew out of a shared locale, a common *raptus*, something the importance of which Ibsen himself emphasized when, in speculating on the way a locality influences the forms within which the imagination creates, he asked: 'Can I not . . . point to *Brand* and *Peer Gynt* and say "Look, that was when intoxicated with wine"?' and in so doing contrasted them with the beery plays that followed when he moved to Germany. On their title pages, they are both designated 'A dramatic poem', a description not given to any other of Ibsen's plays. They are moreover the only 'dramatic' works of his which were not composed for the stage. And together they mark the last use by Ibsen of verse as a medium of dramatic expression. On a number of occasions in later life, Ibsen used phrases that emphasized or admitted the close relationship that these works enjoyed. 'Brand is myself in my best moments,' he once confessed, 'just as I have also, by self-dissection, brought out many features in both Peer Gynt and Steensgaard.' And he went on to add that 'after *Brand*, *Peer Gynt* followed as it were of its own accord'. Towards the end of his life, Ibsen returned to this same point in conversation with William Archer, who reported: 'He wrote *Brand* and *Peer Gynt* (which appeared with only a year's interval between them) at very high pressure, amounting to nervous overstrain. He would go on writing verses all the time, even when asleep or half awake. He thought them capital for the moment; but they were the veriest nonsense. Once or twice he was so impressed with their merit that he rose in his nightshirt to write them down; but they were never of the slightest use.' Ibsen also apparently admitted on this same occasion that 'it was much easier to write a piece like *Brand* or *Peer Gynt*, in which you can bring in a little of everything, than to carry through a severely logical scheme like that of *John Gabriel Borkman*'.

That the two works enjoy a close and distinctive relationship, that they were the result of a largely (but not necessarily completely) homogeneous set of assumptions and attitudes, is therefore a common-place of literary criticism. In itself, however, it is an observation that probably raises more problems than it resolves, and more often than not leaves unexamined the crucial problem of *how* they relate.

Criticism has occasionally found it helpful to think of *Brand* and *Peer Gynt* as two sides of the same coin, for example, or as the positive and the negative of the same exposure. Pondering Ibsen's admission that *both* characters were in their own special way self-portraits, one is reminded of the words of the Thin Man to Peer in the final act of the drama:

> Don't forget there are two ways of being yourself. . . .
> You can either show the straightforward picture
> Or else what is called the negative.
> In the latter light and shade are reversed;
> To the unaccustomed eye it seems ugly;
> But the likeness is in that, too, all the same;
> It only needs to be brought out.

The unbending, uncompromising, sternly self-disciplined Brand is succeeded by the compliant, opportunistic, and self-indulgent Peer; dedication to the principle of 'All or Nothing' yields to the easy evasions of 'To thine own self be—sufficient'. Whereas Peer lives his entire life by illusions, Brand finds fulfilment precisely in destroying them. Where Brand speaks in the commanding tones of a genuine prophet, Peer has the plausible tongue of the spurious one: 'Answering prophetwise', he reassures himself in the scene with Anitra, 'isn't really lying.' Where the call of duty binds Brand ever more firmly to the village community despite the urge that he feels to reach a wider world, Peer's abandonment of his responsibilities—even, in the end, that of burying his dead mother—takes him to all manner of foreign parts; in a spatial and dynamic sense, *Brand* is thus centripetal, *Peer Gynt* centrifugal. And where Brand for ever, even under the descending avalanche, keeps a hard nucleus of his faith in the Will intact though the outer shell has cracked, Peer Gynt—as his own surprised reflections reveal to him—is onion-like, soft-layered, and with nothing at the centre. Brand's life is a rigorously planned economy; Peer's is *laissez-faire* and private enterprise.

But these recognitions should not be allowed to distract from the fact that there were many things about *Peer Gynt* that betokened a positive reversion to Ibsen's earlier practices, and a partial abandonment of some of those more radical notions to which he had given free rein in *Brand*. And one is reminded of the assurance Ibsen gave to his publisher even as he was writing it: 'It will show no resemblance to *Brand*, and is without direct polemics.' It was, for example—despite the bold declarations of 'To my fellows in guilt' of the previous year —not nearly so challengingly contemporary in theme or setting, and not nearly so audacious in its realism, as his declared programme would have led one to expect. Indeed, had Ibsen followed his first inclinations after completing *Brand*, he would apparently have written an out-and-out historical play 'set in the time of Christian IV', as he at first described it to his publisher. Furthermore, there were moments during this year when he was strongly drawn to the theme of Julian the Apostate (which, of course, eventually had its turn in the early seventies); and this would have taken him still deeper into the past and still further away from the contemporary scene. Even when the decision was taken for *Peer Gynt*, its original setting in time took it out of the contemporary world and pushed it half a century and more into the past; only later did Ibsen relent and allow the final scenes of the drama to 'end close to the present day'.

The suspicion is born that, with *Brand* completed, Ibsen had, like his scorpion, discharged his venom, vented his spleen, and now felt better for it. The tension in *Peer Gynt* is notably relaxed; the pressure of the passions much reduced. True, any detailed annotation of the work discovers assaults on a range of specific and often individually identifiable targets: the satirical trouncing of the language fanatics, for example, which left Ibsen hugely and rather smugly pleased with himself; and his pillorying of Count Manderström, so daringly topical at the time but today worth no more than a scholarly footnote. Even when one turns to the broader, diffuser elements of censure, the effect is uncertain, and the strokes ill-timed. It may well have been that the public's expectations were at fault. Certainly, Ibsen later complained that people found much more satire in the drama than he had intended. The view that Ibsen created Peer with the intention of amalgamating in one character all Brand had repudiated in the Norwegian temperament, making a single compound of the *lettsind*, *slappsind*, and *vildsind*, the frivolity, the apathy, the irresponsibility that Brand dedicates his life to defeating, was widely canvassed, and eagerly—perhaps too eagerly—adopted. Admittedly, an itemized catalogue of Peer's actions would seem in sum to define a most reprehensible villain: violent, self-centred, vicious, envious, irresponsible, cowardly, heartless, murderous. And yet, if it really was the drama's intention to indict Peer, something clearly went wrong; for whilst Brand was unlovable though admirable, Peer Gynt is much more the forgivable rogue than the despicable villain. (Perhaps it was too much to expect that a character so given to 'digtning', to invention, to fabulating, to fantasizing, could for long expect Ibsen's censure.)

The ultimate reduction in importance of the role of Solveig's father within the action also seems to confirm something of the same attitudinal shift. In the earliest stages of the drama, he was a *named* character; subsequently he was reduced to anonymity within the *dramatis personae* as 'a Man newly arrived in the district'. An entire scene in which he was allowed to enunciate a stern philosophy of life, in which he exhorted Peer to deliver himself up to justice and to accept the inevitable seven-year prison sentence in order to settle his account of guilt, was cut out of the play at a relatively advanced stage in its composition. In the same way that any direct and fully argued conflict and confrontation of *Weltanschauungen* had been evaded in *Brand* by modifications to the figure of Einar, so the opposition case against Peer's standards of conduct was largely eliminated from the plan of *Peer Gynt*. It could well be, as Arne Garborg has argued, that Solveig's father was in essence a reincarnation of Brand; if this had ever been the case, he is given no opportunity in the finished *Peer Gynt* to practise his earlier eloquence. Nor, when the targets are the quirks and stupidities of 'national character', is *Peer Gynt* nearly so narrowly focused and exclusively Norwegian as *Brand* is. In the North African scenes, Ibsen extends the satire to embrace also Anglo-Saxon, French, Swedish, and German national weaknesses. All seems to indicate a certain damping down of the emotional savagery with which Ibsen began his exile from Norway, and which marked the earlier months of his residence in Italy. Yet, unexpectedly, the less nationalistic it became, the more national it grew, and the more difficult it became for a non-Norwegian reader to follow. Ibsen's own misgivings on this point found expression in his letter in 1880 to his German translator, in which he stated that, of all his works up to that time, he regarded *Peer Gynt* as the one most difficult to understand outside Scandinavia;

few people, he feared, possessed the familiarity with Norwegian literature, people, habits of thought, national character, and landscape necessary for an appreciation of the drama. This seems to have been a strange compensatory side-effect to accompany the more vehement repudiation of things Norwegian of a few short months previously.

Uniquely useful as a kind of tracer element by which to follow through these shifts of attitude and belief is the incident of the youth and the amputated finger. Four stages (one of which is admittedly a sort of nil return) may be distinguished in the fluctuating shape of the incident, and consequently in the purpose it is in each case asked to serve: first, there is the incident as it is narrated in the 'epic Brand'; second, comes the decision to eliminate it as the 'epic Brand' is transposed into drama; third, there is the incident as Peer witnesses it and reacts to it in Act III of the drama; and fourth, as an unexpected extension, we are given the churchyard comments, a whole generation later, uttered by the Priest over the grave of the man. In the 'epic Brand', the incident was pressed into service as a shameful indictment of the Norwegian people: see how this young man will go to any lengths, the story announces, to avoid doing what ought to be his joyous duty of serving as a soldier in defence of his brother Danes. Ignominiously dismissed by the solemn captain, denounced by the whole community, and red with shame, the youth flees the village community; and the memory of this disgraceful scene confirms Brand in the disgust he feels whenever he hears great empty phrases about 'Viking blood' in the speeches on Independence Day. The incident at this stage is unambiguously a device with which to scourge the Norwegian people for their cowardice in evading their obligations. When it came to embodying it in the drama of *Brand*, however, Ibsen clearly found objections to its use. Doubtless he came to realize with time that there were other dimensions to the story, previously unrecognized, that prevented its being used in the way he had first intended: that, after all, it bore witness to a measure of courage of a different but no less valid kind, which thus destroyed its force as a simple parable of non-courage; that one marvelled strangely at the strength of will and purpose that led to an act of this kind, quite apart from its ultimate motive. Such indeed was to become Peer's immediate reaction to the event.

> What spunk! An irreplaceable finger!
> Right off! And no one making him do it.

When it comes to motive, Peer remembers why this might be: that the boy will by this means avoid being called up to the army. But—and how revealing of the change that had come over Ibsen's attitude to the incident and the significance behind it—he then adds:

> That's it. They were going to send him to war;
> And the boy, not surprisingly, objected.

Between this 'not surprisingly' [lit. 'understandably'] and the simpler patriotics of the 'epic Brand' lies a world of difference.

The final long and quite detailed comment on this incident and its consequences, which is incorporated into the last Act of *Peer Gynt*, then invites a different interpretation, supports a wholly new world of values. The recruiting incident remains much as it was in the 'epic Brand': the Captain still spits and tells the boy to go; the company make the youth run the gauntlet, 'stoning the boy with silent stares'. But this is not the end of things; and time gives a new perspective to the incident. The man in question devotes himself to the ways of peace rather than the violence of war; he is revealed as one who has led a life of meekness, reticence, humility, quiet endeavour, and great though inconspicuous courage. 'Not even an avalanche could crack his courage', the Priest reports admiringly. The larger abstractions—mankind, patriotism—meant little to him; but loyalty to wife and children, to farm and homestead, fill his life with meaning:

> He was a poor patriot. To State
> And Church, an unproductive tree. But there
> On the brow of the hill, within the narrow
> Circle of family, where his work was done,
> There he was great, because he was himself.

This funeral oration is positioned within a series of offset but over-lapping and widening contexts (the fifth Act proper, the drama as a whole, and the collective statement of *Brand* and *Peer Gynt*), and as such it articulates a set of values which contrasts sharply not only with Peer Gynt's but also with Brand's; and it seems to offer evidence of a very considerable semantic shift within the drama as a whole, a shift that eventually left things at a substantial remove from the terminus that was apparently originally intended.

Compared with the hard-edge, blueprint world of Brand, with its severe imperatives, its inflexible compulsions, its frozen and intractable topography, the world which Peer Gynt inhabits is one of daunting fluidity, a fairy-tale world of effortless transformation and of disconcerting transpositions. The journey from reality to fantasy and return, from the substance to the shadow and back again, seems to encounter no obvious frontier, to require no particular formalities. Waking and dreaming interpenetrate in a way that was foreshadowed by those lines in the 'epic Brand' that told of an earlier boy who dreamed: 'The dream bound him to look at himself as the vortex binds one who looks at the stream; and the boy looked at it, and could not break free, and was carried round in circles. . . . He tried to distinguish—but it was hard to tell—what was truth . . . and what was dream. He slept. Then he dreamed he lay awake.' When it comes to Peer, it is true that he sometimes becomes aware of his day-dreaming, and feels the need to admonish himself: 'Lies!' he tells himself as he wields his axe at the start of Act III: 'It isn't a giant in armour; it's a fir-tree with a craggy bark. . . . It will have to stop, this woolgathering. . . .' But at other times, when in this same mood of self-admonition, he also betrays that for him the distinctions are blurred, and that fact and fantasy fuse:

> That ride on the Gjendin ridge,
> Invention [*dikt*, lit. 'poetry'] and damned lies!
> Humping the bride up the steepest
> Rock-face—and drunk all day;
> Pursued by hawks and kites,
> Threatened by trolls and suchlike,
> Racketing with crazy wenches;—
> Lies and damned invention!

The line between Dichtung and Wahrheit, between fiction and fact, disappears in one great and imaginative universe. Fears are reborn as only nightmare can shape them; desires achieved as only dream can fulfil them. The frustrations of one moment become the fulfilments of the next: if the girls at Hægstad coldly spurn him, the girls at the sæter are ardent and willing; ousted and displaced as a suitor *here*, he is welcomed as a potential son-in-law *there*; ostracized by the valley's wedding guests, he is made a great fuss of by the mountain trolls; disbelieved and mocked by the village youths when he brags of his exploits, he finds enthusiastic credence from the Woman in Green, so that together they can agree that 'black can seem white, and the ugly beautiful; big can seem little, and filth seem clean'. As Aase knows full well, Peer is intoxicated by make-believe as other men are drunk with brandy; his is a world in which wishes *are* horses (except when they are pigs!) and beggars *do* ride. North Africa and other exotic places are only a dream away; things—such as the blowing up of the expropriated yacht—*are* no sooner said than done. A fantasy world seems at times to counterfeit a real one, and at others a real one to mint again the fantastical; some characters, like the Dovre-Master and the Woman in Green, appear to live a valid life in both; with others, appearances—but only appearances—change, and the Hægstad wedding guests are recognizable again in the trolls; sometimes it seems, as with the sound of church bells, that reality penetrates fantasy; and at other times, as with the Ugly Child, that fantasy invades reality. Nevertheless, taking the strictest view of the logic of the poem, all these things are merely aspects of a single reality/fantasy continuum, in which fact is a function of fiction, invention a function of experience, and lies and life are one.

The role of Solveig in this world is easily misunderstood. It is often held that she is the one truly stable element in the work, and represents the one genuinely positive virtue: constancy. In a spatial sense, she seems at the end to have remained firm and steadfast, having lived her whole life through in the little forest clearing where Peer and she were to make their home. Admittedly, the drama is not overprovided with positive statements of the kind she is assumed to make. Apart from her father, who is allowed a brief advocacy of confession and expiation as a way of life, and also possibly and in some respects Aase, whose deeper loyalty to her son can always be relied on, Solveig is about the only figure who by her actions seems to embody any positive assertion about life's values. The result has been that critical interpretation has tended to burden Solveig with a weight of symbolic significance too heavy for her slight character to bear; and to ascribe a sentimental solemnity to the final moments that relates uneasily to what has gone before. Solveig is by this token seen to be making an almost Brand-like 'all or nothing' commitment to 'love', as offering a counter-statement to Brand's hostile eloquence on this very theme. When Solveig tells Peer he has made her life 'a cause for singing'—or, as a more literal translation brings out even more clearly, has turned her life into 'a lovely song'—there is an echo of the life that Einar and Agnes lived before Brand came storming into their existence, when life was a song to be sung together. The way she receives Peer after a lifetime's absence seems to suggest that her values are wholly contrary to Peer's: that the great wrong he believes he has done her is in reality a great right, and that the transformation has been achieved by her faith, her love, her hope. This, it is suggested, makes her representative of Woman, of 'das Ewig-Weibliche', an archetypal wife and mother figure finding her fulfilment as the patient custodian of man's real essence, preserving, protecting, enfolding: the ultimate refuge where man at last finds his proper dominion, his redemption, his salvation. To expect, however, that a character so sentimentalized, so bloodless, so stylized in her flaxen-haired doll-like unreality, so *absent* as Solveig is—to expect that she should carry all this ponderous significance is merely grotesque. Nor does the 'message' of her life, positive though it is in the *manner* of its dramatic formulation, carry particularly deep conviction: that Woman's redemptive role (if such *is* her role) is adequately performed by sitting and dreaming and hoping a whole life long, by living on her memories, by cherishing the images of the past.

What Solveig really represents in this last scene is not some objectively ideal embodiment of Redemptive Woman, but the realization of Peer's wish-image of Woman at this moment in his life. What he yearns for, and what his fantasy creates for him (as it had so often before in his life created for him) is an essentially maternal figure, endlessly forgiving, entirely devoted to him, who will soothe his fears and chase the bogeyman Buttonmoulder away, on whose love and protection he can *exclusively* count, whose features are compounded of mother and bride, who can be relied upon to create a cosy intimate world and put his own Self at the centre.

Such is the mother fixation of Peer (as others have noted before) that Solveig at this fateful moment takes on not only the role but also the features of Aase, finally mothering Peer in her lap as he seems almost literally to return to the womb. 'You have mothered that thought of the man yourself', Peer says in the final moments of the drama. 'My mother, my wife, purest of women!' He buries his face in her lap. 'Hide me there, hide me in your heart!' She becomes 'real', is *realized*, only when Peer desires it. He re-creates her for his own comfort; she is as much an escape from the pressing realities of the moment—an old man's realities—as his deathbed ride with Aase had been, and the distorted gratifications of the night with the trolls. Certainly, the Buttonmoulder is not taken in by what goes on. He breaks into Solveig's song to remind Peer that he deceives himself if he thinks this means any real 'escape', and that they will meet at the last crossroads; fantasy may have been Peer's refuge time after time in life, but it is no answer to death. Nor, the Buttonmoulder seems to imply, is redemption all *that* easy.

It is commonly felt that *Brand* and *Peer Gynt* must together in the end add up to some kind of moral declaration. In the case of *Brand*, this has led to a perhaps disproportionate amount of attention being paid to the closing moments; surely there, it is felt, we should be able to find the essential clue that will permit us to judge Brand's conduct correctly, and thus draw the appropriate moral. If the Voice is thought of as uttering a reproach, as insisting on the necessity (repudiated by Brand) of acknowledging the cosmic force of love, then the stress is seen as having been placed on Brand's guilt, and the discovered pattern of the drama is one of crime and punishment, of blasphemy and retribution. If, on the other hand, the Voice seems to say 'And yet . . .', the emphasis seems rather to be on the merciful intervention of an all-loving God at the very crisis of defeat and destruction, thus making of Brand's career a thing of error and forgiveness, of transgression and redemption. Or, by extension, the total meaning is found synthetically in the kind of ambiguity that holds *both* these interpretations in suspense, and like the 'Ist gerichtet . . . ist gerettet' of Goethe's *Faust*, implies both judgement and salvation. Conversely, when it comes to *Peer Gynt*, the tendency is to concentrate on the cataloguing of Peer's more reprehensible qualities—his mendacity, his irresponsibility and lack of control, his self-centred conduct—and then, by giving special scrutiny to those scenes with the Strange Passenger, the Thin Man and the Buttonmoulder, to work out how the drama invites us to shape our moral condemnation. In all these instances, the criteria are Schillerian: Brand is adjudged a great but morally flawed hero, and the drama such that both the admiration we feel for this hero and also the suffering he endures in working out his destiny have a moral basis; whilst Peer Gynt, though Brand's antithesis and essentially an anti-hero, is nevertheless similarly defined in moral terms.

Yet this seems to leave important aspects of the works only partially, or awkwardly, defined. Although remorse leads Brand in the end to revise certain of his basic beliefs, there is in his recantation none of that sublimity, that defiantly glad acceptance of destiny that is the essence of Schillerian tragedy. In Brand's last cry there is a note of puzzlement, of remonstrance, of querulousness even, and he seems to claim that he somehow deserved better. In *Peer Gynt*, on the other hand, the final moments seem to promise the anti-hero a destiny rather better than he deserves. In both instances the outlines become confused and blurred if the works are thought of as being structured pre-eminently to making a moral affirmation.

A much more satisfactory interpretation seems to emerge if one takes one's cue not from Schiller but from Hebbel. Exactly how familiar Ibsen was with Hebbel's ideas on tragedy is not very certain. In the present state of knowledge, little more can be said than that Hebbel's theories were closely followed and discussed in the Denmark of their day; that one of his more important theoretical statements—his *Mein Wort über das Drama* of 1843—grew out of a bitter public exchange which he had in the Copenhagen press with the Danish critic J. L. Heiberg, later director of the Royal Theatre; and that Hermann Hettner's influential monograph *Das moderne Drama*, which Ibsen is believed to have read and studied while on his study tour in Germany in 1852, followed a strongly marked Hebbelian line. How persistent the subsequent discussion of Hebbel's views was in those Scandinavian periodicals known to have belonged to Ibsen's reading in the fifties and sixties is difficult to measure. What can be emphatically said, however, is that Ibsen's dramatic practice as it found expression in *Brand*—and negatively in *Peer Gynt*—strikingly matches Hebbel's theory as he expounded it in the 1840s.

Guilt, both in drama and in what he called the 'life process', was for Hebbel something completely divorced from notions of good or evil, something wholly unconnected with the moral basis of individual action. It derived in his view simply and inevitably and automatically from the exercise of the Will, from the sheer act of self-assertion, from the stubborn, autonomous thrust of the Self ('aus der starren, eigenmächtigen Ausdehnung des Ichs'). For him, as for Brand, it was in large measure a quantitative matter, inseparable from individual action and increasing in direct proportion to the degree of intensity of the individual self-assertion. Guilt, Hebbel insisted, 'does not depend upon the direction of human volition; it is present in all human conduct; and it makes no difference whether we turn towards good or evil, for we may overstep moderation just as much in the one as in the other. It is with this alone that the higher drama is concerned. Not only is it immaterial whether the hero is destroyed in consequence of an admirable or of a reprehensible undertaking, but also—if the most affective result is to be achieved—it is even essential for this to happen as the result of the former and not of the latter.' It was a concept of guilt that made of it an amoral and largely technical thing

—a concept which Hebbel only much later discovered was essentially Hegelian.

This was an essential component in Hebbel's view of the 'life-process', and consequently also in his interpretation of the nature of dramatic conflict. Individual initiative, the vigorous exercise of those qualities that in themselves constitute and define individuality, must (he argued) by the sheer nature of things provoke an imbalance, a disequilibrium within the Whole. The more pronounced the individual talent, the more forceful its expression, the greater the tragic dissonance within the wider scheme of things. There is set in train a lumbering, crushing reaction on the part of the 'Universum'—the totality of the age, the environment, the society, the moral climate within which the individual has his being—as a result of which the individual is inevitably overwhelmed and defeated, having at most achieved some slight displacement within the wider framework of life. There is no doubt that had Hebbel lived only a few years longer, he would have recognized *Brand* as an almost perfect embodiment of his dramatic theory; indeed it is striking that when Hebbel attempted in his diaries to find other phrases and formulations for his theory, he was moved to use the same image of melting ice that was later to dominate the final moments of *Brand*: 'Life is a great stream,' Hebbel wrote in his diary of 6 March 1843, 'the individuals are the drops, but the tragic ones are lumps of ice which have to be melted. . . .'

If this absolves the reader from taking moral sides before feeling that he can legitimately assess *Brand*, it also deflects attention in *Peer Gynt* away from the incidentals of Peer's moral constitution and on to the problem of his individuality, his selfdom, and the manner of its expression. In other words, to the topic that Peer himself is endlessly preoccupied with: the Gyntian Self. By these criteria, Peer then takes his place as a *failed* Hebbelian hero. Underlying his conduct generally is the urge to do what Brand does: assert himself as an individual, be a 'personality', make an impact on those about him, influence affairs, control human destinies. But there is seemingly no enduring Self there to assert, no 'stubborn autonomous thrust', no hard nucleus but only layer after soft onion layer of assumed *personae* with nothing at the centre. The Buttonmoulder tells Peer aphoristically what Hebbel might have said in abstract prose. In the Buttonmoulder's phrases, Peer has never really been himself and has defied the purpose of his life; to be oneself is to kill oneself, or in other words to show un-mistakably the Master's intention in whatever one does; right and wrong, good and evil, do not enter into the calculations when it comes to escaping the casting-ladle, for a sinner counts as much as a saint provided things are done 'on a grand scale'. Or transposed into Hebbelian terms: that there has been no authentic self-assertion, and in consequence Peer has failed to participate in the 'Lebensprozess', failed to make any positive contribution to historical development; that those who do properly assert their individuality are inevitably destined for a tragic death by virtue of the reaction of the 'Universum'; that to recognize this, and act in that knowledge, is just what Peer has conspicuously neglected to do; and finally—as was discussed above— that the criteria applicable in this context are essentially amoral.

Interestingly, this is not the only echo of Hebbelian polemics to be heard in *Brand* and *Peer Gynt*. Within the German-speaking world at mid-century, the grandiose theories of Hebbel, tracing the larger patterns of human destiny through centuries of time, selecting the grander issues of historical development for literary treatment, did not go unchallenged. There was also—by that group of writers who came to be known as the Poetic Realists—a gentler insistence on the values of modest, everyday living, of quiet unspectacular endeavour, of the little things in life. Hebbel himself had to a great extent provoked them to this; at least, he provoked one of his contemporaries, Adalbert Stifter, to draft a reasoned defence of his own philosophy of life and literature, and to commend what he called 'the gentle law' (as an alternative to Hebbel's 'life process') as the essence of authentic living. In response to a somewhat clumsy and heavy-handed epigrammatic poem published in 1848, in which Hebbel accused some of his contemporaries of smallmindedness and lack of vision, of devoting themselves to insignificant themes because they had no understanding of life's cosmic forces, Stifter appended to his collection of short stories, *Bunte Steine*, a preface, dated 1852, in which he set out his own literary credo:

The wafting of the breeze, the rippling of water, the growing of the crops, the swelling of the sea, the green of the earth, the gleam of heaven, the shining of the stars I consider great. . . . The tremendous tempest, the lightning that destroys houses, the storm that rages in the surf, the erupting volcano, the earthquake that destroys whole countries, these I do not consider any greater than the things above; indeed I consider them smaller because they are only the outer effects of much greater laws. . . . As with external nature, so with inner nature, human nature. A whole life full of righteousness, simplicity, self-control, reasonableness, activity within one's own circle, love of beauty, combined with a benign calm death I consider great. Powerful and tempestuous emotions, terrible fits of anger, the desire for revenge, the fiery spirit that strains for action, demolishes, alters, destroys, and in its excitement often throws away its own life, I consider not greater but smaller. . . .

As Stifter, by this declaration, was to Hebbel, so Agnes was to Brand—not only by the manner of her living and dying, but also by the literal terms of the phrase with which Brand characterizes her: she could discover (he says) the great in the small. In contrast to the strident heroics of Brand, hers is a temperament guided by this 'sanfte Gesetz' of Stifter. Similarly, it is this same set of values that the Priest in his graveside oration is concerned to assert, and which the boy who cut off his finger exemplifies by his later life—a life that stands in conspicuous contrast to the restless, unsatisfied questing of Peer. If it is in fact important to seek for positive moral declarations in these two works, it is surely here in the characters of Agnes and the peasant man that they are to be sought. It is wholly characteristic of Ibsen's art, however, that in both instances this positive statement, though not inconspicuous, is peripheral.

THE 'EPIC BRAND'

A FRAGMENT
[1864–65]

Translated into prose by James Walter McFarlane

THE 'EPIC BRAND'

To my fellows in guilt

1. My people, my fair country, my Northern home, where the sun is shut out by glacier and mountain, where the foot's way is barred by rock and fjord, and the soul's flight by even worse forces—to you I will sing a melancholy song, perhaps as Norway's bard my last; for no poet sings again where once the hymn has been sung over the people's coffin.

2. And the plague has begun. I see a corpse, monstrous as Ymir's body, lying and spreading its pestilential air over field and fjord, infecting rich man and beggar alike. Wrap the corpse in all the flags of Norway! Help, youth, to sink it deep in the sea! The giant corpse best lies buried where the great jarl once met Jomsborg's men in battle.

3. Madmen, hold no longer to your dead as Harald kept his Snefrid's corpse. Do not, as he did, think to glimpse red cheeks, or hear the heart beneath the shroud. What is dead no lie will bring to life. What is dead must down into the dark. The dead has only one purpose: to yield nourishment for the new-sown seed.

4. And this lying pretence with the dead is a game you have played for long years; this is your youthful sin, your manhood's crime, and the source of all your future sickness. Yet punishment cannot fall on all men equally; with tenfold force it must strike those who have been foremost in leading the people—and a hundredfold strike your skalds.

5. For we have conjured up a burnt-out race, painted the corpse in the colours of past glory, and hung the walls of memory's hall with the weight of a warrior's weapons—for a dwarf's delight. In the night of the present we sang of ancient day; but one great thing we forgot to consider: can he rightfully accept his inheritance whose hands are too weak to raise the treasure?

6. Now a hush falls over the land. A stagnant mist envelops the mountains. It is as if some treacherous poison were by some

sorcery mixed in the springs of the people's life. Like birds at the sun's eclipse, listless, I see my people sitting silently and alone; their sinews flabby, their sap dried up, while the midday gloom invades the coasts and valleys.

7. Let the poet keep moving with the stream of his people? Indeed —his banner must fly at the head. But he *must* make straight for the goal indicated by the mysterious signs of the age. He resolves the people's longings by his song, hearing confessions, interpreting remorse, sighing at their fears—clothing in words their secret urges. This is why he sings.

8. Therefore I have turned my sight and mind away from the soul-dead tales of our past, away from the lying dream of a bright future, and I enter the misty world of the present. I shall wander in the loneliness of the pine forest, clammy in my cloak under the weight of the rain, in the dark of the autumn night that gives refuge from shame, gives sleep for sorrow—for me as for the others.

9. My poem is like the heather-grown hill that steadily rises aslant above the peasant farm. But beyond the hill—so long as you stand free—you clearly glimpse a ring of white peaks. My lute is tuned to play a muted song; but deeper strings lend colour to the chords. A poem is thus concealed within the poem; and he who fathoms *this* will grasp the song.

From the time of ripening

10. It was a Saturday evening, peaceful and still—that strange peace which every man has known, that peace so rich in rest and gentleness, as the sun stands low and the week's work is done—that peace akin to such excitement as fills a house when the lamp is brought, when the feast is ready and the table covered, and the clock strikes and the guests can be expected.

11. Half-veiled in red mist the great city stands in the fjord valley, set among summer cottages. It is so white, so shining, so new—a child of today dressed in its best. Pennants flutter across the harbour and the bay where a host of ships lie, scattered and in rows. But only *one* spire reaches towards heaven, pointing up to Him who gave it name.

12. It is as if life's busy tumult spared but one single finger to point to heaven—as if the throng of people found a thousand better purposes to build for. See how the city spreads on every side; see how it grabs greedily at the lush valley. For such uses it has hands without number; ceaselessly growing—only not in the heights.

13. Viewing the district from the broad hillsides running up from the valley floor to the North, one sees tree-clad islands rising from the fjord, cradled like some wreathed sea-god's head. But beyond, towards the other side, the land falls away towards an inland region, with freshwater lakes, and forest, with rushing rivers, with wilder country and a row of steep hills.

14. On the ridge where this double view was to be seen lay a couple of lads of about twelve or thirteen. Autumn was approaching. Only stubble remained in the fields where the corn was binding. But the sun still had a summer's warmth; and the yellow trees still had their leaves; and it was Saturday evening, and no school; so here the two boys lay in the grass.

15. The one was blond and open-featured—one who looks at the world with sparkling eyes, deep-set, rather small, but bold and gay, sun-drenched, made for laughter. With his hat tipped back for shade, and his hands folded under his chin, he lay on his stomach, at ease, looking at the fjord, the houses, the city, where the sun was shining.

16. The other sat with his back turned to the sun. He looked to the North, down into the landlocked district, where the river leapt, where the charcoal fires burned, where the lake lay black in the evening shadow. Far in the distance came the noise of hammers, mixed with the sound of the falls and the rattle of wheels; a rowing-boat glided forward with quiet strokes; a solitary wild duck flew swiftly across the lake.

17. But it was not so much the view that attracted him; he scarce seemed to realize what it was he saw. He sat, his knee drawn up to his breast, whistling occasional notes from some tune. It was as though his thoughts came and went at random, as though he sang what he had himself forgotten, as though he looked *beyond* what he saw—as though something unseen lay hidden behind the view.

18. He was one of those children who seem old, one whom his play-
mates in the break never succeed in drawing into their romping
games, who quietly look on and are sufficient to themselves. His
hair was black, but thin and long and smooth; his features drawn
and sharp and tense, though something in them had a *committed*
look. He looked like one who *wills*, but can well wait.

19. A puff of white rose up behind the town, then another, and
gunshot followed gunshot until the city and the bay lay concealed
in smoke as though under the wing of some great dragon. The
blond boy gave a start; he lay counting: 'Sixteen, seventeen,
eighteen . . .' and so on, until the thundering was over. Then
he cried: 'Look there! There goes the frigate!

20. 'There's a band on the quarterdeck. Listen to the sound! And
look at the spray and foam at its bows! Look how it goes! Before
the bells ring early tomorrow it will have reached harbour.
Imagine being there at home then; being able to go along with
the others, and go aboard. There are great beech groves down
there, and the town lies by the open fjord.

21. 'Away over there, behind the high land standing blue on the far
side of the fjord, it is beautiful, believe me. My father has a farm
where the hillside runs away to the South, down to a wooded
bay. It is lovely at home on Sunday mornings. Especially in
summer, you understand. The picture Bible lies on the table, and
all people are dressed in their best.

22. 'The glass doors stand open to the garden, and sand and juniper
twigs are strewn on the steps; and the flag is hoisted on the gate
pole, and the rose hedge gleams red; and the doves are fed with
peas—one of them is blue and quite tame. These we make our
guests; we are the hosts, and the front steps are our reception hall.

23. 'In the passage stands a brig with sails and masts. It has galleys
that *must* puff out smoke. We *must* play with that. Then my aunt and
her children come from town on a visit. There is an old man
who drives them; he has a yellow carriage, big and broad. Long
before we can see them, we can hear them; and if we go to meet
them, we can ride with them.

24. 'Then we run about the garden all day long, and play tag around
the great hayrack. And my aunt has a daughter—she is nice.

She is called Agnes; she never gets caught. For dinner we get roast meat with cranberry sauce, and we are allowed to eat at the grown-ups' table. But the nicest thing is what follows—when mother and father and auntie always join in the game.

25. 'Late in the evening the carriage is brought out again; they don't want to leave, for nobody is tired. But it is a long way back to town, and they must return home, and we are allowed to accompany them to the turn in the road. There we say goodnight, and they must drive on. How quiet! How white the mist lies over the fields. We can hear the corncrakes up on the hillside. Then mother calls to us. We must go to bed.'

26. He listened—he who turned his back to the sun. He half turned round towards his friend, and asked: 'Tell me more things like that from yonder—before you came here to go to school. Take care to remember everything well. Nor must you forget what you have dreamed. But tell me first whether it is customary to play with your mother, where your home is?'

27. And the boy told of all sorts of things, just as they came into his mind. And the other looked at him. His look was keen, as though he wished to look deep within him. And then he laughed, and cried out: 'Better stop now! I wouldn't believe a thing like that, even if the priest swore it. You must have read what you are telling! Pah! These are lies—every word's a lie!'

28. He lay on his back, his thoughts awhirl; he rested his head in the hollow of his hand, pushed his stick into the band of his hat and swung his hat round in wide circles. And as he lay and played, he looked at the sky. But after a while—as though he found the game an empty one—he threw the stick away, half turned and pointed over the hills towards the North.

29. 'Home—always it lies far to the North', he said, scarce attending to the other, as he once more resumed speaking, brushing his long black hair from his face. 'A Saturday evening—words with the sound of bells; a song—a word with the taste of pine stalks; a lie—a word you can stroke like silk; home—a word always shut towards the South.

30. 'Now it seems to me I can see a home. It is winter. No snow, but hard frost. On the beach lies a splintered boat. The rim of the

glacier shines on the mountain ridge. How gloomy and black the fjord lies! It sleeps. The great clouds see themselves in it. How good to fly out and be free—but there is nobody who can ferry across.

31. 'And what bad dreams one can have at home! I know a boy who once so dreamed that he dreamed away both sun and song—and everything about his home grew strange to him. For the dream bound him to look at himself as the vortex binds one who looks at the stream; and the boy looked at it, and could not break free, and was carried round in circles. . . . Now you shall hear his dream.

32. 'It was a Christmas Eve, and he lay sick. It felt like an iron band around his head; his temples throbbed, his arms were limp and feeble; fire and ice seemed to be coursing through his blood. His mother lay in the next room, even sicker; and in the third somebody could be heard groaning. There lay his father, bent and twisted with pain—the sickest of them all.

33. 'It had been a busy day that day at the farm; for the doctor had been there, and the priest as well. Now it was quiet again, as before a feast; only the sound of the bell was borne across the fjord. They rang in the festival time, and the boy listened with eyes closed, as he froze in his sweat. Then he heard somebody looking in at the door . . . and a moment later he heard somebody weeping.

34. 'It was the old maid who had crept in. Doubtless she thought he was in a deep and heavy sleep. He felt the tears fall; she sighed and sobbed: "Now your father's dead, poor little mite!" She fumbled at his bed which had not been touched for many days, lightly patted his cheek, drew up the pillow and smoothed the blanket and slipped out of the room as soundlessly as the wind.

35. 'He heard the bell whilst she was in there. His thoughts bubbled like a muddied stream. He tried to distinguish—but it was hard to tell—what was truth in this and what was dream. He slept. Then he dreamed that he lay awake . . . and it was dark. He called —no answer. He glimpsed, like a dim light in the mist, what the maid had whispered about his father.

36. 'He dreamed that he sat up, stood up. Since no one came, he decided to see for himself. He fumbled his way out; shivers ran

through his body; his ears sang; his knees had no strength. He dreamed that all was dark, the fire out . . . that all were asleep . . . that it was dead of night. But in the room where his father lay, candles were burning. . . . He made for them, and found the handle.

37. 'He crept in . . . along the wall . . . to a corner. Two lighted candles were set at the ends of the bed. Stretched out on his back, his father lay, with a book clutched between his hands and held to his breast. His face seemed more yellow than pale; his skin was taut, his wrists were so narrow. His legs, stretched straight, were thin and bony, and over them fell the linen folds.

38. 'There it was as quiet and cold as in a church. He recognized the smell of the clammy linen. Then outside he heard the sound of soft footsteps. . . . And heard somebody fumbling at the door. He trembled. Terrified he looked about him, and shrank back deep into his corner. And at that moment he thought he saw a woman in a nightgown, carrying a candle.

39. 'With stumbling steps she went over to the bed. He saw her falter at every step she took; she shielded the candle with her fingers. He heard how hard she breathed. Then all at once she raised, stiff and straight, her arm, and cried with a strangled voice: "This is because you spoilt my life", and dealt the corpse a blow across the head.

40. 'And with that blow across the dead man's cheek, it was as if a long day's task was ended. She turned and went—and the lamp-light fell upon a face he surely knew. She resembled *two* things which had terrified him before he was able to express the power of terror in words: she resembled the eagle pinned above the outhouse door; but even more she resembled his mother.

41. 'On the third morning he woke as strong as steel. His father was dead, but the rest was all a dream. He kept silent about it. All the girls sat around sewing black dresses, trimmed for mourning. And the local tailor arrived in the house before midday, to sew something for the boy. . . . Ah, how fine! Then the carriage left for town. All went smoothly. Quietly they drank coffee, mourned, and kept the day free.

42. 'One evening the coffin arrived, expensive and fine. It had silver fittings, I remember. Then from the town came new-sewn

folded linen, and greenery for the wreathes was bought in town. Then came the spruce twigs. And as the final preparations were made, the widow's house gave off a scent so rich of flowers, twigs, and all things green that since that time it seemed to the boy that summer smelled of corpses.

43. 'Finally the funeral day arrived. Boat upon boat brought the men of the parish rowing across to the house. Half-suppressed weeping could be heard in the house of mourning; the black bier stood in the great hall. There the procession assembled, and the priest spoke of suffering and death and the peace of the grave; but above all he described the widow's grief so that all the women wept—but the boy laughed.

44. 'Many days he laughed, but secretly. Yet once he laughed so that it sounded like a shriek to heaven. That was one day when, following custom, he found the newspapers which had arrived from town. There stood in print, with cross and black surround, in the edition of 7 January: "Last month my beloved husband departed from me and this life on the 24th."

45. 'How active she was when once she had recovered! From early morning until late evening she occupied herself with the affairs of the house; she took a personal hand in all things; she trusted no one. And all was done quietly and in haste, as though by one who suffered from some tormenting duty; it was as though she was afraid of rest, of the dark, of her thoughts and similar things.

46. 'There was on the farm a little spotted dog, of which the boy was immensely fond. One day in late spring it happened that the boy was playing with the little dog. They lay in the sand outside, beside the wall, and the dog wagged his tail as the boy stroked its coat. Then some troll-like power passed through his mind; he rose, went off and fetched a sledgehammer.

47. 'He swung it; the dog whined; and the boy struck; it fell, yelping, and rose again and fell; it seemed to ask for mercy; then it dragged itself under the steps, howling and lame. But at that same moment, even before he fully realized the savageness of his deed, his mother stood beside him at the outhouse door, tall, lean, grey, asking what was wrong.

48. ' "Why did you hit him?" she shouted angrily. He trembled— his blood turned to ice. As you know, one stands in terror of

one's mother. But, composing himself, he raised his head, standing there still with the hammer poised, his hand gripping the shaft, stiff and straight, and answered with a defiant look in his eyes: "That was because it had spoiled my life!" '

Over the great mountain

49. A region rises high in Norway's land; in the east it rises slowly up from the valley; to the west it plunges abruptly to the fjord's edge, and this is the bare region of the highland wastes. Brown heather grows in place of forest, and moss grows only among fierce rocks; here the glacier spreads his broad cap; here the reindeer lives alone and undisturbed.

50. No beaten path leads through this region; it is wild country for both foot and thought. Now the glacier's whirling snow is like the smoke from a forest fire, now it lies in slender folds like linen, now naked crags nod above the heights, now they wrap themselves in a veil of mist. A single pole, a cairn, denotes the way through the pass, barred both to north and south.

51. There was once a summer morning, cool and still. Close by that place on the wasteland's broad breast where the river, shrunken to a double source, trickles out of the marsh to east and west— there sat a small group of happy friends and their girls gathered together. The heather burns in the trench beneath the pot, and the vine sparkles in the clear light of day.

52. These must surely be gentlefolk, sitting out here, for they have guides and horses and pack animals, and flags on sticks, and their hats are decorated with leaves, and covers are spread out on the heather. Among these young people is one who sits and sings; the sun seems to shine on the song; close by him a young girl rests, lightly as a bird that swings up and down on a willow wand.

53. Now there are jests, gusts of hearty laughter; now the joy grows silent after being at its height; it is clear to see from words and faces that the company is gathered for a leave-taking. Within the group a man—not altogether elderly, nor yet young, but strong and at the height of his powers—turns to two among them, the couple whose features are radiant with happiness.

54. He fills his glass, and strikes on it for silence; he smiles a little, then begins to speak: 'Our Lord knew splendidly what he was

doing when he allowed you two to meet in my house. You, Agnes, were sent from town, ailing; you were to enjoy fresh mountain air, and drink the sun and the dew and the pine tree's scent. . . . And then *he* arrived as though he had fallen from the sky.

55. 'He came, a paint box on his back, returning home from the South, from distant journeys. He was so strong and healthy, so bold and confident, and his breast was filled with a thousand songs. He was seeking beauty in the mountains, he said, among the moor's pines and along the forest river, in the scudding clouds under the vault of heaven—then he met you . . . and he found the power of beauty.

56. 'Then he painted his best masterpiece; he painted healthy roses on your cheeks; two eyes he painted radiating happiness, and then a smile that laughed its way into the soul. I soon realized that I, your old doctor, was superfluous to such a cure. His songs worked better than any medicines, better even than bathing in God's nature.

57. 'And yet, superfluous? No, hardly that! Was it not I who stopped him one day as he stood all dressed to leave, with his knapsack packed, and reminded him of something he'd neglected—a matter which you two had dreamingly overlooked in your games and play? What matter? That of getting engaged. And why? Because he had forgotten to ask!

58. 'He had forgotten to ask for your hand, and you had forgotten to answer. You needed but the hour, and that was granted. You thought the game could last like the feast of summer, enduring the whole day through. You *thought*? No, indeed you did *not* think, and least of all about your future house. You sang in your souls, laughed with eye and mouth, and weeks passed as in the delirium of a festive night.

59. 'So then I had to act, I thought. For him I paid court, and for you I answered, and placed your two hands together and thus the whole thing was settled. Then the party lasted three whole days, and then we accompanied the young couple on their way. Now, friends, the hour of parting strikes; for here we must part from him and from her.

60. 'So it will be quiet for us in the valley, as it was before; only the river will sing us his old song; soon the sun will sink, soon the swallow depart, and we shall only have the echo of a memory. Then hedge and hazel will turn yellow as the leaves drop, and field and marsh will stiffen and winter come. One night the meadow and the hillside will lie white—but you go on to the radiant summer of happiness.

61. 'First you cross the silent peaks of the highlands, then deep down to the fjord in the west; there waits Aegir's horse with steam up, on which you will ride home to your wedding feast. Then together you will set your course for Southern lands, like young swans on their first flight. There you will live a joyous summer life, delightful as a dream, and lovely as a fable.

62. 'For the fair weather of joy shall sustain your boat on its journey over life's sea; you must swear loyalty to the flag of happiness— a crusade of sorrow would bring you to your graves. You were created—and for this praised be the hand that spins the long thread of fate—to make your pilgrimage to paradise through kingdoms fair, and with song.

63. 'That is why, this Sunday morning, though doctor and layman only and no priest, I declare you protected from want and from sorrow, and dedicate your life to the festival of joy. Through the throng you shall make your way in sunshine; for you the stars will shine every night; your life shall be like one long game of tag until, playing like children, you find Heaven!'

64. Here he fell silent. Behind his jesting speech, a serious content peeped as though from behind a cloak; lightly he brushed his hand across his eyes, and emptied his glass to the last drop. But the young people rushed forward in a group round the couple, their glasses filled; any sorrow that might weigh heavily on the light foliage over their dwelling-place was declared outlawed.

65. They banished from the language every word that carried any hint of distant storms; they garlanded them with leaves and hailed them as the true and legitimate children of happiness. And wilder and wilder the group wove their ring-dance across the brown strip of heather. They bade defiance to all the powers of darkness, and conjured up all daytime's elfin creatures.

66. Then a kind of weariness followed their exertions; they drained the last drops of their exuberance. They pressed the couple's hands firmly and silently, and bade them long and earnestly farewell. Then the group made eastwards for the valley, and the guide rode slowly to the west; but, in the middle of the mountain hall, waving, stood alone the painter with his bride.

67. He swung his hat, she stood with fluttering veil, to thank them for each parting word, for each farewell greeting that echoed, ever fainter, till the group disappeared down the steep pass. Silently they looked at each other a while in the earnest afterglow of the leave-taking; then a smile trembled on both their lips like sunlight trembling through the forest's leaves.

68. And the smile spread until a world of youthful happiness lay radiant in it. Forgotten were their friends and what they had done, as a quickly passing cloud is soon forgotten. They looked neither forwards nor backwards, but saw only the radiance of the present moment. They did not see the terrified storm birds, their wings spread as they flew up from fjord and sound.

69. Like a happy brother and sister, hand in hand, they ran towards the west across the brown carpet of the highland wastes. He was as slim and supple as a wand, and her feet scarcely touched the ground. She tore herself free, and laughingly ran away, and he was quick to try to catch her again; and the jest became a game as they ran free, and then their words and laughter turned to song.

70. 'Agnes, my lovely butterfly, I shall catch you in our play. I shall make a net of finest mesh, formed of my songs.'

71. 'If I am a dear little butterfly, then let me drink of the flowers; and if you're a lad who is longing to play, then chase me but do not catch me!'

72. 'Agnes, my lovely butterfly, now I have fashioned my net; your fluttering flight will be of small help, and soon you'll sit captive in the net.'

73. 'If I am a young bright butterfly, I will gladly join in the game; but if you catch me in your net, please don't touch my wings!'

74. 'No, I shall lift you carefully on my hand, and shut you in to my heart; there you may play your whole life long, the merriest game you learnt.'

75. 'Ah, if I'm a butterfly, happy and free, a cage is not for me; I do not know whether life's long or short, but I know it's wholly delightful.'

76. Then suddenly they stopped. They stood on the edge of the steep drop that falls away to the west. Far below their feet a falcon soared; and the guide cautiously dismounted from his horse. 'Go slowly here,' he said to the couple, 'and in that way you can guard against any bad or evil things you might meet in the pass. . . . Throw crossed twigs in front of you at your feet.'

77. Then he strode on, and the young ones followed, their hearts beating with silent terror, whilst now and then a gust would disperse the mist and show the gorge, which would then be hidden again. She clung to him as a frightened child does at night. She whispered: 'Is it not as though we were leaving life and the warm power of light and descending deep down into the kingdom of death?'

78. Then a cloud, which had brooded threateningly on the mountain's bosom, lifted; and far behind the land of shadows, deep within the gorge, a world emerged, cradled and warm. It was a sight no hand can paint: there was the great endless sea which lay sparkling beyond the dales as eternity glistens beyond the grave.

79. And golden sunshine trembled on the broad waters, and brilliant white sails streamed out from the shore like happy yearning thoughts across the countenance of the world, on their flight to infinity's land. And like a frame round some great picture stood the dark walls of the gorge, the roof of clouds, whilst the desolate wastes in the foreground stood in strong shadowy contrast to the distant light.

80. Then on the horizon a gale arose and whipped the waves to foam; then the cloak of mist fell over the view, and veiled the distant world. And the path fell away steeper and more narrow, and the river leapt still wilder at the rim, and blacker the rocky face that barred the valley, and the mountain sunlight vanished.

81. Like the remnants of a shattered world, boulders lay like churches strewn about the path; no blade of grass grew on the gorge's floor, and no traveller met them on their way. Pale, sick in spirit,

she walked by his side; he heard her heart beating in her breast; she looked at him as a child might in distress; then he smiled and sang out loud:

82. 'Agnes, my lovely sister, say why your heart is beating. Do not let the mountain fill you with fear and terror; you are in your mother's house.

83. 'Agnes, girl of the open air, there is no need for us to feel terror; dutiful children may go at night through the dark and haunted room.

84. 'You are in your mother's haunted room; but do not be anxious in spirit. Your brother accompanies you with songs, and holds you faithfully by the hand.

85. 'Do not be afraid whatever you may hear, whether shrieks or the howling of dogs. It is not evening, it is not night; it is merely the mist at the window.

86. 'Outside it is sunlight and bright day; and soon the door will open. Let us simply go trustingly, singing a song, through the dark and haunted room!'

87. And as the song rose from his breast, so the cloud was lifted from her face; no longer did she walk anxious and in dread, and she hummed as a smile came to her lips. She took two stones, and one she threw into the waterfall and the other she flung against the rocky wall where the giant stood threateningly like some frozen petrified Jutul with a Moses beard.

88. And boldly, excitedly, she called: 'River nixie, away with you and your sobbing and sighing. You will never fill us with frost and trembling, for we have ears only for songs of joy! You evil mountain troll with your furrowed forehead, stand there if you like to threaten us as we pass by. You will not bar our way. We are on the road to life and gaiety in the land of joy, you know!'

89. Then a singer's voice resounds from the mountain, full as when the organ sounds in church. It deafens the river's roar and the noise of the falls, and far and wide it echoes and re-echoes. It halts the happy children on their path where, despite nixie and Jutul, they make their way. They stop, listen, stare up at the heights where the voice runs on through the words of the song:

90. 'Lord make me rich in sorrow; protect me from each tempting joy! Whip me into the ways of renunciation! Lord God, Father in Heaven, teach me to suffer and pray!

91. 'Teach me to walk through the land of the flesh, blind to sun and to summer. Teach me to *will* more than I *can*. Call on me, my Lord and Saviour, and bend my soul that I come!

92. 'The earth is like a winter's night; all sorrows are sparkling stars. They are set as lights for erring souls; if they are quenched, I lose my way. I know not who will protect me.

93. 'Sorrow sits like a proud queen in her frosty robe of Northern lights. Follow me, all, into the night! Lord, Lord, God of Heaven, teach us to suffer and pray!'

94. The sound came from high up, where a path emerged from a side valley through the desolate rocks; trumpet-like it called to the society of men far across hill and dale. It was then that the couple remembered, with secret regret, how they had forgotten to cast crosses of twigs before their feet. Too late. No tree took root here; and down towards them came the powerful singer.

95. He was a fine-featured man, dressed in black, rather pale, rather sharp, with a high receding forehead; with his right hand he wiped the sweat away, and held his hat in the other as he walked. His eye was like a tarn in shadow, something deep and secret and hidden. He carried a laced knapsack on his back, and held his stick firmly under his arm.

96. Like theirs, his path led down to the township. He greeted them politely as he passed. Yet there was a question in it, as though he thought: 'Do we not know each other?' And the same thought seized the young painter; uncertainly he stopped the man on his way, and asked: 'Brand, is it you?' Then the other answered: 'Yes—Einar, is it you!'

97. They were that pair of schoolboy friends who once lived close as brothers, but who had parted and never met again, until like half-strangers they met each other here. How much did there not lie between now and when they were at school! Each had gone his own way into the world; each strove to reach God in his own fashion—one by his palette, and the other by the pulpit.

98. But Einar was the first to give tongue to all the memories
sleeping in his soul. He seized his friend's hand as though it were
some prey he would not wish to share with any man on earth.
Then quickly, in a fever of joy, he spoke of the bond he had
formed that summer, of all his hopes, fully believing he had
found a way to his friend's heart.

99. Yet Brand stood silent. Gently he freed his hand from his friend's
warm grip. A slight twitch played about his lips; he seemed to
fight a battle with himself. He answered, half absently, half
embarrassed: 'It is good to know that one has reached one's
haven. You are a painter now, and have made your name—each
road is right as long as it is one's own.

100. 'But two kinds of road one's will may choose: *one* resembles a
navigable river, where progress is like some game on the dance
floor; the other is the way you must cut through yourself. The
first lies broad for you and for a thousand others; the second you
must boldly open up with steel. On this one, no other man but
you dare go, until the world sees that it leads to some goal.

101. 'And two kinds of call can rouse a man's powers. The one draws
him on by inclination and desire; the other, which might be
called the spirit of baptism, buries its tongue of flame within his
breast. By *its* power he speaks an unknown language; by *its*
power, victory belongs to him. And if you have known the grace
of such a flame, I can understand why you have become a painter.

102. 'Then you can go out into the heathen land and interpret the
things of the Light in form and colour, that souls may be released
and raise themselves to God like butterflies that burst from the
chrysalis. Then you can melt the people's glacier hearts, for then
you are in partnership with Heaven. But don't forget that if you
have this power you are probably unique among your kind.'

103. He spoke with a certain restless fire, in a low voice and with
flaming cheeks; the glow in his eyes was like blood that gleams
on the arrow's point by lightning flash. He seemed to writhe
under the words, as though he battled with some secret force, as
though his thoughts bored their way through against resistance
and, resonant, were placed on his lips.

104. The young girl observed him closely like one who spies out an
enemy camp. Then, confidently, she sought her betrothed's eye

and demanded, though in silence, the triumphant reply. She was so sure, so certain of her case, as earnestly the painter began to speak: 'My friend, this is the second time today you have tried to depress our good spirits.

105. 'First you cast over us the shadow of your song; now you wish to darken things for us by your speech. But give what name you will to the glad urge that whispers in me: "To live is to paint!" I do not require any elucidation; I do not wait for some angel to appear out of the blue. God does not send all men his revelation. For me it is enough to go the way I *must*.

106. 'Little have you grasped the mystery of beauty; you show poor understanding of what art can and must do if you suppose that salvation's laws shall rule the happy childhood land of painting. Do you think a flower's right to blossom is greater if it holds medicinal properties in its sap or leaf than if it simply has scent and colour?

107. 'And do you think that a bird should sit silent in the forest unless its song can ease somebody's grief? Is everything from which you cannot derive knowledge without meaning in the book of nature? I believe in the soul's right to joy in life, in the voice's right to sing for the sake of singing; that the same right is given to the spring snowdrop as is given to the cherry and the eldertree.

108. 'And tell me finally, with hand on heart, with the truth and nothing but the truth on your lips: did you receive that call of grace that clearly intimated that you were chosen the standard-bearer of the Light? Have you known the Pentecostal morning? Have you felt the Dove descend upon your soul? Have you heard the mighty voice from the vaults of Heaven instructing you to dedicate your life?'

109. It took some time for the priest to collect his words for the answer that lay fermenting in his breast. A flush rose to his cheeks. He whispered, as he gripped the arm of his friend: 'Yes, I have the call; but it comes at different times. Like the moon it waxes and wanes; I rise and fall like a ship at sea; in battle I pray and in prayer I battle.

110. 'But I will conquer; first my inmost self, and then my brothers in the earth's wide circle. I may not haggle; I am not content

with *something*; *all* must be done, nothing less. Division of labour is the cancer of the age; it consumes everything that is *whole*. One man cares for his belly, one for his soul, one for his learning, one for his pleasure.

111. 'That is why our generation has sunk in the mire. The slave still longs for the promised land, but slinks through life, lame and sullen, content to finish up wherever he finds himself. Tell me, where is the man who *wills* and *believes* and *sees*, who *fights* for the selfsame thing for which he *burns*? I see no longer *men* upon the earth; I see but *stomachs*, *heads*, and *hands*.

112. 'But it was *men* the Lord created; it was to *men* that Christ came; for it was men who had strayed and had to be redeemed from the judgement of the law. Now this great work has crumbled into dust. Stand on the peak, man, and look. Weep if you can . . . and laugh, if you are strong. And then shout: "What waste of splendid powers!"

113. 'That gives you an index to my soul. I know precisely what there remains for a man to make his life's work in our days: it is to make this generation once more *whole*. The age of miracles is past. God will create no more Adams here on earth. It is human help the Lord requires, if this generation is to be brought back to its rightful path.

114. 'This is why I will go out into the world and collect the dismembered and scattered parts and create Man, whole and true, in God's image for a second time. This is why I wage war on you and yours, on all whose distorted vision has destroyed this generation . . . who worshipped truth in its individual features, whilst truth is in nothing if not all.'

115. With eyes like a frightened bird in a trap, the girl was carried along on the swirling flood of his thoughts. It was as though she was bent low under the tempestuous force of his will and courage. But Einar shook his blond head and answered in friendly fashion with a smile: 'I see you fulfil as a man what you promised as a child—to become a scourge of the world.

116. 'I well remember many moments at school when in our imagination we lived in the ancient sagas, with all their violence, their injustice and their pain, and we added stories to them from our

other knowledge. You never came with help and sympathy in cases of need; you never opposed the doings of evil men. You let the worst things happen; but *after* the crime, you stormed forth with the sharp sword of vengeance.

117. 'This is the same spirit that drives you now violently to turn the world all upside down. But remember, every seedling you tear up by the roots requires some better plant in its place. Do not extinguish the match, although it splutters, before you have lit the torch to light the people's way. Do not expunge the old words from our tongue before new thoughts require new words.

118. 'And remember, one's call can often be on hostile terms with the conditions of one's life. A diocesan curacy is hardly the appointment from which to start a reformation. Shut in by mountains, the voice does not carry far. Understand me well. I know that many a giant has sprung from a modest position. But our people have been minted as farthings; do not counterfeit the stamp they were given by God.'

119. There was a rattle in the priest's throat, like a laugh that died before it reached his lips; a touch of scorn played about his lips, as he once again began to speak: 'Yes, our people have a double nature! Given to great deeds when the glasses clink, when song and speech release the spirit's wings and thought flies out from its workaday cage.

120. 'It is a people with an unrivalled past; a people that once was great, its men and women of heroic stature . . . whenever the skald is commissioned to sing. It is a people so strong, so undaunted; a people that shakes its fist towards the East; a people that stands on guard to the South . . . when the banquet speaker raises his voice.

121. 'It is a people, each man of which is so distinguished that from him the whole world may learn those splendid qualities that bestow honour—as one witness to the truth once said. It is a people that confidently believes in its right to guide the world from its rocky corner, a people that grew and throve while the spirit of the age grew weary. . . . Such is our people . . . in our own estimation.

122. 'But when the times become tempestuous, and talk fades and words must yield to deeds, and bare steel replace wooden staves,

and scabbards are to hang empty at the left hip—what is this people *then*, these men, these women? A people deficient in every capacity; a people which ultimately makes itself so small that it almost loses sight of itself.

123. 'Then women scream, and men draw aside; deaf ears are turned to all prayers and pleas. Then we call ourselves "the poor folk on the shore", a people which (God be praised) were minted farthings. When great powers meet, what have we to offer? What influence has the rockbound people's mite? The job it was given, once and for all, is to drive a plough and steer a boat.

124. 'What can we do if some enemy advances? Making sacrifices is for other people. It was only for empty show that some vague enthusiast split the Norwegian flag and gave it tongues. No, let the cheeks of the greater nations flame when the arteries of time course hot and full. We were made to plough the soil and seas; our task in life is to sweat, not to bleed.

125. 'Ten more years—and the nation will be in darkness, that clammy half-night fit for a race of pygmies, where the will vacillates between good and evil, where every man's outlook is foolish, his breast drained dry. Clouds of soot will descend over the country, like that rain of ashes over the ancient city; but nobody sees that the region is accursed, and it occurs to nobody to flee.

126. 'On the contrary! In the crooked passages of the mine the pygmy crowd will feel secure, and hew the ore to the sound of dripping water, hunchbacked in soul as in body. Each heartbeat will be drowned by hammerblows, and each cry of the soul by the whine of sawblades. No heart will rend at any friend's distress; no smile be quenched by any kinsman's death.

127. 'And even if our Nordic sun of faith were threatened by the baying Fenri-wolf of doubt, the pygmy race will find it all in order; this is a matter for others, not for him. He belongs to a people made only for brawling, not for the battle for victory or for fame; he is content to achieve in afterlife a modicum of bliss or a little damnation.

128. 'What to him are nail-wounds in the hands? Or the agony of death in the olive grove? Or the rubies of blood where thorns ripped the Lord's brow in his hour of destiny? Was it not for

others that Christ died? He came to them as the interpreter of love. Only the thong's lash from the Wandering Jew was what our Lord suffered for our nation!'

129. No word was answered. Silent like frightened children who, happily picking berries on the hill, suddenly meet the grim mountain bear, the couple stood spellbound by him on the path. With their eyes fixed on this angry apparition, with their cold hands clasped together, staring back in wild terror they silently slipped away to seek some refuge.

130. Soon they were out of sight. Einar was breathing like a man who had fought heavily and hard; he drew breath as one does who has suffered the agony of nightmare. He tried to sing, but his voice failed him; he tried to laugh, but the sound was empty. He tried to jest, but the joke was a bird that fled as it sensed the hunter take aim.

131. So he turned his vision towards a Southern landscape, to laurel bushes and golden orange groves, to summer life in the warm vineyard, and clustering grapes sparkling and full. Her ear alone caught what his words described; half-seeing only, she looked out over the fjord, her only answer the simple words: 'But did you see how, as he spoke, he grew!'

The ways to church

132. There is a story of a troll who came walking along at one place and had to cross a fjord, but did not step out far enough and was left standing in a hundred fathoms of water. It came up to his knees. It is for his kind that the path down from the mountain tops to the fjord seems to have been made. Two valleys divide the land into three layers—a three-step stairway from the heights down to the sea.

133. Walk for hours, then look upward and you think you are standing at the very root of the mountain; yet down below, where the valley curves away, you have yet another abyss at your feet. The upper valley is narrow and black, though without snow; there the streams of melted ice rush past. The next lower valley is narrow and grey and treeless—*there* men like us are born and die.

134. But do not believe that you have reached the fjord—here where
scattered souls live poised between life in the fields and death on
the mountains, where the sun is cold, and poverty has its home.
You must descend the lower slopes; there you will see townsteads
of a different kind. Yellowing grain fills broad acres; fruit ripens.
The rich live down there.

135. It was in the upper valley that they met. They came rolling like
angry thunderclouds; they clashed; the storm flashed and rolled,
then they were thrown apart. The couple took the path down the
hillside; but Brand followed the edge of the abyss—he knew the
district. He hoisted his rucksack higher on his back, advanced
foot by foot, his eye turned inward.

136. Crusading zeal shone in his face. He revelled in the agonized
delight a soul can draw from the word 'regret'—poised between
embracing and condemning. He had met the summer-glad
singer; he had deadened the song by his words; he had turned
the man's eyes from sun to ground—he saw what he had done
and writhed in his remorse.

137. He spread his arms wide to the wind, running forward with open
embrace. A hot salt tear burned on his cheek. He called Einar's
name, as though in dread. It went unheard. He slackened his pace,
and the smart cooled once more in his blood. He walked out and
stood on an overhanging crag where the path wound down to
the mountain's foot.

138. Far ahead and deep below the couple went, though horse and
guide were long since out of sight. She tried the plank serving as
a bridge; he seemed to be afraid it might give way. Yet over it
they went, and with sunken heads they walked along the edge
of the chasm. Like mankind's mother, she seemed to bear the
fruits of her knowledge, the loss of paradise.

139. Soon they vanished among the woods and the scree; but Brand
continued staring, searching, looking down into the valley from
the heights where he stood. It was his native village he was
looking at. He recognized the fjord waters, narrow and twisted
and black; and the landslide slope with its stunted birches; the
round churchyard with its stone-roofed portico, the dilapidated
bridge, the tarred church.

140. He recognized again the scattered homesteads; he could remember every bend in the road; the red marquee he saw still stood there; yet everything seemed to him to have grown smaller. He saw the broad cleft where the fjord broke through; he saw a sloop which was putting in for loading; he saw a wharf and a white-painted house—that was the headland where the storekeeper's widow lived.

141. That was his mother's house, his childhood home where he had grown up among the rocks on the shore. Now a multitude of memories came thronging which earlier had been banished into the night by one thing. He rejected them, tried to drive them away but they kept returning, grinning, mocking: 'Brand, can you remember . . . ?' they asked him tormentingly; his breast tightened as he recognized the terror of home.

142. He felt the anguish of knowing kinship with something that lay beyond himself; half his strength seemed to drain away under the burden of sharing common cause. Those great things he had recently planned became alien to him; his powers grew sickly and his determination weakened; as he drew near his home he felt like a shorn Samson in his concubine's lap.

143. He threw himself down upon a slab of stone by the wayside and said, half in thought, half in words: 'It is as though spectres stood by the fjord and wept; as though trolls shrieked from all the mountains. Yes—you may well recognize me again, though I have grown tall since last you saw me. I am sprung from your kinsmen's loins; we are related and you wish to greet me.

144. 'Look how dark and cold it grows for this our meeting; storm clouds are gathering. That is right! Out yonder the rain is streaming down; the sloop reduces sail, its foresail has been carried away. Blow, wind, and cool my brow, cool my cheek; sweep the air clean of all the mists of memory. A plague lies in them such as no arts can combat except the distant wind.

145. 'My mother's house! Look, it's newly painted, has a tiled roof and green shutters. But it lies exposed, lacking the shelter of trees; it seldom has sun and never midday warmth. There she goes, year after year, unchangingly, forever a victim of her restlessness, looking to her own interests and calculating and growing rich— so rich, so rich it is unpleasant to think about.'

146. Suddenly he laughed, but bitterly as through tears, as he let his eye run along the hillside. His voice was low and curt and sharp and wild, as, half dreaming, he half spoke his thoughts aloud: 'Look, there's the clump of hazel-trees. *That* has memories! There for the first time I saw Norwegian courage; there for the first time I saw Norwegian blood, and the manner it is shed in our times.

147. 'It was a clear autumn day. I well remember the rustling hazels, brown and yellow. Red berries hung in great clusters on the rowan tree—and such swarms of singing birds! We were already on our way home; I was the last. One nut hung high, and was difficult to reach. Then I heard the sound of dry twigs crackling; I heard footsteps. I saw a man.

148. 'He was carrying an axe beneath his jacket. At every step he glanced behind him; then he sank down as though exhausted after effort. Some time after, he stood up again and seemed more certain of himself. He placed the axe on a fallen tree-trunk, drew a cloth—a bandage—from his pocket, again looked round, then suddenly chopped a finger off his right hand.

149. 'I saw only the spurt of blood. I know no more. I ran home and kept silent about what I had seen. But the next morning I and several others went along to the local offices where recruitment was taking place. In the room a captain sat at a table along with the doctor, the sheriff, the clerk and the constable. The men of the village stood around in groups, exchanging words. They were whispering that war could be expected.

150. 'The names of the young men were called out one by one; they were measured, examined, and inscribed. When that was done, each one returned with a serious face to his apprehensive group. Finally one went up, his hand wrapped in a cloth. How deathly pale he was as he walked across the floor! His eyes were cast down; I saw him sweating. I recognized him again at first sight.

151. 'Hesitantly he held out his hand in the bandage to show it to those who were sitting round the long table. He mumbled something about a sickle slipping on his finger and cutting it to the bone; he mentioned something about an accident. He stood like some symbol of the world's distress; he stood like one who lied and yet repented—like hopelessness itself begging for mercy.

152. 'All the people crowded round, standing on their toes, climbing on stools; they stared, they gaped, they forgot to speak, and every look met the lad like a sting. The men round the table conferred quietly for a moment. Then the old, grey-haired captain stood up. He was about to speak, but he swallowed his words. He spat, pointed, and said "Go!"'

153. 'And the boy went. The people drew back, made a lane along which he was allowed to pass without hindrance. Red as the blood that spurted from his finger was the blood-red flush now upon his cheeks. He left the farm, went far up into the mountains; they watched him from the village, talking among themselves. He climbed and climbed till you could no longer make him out —he belonged at home in among the mountains.

154. 'Many's the day I have thought about that lad—especially on Independence Day when people gathered in the market-place and walked, singing and carrying flags, to the liberator's statue. The first time I joined them was as a schoolboy, when I marched along with other youths, eager, merry. I felt there was something infinitely inspiring about that singing and marching flood of people.

155. 'The broad street was too narrow for the procession. Every vantage point was occupied, every window crowded. Fair women smiled graciously upon us. Ribbons fluttered, gaily coloured flowers abounded, cannons thundered, flags flapped and fluttered, the dust rose as on a battlefield, patriotic songs resounded, small boys beat their drums, and all hearts witnessed: "Glorious is our North!"

156. 'The country's promise and budding hopes, we stood around the monument, many thousand strong. Now it grew quiet; somebody seemed to be expected. Then a man climbed up on the plinth. Shouts and applause surged like some great wave; there were shrill cries of "Hurrah" among the peal of trumpets. "There he is," the cry ran through the crowded throng. The people gave a greeting to their skald.

157. 'For this man was the nation's great poet. Blond, broad-shouldered and strong, hatless, he stood by the lion, gripping the stonework, gratifying the eyes of the crowd, as greatness requires. And when he had reaped the approbation of renewed shouts and

clapping from all directions, he lifted up his voice, filled his lungs and spoke, first in prose and then in verse.

158. 'First he spoke of the morning sun's new dawn in Eidsvoll's groves after the night of thraldom; then he spoke of freedom's treasure found, and then of the great significance of this festive day. His eyes shone mistily, and the crowd shared his vision— the kind of glow that comes from devoting a day and a night to the punch bowl and to abandoned dancing.

159. 'Then he spoke of the linking generations between past and present. The effect of his speech was great. He condemned all those who denied popular gods, and far over the multitude there re-echoed these words: "The blood that runs in every Norseman's veins is the blood that coursed in Jarl Haakon; the glow that burns upon a Norseman's cheeks once glowed upon the cheeks of the Thundergod."

160. 'Then I remembered the blood that ran in the forest, and the cheek that flamed by that long table. The blood in my limbs ran cold; a lightning flash broke my daydream, and I awoke. I looked about me. Would anyone guffaw? No, on the contrary. They listened breathlessly; only a murmuring sound like the purring of a contented cat whose coat is stroked and whose chin is scratched.

161. 'He tickled the crowd, and they allowed themselves to be tickled; only I stood crushed under the weight of the truth. I knew why the blood trickled and why the cheeks of the people flushed. I ran away as if I had seen devils from the thousand swamps of hell celebrating the festive day. But behind me shouted and roared a thousand mouths—that was my people endorsing those skaldic lies!

162. 'The trumpet's sound seemed to add its oath to the lies, and the poet stepped down, his speech finished. But the seed he sowed will be scattered again in print in all of Norway's valleys. It sprouts here, sends roots down there; what harvest can be expected in a hundred years? When the prince of lies speaks through the priest, how will it fare with the rest?'

163. He leaped up from the rock; he looked down where the village lay in shadow, wet and black; his face was like a gathering storm,

his look not merely stern but dark and hard. He resembled Moses, this young priest. With all the wrath of the Old Testament, he stood there like the eagle of the Lord looking down on his people in the desert as they worshipped the golden calf.

164. Yet once again a ray of sunshine passed across his face; his features cleared and became composed. He saw a boat putting out from the far shore, and away beyond the headland saw two more. Soon there were ten, gliding in towards the spit of land; and along the roads there was bustle and activity, with groups of people all converging on the same objective, the old village church.

165. It was church time. He lowered his gaze to that strange and quiet event; and compulsively, the words came in a low voice from his breast: 'What worth are these souls to the Lord? Over wide areas of the earth it is now the holy hour; *there* a thousand spires point towards the sky; *there* the organs roll, the bells ring out, calling to worship in the house of peace.

166. '*There* the sun shines; *there* the sky is open; out *there* the one soul rubs bright against the other; *there* the ore of thought is shaped into a handle to lift each single soul above the tumult. *There* angels hover—great and strong and silent—and offer to bear the message of mankind. *There* it is possible to approach God—all one needs is the courage and the will.

167. 'But *here*! Look at the church with its wooden shingles. No tower, no spire, no cross to point on high; no bells call, no organ plays. It lies shut in by the mountains, with the strip of sky made narrower by the snowdrifts! How the mist bears down upon the hills! Yet see how the congregation swarms and creeps and throngs upon the road to church.

168. 'These quiet people also wish to join their voices in the world's chorus. What did the Lord God give them to sustain them? What dove did He send to them with the Word? What did they get beyond bare life? What bids them to give praise and prayers of thanks? He commanded; He uttered his stern "Be!"; and the people became—the sons of misery.

169. 'One thing I'd like to know. Suppose the whole of mankind had been destroyed just as the hour of salvation was at hand, and only

these were left—I wonder whether the weight of sin would have been atoned by blood, as it now is? Would the Lord have sent His Son for these? The agony of the cross been endured for *these* —so great a solution for so little? I believe, I believe He would have for sure!'

170. He started to hasten down; but at that moment a little stone rolled into his path, rolling and leaping till it came to rest far down the hillside. He glanced up: there stood an unkempt dog looking at him expectantly, its ears cocked, and behind the dog a girl, laughing and holding a rag to her mouth.

171. She seemed half woman, half child; warm-blooded and shapely, vital and eager, uncertain of herself though not wholly innocent, wanton and wondering though inexperienced. She stood as though she jested through her tears; she breathed as though she felt both pleasure and pain; her skin was golden-brown. It was easy to see that gypsy blood ran through her veins.

172. Her hair was cut short like a boy's. Her eyes, deep-set and black, looked hard and unswervingly at the priest, strangely appealing and yet mocking. Her short skirt flapped round her legs, and her feet were bound in skins. She carried a goat-horn in her right hand. She held on to the branches of a bush behind her.

173. Wonderingly, like some new-born child, she stared down; the priest gazed up. Then, between path and hillside, two questions passed unspoken, and met halfway. Soon, however, the priest found speech; with a nod, he asked gently: 'God's peace—how far is your road?' But the girl screamed as though stung; she let go the bush and clambered back up the hill.

174. She gave no answer, but merely climbed. He heard the rattle of pebbles, the crackle of the heather. High up she stopped. Coldly, dully, she looked at him and called down: 'To Church!' Again she climbed, higher and ever higher; then again she stopped, and cupped her hands to her mouth: 'To church, I tell you!' she shouted down, this time with laughter.

175. She climbed till she vanished behind a corner of the overhanging glacier, cold and jagged. 'To church!' she shrieked, and this time the cry came through her horn. 'To church', she shouted, now here, now there, but always higher and more distant, now from

the glaciers, now from behind the boulder-strewn slopes of the bare mountain.

176. 'To church', the girl shouted, sometimes through her cupped hands, sometimes through her horn; it sounded far over the valley floor, echoing again from the rock face to the North. 'To church' it boomed, now like song, now like laughter, now like distant bells; sometimes it was like a shriek, sometimes like a beguiling tune in the wasteland.

177. Something seemed to freeze the priest's blood. Silently he stood there, staring and listening, as the voice sounded, shifting, fleeting, sometimes from behind him, sometimes to the side, sometimes in front. She was going to church; but the church lay far below him in the valley, and she climbed upwards. How far? Whither? In among the peaks, away among the pillars of the mountain hall.

178. And yet to church! Church? A name flashed like flickering lightning through the night of his memories, coming and going, hissing and beckoning. It escaped his tongue; but at last he grasped it. At first it sounded so foreign to him, so strange; but gradually its features grew familiar, until finally all the mists of time rolled away and the name stood out sharply in the light of home.

179. He remembered a remote valley, far within, where the mountain wastes lie under frozen snow—a cleft between mountain peaks, with an overhang running between snowdrift and glacier. By frost and thaw and whirling snow, winter builds this gleaming vault across between the rocky walls; through the valley runs a raging river; the mountain side throws blue-black shadows.

180. Often the dome reaches halfway across the valley; it extends far across, brittle; the melting ice secretly hollows it out, but the drift increases from year to year. But if there should come a sun-warmed summer, the ice structure collapses with a thunderous roar; the streams are swollen, the rivers rush and foam, and the snow drift cracks across the sloping crest.

181. The foundation supporting it is washed away as melted ice, and booms and cracks give warning of its collapse. A gust, a flurry of snow, then a crashing roar, and away goes the avalanche,

filling the entire valley. A clap of thunder, a rifle shot is enough when the glacier hangs in its brittle state—then for many long years the river must force its way through the depths, submerged.

182. He recalled, from when he was little, how a strange discovery had been made. Long long ago a man had gone off hunting, and since then nobody had seen or heard of him. He had been hunting reindeer somewhere deep in the mountains; a shot had been fired and an avalanche started. People still mentioned the precise time and place, even though the events happened long before living memory.

183. Nearly a hundred years later they found the marksman. The crushed reindeer flock, the shot beast, the rifle, pouch, the hunting cabin—all came to light on the frozen marsh. Then old and young had to see the discovery; he remembered that he had been allowed to go along. Now, despite all the time that had elapsed, he remembered what people called that uncanny place.

184. It was called the Ice Church. Far above his head, a path led up there along the edge of the precipice. Anyone making for it would have to pass this spot—and it was exactly here that the girl had passed. She was making for the Ice Church. When she stood near him, he seemed to feel a gust from the glacier, a blast of whirling snow and ice. She came from the snow, and to the snow she went.

185. All things presented themselves to him in this cold light. He saw the life of his native village, its apathy, its struggle, as through a veil of frozen mist. And it was through *here* that he had to go. He wished he had a horse, wished that he could gallop past every homestead, every farm, particularly his mother's. He wished to hear nothing but the sparks struck by his horse's hooves—then straight on for the fjord.

186. On board, on board! Who wants to shut himself in when the world lies open to him, and ample? Who wants to blast the barren rock when there is cultivated soil to find? Who plants kernels to gather fruit when there are young trees, soon to mature? Who shouts himself hoarse in daily labour when he has brilliant visions and soaring thoughts?

187. Who sells his life's work for so little? He remembered Einar's words: 'A diocesan curacy is hardly the appointment from which

to start a reformation; shut in by mountains, the voice does not carry far!' So out of the mountains and into the light! He rose, and straightened himself; his determination was strong. The Lord waited for his work. To make mankind whole—that was the task.

188. No longer did he see the people swarming at his feet; his eyes were fixed on higher distant paths. He saw a great procession, with music and banners, with victory following sacrifice, with death and blood. With all the force a lonely soul can muster, he yearned to be outside his narrow home. There he caught a glimpse of *his* way to church, like sunshine through a partly open door.

189. What concern to him was that churchgoer up in the snows? Or those two who chose the way to church through joy? Or the crowd that crept along the deep and narrow valley? *He* was to cure the whole world's pain! *His* voice was to ring out for all. He walked as proud as though the work were already accomplished—as tall as if he wore a crown of thorns. Then he looked up. He was standing by the church door.

By the church

190. There are many townships along the length of Norway where to live is to hunger until one drowns, where whole generations toil until they die, like their fathers and their grandfathers, in flood or in avalanche. There is many a parish assembly that would find room enough to meet in the servants' quarters of some rich man; many a church can be found where the low roof would bend each back not already bent by a hard life.

191. This was such a township; and so also was its church. Storms had taken away its tower, and now it stood lopped; the rain had stained its painted walls; its carvings had crumbled with the weather. The serpents and the tendrils on the door-frame could scarcely be distinguished under the coats of tar, and the dragons on its roof had been replaced by boards and planks.

192. On the hill slope was a fenced plot where the women and children of the township lay buried; the bodies of the men all lay elsewhere, some beneath the rocks, some in the sea. It was badly kept, that holy ground; but the gate indicated a thoughtful founder; for

it was arched, spacious and big, as though the broad highway ran beneath it.

193. Here stood our midwife of the age. He listened; all was quiet as in the house of the dead. Neither hymn nor service met his ears. He grasped the latch; the lock held. This little house of God was shut; no deacon read in the chair, nobody preached the Word. Then he climbed over the churchyard fence, but there too it was deserted. Where were the people?

194. He listened; the air hung heavy and dank. Yet there was something that cut through the silence. He heard a shout, and then an answer; now a name was mentioned, now a number. It seemed to come from behind the church. He approached; now it sounded close at hand; he stepped over the boundary. There he stood, high and free. Then a strange picture caught his gaze on the hillside below.

195. The red marquee stood where the river runs in a curve round a nearby spit of land. The whole parish, men and women and children, were collected here in a group. They looked more dead then alive. The sunken temples, the dark-ringed eyes, the hoarse voices proclaimed that hunger held sway here.

196. It was the old song that never ends: a bad year, then a winter without bread; a spring with empty mouths and empty hands, and then a summer with disease and death. And then an appeal that failed, then poor relief sullenly and reluctantly offered, a cautious groping into sack and purse—a meagre mite to those who lacked everything.

197. By the steps there sat a man in city clothes, a meerschaum pipe hung from the left corner of his mouth; and every time he turned, an old gold-embroidered tobacco pouch swung from his jacket button. He seemed to be the man in charge. He wrote notes on his knee, read, and shouted to this man and that in the pallid crowd, and meted out corn and bread in fragmentary portions.

198. He found time in his activity for jokes and other remarks, humorous, frivolous; he looked about him with a contented smile, and laughed with lack-lustre pewter-blue eyes; his round cheeks glistened with well-being, and he addressed each man as a comrade; to many he nodded and shook hands—and was nice to the children—talking all the while.

199. 'There, Nils, is corn and money; home now, and keep hunger
and Satan away from your door. Don't squander it now, my
man—and forget about those nips of brandy! Here's yours,
Aslak—away now, you waster, feed those who wait, eat and be
merry. But, Kari dear, burn his hymn book—I mean the one
with the fifty-two leaves!'

200. Thus it went without pause. Bread, morals, corn, well-meant
advice all went together; a man with a golden chain laughed like
mad, holding his belly as though ready to burst. But among the
little pallid crowd there was silence; only a strained smile passed
over the group. Each one took his share, big or little, and without
thanks slipped off through the crowd.

201. It was as if distress had burnt out their souls, as though their wills
no longer resided there, as though a leaden weight of hopelessness
had attached itself fast to their heels. It was as though life was a
punishment, the cruel meaning of which was that it had to be
lived. It was as though all assertion were pointless, all rebellion
futile, all striving empty.

202. Brand stood looking down. He saw his friend, the young girl,
the guide and the horse; the pack animal was being loaded up
again. The remnants of their food were being shared out. Then
the contents of the purse distributed, coin by coin, and those who
stood around stared silently, took what was offered them, and
left, confused. And the man on the steps almost forgot his duties.

203. But soon he regained his composure and looked round as though
he had had some part in that miracle. He shouted to the couple:
'Take your time! Do good, to some purpose! You are welcome!
Share out in fingerbowl and share out in bucket; we accept great
things and small.' And his eye glistened in a juicy smile; then he
looked round, and his gaze fell upon Brand.

204. He pointed up with his pipe, nodded, laughed and called out:
'Turn around, good people. There are others. I fancy I was lucky
in my choice of time. I swear you'll get something more!
Welcome! Come down here! We are short! You have doubtless
heard of flood and of drought? Here I sit with my people in the
desert, and my few small fishes will not stretch very far!'

205. But Brand remained standing, cold, pale, and earnest; in that
moment the priest looked handsome. And yet it sounded as

though he was insensitive to the silent grief and the sighs of the crowd. He shook his head, remained silent for a moment, and then replied: 'Yes, I have bread to give, but before I would give the smallest slice to you, I would throw it all to a dog.

206. 'Where is the heart among you that dare freely take? Where is the power here that dare distribute? Where is the spirit amongst you who will accept God's chastisement without complaint? Follow me! I have a better gift to offer than compensation for your wasted efforts. Cast your burdens off, and I shall interpret the Lord's writing on the wall for you!'

207. It was as though a king stood amongst them, so obediently they hearkened to his words; and when he turned to go it was as if something pulled them in this unknown man's path. Soundlessly they set down what they had been given, regardless of whether it was great or small; they followed him to the gate of the church silently, and moved by a strange excitement.

208. Somebody unlocked it. Brand climbed up to the pulpit. They whispered quietly among themselves: 'This is a priest!' But the man whose face had shone like the sun stood sullenly by the door like an uninvited guest. Inside it was deathly still in the gloom, and the benches in the church filled row by row; the priest could be heard murmuring in the pulpit, but nobody could hear what he said.

209. His prayer was short, and then he spoke: 'Man, remember, you do not live by bread alone. But if your body's needs alone are met, then it is as though you were offered stones for bread. And if your pangs of hunger can be stilled by gifts handed out to you, then you have no relation to your God—and there is no bridge between you and the spirit.

210. 'This morning I stood high on the mountain peak and saw you flocking hither on every path; and I thought then that your minds were fixed on Him, who raises up and makes free in the valley of distress. I thought life among you was following its old course, with no thought of a new awakening. Yet I was glad that you nevertheless felt the need to reach for Him as for a saving raft.

211. 'How easy to believe oneself forgotten by the Creator, how quickly one believes oneself abandoned by one's God when

neither stars nor sun move in their courses, when there is neither morning nor night, when everything is grey upon grey, all things the same, the same need today as yesterday, the old picture in the old frame as long in time as the eye can reach.

212. 'When nothing rises and nothing sinks, when life oppresses like a canopy of mist, when nobody is angered and nobody whimpers, when the judgement is taken as it is passed, when no terror and when no joy cast light and shade on the progress of the day, the soul is tempted to collapse and to believe itself struck out of the book of the Lord.

⟨*The manuscript ends abruptly here.*⟩

BRAND
[Brand]

A DRAMATIC POEM
(1866)

Translated by James Kirkup
in collaboration with James Walter McFarlane

CHARACTERS

BRAND

HIS MOTHER

EINAR, a painter

AGNES

THE MAYOR

THE DOCTOR

THE DEAN

THE SEXTON

THE SCHOOLMASTER

GERD

A PEASANT

HIS YOUNG SON

A SECOND PEASANT

A WOMAN

A SECOND WOMAN

A CLERK

PRIESTS and OFFICIALS

MEN, WOMEN and CHILDREN of the district

———————————

THE TEMPTER in the WILDERNESS

INVISIBLE CHOIR

A VOICE

The action takes place in our own time [1866], in part in and around a fjord township on the west coast of Norway.

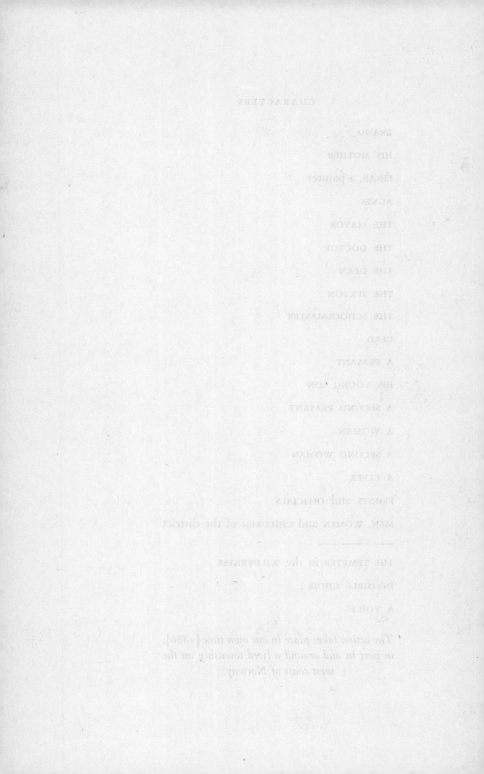

ACT ONE

In the snow, high up in the mountains. The mist lies thick and heavy. It is raining and nearly dark. BRAND, *dressed in black, with a staff and a pack, is making his way with difficulty towards the west.* A PEASANT *and his young* SON, *who have joined him, are some way behind.*

PEASANT [*shouts after* BRAND].
  Hey you! Slow down a bit!
  Where are you?

BRAND.   Over here!

PEASANT.   Ye'll get lost!
  The mist's that thick, ye can
  Scarce see the fist afore your face. . . .

SON. The ice's cracked, Dad!

PEASANT.   It's a crevasse!

BRAND. And now we've lost all trace of the path.

PEASANT [*shouts*]. Give over, man! For God's sake . . .!
  The ice just here's as crisp
  As crackling! Don't go stamping on the snow!

BRAND [*listening*]. I hear a waterfall roaring.

PEASANT. That'll be the torrent
  Has worn it out all hollow underfoot;
  There's a chasm under here, dear knows how deep . . .
  It could swallow up the lot of us!

BRAND. I told you—I *must* keep on.

PEASANT. It's more than any man can—Look you here!
  It sounds all hollow and brittle underfoot . . .
  Come on back, man! Ye'll be the death of all of us!

BRAND. I *must* go on. I am doing
  What my master bids me do.

PEASANT. What do they call him?

BRAND.   They call him God.

PEASANT. And who d'ye think *you* are?

BRAND.   A priest.

PEASANT. Very likely; but I'm telling ye,
Ye could be the Dean or the Bishop himself,
But ye'd be a goner afore the night's out—
That's if ye keep on along the hollow
Rim of this glacier.

[*Approaches cautiously, speaks persuasively.*]

Now listen, priest.
Even if a man's got book-learning,
There are some things he cannot do.
Come on back; don't be so daft!
A man's got only one life.
If he loses that, what's left?
It's six miles to the nearest house,
And the fog's getting that thick
Ye could cut it with a knife.

BRAND. When the fog is thick, there can be no
Will-o'-the wisp to lead our steps astray.

PEASANT. But there are ice-holes all round us;
Those ice-holes are nasty things.

BRAND. We shall walk across their waters.

PEASANT. Walk the waves? I think your tongue's
Too big for your head.

BRAND. Someone once proved . . . that faith
Will carry a man dry-shod over water.

PEASANT. Yes, but that was a long time back.
These days he'd sink like a stone.

BRAND. Farewell! [*He turns to go.*]

PEASANT.   You'll kill yourself.

BRAND. If the Lord has need of my death . . . I gladly
Give myself unto flood and waterfall and chasm!

PEASANT [*in a low voice*]. He's mad! He's out of his mind!

SON [*almost crying*]. Come on, Dad, let's turn back!
The sky's looking blacker than ever!

BRAND [*stops and walks back again*]. Look, man! Didn't you just tell me
Your daughter down by the fjord
Sent you word she was dying; and cannot
Depart this world in peace, if she may not
Look one last time upon your face?

PEASANT. That's the God's own truth.

BRAND. And so she gave you until today?

PEASANT. That's right.

BRAND.   No longer?

PEASANT.   No.

BRAND.   Come on then!

PEASANT. It can't be done. Turn back!

BRAND [*looks hard at him*]. Listen! Would you pay a hundred daler
For her to die happy?

PEASANT.   Yes, sir!

BRAND.   Two hundred?

PEASANT. I'd gladly sign away house and home
If only she could die in peace!

BRAND. But—would you give your *life*?

PEASANT. What? My life? Now wait a . . . !

BRAND. *Would* you?

PEASANT [*scratching his head*]. Well, now . . . there's a limit . . . !
For Christ's sake, remember
I've a wife and children at home.

BRAND. He whose name you utter
Also had a mother.

PEASANT.   Yes,
But that was a long, long time ago.
There was plenty of miracles and things then;
Life's different these days.

BRAND. Go back home. Your life is the way
Of death. You know not God,
And God knows not you.

PEASANT.   You're a hard man.

SON [*pulling at his coat*]. Come on, Dad.

PEASANT.   All right. But *he's* coming with us!

BRAND. Am I?

PEASANT.   If ye get lost in this perishing cold,
And it gets around—can't be kept dark, can it?—
That we set out together, then one fine day
I'll be up before the judge . . .
And if ye get drowned in some bog or lake,
I'll find myself behind bars. . . .

BRAND. Then you'd be suffering in the service of the Lord.

PEASANT. I'm having nothing to do with either you or Him;
I've enough to see to, looking after my own.
Come on, lad!

BRAND.   Farewell!

[*A hollow roar is heard in the distance.*]

SON [*screaming*].   It's an avalanche!

BRAND [*to the* PEASANT *who has seized him by the collar*].
Let me go!

PEASANT.   No!

BRAND.   Let go of me!

SON. Dad! Come on!

PEASANT [*struggling with* BRAND]. I'll be damned if . . .

BRAND [*tears himself loose and hurls the other into the snow*].
    You will be in the end; of that
    You can be certain. [*He goes.*]

PEASANT [*sits and rubs his arm*]. Oh! Oh! He's stubborn!
    And he's got some muscle on him! So this
    Is what he calls doing the Lord's work!

          [*Shouts as he gets up.*]

    Hey, preacher!

SON.   He went over the ridge.

PEASANT. I can still see him. [*Shouts.*] Hi, there!
    D'ye remember where we went off the path?

BRAND [*in the mist*]. You need no signpost. . . . Your way
    Is already all too broad enough.

PEASANT. I hope to God it is, for then
    I can be safe and snug at home tonight.

    [*He and his* SON *make again towards the east.*]

BRAND [*appears again higher up, looking in the direction in which the*
    PEASANT *went*].
    There they go, groping their way back home.
    You spineless wretch! If only you'd shown some spirit,
    If it had only been the flesh that was weak,
    I would have lightened the burden of your way;
    Though weary unto death, and with bleeding feet,
    I would have gladly borne you on my back;
    But what use is help to a man
    Who will do no more than he knows he can?

          [*Moves on again.*]

    Ah, life, life! To people like these,
    How very dear life seems! Every little runt
    Lays so much store by life, you might think
    The salvation of the world, the spiritual welfare
    Of all mankind lay on *his* puny shoulders.
    Any sacrifice they'll make . . . as heaven is my witness!
    Except life! Life must be saved at all costs!

    [*Smiles as though remembering something.*]

When I was a boy, there were two secret thoughts
That made me shake with inward laughter;
They got me many a hiding
When the old schoolmarm was feeling nasty:
I tried to imagine an owl afraid
Of the dark, and a fish afraid of water.
They used to make me laugh out loud.
I tried to put them from my mind, but still
They stuck there, like burs. . . . What gave me
Those sudden fits of laughter? Well, I suppose
It was the dimly-apprehended gulf
Between what is, and what ought to be . . .
Between having to bear the burden, and
Finding the burden too heavy to bear. . . .
       Nearly every man in this land, whether sick or well,
Is just such an owl, just such a fish.
He was created to toil in the deep,
And meant to have his being in the dark.
Yet those are the things that make him tremble.
He flounders in fear towards the shore;
He dreads his own star-bright chamber,
And from him the cry goes up
'O, for air! O, for the fires of noon!'

            [*Halts for a moment, listening.*]

       What was that? It sounded like singing!
Yes, it is singing, mingled with laughter.
Hark at them! Such a joyful shout!
And another . . . and another . . . and yet another!
       How the sunlight streams down there!
The mists are lifting. Now
I see the fields, all white with snow.
Look! Up there in the morning sunlight,
On that high ridge, there I glimpse
A happy band of friends, their shadows
Cast westward across the desolate snowfields.
They are exchanging a few last words;
They are giving each other their hands.
And now they are parting. They are all
Turning to the east, all but two,

Who now are turning towards the west.
They are shouting their last goodbyes,
Waving caps, veils, hands.

[*The sun is gradually breaking through the mist. He stands for some time looking down upon those coming towards him.*]

These two approaching—light shines about them,
As though the mist gave way before them,
As though the rough heather were spreading
Soft carpets on the rocks at their feet,
And the heavens seem to laugh around them both.
They must be brother and sister.
Hand in hand, they dance
Over the springy heather. Look! That girl
Scarcely seems to touch the ground, and he
Is as lithe as a willow-wand. Now
She's running away from him! She slipped away
Just as he was about to catch her. . . .
Now their chase is like a children's game!
Their laughter is turning into song! Listen!

[EINAR *and* AGNES, *in summer clothes, both of them warm and glowing, come frolicking across the snow-covered fields. The fog has lifted; the mountain lies in clear morning light.*]

EINAR.

> Butterfly, sweet butterfly,
> Come and let me catch you!
> In the net of songs I made
> Come and let me snatch you!

AGNES [*dancing backwards in front of him, always just out of reach*].

> If I am a butterfly
> Do not try to smutch me,
> Let me sip the heather bells,
> Chase but do not touch me!

EINAR.

> Butterfly, sweet butterfly,
> Now my net's above you!
> Soon you will be mine, and
> Wings will never save you!

AGNES.

> If I am a butterfly
> I will gladly play, sir!

But if you should net my wings,
Keep your hands away, sir!

EINAR.   O, but I shall hold you
Tenderly, and warm you
Always in my heart, where
None shall ever harm you!

[*Without noticing it, they have approached a steep precipice; they are now standing right on the very brink.*]

BRAND [*shouts to them*]. Stop! You are right on the edge of
A precipice!

EINAR.   Who's that shouting?

AGNES [*points upwards*].
Look up there!

BRAND.   Save yourselves
Before it is too late! You are standing
On a hanging ledge of snow, suspended
On the very brink of a precipice!

EINAR [*puts his arms about her and laughs*].
You need have no fears about us.

AGNES. We have a whole lifetime to play away!

EINAR. A sunlit future lies all before us—
One hundred years of it!

BRAND. So the end will not come till then?
Is that what you mean?

AGNES [*waves her veil*]. No,
After that, our play will still go on,
And rise and soar into the infinite.

EINAR. First, one hundred years of festive gatherings,
With wedding lanterns lighted every night . . .
A whole lifetime, a hundred years of play . . .

BRAND. And then?

EINAR.   Then home again . . . home to Heaven.

BRAND. Ah, so that is where you have come from?

EINAR. Of course, where else?

AGNES.   Well, strictly speaking,
  The last place we came from was
  The valley east of the mountain.

BRAND. Yes, I thought I caught a glimpse of you
  Over there on the ridge.

EINAR. Yes, there we parted from our friends;
  We shook hands, embraced, and kissed
  To put the seal on all our happy memories.
  Come and join us! I shall tell you
  How great is the glory of God . . .
  Then you will grasp the depth of our joy . . .!
  Oh, don't stand there like a snowman!
  Come on! Thaw out! That's better.
  First let me tell you I'm a painter
  And that in itself is happiness enough . . .
  To be able to let my thoughts take flight,
  To be able to charm life into colours,
  Even as He makes butterflies from worms.
  But God was greatest in His glory
  When He gave me Agnes for my bride!
  I had come from the south, after long journeyings,
  My painter's gear upon my back . . .

AGNES [*eagerly*].   Happy as a king,
  And his head filled with a thousand songs!

EINAR. Just as I was passing through this village,
  She happened to be there on a visit. *She*
  Was sent there to drink the wild mountain air.
  And *I* . . . some divine power drove me to that mountain.
  A voice kept singing within me: seek out beauty
  Among the pine forests, by the forest streams,
  In the clouds coursing the vault of Heaven!—
  There it was I painted my masterpiece:
  A rosy blush upon her cheeks,
  Two eyes shining with happiness,
  A smile that sang its way into my soul. . . .

AGNES. But you scarcely saw what you were painting . . .
　　　You drank blindly from the cup of life,
　　　And then, one sunny day,
　　　With staff in hand and your rucksack ready—

EINAR. Then it suddenly occurred to me:
　　　I'd forgotten to ask her . . . !
　　　Aha! No sooner said than won!
　　　'Yes', said she, and that was that!
　　　Our old doctor was over the moon.
　　　He threw a party for us,
　　　Three whole days of singing and dancing
　　　With the young folk of all the local families . . .
　　　The sheriff's, the constable's,
　　　The magistrate's, the minister's.
　　　We set off from the farm last night;
　　　But the party still wasn't over. . . .
　　　They came to send us on our way,
　　　Waving flags, with leaves and flowers in their hair,
　　　Up the mountainside and over the ridge.

AGNES. We just danced our way over the mountain . . .
　　　Couples dancing together, or all dancing in a ring.

EINAR. We drank sweet wine from a silver cup. . . .

AGNES. Our songs rang out on the summer night. . . .

EINAR. And the heavy mist from the north
　　　Gave way before our dancing.

BRAND. And whither does your way take you now?

EINAR. Straight on down into the town.

AGNES. That's where I come from.

EINAR. But first we must pass the final peaks;
　　　Then westwards down to the fjord;
　　　Then full steam ahead on Egir's horse
　　　And home to our wedding-feast;
　　　After that . . . on together to the south,
　　　Like swans on their first flight from winter.

BRAND. What then?

EINAR. A happy married life,
Radiant as dreams, lovely as legends.
This very Sunday morning, you know,
Deep in the mountains, no minister mind you,
Our lives were hallowed against all grief and guilt,
And dedicated to a festival of joy.

BRAND. By whom?

EINAR. By all our happy band.
As our wine-glasses clinked, we banished
Every storm-cloud threatening our leafy bower
Of sweetness and light. And kissed goodbye
To every word bearing even a hint
Of the sound of a storm. Our friends,
With leaves in their hair, proclaimed us
True children of joy.

BRAND. I bid you both farewell. [*About to go.*]

EINAR [*starts, looks more closely at him*]. No, stop! Wait!
Your face is familiar. . . .

BRAND [*coldly*]. You know me not.

EINAR. Was it at school, or was it at home . . .
I do believe I can remember . . .

BRAND. It was at school. Yes, we were friends there.
I was only a boy then; now I am a man.

EINAR. Surely it can't be . . . ? [*Suddenly cries out.*] Brand!
It's Brand! Now I know who you are!

BRAND. I knew who *you* were from the start.

EINAR. How glad I am! How good to see you again!
Let me look at you! Yes,
You're the same old Brand, the same old loner—
We could never drag you into our rowdy games.

BRAND. They had no appeal for me.
You I do believe I was fond of,
Though all of you down in the south
Were made of different stuff from me . . .

I who was born on a bleak headland by the sea.
Born in the shadow of a barren crag.

EINAR. Your native village . . . Isn't it in these parts?

BRAND. My way shall take me through it soon.

EINAR. *Through* it? Are you going further, then?

BRAND. Yes, much further. And straight away,
Leaving house and home behind.

EINAR. Are you a priest?

BRAND [*smiles*].   A diocesan curate.
Like the creatures of the pine-wood,
I have my house here one day, there the next.

EINAR. And where are you finally bound for?

BRAND [*quickly and sternly*].
You must not ask me that!

EINAR.   Why?

BRAND [*altering his tone*].
Well, why not? The ship awaiting
You down there will also carry me.

EINAR. Our sea-borne wedding coach? Wonderful!
Agnes, think of that! He's going our way!

BRAND. Yes. But *I* am going to a funeral.

AGNES. A funeral?

EINAR.   Who's being buried?

BRAND. The God you just called *yours*.

AGNES [*shrinks back*].
Einar, let's go.

EINAR.   Brand!

BRAND. The God of hacks and time-serving drudges
Shall be wrapped in his shroud and laid in his coffin.
And in broad daylight. This thing must have an end.
It is time, don't you see? He has been ailing
These thousand years.

EINAR. You're sick!

BRAND. No!
I'm strong and fit as the mountain pine,
As the wild juniper on the hill.
It is our sick generation needs a doctor.
All you want to do is flirt, play, laugh.
Your faith comes easy, but you will not see. . . .
You want to unload the whole burden of anguish
On one who, we are told, paid the supreme penalty.
Don't you see? It was for *your* sake
He bore upon his brow the crown of thorns,
And that is why you are now free to dance.
Well, dance on! Dance away!
But where is your dancing leading you?
That, my friend, is another matter!

EINAR. Oh, I see now! This is the new cry,
And everyone seems to be taking it up now.
You belong to that group of young people
Who go about calling life stale and vain,
Who want to put us all into sackcloth
Out of fear of hell-fire.

BRAND. No. I'm no preacher.
I do not speak as a priest of the church;
Indeed, I hardly know if I am a Christian;
But I do know this: I am a man, and I do know
There is a canker devouring the marrow of this land.

EINAR [*smiles*]. Well, this land of ours never did have
Much of a reputation for the joy of life.

BRAND. No. Our hearts are hardly bursting with joy.
If it were so, then all might be well.
What matter if you are a slave to joy . . .
Just as long as you stay that way? But
Don't be one thing today, one thing yesterday,
And something quite different a year from now.
Be what you have to be
Wholly and completely, not
A little bit here and a little bit there.
You know where you are with a Bacchante, but

G1

A drunk is neither one thing nor the other.
Silenus is a magnificent animal;
Your common tippler's a mere travesty of that.
Just move around this country, and listen,
Listen to what people have to say,
And you will find that each man
Has taught himself to be only a bit of everything.
A bit solemn when it comes to Sunday,
A bit loyal to the ways of his ancestors,
A bit randy after supper—for those same ancestors
Were like that, too—
A bit sentimental on festive occasions
When songs of praise are sung
For the small but sturdy nation
That never bowed to an alien lash:
A bit lavish with his promises, but also
A bit stingy when, in the sober light of day,
He weighs up what he promised;
'Oh, I must have been drunk', he explains
When the day of reckoning arrives.
Yet, as I said, he's only a bit of everything.
Neither his faults nor his virtues go very far:
In great things and in small
He is but a fragment, a vulgar
Fraction of evil, a fragment of good.
But the worst thing of all is:
Each bit of each fraction
Smashes the whole to smithereens!

EINAR. It's easy enough to scoff.
It'd be more charitable to spare them . . .

BRAND. Perhaps, but not so salutary.

EINAR. Oh well! I suppose I must admit you're right
In all your charges against our people.
But I don't see what this has to do with
The one you want to bury—
The God I still call mine.

BRAND. My merry friend, you are a painter.
Show me the God of whom you speak.

You have painted him, so I have heard,
And the picture has moved men. I expect
You made him old, didn't you?

EINAR.   Well . . .

BRAND.   Of course.
And grey? With an old man's bald pate,
And a long beard like threads of silvery ice?
Kindly looking, but forbidding enough
To scare the children off to bed with?
Did you put him in carpet-slippers?
Well, we won't go into that.
But I'm sure he would really look the part
If he were given a pair of specs and a skull cap.

EINAR [*angrily*]. Look here . . .

BRAND.   I'm not joking.
That is exactly the way he looks,
This household god of our native land.
Just as the Catholics have made
A baby-faced brat of our Saviour here.
The people of this land make of our Lord
A doddering old man in his second childhood.
Just as the Pope on St. Peter's throne
Has little more to show than a couple of crossed keys,
Even so shall the Kingdom of God
Be confined to churches only, the length
And breadth of the creation.
You separate life from faith and teaching;
Nobody makes the effort to *be*;
You strive to elevate your souls,
But not to live the full life.
For this kind of holy decrepitude
You need a God who turns a blind eye.
Like men themselves, this God of yours
Is turning grey and thin on top, and so
Must be depicted wearing a skull cap.
But this God is not *my* God!
Mine is a gale where yours is a zephyr,
Mine an obdurate judge . . . yours hard

Only of hearing. Mine is all love
Where yours is passion-spent. And mine
Is young like Hercules—not
Some old greybeard in his dotage!
O, but that voice of his did strike
With lightning and with terror when
Like a blazing fire in the bush of thorns
He stood before Moses on Mount Horeb,
A giant before the dwarf of dwarfs.
He did stay the sun in the Vale of Gibeon,
And did perform unnumbered miracles. . . .
Yes, would still be working wonders, if only
Men were not all gutless, like you!

EINAR [*with an uncertain smile*]. So now
You want all men to be created anew?

BRAND. That I do, sure as I know
I was born into this world of ours
To heal its sickness and its wrongs.

EINAR [*shakes his head*]. Do not blow out the match
Even if it does splutter a little,
Before the lantern lights our path;
Do not expunge the old words from our tongue
Before you have created new ones.

BRAND. I am not aiming at anything new;
I want to uphold eternal truths.
It is not dogmas and churches I want to exalt,
For they have both seen better days; and so
They'll soon see worse, the final dark.
All things created have their measured end.
Moth and worm corrupt them; they give way,
By nature's law, to forms unborn. But there is
One thing that does prevail and endure—
That is the uncreated spirit, once redeemed
From Chaos in the first fresh Spring of time, and still
Extending bridges of unalterable faith
From banks of flesh to banks of spirit.
Now it is hawked from door to door, and cheap . . .
Thanks to this generation's view of God.

But out of these dismembered wrecks of soul,
From these truncated torsos of the spirit,
From these heads, these hands, there shall arise
A whole being, so that the Lord
May recognize his creature Man once more,
His greatest masterpiece, his heir,
His Adam, powerful, and tall, and young!

EINAR [*interrupting*]. Farewell. I think we'd better part here.

BRAND. You to the west, I to the north.
Two paths lead to the fjord, both
About the same length. Farewell!

EINAR. Farewell.

BRAND [*turns as he is about to go down*]. Learn to tell
The true light from the false. And remember . . .
Living is also a work of art.

EINAR [*waving him away*]. Go, turn the whole world upside-down;
I shall stick to the God I know!

BRAND. All right! Paint him with crutches . . .
But *I'm* going to lay him in his grave!

[*Walks off down the path.* EINAR *walks over in silence, watching* BRAND *go.*]

AGNES [*stands for a moment lost in thought; then she starts, looks around
uneasily and asks*].
Has the sun set?

EINAR.   No, nothing but
A passing cloud. It's coming out again.

AGNES. The wind blows cold.

EINAR.   Only a gust
Sweeping through the pass. Here we go down.

AGNES. That mountain to the south did not seem
To bar our way before, nor look so black.

EINAR. Because we were singing and playing.
You did not notice it until
He frightened you with his ravings.

But let him follow his own steep path;
We'll continue our game where we left off.

AGNES. No, not now. I'm tired.

EINAR.　　　　　　　　　　And so am I.
And the path down is not as easy
As it was over there on the moors.
But once we have the heights behind us
We shall dance for sheer devilment—Yes,
A hundred times faster and wilder
Than we might have danced before.
Look here—look at that stretch of blue
On which the sunlight glistens now!
Sometimes it ripples, sometimes it laughs,
Sometimes it's silver, sometimes it's amber,
That is the great open sea out there.
You see that dark smoke hanging over the strait?
And that black dot just rounding the headland?
That's our steamer—yours and mine!
Now it's beginning to turn into the fjord . . .
This evening, it will steam out again,
Out to sea, with you and me aboard!
Now, a heavy, grey fog is starting to fall again—
But didn't you see what a beautiful composition
The sea and the sky made, just for a moment?

AGNES [*looks unseeingly, lost in thought*]. Yes, of course. But tell me,
Did you see—something else . . . ?

EINAR.　　　　　　　　　　What?

AGNES [*without looking at him, and speaking softly, as if in church*].
As he was speaking . . . how he seemed to grow?
　　　　[*She goes down the path.* EINAR *follows her.*]

———————

[*A path along the flank of the mountain, with a fearsome abyss falling
away to the right. Above and behind the mountain can be seen even
higher peaks, covered with snow.*]

BRAND [*comes along the path, making his way down, stops halfway on a
projecting rock and looks down into the valley*].
Ah, now I know where I am!

Every boathouse, every cottage,
All the dead falls of rock,
The birches at the river mouth,
The elder-bushes by the stream,
And the old brown church. . . .
I remember it all from my childhood.
But it seems to look greyer now,
And smaller; the mountain's suspended
Avalanche of snow hangs over
Even more than it did then,
And has narrowed even more
The valley's narrow sky. How it
Glowers, threatens, overshadows,
Robbing us of the light of the sun!

[*He sits down and stares into the distance.*]

There's the fjord. Was it quite
So gloomy and narrow in those days?
Look at those rain squalls driving across it!
That sailing ship scudding before the wind.
To the south, in the shadow of the crag
I see a building by the jetty;
Behind it a cottage with dark red walls . . .
The cottage, by the estuary—
The widow's cottage—my childhood home.
Memories and memories born of memories.
There among the stones along the shore
My child-soul dwelt alone.
  My soul was ever weighed and oppressed
By this burden, by this kinship
With a spirit ever earthwards-trending,
Ever away from my true self.
Everything I yearned for then
Now seems lost in the mists of time.
My courage and my strength have failed me,
My mind and soul grown slack and feeble,
And coming home, I feel a stranger. . . .
I wake bound and tamed and shorn,
Like Samson in Delilah's bosom.

[*Again looks down into the valley.*]

But what is going on down there?
Men, women and children coming out
Of all the cottages. Long lines
Of folk moving between the broken rocks
And reappearing once again
Over there by the old church.

[*He gets up.*]

O, but I know you through and through,
Ye sluggard souls, ye laggard minds!
None of your prayers has wing enough,
Nor groaning anguish, nor reverberating voice
Enough to thrust its way to heaven—
Except when begging for daily bread!
That is the motto of this country;
That is its people's battle cry.
Torn from its roots, stamped on each heart,
It drifts along upon the air
Like a shipwrecked fragment of your faith!
Get out of that stagnant pit! The air
Is as stale as the bottom of a coal mine.
No fresh breeze can ever blow
Down there upon the flags of freedom.

[*He is about to go. Someone throws a stone from above. It rolls down the slope close beside him.*]

BRAND [*shouting upwards*]. Hey, there! Who's throwing stones?

[GERD, *a fifteen-year-old girl, runs along the edge of the cliff with stones in her apron.*]

GERD. Did you hear? It screeched! I hit it! [*Throws again.*]

BRAND. Now hold on! Stop this nonsense!

GERD. There it is—I've still not got it . . .
It's hopping along that fallen branch!

[*Throws again, screaming.*]

Here it comes, the big brute!
Help! Aaagh! It's tearing me with its talons!

BRAND. In God's name . . . !

GERD.   Shut up! Who d'you think you are?
     Keep still! Keep still! There, it's flying away now.

BRAND. What's flying away?

GERD.   Didn't you see the hawk?

BRAND. Up here? No.

GERD.   That great ugly bird
     With its crest flattened against its head
     And its red and gold rimmed eyes!

BRAND. Where are you making for?

GERD.   The church.

BRAND. Oh, then we can go together.

GERD. With *you*? No. I'm going up there.

BRAND [*pointing downwards*]. But the church is down there.

GERD [*looks scornfully at him, then grins and points downwards*].
     That one down there?

BRAND.   Naturally. Come on.

GERD. No. It's too ugly.

BRAND.   Ugly? What do you mean?

GERD. Well, for one thing, it's so mingy.

BRAND. And do you know of a better one?

GERD. Better than that? I should say so. Farewell!

                    [*Continues her way upwards.*]

BRAND. Is *that* the way to your church?
     The way leads into wild mountains.

GERD. Come with me, and you shall see
     A church that is builded of ice and snow!

BRAND. Ice and snow! Now I understand!
     High up between the mountain peaks—
     I remember hearing when I was a boy—
     There is said to be a chasm at the valley head;

I believe they used to call it the Ice Church.
We used to hear all kinds of things about it . . .
How its floor is a frozen tarn,
And the snowdrift piled above it
Poised just like a roof
Over the cleft in the rock wall.

GERD. Yes, it looks just ice and rocks, like . . .
But it's a church, a real church.

BRAND. Don't you ever go near the place!
One gust of wind could dislodge that snow . . .
Or a shout, a rifle shot . . .

GERD [*not listening to him*]. Come with me,
I'll show you a reindeer herd
Buried alive under an avalanche—
And reappearing only with the Spring thaw.

BRAND. Don't go there! It's dangerous!

GERD [*points down*]. Don't go there. It's ugly!

BRAND. May the peace of God go with you.

GERD. I'd rather *you* go with me! Up there,
Mass is sung by waterfall and avalanche.
The wind prays from the glacier cliff,
Till you're burning and freezing both at once.
And the hawk never gets within my church;
It comes swooping down upon the black peak—
And it just sits there, the ugly beast,
Like a gloomy weathercock upon
My church's steeple of glittering ice.

BRAND. Stormy your path, and stormy your soul,
A harp of the winds with a broken frame.
Bad breeds nothing but badness, though
Evil may sometimes be turned to good.

GERD. Here it comes with its great wings
Flapping! I must run and hide!
I'll be safe inside my church!
Aaaagh! How fierce and ugly it is! [*Screams.*]

Don't come near! I'll throw this stone!
Claw at me, and I'll club you with this, you brute!

[*She runs away up the mountain.*]

BRAND [*after a pause*]. So, she's a churchgoer too.
There's the valley . . . and the mountain. . . .
Which is right? Which of us has lost the way?
Which is the blinder, stumbling further
From peace and home? Is it
That rashness of mind, garlanded in leaves and flowers,
Dancing at the brink of the deepest abyss?
Or that dullness of mind, plodding along
Because that was the way it always went. . . .
Or that madness of mind, so wild in its flight
That all evil seems good! I must gird up my loins
And do battle evermore against this Triple Threat!
I now behold my vocation; it shines
Like a shaft of sun through a chink in a shutter.
I behold now the nature of my mission upon earth!
The downfall and death of those three demons
Would cure this world of all its sickness.
If we can send them to death and damnation,
The sickness of this world will be banished!
Come, my soul, let us take arms and fight!
Unsheath your bright blade! And fight,
Fight for the inheritors of Heaven!

[*He descends into the valley.*]

ACT TWO

Down by the fjord with steep mountain walls all round. The dilapidated old church stands on a little hill near by. A storm is gathering. The people of the parish—men, women and children— are gathered in small groups, some on the shore, some on the hillsides. The MAYOR is sitting in the midst of them, on a stone; a CLERK is helping him; grain and other provisions are being distributed. EINAR and AGNES are standing some little distance away, surrounded by a group of people. Some boats are drawn up on the shore. BRAND appears on the hillside by the church without being noticed by the crowd.

A MAN [*forcing his way through the throng*].
Out of my way!

A WOMAN.   I was first!

THE MAN [*pushing her aside*].
Get away with you!

                    [*Pushes through to the* MAYOR.]

                                See here!
Fill this empty sack!

MAYOR.   Give me time.

MAN. Can't! Got to get home! There's four . . .
Five of us sitting at home starving!

MAYOR [*jokingly*].
Sure it wasn't six . . . or seven?

MAN. One was dying as I left.

MAYOR. Wait! I suppose you are on the list?

                    [*Thumbs through his papers.*]

No . . . Yes, you are. Lucky for you.

                                [*To the* CLERK.]

Let Number Twenty-nine have his. Now, now, folks,
Steady on, steady on! Nils Snemyr?

A MAN.   Yes!

MAYOR. Today you get only three-quarters of last time's.
There's not so many of you now.

THE MAN. Yes, my Ragnhild died yesterday.

MAYOR [*makes a note*].
One less. Something lost, something gained.

[*To the man who is moving away*.]

Now don't you go running off
And getting yourself married again!

CLERK [*giggles*].   Tee-hee!

MAYOR [*sharply*]. What are you laughing at?

CLERK.   I was laughing
Because you were so witty, your Worship.

MAYOR. Shut up. This is no time for playing the fool.
Well, maybe the best thing for sorrow is a good laugh.

EINAR [*steps out of the crowd with* AGNES].
Now I have emptied all my pockets.
My purse and my wallet are empty, too.
I'll go abroad like some tramp,
Having to pawn my watch and stick.

MAYOR. Yes, you two have come just in time.
What I've scraped together doesn't come to much.
It doesn't go far, I needn't tell you,
When careworn hand and hungry mouth
Have to share crust and crumb
With those with even less than themselves.

[*Catches sight of* BRAND *and points*.]

Here's another! The more the merrier!
There's famine, flood, and drought among us here.
Loosen your purse-strings. All's grist to our mill.
We'll soon be scraping the bottom of the barrel.

In the wilderness of poverty, five small fishes
Don't make much of a meal nowadays.

BRAND. Even ten thousand, shared out in an idol's name,
  Would not profit a single soul.

MAYOR. I wasn't asking you for a sermon. Words
  Are no better than stones when the belly's empty.

EINAR. You cannot possibly know how long
  And how severely people have suffered!
  Brand, this is a bad year, with famine and sickness.
  People lying dead of hunger . . .

BRAND.   I can see that.
  The dark, leaden ring circling every eye
  Proclaims who holds court here.

MAYOR. And still you stand there as hard as flint!

BRAND [*steps down among the crowd and speaks emphatically*].
  If life here ran slowly and gently,
  Ran the sluggish course of everyday need, then
  I could have pity on your cries for bread.
  If you have to creep home on all fours
  Then the beast in you comes out.
  If day follows day in drowsy lassitude,
  And time moves at a funereal pace, then
  It's all too easy to think one has been banished
  From the Lord's good will. But to you
  He has shown the best will on earth!
  He has dripped terror into your blood;
  He has scourged you with the whip of death!
  Those precious gifts of his he has taken away . . .

SEVERAL VOICES [*interrupting him threateningly*].
  We're starving, and he mocks us!

MAYOR. We give you bread, and he abuses us!

BRAND [*shakes his head*]. Oh, if all the blood within my heart and body
  Could restore you like a healing stream of life,
  Then it would pour forth in such a flood
  That all my arteries and veins would soon run dry.
  But here—giving help here would be a sin!

Don't you see? God wants to raise you from the mire.
A living people—even when scattered and weakened—
Draws strength and marrow from affliction.
The dulled vision soars like a falcon then,
Seeing far and seeing clear. The weakened will
Is given backbone once again, and confidence
Of victory beyond the present conflict.
But where adversity breeds no nobility of mind,
Those people are not worthy of salvation!

A WOMAN. The storm's breaking, out over the fjord,
As though it had been awakened by his words!

ANOTHER. He'll bring the wrath of God on us, you'll see!

BRAND. *Your* God can perform his miracles no more!

THE WOMEN. Just look at the sky! The sea! Look!

VOICES AMONG THE CROWD. Drive this hard-hearted creature from our
      village!
Drive him out with stones and knives!

[*The people swarm threateningly round* BRAND. *The* MAYOR *intervenes.
A woman, wild and dishevelled, runs down the hillside.*]

THE WOMAN [*shrieks to the crowd*].
  Help me! In the name of Jesus,
  Help me, someone, help me!

MAYOR.   What's the matter?
  Tell us. What do you need? What do you want?

THE WOMAN. It's not a question of needing or wanting!
  O, it's the most horrible thing . . . horrible . . .

MAYOR. What is it? Tell us, woman!

THE WOMAN.   I cannot tell you!
  Where is the priest? O, help me, help me, God!

MAYOR. There's no priest here . . .

THE WOMAN.   Lost, lost!
  O, God, how could you be so cruel,
  To let me be born into this world . . . A priest . . .

BRAND [*approaches*]. Perhaps one might be found.

THE WOMAN [*grips his arm*].   Then bring him now!
  What's keeping him?

BRAND.   Tell me your trouble. He will come.

THE WOMAN. Across the fjord . . .

BRAND.   Yes?

THE WOMAN.   My husband . . .
  Three starving children, and the house
  With nothing in it . . . No, no!
  He can't be damned for that!

BRAND. Come, tell me.

THE WOMAN.   I had no milk.
  Neither man nor God would help us.
  The youngest was fighting hard against death.
  It broke his heart to watch . . . He killed . . . !

BRAND.   Yes?

THE WOMAN. He killed his own child!

THE CROWD [*fearfully*].   His own child!

THE WOMAN. As he did the deed, he stared in the abyss!
  The tears rushed from him like a river!
  He tried to kill himself! Come now and save his soul!
  He cannot go on living, and he dare not die.
  He's lying there, holding the dead boy, and
  Calling on the Devil to come and take him!

BRAND [*quietly*]. Yes, he has great need of me.

EINAR [*pale*]. Can this be true?

MAYOR.   He's not in my ward.

BRAND [*curtly, to the crowd*].
  Get a boat and take me across!

A MAN. In a storm like this? No one would dare!

MAYOR. There's a footpath running round the fjord . . .

THE WOMAN. No, no! It's not passable now.
    I came that way, but the river in flood
    Carried away the bridge behind me.

BRAND. Get me a boat.

A MAN.   Impossible.
    The waves are dashing on the rocks!

ANOTHER. Look there! The wind off the mountains
    Has got the whole fjord in a turmoil!

A THIRD. With weather like this, with such pounding waves,
    The minister usually calls the service off.

BRAND. A sinner's immortal soul, so close to perdition,
    Cannot wait upon wind and weather!

        [*Steps down into a boat and loosens the sail.*]
    Will you risk your boat?

THE OWNER.   Yes. But you can't go in this!

BRAND. Good! Now who will risk his life as well?

A MAN. I'm not going.

ANOTHER.   Nor I!

SEVERAL.   It's certain death. We'd be drowned!

BRAND. *Your* God would help not one of you across the fjord!
    But remember that *mine* is here on board with me!

THE WOMAN [*wringing her hands*].
    He'll die in mortal sin!

BRAND [*shouts from the boat*].
                  Give me just one man
    To help me bale and haul the sails! Come,
    One of you who were so generous just now!
    Who will give again, give in the face of death?

SEVERAL [*recoiling*]. You can't ask us that!

ONE MAN [*threateningly*].   Out of that boat!
    You'll go too far. You'll bring the wrath of God
    Upon us all!
    H1

SEVERAL VOICES. Look! The sea! It's a storm!

OTHERS. The rope's snapped!

BRAND [*holding on with the boat-hook and shouting to the woman*].
                    All right, then!
       You come with me. Come on! Now!

THE WOMAN [*recoiling*].
       What, me? When no one . . . !

BRAND.   Leave them!

THE WOMAN. I cannot!

BRAND.   You cannot!

THE WOMAN.   Remember my little ones . . . !

BRAND [*laughs*]. You built your house on sand!

AGNES [*turns with flaming cheeks quickly to* EINAR, *places her hand on his
       arm and says*].
       Did you hear that?

EINAR.   Yes, he's brave!

AGNES. God bless you! You know where your duty lies!

                    [*She shouts to* BRAND.]

       Look! There's one man here who's fit
       To sail with you to the rescue.

BRAND. Come on, then!

EINAR [*pale*].   What! I . . . ?

AGNES.   Go with him!
       I release you from our vows. My eyes
       Were fixed upon the ground, but now I see the stars!

EINAR. If it had been before I met you, then gladly
       I would have offered myself, and sailed with him.

AGNES [*trembling*]. But now, you . . . !

EINAR.

No, I cannot do it!

I am young. Life is so sweet.

AGNES [*shrinks back*]. What did you say?

EINAR. I dare not . . . dare not do it.

AGNES [*cries out*].
Then now there lies between us
An ocean that can not be crossed,
All raging foam and tempests!

[*To* BRAND.]

I shall come with you in your boat!

BRAND. Come on, then!

THE WOMAN [*in terror as she springs on board*].

Jesus! mercy!

EINAR [*desperately tries to seize her*].
Agnes!

THE WHOLE CROWD [*rushes forward*].
No! Stop! Come back!

BRAND. Where's the house?

THE WOMAN [*pointing*].   Over there!
On that headland, behind the black rocks!

[*The boat moves away from the shore.*]

EINAR [*shouts after them*].
Think of your brothers and sisters!
Remember your mother! Save yourself!

AGNES. There are *three* of us on board!

[*The boat sails off. The crowd gathers on the hillsides and gazes after them, tense.*]

A MAN. He's cleared the point!

ANOTHER.   No, he hasn't!

THE FIRST.   He has!
It's astern now, and to his leeward!

THE SECOND. That squall! It's hit them!

MAYOR. Look, the gale's carried off his hat!

A WOMAN. Black as a raven's wing, his dripping hair
Streams behind him in the wind!

FIRST MAN. The waves boil and smoke.

EINAR. What was that cry I heard
Above the storm?

A WOMAN.   It came from the mountain.

A SECOND WOMAN [*pointing*].
Look! It's Gerd! Look at her!
Standing there laughing and screaming at him!

FIRST WOMAN. She's blowing on a ram's horn, and throwing
Stones like a witch's curses.

SECOND WOMAN. She's flung away her horn; now
She's hooting through her cupped hands!

A MAN. Howl on! Shriek away, you ugly troll!
That man has someone watching over him.

SECOND MAN. With him at the helm, I'd put to sea again,
And in far worse storms than this!

FIRST MAN [*to* EINAR]. What is he?

EINAR.   A priest.

SECOND MAN. Whatever he is, he's a man, all right!
What courage! What strength! And what a will he has!

FIRST MAN. Now there's the man we need for a priest!

MANY VOICES. Yes! He's for us! He's the priest for us!

[*They disperse over the hillsides.*]

MAYOR [*gathering up his papers and books*].
But when all's said and done, I think
It's most irregular to interfere in other people's
Private affairs, risking others' lives for no good cause.

I think I can say I always do my duty,
But never overstep the bounds of my electoral ward!
[*He goes.*]

[*Outside the cottage on the point. It is late in the day. The fjord lies
smooth and still.* AGNES *sits down by the shore. A moment or two later*
BRAND *comes out of the door.*]

BRAND. So that is death. It has washed away
   The stains of all his guilt, and all his fear.
   Now, he lies there with a face of perfect peace,
   In rest and silence, his burden cast away.
   Can night be altered into day like this, and changed
   So easily, as if it all were but a vain illusion?
   Of his wild and hellish crime he understood
   Only the empty outer shell, so many empty words,
   The dead matter that is all the fingers grasp,
   The mere name of the deed that branded him, and wrought
   Its mindless violence upon a dying child . . .
   —And now there are those two little ones,
   Who crouched there terrified, staring wide-eyed,
   Like lost fledgelings huddled in the chimney-corner . . .
   Those two, who could only watch till it was over,
   They themselves not understanding what it was . . .
   Those two, upon whose souls a scar was seared
   That they can never heal in all the weary toil of time.
   Nay, not even in their bent and white-haired age
   Will they from whose contaminated memories
   The river of their lives must flow, illumined
   By the ghastly flare of one night's horrifying hell,
   Will they have burned away to ashes of oblivion
   This foul carcase of their father's twisted mind;
   A father who did not have the wit to realize
   It was these little children who would bear for ever
   His condemnation and his shame. Or that the seed of crime
   He planted in them might put forth still more inhuman deeds.
   O, why? Why? Why? The answer, like an echo's
   Hollow mockery, reverberates from the abyss:
   They are their father's sons! Can the silences of time
   Unwrite their book? Can mercy wipe away their fate?

Deep in the darkest springs of human life, O where
Does our guilt and our inheritance of shame begin?
What great trial that will be, that final hearing
From which all judgements come! Who shall plead innocence,
And who shall testify against him, when all are guilty?
Who shall dare produce the filthy record of his sins?
—And on that day of judgement, can man's one plea be
This defence: the fault was in my father? O, riddle,
Lost immeasurably deep within eternity's long night,
No man can yet unravel all your mystery. But on the brink
Of the abyss, the masses dance on, mindlessly and heedlessly.
The soul should cry aloud against its horror, but
Not one man in a thousand who has eyes to see
What awful, overwhelming avalanche of guilt
Hangs suspended on that little word—the one word, Life!

[*Some of the villagers peep out from behind the cottage and approach* BRAND.]

A MAN. So we meet again.

BRAND.   He no longer needs your help.

MAN. He's gone. He's past all saving. But
There are still three left behind.

BRAND.   Well?

MAN. We've brought a bit of the scraps we got . . .

BRAND. Even if you were to give everything, but not your life,
It would still be as if you had given nothing at all.

MAN. If that man lying dead there now were suddenly
To find himself in mortal peril, and shout to me for help from
His overturned boat, I'd risk my life for him.

BRAND. But the cry of his immortal soul would fail to move you?

MAN. Remember, we lead a poor and harsh existence here.

BRAND. Then turn your eyes away completely from
The light beyond the mountain; stop squinting
With your left eye on heaven, your right eye on the earth,
Where like some beast your back is harnessed to the yoke.

MAN. I should have thought you would advise us rather
To cast the yoke aside.

BRAND. Do so, if you can.

MAN. You have the power.

BRAND. I do?

MAN. Many a man
Before now has told us where the way lies.
They told us, but you *took* it.

BRAND. You mean . . . ?

MAN. Not even a thousand words can leave
A mark like that left by one deed.
We have come to you in the name of the parish.
We see that what we need is . . . a *man*!

BRAND [*uneasily*]. What do you want of me?

MAN. Be our priest!

BRAND. Me? In this place?

MAN. You have doubtless heard
And read that our parish is without a priest.

BRAND. I do recall . . .

MAN. In former times this parish was big.
But it's declined. When the bad years came,
And when the corn was killed by frost,
When sickness felled the people and their beasts,
When poverty brought every man to his knees,
When destitution numbed our souls,
When meat and grain grew dear and scarce,
Then priests too grew scarce.

BRAND. Ask anything but that of me!
It is a greater burden I must bear.
I need the broader currents of existence,
I need the open ears of all the world. But here,
What can I do? Imprisoned by these mountains,
A man's voice cannot reach the outer world.

MAN. But when it is the mountain that replies to it,
  Words boldly and bravely spoken reverberate the longer.

BRAND. What man would bury himself in a pit
  When there are free, open meadows beckoning?
  Who will plough barren wastes, when there is tilled land?
  Who grows his fruit from seed
  When there are young trees ready to bear?
  Who drudges on at some monotonous task
  When he has visions, fire, and wings?

MAN [*shakes his head*].
  Your deed I could understand. But not your words.

BRAND. Bother me no more! I must go back on board.
                      [*Is about to go.*]

MAN [*standing in his way*].
  This call which you will not give up—
  This work you yearn for—is it so dear?

BRAND. It is my life!

MAN.   Then stay! [*With emphasis.*]
  Even if you were to give everything,
  But not your life, remember, it would still be
  As if you had given nothing at all. . . .

BRAND. One possession you cannot give away;
  And that is your own inner self.
  You may not stop, may not deflect,
  May not obstruct the river of your call. . . .
  It must seek its own course to the open sea.

MAN. Even if it were lost in marsh or lake,
  It would finally reach the ocean, as drops of dew.

BRAND [*looks hard at him*].
  Who was it put such words into your mouth?

MAN. You gave them to me in the heat of action,
  When the tempest raged, and waves lashed the shore.
  When despite storm and tempest you went forth,
  When to save a helpless sinner's soul
  You staked your life upon a plank—then your voice

Rang through the minds of all of us, now icy cold,
Now hot as fire, like sun and wind together—
It rang through us like the beating of a brazen bell . . .

[*Lowers his voice.*]

Tomorrow, perhaps, it will have been forgotten;
Then we shall haul down the colours of the inspiration
That you hoisted over us today.

BRAND. Where there is no strength, there can be no call. [*Hard.*]
If you cannot be what you ought to be,
Then try to be whatever you honestly can.
Be utterly a man of clay.

MAN [*looks at him a moment before speaking*]. Cursed be you
Who stamped out the very light you lit!
Cursed be we, who for a moment saw that light!

[*He goes; the rest follow him silently.*]

BRAND [*follows them with his eyes*].
One by one, with bent heads, the silent little group
Goes home again. Their spirits sink, their feet drag
And stumble heavily and wearily along the way. Each one of them,
Worn out with care, moves as if threatened with the whip,
Moves like the first man being driven out of paradise . . .
Moves like him with a brow furrowed by guilt . . .
Gazes like him into a dark void . . . bears like him
The burden that is all the profit knowledge brings . . .
Bears like him the blinding of the eye of innocence.
I have to dare to create that man anew—a whole man,
Clean and sound. To work here would be to toil in guilt,
And not a labour to the glory of the Lord,
As it is meant to be. I must leave this place for wider fields;
There is no room here for noble deeds.

[*Is about to go; stops when he sees* AGNES *on the shore.*]

See how she sits, listening as if to some
Music in the air—even so she sat, listening,
In the boat as it cut its way through the raging waves,
Listening as she clung to the plank she sat on,
Listening as she wiped the sea-spray from her open brow.

It is as if her hearing had changed its source,
And she were listening with her eyes alone. [*Approaches.*]
Is it the fjord's crooked course your eyes are following . . . ?

AGNES [*without turning round*].
   Neither the fjord's nor the world's; for both
   Are hidden from my sight. No, I glimpse a larger world;
   Its image stands out sharp against the sky.
   I see oceans, and the estuaries of rivers. I see daybreak,
   And sunlight gleaming through the mists,
   Fiery red, smouldering on cloud-topped peaks;
   I see an immense waste of desert. Giant palm trees
   Stand there swaying in the keen winds,
   Casting sombre shadows behind them. No sign of life.
   It is like a world about to be created. I hear voices
   Ringing, and I hear other voices, telling what they sing:
   Now thou art either saved or lost. Do thy work,
   This appointed, heavy task. For thou shalt people this earth!

BRAND [*carried away*]. Tell me more of what you see!

AGNES [*placing her hand upon her breast*].   Here, within me,
   I can feel secret forces stirring, can feel
   Floods rising, can see a great dawn breaking.
   My heart, like the world itself, expands into infinity,
   And I hear again the other voices, telling me:
   This is the world that thou must people!
   Every thought that is to come, every deed to be performed,
   Wakens, whispers, breathes, and moves as if
   The moment of some mighty birth were now at hand.
   And—no, I do not see, but rather
   Sense that One who sits on high, and know
   He gazes down upon us full of love and sadness,
   Radiant and gentle as the dawn, and yet
   Sorrowful unto death. And again I hear the voices ringing:
   Now thou shalt create and be created; do thy work;
   Now thou art either saved or lost;
   Do thy appointed, heavy task!

BRAND. Within! Within! That is my call!
   That is the way I must venture! That is my path!
   One's own inmost heart—*that* is the world,

Newly created, and ripe for God's work.
There shall the vulture of the will be slain.
And *there* shall the new Adam at last be born again.
So let the world go on its way, singing or in chains;
But if that world and I should ever meet as foes,
Or if that world should ever try to wreck my work . . .
Then, by Heaven, I shall smite it to the death!
O, for room in the world's wide arch, a place
Where I may be myself entirely! That is the lawful right
Of every man! This granted, I should demand no more.

[*Reflects silently for a moment, then says:*]

To be myself entirely? But what about that burden,
The weight of one's inheritance of guilt?

[*Pauses and looks into the distance.*]

Who is this comes toiling up the hill,
Stooping, stumbling, bent almost double?
She keeps stopping to get her breath, and leans
Upon a stick to keep herself from falling.
Her skinny fingers clutch at her pockets, as if
She carried some great treasure there. Her skirt
Hangs in rags and tatters round her withered limbs.
Her hands are clenched like pincers. She flaps
Like a moulting eagle nailed to a barnyard wall. [*With sudden fear.*]
O, what ice-cold childhood memory, what chill blast
From home and farm and fjord casts its bitter frost
About this woman . . . and casts an even sharper frost within . . . ?
God have mercy! It is my mother . . .

[BRAND's MOTHER *climbs up the slope, stops when she is half visible
above the hill, shades her eyes with her hand and looks about her.*]

MOTHER.   They told me he was here.

[*Approaches.*]

Drat this sun—it fair blinds me! Is that you, son?

BRAND.   Yes.

MOTHER [*rubs her eyes*]. Ugh! This glaring light! It burns your eyes out.
You can't tell a priest from a peasant.

BRAND.   At home,
I never saw the sun from leaf-fall till the cuckoo's cry.

MOTHER [*laughs silently*]. Ah, yes, now *there's* a good place to be. Back
    home
You freeze hard, a waterfall frozen into a man of ice.
You're so strong, you dare anything, and still
Feel your soul's in safe keeping.

BRAND.   I must be going.

MOTHER. Yes, you were always in a hurry. Even as a boy
You ran away from home. . . .

BRAND.   You wanted me to leave.

MOTHER. Ah, well, there's reasons for everything, then as now.
Yes, I suppose you had to go and make yourself a priest.

                    [*Observes him more closely.*]

Hm! How big and strong he's grown! But mark my words—
Watch out for your life!

BRAND.   Nothing more?

MOTHER. Well, what more is there than life?

BRAND. I mean the warning that you gave me.
Is that all?

MOTHER.   If you know of something else,
Take heed of it. But life . . .
Keep that for me. It was I gave life to you.
[*Angrily.*] People have been talking of you. It scared
And horrified me. You went out on the fjord today!
Why, you might have robbed me of what
For *my* sake you should preserve and treasure.
You are the last of our line . . .
You are my son, my flesh and blood.
You are the final roof-beam of the dwelling
I have built with my own hands, bit by bit.
Hold fast to life! Stand firm! Endure!
Be careful of your life! Keep on!
It is the last son's duty to stay alive . . .
And some day . . . in the future . . . you'll be my . . .

BRAND. Ah! So that's why you came seeking me . . .
To buy me back?

MOTHER.   Are you mad?
[*Draws back.*] Keep away from me! Don't touch me,
Or I'll lay about you with this stick!
[*Calmer.*] What's got into you? Listen here!
I'm not getting any younger, son. Sooner or later
I'll be in my grave . . . and it won't be later.
Then you'll be left everything that I possess.
I have it there, all counted, measured, weighed.
I've brought nothing with me. It's all at home.
There's not all that much, mind you. But it's enough
To keep you in comfort for the rest of your days. . . .
Stay where you are! Don't you lay hands on me!
I promise you, I won't hide my stuff in secret cubbyholes,
Or push my gold into crevices or bury it in the woods.
I won't hide anything under stones, or in walls,
Or under the floorboards. It's all for you, my son,
The whole inheritance. You shall come into the lot.

BRAND. On what conditions?

MOTHER.   Only this . . .
That you do not throw your life away.
Keep up the family name, hand it on from son to son.
That's not much for a mother to ask, is it?
And see to it that the money's not squandered.
Don't divide the property, or share it out.
Whether you build it up or not is up to you.
But above all—hold on to it!
Hold on to it through thick and thin!

BRAND [*after a short pause*]. We must get one thing clear between us.
Ever since I was a boy, I've been against you.
I was no son to you, you were no mother to me
Until your hair was grey, and I was grown.

MOTHER. I'm not the sort that needs petting and fussing.
Be what you will—but I'll never be soft.
Be hard, be stubborn, be cold as ice . . .
You'll never best me. Hang on to what's yours. . . .

What though it might be dead and barren
So long as it stays within the family.

BRAND [*takes a step forward*]. And what if I did just the opposite,
And scattered it to the four winds?

MOTHER [*staggers back*].   What? Throw away
All those years of work that bent
My back and turned my girl's hair grey?

BRAND [*nodding slowly*]. Yes. Scatter it to the four winds.

MOTHER.   If you do,
It's my soul you'll be scattering to the winds!

BRAND. And what if I do? I can see myself,
Standing by your bed at night,
With all the candles set and shining round you
With your prayer-book in your folded hands
As you sleep through your long first night of death—
What if then I were to rummage round
And snatch your hoard away bundle by bundle . . .
And what if then I were to take a candle,
And set it all alight . . . ?

MOTHER [*tense, approaching him*].
What puts this idea into your mind?

BRAND. Do you really want to know?

MOTHER.   Yes! Tell me!

BRAND. It comes from something in my childhood, something
I can never forget. It seared my soul, and left a scar
That marked me for life. It was an autumn evening.
Father was lying on his deathbed,
And you were ill. I crept in,
Where he lay white and still in the candle-light.
I stood in a dark corner, staring at him.
I saw he was holding his old prayer-book.
I wondered why he slept so silently and deep,
And why his bony wrists had grown so thin.
I caught the smell of cold and clammy sheets.
Then there were footsteps: a woman came in,

But did not see me. She went straight over
To the bed, and started to grope and fumble.
She shoved the dead man's head aside,
And snatched a bundle, then several more.
I could hear her whispered counting of the notes:
'More, more, more!' Then from the pillows she
Pulled out a packet tied with knotted string.
She clawed at it, tore at it with trembling hands,
And finally had to bite it open with her teeth.
She groped about again, found several more,
And whispered hoarsely: 'More, more, more!'
She wept, she prayed, she moaned and swore.
She seemed to root out hidden treasure
Like a hog, by smell; and, striking lucky,
Time and time again would pounce,
In ecstatic anguish, like a falcon on its prey,
And pounce again. And at the end,
Every hole and corner had been rifled.
She left the room, moving like one condemned.
With her ill-gotten gains all bundled in a shawl,
She went out moaning to herself: 'So this is all!'

MOTHER. It was a desperate time for me. There wasn't much,
And what I found that night I paid for dear.

BRAND. And had to pay for dearer still. It cost you the affection
Of your only son.

MOTHER.   That may well be.
It's the common custom here to give
Your heart and soul away for property and gold.
Right from the start I paid the price in full—
I see now I paid it with the shipwreck of my life.
I gave it all away—and now it's gone for ever.
I seem to see it now as something bright and fleeting,
Something foolish, light as air, but beautiful,
Something I now hardly know the meaning of . . .
People used to call it love.
I still remember well how hard it was;
Remember too my father's words of advice:
'Forget the cottager's young son. Take

The other one. Forget his wizened body.
He's got brains. He'll be a money-maker.'
I took him, but he brought me only shame.
He never made his fortune; but since his death
I've toiled and slaved, and now
I'm not far off making one myself.

BRAND. So now, when you are near to death,
    All you remember is that you sold your soul?

MOTHER. That's all I remember. And the proof of that is,
    I made my son, my only son, a priest.
    When my time comes, you will ease my soul,
    And in return the inheritance is yours.
    The property and gold belong to me:
    Yours are the words of strength and comfort at the last.

BRAND. Shrewd as you are, yet you deceived yourself when you
    Projected on your son the image of house and home.
    Many a mother in these valleys, by the fjords and the lakes,
    Possesses this form of parental love, looks upon her child
    As someone to tidy up the mess she leaves behind.
    From time to time, faint apprehensions of eternity
    Pass through your mind. You snatch at these,
    And so delude yourself eternity is yours
    Because you've chained the family to the inheritance.
    You mistakenly imagine you're uniting life and death, and fancy
    The vastness of eternity to be the sum of earthly years.

MOTHER. Now, son, don't go prying into wiser heads than yours.
    Just take what's coming to you. Leave the rest alone.

BRAND. And what about your debts?

MOTHER.   My debts? What debts?
    There are no debts!

BRAND.   Oh, very well. But if there were,
    You know I'd have to be responsible
    For everything, and settle every claim.
    It is the duty of the son to settle all demands
    As soon as his mother is laid within her grave.
    You might leave me nothing but an empty house.

The sum of my inheritance would be the debts you leave behind.

MOTHER. There's no law says that.

BRAND.   Perhaps no written law.
But in the mind of every honourable son
Another kind of law's engraved, a law to be obeyed.
Woman, are you blind? Then learn to see!
You have diminished the estate of God on earth,
And squandered the soul he graced you with.
The image in which he created your humanity
You have defiled with dirt and filth. The spirit
That should have soared is bound now to earth
Because you clipped its wings. These are the debts I mean.
Where will you turn to when the Lord demands
The restitution of all these precious things he gave you?

MOTHER [*timidly*]. Where shall I turn to? Where?

BRAND.   Have no fear.
Your son will take upon himself all debts that you have made.
The image of God which you defiled shall be restored,
Cleansed by the fire of my will. Go then to join the dead
In comfort, with a mind at rest. It shall not be said
My mother was laid away within a debtor's grave.
I shall settle all your debts.

MOTHER.   All my debts. And my sins, too . . . ?

BRAND. Your debts, and those alone. Mark well what I say.
Your son shall settle the debts laid on your soul;
But you yourself must answer for your sins.
All that human good that you destroyed within yourself
Through shabby greed—this can be paid in full by someone else.
But the real sin lies in the waste itself, a crime
That can be expiated only by repentance—or by death!

MOTHER [*uneasily*]. I think now I'd better be getting back home,
Back to that shadowy home beneath the glacier-cliff.
Here, in this sultry sunlight's uncanny glare,
Poisonous thoughts begin to sprout like evil weeds.
My senses reel with their suffocating fumes.

I I

BRAND. Return to your shadows. Remember I am never far from you.
   And if one day you again desire the light of heaven,
   And want another meeting, send word, and I shall come.

MOTHER. Yes, with more talk of penalties to pay!

BRAND.   No.
   As befits both loving son and gentle priest,
   I shall protect you from the icy blasts of terror.
   At the foot of your bed I shall stand,
   And cool the fever in your blood with hymns and prayers.

MOTHER. Do you pledge me that, with hand on heart?

BRAND.   I shall come to you
   The moment you repent. [*Approaching her.*] But I, too, have my
      conditions.
   You shall of your own free will cast off
   Everything that binds you to this earth, and go
   Naked to your grave.

MOTHER [*strikes him wildly*]. Bid the fire have no flame, the snow
   No cold, the sea no salt! But do not ask so much of *me*!

BRAND. Cast overboard your child in mid-fjord,
   Then pray to God to bless the deed!

MOTHER. Ask any other penance—I'll starve and thirst—
   But not to cast away all that I value most!

BRAND. No. Unless you pay the highest price,
   Nothing else you do can moderate the wrath of One on high!

MOTHER. I'll put silver in the poorbox!

BRAND.   *All* of it?

MOTHER. Is it not enough to give *much*, my son?

BRAND. For you there can be no penances enough, until,
   Like Job, you die at last upon a heap of ashes.

MOTHER [*wringing her hands*]. My life is wasted, my soul a hopeless
      wreck;
   Soon my earthly treasures will be scattered too!
   I'll go back home, then, and gather to my breast

All I can still call mine—my property,
My child of sorrow, my goods and chattels.
For *you* I tore my breast until it bled.
So now I'll go back home, alone, and weep
As a mother weeps at the cradle of her dying child.
Why was my soul housed in this flesh,
If passion for the flesh is death unto the soul?
Stay with me, son, my priest! For how can I tell
What thoughts may come upon me in the hour of my dread?
If it must be, if I must lose all I possess,
Then I shall keep it by me to the end! [*She goes.*]

BRAND [*watching her go*]. Yes, your son shall be with you, shall wait
Until you cry out for repentance and forgiveness,
And warm your poor, cold hand
The moment you hold it out towards me. [*Goes over to* AGNES.]
The evening is not as the morning was.
Mind and heart were ready to do battle then.
From afar I heard the thunderings of war,
I burned to raise on high the sword of wrath,
To crush all falsehood, kill the trolls of untruth,
And crush the world between my clashing shields!

AGNES [*turns round joyfully to look at him*]. Compared with now, this
    evening,
How pale the morning was! Then all I wanted
Was false frivolity. I wanted to live a lie
Whose loss is now my gain.

BRAND.   How passionate
And lovely the dreams that beat about my head
Like flights of wild swans, uplifting me on throbbing wings!
I saw my path before me, reaching out into the world. . . .
Champion of my age, spokesman for our generation,
Summoned to great things by tumultuous youth!
My life's work a glittering and glorious pageant
Of processions, hymns, choirs, incense, silken banners,
Golden chalices, and chants of victory and joy, all mingling
With the shouts of exultation from the clamouring throngs!
It all lay there before me, in a rich and tempting glow
Of visionary rapture. . . . But it was—nothing.

An idle fabrication, a mirage upon a mountain peak,
Glimpsed half in sunlight, half in a rainbow's thunderclouds.
   I stand here now, where twilight turns to grey
Before the day declines—long long before.
I stand here between the mountain and the sea,
Far from the tumult of the world,
With only a faint strip of sky above . . .
But I stand where I belong.
My matins now are sung; my winged steed
I must unsaddle. But I behold a greater goal
Than knightly tournaments of high romance.
I shall perform my daily work, my humble toil,
With such devotion that it becomes a holy task.

AGNES. And what of that God who was to be brought so low?

BRAND. He shall be brought low. But his fall shall be
A silent plunge, a secret well concealed—an obscure iconoclasm.
I see now I had the wrong idea, a false perception
Of how to cure the sickness of mankind. I see now
This age can never be transformed by vainglorious conceit.
This generation's failings cannot be corrected merely
By wakening a sense of its neglected capabilities.
No. It is the *will* that must be brought to life again.
The will alone can liberate or bring man low . . .
The will, the one whole thing in a fragmented world,
The will that bears on all tasks, great or small!

[*Turns to face the village, where night is falling.*]

   Come then all you who wander as in living death
Here in this landlocked prison of my valley home!
Let us have converse one with the other, man to man,
And labour side by side to free and purify our souls!
Abjure half-measures, half-truths! Vanquish falsehood!
Come, and rouse from sleep the lion of the will!
Whether we lay our hands upon the plough or on the sword,
We serve, each in his own way, to demonstrate the dignity of man.
This is our common aim—to make our bodies and our souls
Like open books, upon whose virgin pages God can write his name.

[*He is about to go.* EINAR *confronts him.*]

EINAR. Stop! Give back what you stole from me!

BRAND. Take her. There she is.

EINAR [*to* AGNES].   Choose now
Between the sun-topped mountain peaks
And this dark pit of misery.

AGNES. There is no choice left for me.

EINAR. Agnes, Agnes, please listen! Remember the old saying:
'A burden lightly lifted is a burden hard to bear.'

AGNES. For God's sake, do not tempt me any more.
I shall bear this burden to the bitter end.

EINAR. Remember all who love you back at home!

AGNES. Give my greetings to them—mother, sisters, brothers.
I shall send letters, if I can find the words.

EINAR. Out on the shining waters, the white sails
Lean to the wind like hopes and longings
Lighting a dreaming brow, their prows,
High-arching in the rainbow spray,
Are winging freely to far-off harbours
In our land of heart's desire!

AGNES. Sail where you will, to east or west; but think of me
Only as dead and lying in my grave.

EINAR.   Let us go simply
Hand in hand, in pure friendship, like sister and brother!

AGNES [*shakes her head*]. The boundless ocean lies between us now.

EINAR. Then come back home to your mother!

AGNES [*quietly*]. And leave my teacher, my brother, my friend?

BRAND [*moves closer to her*]. Consider carefully the step you are to take.
Imprisoned in these mountain walls, and ever
Overshadowed by the gloom of crag and precipice,
My life, confined within the dungeon
Of this dark abyss shall move
As through some long and sombre autumn night.

AGNES. I no longer dread the dark.
A bright star shines above me now.

BRAND. Remember, my demands are severe and stern.
I shall require All or Nothing.
If you should falter, then your life
Is but a straw cast out upon the sea.
There can be no compromise,
No concessions to a woman's weakness.
If more than life is asked of you,
You must be ready to meet your death.

EINAR. Give up this madness! Reject this grim suitor
And his dark demands! Live your own life!

BRAND. Choose. You stand at the crossroads of life. [*He goes.*]

EINAR. Choose between calm and tempest!
The choice between leaving and staying
Is the choice between joy and sorrow,
The choice between night and morning,
The choice between death and life.

AGNES [*rises, and says slowly*].
I choose the night. Through the way of death.
Beyond them shines the crimson dawn of day.

[*She follows* BRAND. EINAR *for some time follows her with his eyes,
then bows his head and walks out in the direction of the fjord.*]

ACT THREE

Three years later. A little garden at the parsonage. Round it a stone wall; above it rises the steep face of a mountain. The fjord lies in the background, narrow and shut-in. The house door leads out into the garden. Afternoon. BRAND *stands on the steps outside the house.* AGNES *sits on the step below him.*

AGNES. My dear, why do you keep watching the fjord so anxiously?

BRAND. I am expecting a message.

AGNES.   So that's why you're restless!

BRAND. I am expecting a message from my mother.
　　Three years I have waited faithfully
　　For this message that never came.
　　This morning, I finally received word
　　That her hour is near.

AGNES [*softly and affectionately*]. Brand, you should go
　　Without waiting for the message to arrive.

BRAND [*shakes his head*].
　　If she does not repent of her sin,
　　I can find no words to bring her comfort.

AGNES. Your own mother.

BRAND.   I have no right
　　To set my family up as gods.

AGNES. Brand, how hard you are!

BRAND.   Hard towards you?

AGNES.   Oh, no!

BRAND. I warned you it would be a hard existence.

AGNES [*smiles*]. Well, it has not been so. You did not
　　Carry out your threat.

BRAND.   Yes, I did.
  This place is bitter cold.
  You have lost the roses in your cheeks.
  Frost withers your gentle soul.
  In this house, nothing thrives.
  It is all rock and stone.

AGNES. And for that reason stands the more secure.
  The glacier overhangs us now so far
  That when it thaws, in spring, it rushes right above
  And past us, and the parsonage remains untouched
  As though within the cavern of a hollowed waterfall.

BRAND. But what of the sun, that never reaches us?

AGNES. Oh, it dances so warm and gay upon
  The shoulder of the mountain opposite.

BRAND. Yes, for three weeks only, in summer time.
  But never warms its foot.

AGNES [*looks hard at him, rises and says*]: Brand, are you afraid of
  something?

BRAND. No! Are you?

AGNES.   No, but you are!

BRAND. You are hiding some secret fear.

AGNES.   And so are you!

BRAND. You're swaying, as if you stood upon the brink of a precipice!
  What's the matter? Tell me!

AGNES.   Sometimes I shake with fear . . . [*Stops.*]

BRAND. What for?

AGNES.   For Alf.

BRAND.   For our son!

AGNES.   Do you never feel the same?

BRAND. Yes, at times. Oh, no! He cannot be taken away from us!
  God in his great goodness will . . . my little boy will one day
  Grow up big and strong. Where is he now?

AGNES.   Sleeping.

BRAND [*looks in through door*]. Look there! There is no pain or sickness
In such quiet dreams. His little hand is plump and round . . .

AGNES. But pale.

BRAND.   Yes, a little pale. But he'll grow out of that.

AGNES. How sweetly and peacefully he sleeps.

BRAND.   God bless you, little boy.
Sleep tight. [*Shuts the door.*] When you and he came into my life,
Peace and radiance shone around my daily work. Being with you
Has made each time of sorrow, every difficult task,
Easier to bear. Living with you, my courage never failed;
Even his little childish games can give me strength.
I followed my call as to a martyrdom. But now, all that has changed.
Look how success has attended me along our way . . .

AGNES.   Yes, Brand.
But you deserved success. How you fought, suffered, strove . . .
You endured, despite of evil, and toiled and slaved . . .
I know how in secret your heart wept tears of blood . . .

BRAND. Yes, yes. And yet it all seemed easy to me then.
With you, love opened up my heart,
Like the warmth of spring's first sunny day. . . .
Something I had never known before. Neither my father
Nor my mother brought me such tender warmth;
Rather, they damped the fleeting spark
That leapt from the cooling ashes now and then.
It was as if all that tenderness I had borne
Within me, in secret and in silence,
I had treasured up for him, and for you, my dear wife.

AGNES. Not just for us alone, but for all those
Who now belong to us, our house and home—
Each son of sorrow, each brother in need,
Each weeping child and sorrowing mother,
All found a welcome at the full, rich table
Spread with the banquet of your love.

BRAND. It all came to me through you, and him. It was you two
Who built the bridge of tenderness between my heart

And theirs. A man cannot love all men unless
He has first loved *one*. I longed for love,
But I was starved of it, until my heart
Turned to a stone.

AGNES.   But even now, your love
Is still hard. It has a touch that hurts.

BRAND. Hurts you?

AGNES.   Me? Oh, no, my dear.
It was easy to bear what you demanded of me.
But many were repelled by your severe requirement—
That harsh and unrelenting 'All or Nothing'.

BRAND. What the world calls love I neither need
Nor know. I recognize the love of God;
That is not weak, or mild, but hard . . .
Hard as the fear of death itself.
Its caresses strike like blows at the heart.
In the olive garden at Gethsemane,
When His dear Son prayed in an agony of tears and sweat,
Pleading 'Let this cup pass from me' . . .
Did His Father in Heaven take from His lips
The bitter cup of pain? No, child:
He had to drain it to the dregs.

AGNES. Seen in so harsh a light, every mortal soul is doomed.

BRAND. No man can say who shall be doomed, or saved.
But it is written, in letters of eternal flame:
'Be steadfast! Endure unto the last! The crown of life
Was never won by compromise!' You may be drenched
In sweats of terror; but that is not enough.
You must pass through the furnaces of mental torment.
That you *cannot* endure may be forgiven you;
But that you *will* not—never! Never!

AGNES. Yes, it must be as you say. Oh, raise me up,
Lift me with you, wheresoever you may climb.
Lead me ever upwards to your high heaven.
My desire is strong, but I am faint of heart.
Unknown fears bring terror to my mind,
And my footsteps grow tired and heavy.

BRAND. Listen—I have but one command
For all my followers: 'No coward's compromise!'
A man's whole work is doomed
If done only by halves, or scanted.
'Not words, but deeds!' This rule
Shall be my first commandment.

AGNES [*throws her arms round his neck*]. Lead me,
And I shall follow always where your foot has trod!

BRAND. No cliff is too steep to climb if we are side by side.

[*The* DOCTOR *has come down the road and stops outside the garden wall.*]

DOCTOR. Hm! I never expected to hear the song
Of turtle-doves in these dark and desolate crags!

AGNES. My dear old doctor! Come in!

[*She runs down to open the gate.*]

DOCTOR.   Thanks, I'd rather not.
You know quite well that I'm cross with you
For burying yourself away in a hole like this,
Where mountain blasts and winter gales
Cut like blades of ice through body and soul . . . !

BRAND. Not through the soul.

DOCTOR.   No? Well, have it your own way.
It certainly does seem as if your hasty compact
Stands as firm and fast as ever. Though I still think
There's much truth in the saying: 'Marry in haste,
Repent at leisure!'

AGNES.   Things as fleeting as a sunbeam's kiss
Can herald a whole long summer's day. You know that!

DOCTOR. Mm, yes. Well, I must go. I have a patient waiting.

BRAND. Is it my mother?

DOCTOR.   Yes. Are you coming with me?

BRAND. Not today.

DOCTOR.   Perhaps you've been already?

BRAND. No, not yet.

DOCTOR.   You're a hard man.
I've slogged all the way across these barren moors,
Through fog and sleet, just to attend her, though I know
She's an old skinflint when it comes to payment.

BRAND. God bless your devotion and your skill.
Ease her suffering a little, if you can.

DOCTOR. God bless my *will*! It was my duty to go to her
As soon as she sent word she needed me.

BRAND. It was *you* she sent for. *I* am ignored.
It makes me sick at heart. But I can only wait.

DOCTOR. Don't wait any longer. Come with me now!

BRAND. I have no duty to attend upon her, until she sends for me.

DOCTOR [*to* AGNES]. You poor, helpless child, abandoned to
Such unfeeling hands!

BRAND.   I am not unfeeling.

AGNES. He would shed his own heart's blood to cleanse her soul!

BRAND. Like a good son, I freely take upon myself
The burden she has left me with—
An inheritance of guilt and sin.

DOCTOR. First pay your own!

BRAND.   In the sight of God,
The sins of many can be paid by *one*.

DOCTOR. Not by one who is himself a beggar,
And up to the ears in his own debts!

BRAND. Rich man, beggar man—whatever I may be, I know
My *will* is whole and unbroken. That is enough for me.

DOCTOR [*looks hard at him*]. Yes, in the heavy ledger of your days,
Your account shows more than enough credit to your will.
But in your current statement of account
The page that shows the credit to your heart, to love,
Is a total blank. [*He goes.*]

BRAND [*following him for some time with his eyes*]. Love, he says! Has
    any word
  Been more debased, more befouled with insincerity?
  With the connivance of the Devil, they spread this word
  Like a deceptive veil upon the failures of the will, and thus
  Conceal the fact that earthly life is but a mockery.
  If our path is narrow, steep and perilous,
  It can be smoothed . . . by 'love'.
  If we pursue the broad path of sin,
  We can be saved . . . by 'love'.
  If we seek for but do not fight for higher aims,
  Still we can win through . . . by 'love'.
  If we go astray, though we know we are wrong,
  We still may find refuge . . . in 'love'.

AGNES. Yes, love seems a vain delusion. And yet,
  I often ask myself—is it really so?

BRAND. One thing we must not disregard. It is the will alone
  Can satisfy man's thirst for purity and truth.
  First comes the will—the will not only to achieve
  What's feasible in life both great and small;
  The will not only to surmount a measure
  Of pain and misfortune, but that greater will
  To fight one's way with joy and resolution
  Through life that is continual terror and despair.
  To suffer death in agony upon the cross—
  That is no martyrdom, no sacrifice at all.
  But to desire, to *will* that death upon the cross,
  To *will* that anguish of the flesh, to *will* that pain,
  To *will* that desolation of the spirit—*that*
  Is martyrdom! *That* is to seize salvation!

AGNES [*clings tightly to him*]. My dear husband! When my steps falter,
  Give me strength to follow in this steep and stony way!

BRAND. Once the will has triumphed, then is the time for love.
  Then, like a white dove bearing the olive branch
  Of peace and life, love descends upon us.
  But here, in our slack and gutless times,
  A man's best love can only be [*shouts in terror*]—Hate! Hate!

But the will to shout that one, simple little word
Must bring our generation into total war!

[*He goes quickly into the house.*]

AGNES [*looking through the open door*]. He's kneeling beside his little boy,
Rocking his head as in a storm of tears.
Like someone beyond the reach of comfort, or advice,
He clings to the child's bed.
Oh, in that manly breast, what a wealth of love!
He loves his boy. The serpent of the world
Has not yet poisoned that child's soul.

[*She cries out in alarm.*]

He jumps up, wringing his hands! What's the matter?
His face is white as ash!

BRAND [*outside on the steps*]. No message yet?

AGNES. No, no message.

BRAND [*looks back into the house*]. His skin is tight and burning.
His temples throb. His pulse is hammering with fever . . . !
Oh, Agnes, don't be afraid . . . !

AGNES.   Oh, God, what do you mean?

BRAND. No, don't be afraid . . . [*There are shouts down the road.*]
Here comes my message!

A MAN [*comes through the garden gate*]. You must come now, sir.

BRAND [*hurriedly*].   Yes, I'm coming.
What's the news?

THE MAN.   I don't know how to put it.
She sat up in bed and leaned forward, crying:
'Go and bring him! Half my worldly goods
If he will bless me before I die!'

BRAND [*taken aback*]. Half! Only half! No! Don't say that!

THE MAN [*shakes his head*]. Then I should not be speaking the truth, sir.

BRAND. Half! Only half! But I meant *all*!

THE MAN. That may well be. But there's no mistake.
I heard her clearly.

BRAND [*seizes him by the arm*]. Before the Lord on Judgement Day
Will you confirm she spoke those words?

THE MAN. Yes.

BRAND [*firmly*]. Then go and tell her
This is my reply: no priest, no sacrament.

THE MAN [*looks at him uncertainly*]. But you mistake my meaning, sir.
It was your *mother* sent me.

BRAND.   I have one law for all.
For my family as for others.

THE MAN.   That's a hard way to talk.

BRAND. She knew well she was to give me All or Nothing!

THE MAN.   But, sir . . .

BRAND. Go tell her the least fraction of the golden calf
Is just as much an idol as the whole.

THE MAN. This is a harsh and stinging answer.
I shall break the news to her
As gently as I can. She has one comfort:
God himself is not as hard as you! [*Goes.*]

BRAND. Yes. That false comfort has often breathed
Its pestilential vapours on a world grown sick with promises.
To think that in their hour of need, they hope
To mitigate their judge's wrath with pious psalms and tears!
But naturally, that's how it always seemed to them!
That is the only kind of God they know. To them,
He is a kind old gentleman open to bargaining.

[*Out on the road, the* MAN *has met a* SECOND MAN: *they both come
back together.*]

BRAND. A new message?

FIRST MAN.   Yes.

BRAND.   What is it?

SECOND MAN. Now she says 'nine-tenths'.

BRAND.   Not all?

SECOND MAN. Not all.

BRAND.   She knows my answer: no priest, no sacrament.

SECOND MAN. In pain and sorrow, she begged and pleaded . . .

FIRST MAN. Remember, priest, it was she who bore you!

BRAND [*clenching his hands*]. I cannot use two sets of weights,
One for my own family and one for strangers.

SECOND MAN. Her need is desperate. Come with us now.
Or send her a kindly word . . .

BRAND [*to* FIRST MAN].   No, go and say:
The table must be cleared completely
Before the sacrament of bread and wine can be prepared.

[*The* TWO MEN *go*.]

AGNES [*clings tightly to him*]. Sometimes you terrify me, Brand. You
seem to burn
With holy fire, like the flaming sword of God himself.

BRAND [*with tears in his voice*]. Then why does the world defy me
With an empty scabbard? Why does it not strike blood,
And slay me with its dull and stubborn blade?

AGNES. You drive too hard a bargain.

BRAND. Have you an easier one to offer?

AGNES. Can any man on earth accept such terms
As yours?

BRAND.   You may well ask!
No man on earth can accept such terms as mine,
So false, so empty, so paltry and so mean
Has this entire generation's attitude to life become.
A man who passes on his wealth to benefit humanity
Enjoys high praise. But bid this hero be anonymous,
So that the good he can perform is done by stealth—

Offer an emperor, a conqueror, a king such terms as these,
And see what answer you will get? You might as well
Command the poet to release his nests of singing birds in secret,
So that no one realizes it was *he* who gave them song and wing!
Bid the green branch or the withered to disown its roots—
Not one of these, not one will make the sacrifice of self.
This earth-bound selfishness runs through the whole of life.
Even suspended over a wild and steep abyss, a man
Still clings to the breaking branch of an existence made of dust
And when that gives way, he claws with frantic nails at rotten roots.

AGNES. And when they no longer hold, your cry to those who fall
Is 'All or Nothing'.

BRAND. A man must never weaken, or he loses all.
He who falls into the pit may live to rise again.

[*He is silent a moment: his voice changes.*]

Yet when I command each individual soul to rise again,
I feel a castaway upon a stormy sea, swimming on a broken plank.
Often I tried to silence the reproaches on my lips.
And the arm I raised to strike longed for the embrace of love. . . .
    Agnes, go and watch him as he sleeps.
Sing softly to him, give him sweet dreams. A child's soul
Is as clear and tranquil as a tarn in the summer sun.
A mother can glide across it like the bird which,
In silent flight, is mirrored in the deepest depths.

AGNES [*pale*]. What is it, Brand? Wherever you shoot the arrow
Of your thought . . . it flies to him!

BRAND. It is nothing. Watch over him well.

AGNES. Give me a text.

BRAND. A stern one?

AGNES. No, a mild one.

BRAND [*embraces her*]. He who is without guilt shall have eternal life.

AGNES [*looks up at him happily and says*]:
One thing God cannot demand of us!

[*She goes into the house.*]

BRAND [*stands gazing in silence*]. But if He did? The Lord can test me
As he tested Abraham. [*Shakes off his thoughts.*] No, no!
I have made my sacrifice. I have renounced
My life's most dear ambition—to speak
With a tongue like the thunder of the Lord,
And wake the sleepers of the earth.
All false! There was no sacrifice in that!
That was all over when the dream was done,
When Agnes woke me, and joined me in this modest work.

[*He looks down the road.*]

Why does that sick woman send no message, no word
Of sacrifice, repentance, that would root out all her sin
In every branch and fibre, down to its deepest shoots?
Is that another messenger? No, only the Mayor,
Genial, active, stout and full of the joy of life,
His hands in his pockets like brackets round a parenthesis.

MAYOR [*through the garden gate*]. Good afternoon! It's not often I have
    a chance
To talk to you. I hope I've not come at a bad time?

BRAND [*pointing to the house*]. No. Come in.

MAYOR.   Thanks, I'll stay where I am.
    If only my request could be granted—then I'm sure
    All would be for the best in the end.

BRAND.   What is it?

MAYOR. I hear your mother is ill, gravely ill. I'm very sorry.

BRAND. I'm sure you are.

MAYOR.   I am very sorry indeed, I can tell you.

BRAND. What's on your mind?

MAYOR.   Your mother's old.
    We all have to come to it, some day.
    Well, I just happened to be passing, so I thought:
    'Might as well be killed for a sheep as a lamb.'
    You see, I've heard a lot of folks say

As how you and she had a sort of family quarrel
After you arrived here . . .

BRAND.   Family quarrel?

MAYOR. They do say she keeps a tight hold
On what she's got put away. Maybe you feel she's too
Tightfisted. After all, you've got to look after number one,
Haven't you? So there she lies dying, and in full possession
Of all the family inheritance . . .

BRAND.   Yes, that is so.

MAYOR. There's often disagreement among relatives about such things.
Now, as I have reason to believe you're awaiting her demise
In a philosophical frame of mind, I hope you'll not be offended
If I speak out plainly, though obviously it's not
The happiest of moments . . .

BRAND.   Now or later, it's all one to me.

MAYOR. Well, then, let me come straight to the point.
Once your dear mother has passed away, and is laid to rest
In the bosom of the earth—which won't be long—
You'll come into a tidy bit of cash . . .

BRAND.   Do you think so?

MAYOR. Think? Why, man, I'm certain. She owns land round every
    bay,
As far off as the telescope will reach. You'll be a wealthy man, sir!

BRAND. What about the inheritance law?

MAYOR [*smiles*].   Nothing to worry about there!
That's only to settle disputed cases, where
There are several who have to divide the debts
And the inheritance among them. But here it's a straight case.

BRAND. What if some co-heir to the property and the debts
Were to appear, saying: '*I* am the rightful heir'?

MAYOR. That could only be the devil in person! Now look here,
Nobody else has any claim. Believe me, I know. So
You'll be well-off, a rich man indeed. No need
To hold on to this remote parish, no need at all.
You have the whole country to choose from now.

BRAND. I think you're trying to tell me, quite simply, 'Go away'?

MAYOR. If that's the way you want to put it, yes.
    I think it would be best for all parties.
    If you'd only take a closer look
    At folks round here, to whom you bring the Word of God,
    You'd realize how little you fit in here—
    Like a wolf in the fold, in fact.
    Now don't misunderstand me! You have great gifts.
    But I feel they'd be more suited to
    A broader and more sophisticated range of society.
    Here they are more likely to distress
    Our simple country folk, who call themselves
    'Heirs of the rocky gorges', 'Sons
    Of the valley deeps' and that kind of thing.

BRAND. The place where he was born is to a man
    As natural a spot to plant his feet
    As is the soil around it to the rooted tree.
    If there be no call *there* for all his labours,
    His deeds are doomed, his song is ended.

MAYOR. The first rule in any undertaking
    Is that it be adapted to the country's needs.

BRAND. But the country's needs are best viewed from the heights,
    Not from some rock-bound corner of the parish.

MAYOR. That kind of talk is for a larger audience,
    Not for the folk in these poor valleys.

BRAND. Oh, you with your boundaries between lowland and
    mountain!
    Like some Great Power, you demand your national rights,
    But you evade responsibility towards society. Like cowards,
    You cry out 'We are only a small nation', hoping to be spared.

MAYOR. Everything in its own good time, sir. Every generation
    Has its own task to perform. Even our small village
    Has added its mite to the world's great treasure-chest
    Of human achievement. I grant you, that was long ago.
    But the mite was not so tiny. See, the village
    Is small now, and the people few. Yet its fame

Lives on in legend. Its day of vanished greatness
Were in the age of old King Bele. Many tales are told
Of the two brothers, Ulf and Thor, and scores of daring men
Who set their prows for Britain's coasts, and there
Plundered to the heart's delight. In a cold sweat of fear,
The weakly southerners would scream: 'God save us from
The fury of these devil-men!' Yet these very men,
I have no doubt, were lads from these parts.
Vengeance was in their blood, and a fiery thirst
For death and destruction, rape and murder! Indeed,
Legend tells us of that hero's name,
That hero of the Lord who took the cross—but
It is not recorded that he actually went . . .

BRAND. Doubtless there exists a mighty host of sons
   Descended from this paragon . . .

MAYOR.   True. But how did you know . . . ?

BRAND. Oh, it seems obvious to me. Even today, the strain
   Can be recognized in those who make heroic promises,
   And whose crusade is of the same persuasion.

MAYOR. Yes, the family still survives. But we were talking about
   King Bele's times! First, then, we fought across the seas.
   Then we laid waste our neighbours' and our kinsmen's lands.
   We trampled his crops into the mud, set fire
   To church spire and dwelling house
   And wove ourselves a garland of heroic deeds.
   Perhaps we have boasted far too much
   Of all the blood spilled in far-off days.
   Yet, from what I have just been saying, I think
   We may, in all modesty, claim the leadership
   Of that great age, so long ago; and I shall maintain
   To the end of my days that this village of ours
   Added its mite, with fire and with the sword,
   To the great cause of progress in the world.

BRAND. It seems to me you are denying
   The essence of the motto *noblesse oblige*.
   You seem to be destroying the inheritance of old King Bele
   With commonplace and vulgar weapons—harrow, plough, and hoe.

MAYOR. That is not so. If only you could bring yourself to visit
Some of our village celebrations, where I and the constable,
The sexton and the magistrate are given the seats of honour,
Then you would see, when the punch goes round,
That King Bele's memory is far from dead. We remember him
In rousing toasts, the clink of glasses, drinking songs.
We drink to his shade, and make speeches in his praise—
Speeches both long and short, but usually rather long.
I myself have often felt a deep, mysterious urge
To weave my thoughts about him into some literary masterpiece,
Some flowered tapestry of words and epic deeds, and so
Elevate the minds and tastes of many local folk.
I like a bit of poetry myself. So do we all, really,
Here in our village—but in moderation, naturally.
Poetry—there's no place for that in *real* life.
But maybe of an evening, between seven and ten,
When folks have a bit of spare time, and all that,
When, weary with the toil of day, one feels the need
Of some edifying restorative. Now, sir, the difference
Between us and you is that you want to plough with might and main
And fight at one and the same time. The way I see it, your idea
Is to combine the practical and the ideal in life—
To create an eventual union of God's holy war against sin
And the back-breaking labour of the potato-patch—an amalgam
As intimate as charcoal, as sulphur and saltpetre,
The elements of gunpowder.

BRAND.   Yes, more or less.

MAYOR. But that'll never do out here. Now in a larger community,
I'm not saying it mightn't go down well. So I'd advise you
To take your lofty notions somewhere else, and let us folks
Get on with ploughing the bogs and fishing the deep.

BRAND. First, send to the bottom of the sea
All your boasts about the glory of your ancestors.
A dwarf cannot reach the height of a grown man,
Even if his grandfather was Goliath.

MAYOR.   Future growth depends
On memories of greatness past.

BRAND.   Only when memory allies itself
  With *life*. But out of the rocky cairns of memory
  You have only built yourselves a castle of indolence.

MAYOR. Well, I can only repeat what I said at the beginning.
  It would be best if you were to go.
  Your work will never flourish here;
  No one will ever understand your view of life.
  When a touch of the eternal seems to meet the ticket,
  The bit of uplift each man feels the need of now and then,
  You can depend upon it, I shall see to that.
  During the entire tenure of my office, I think I can say,
  Though I do say it myself, that I have given proof
  Of diligence and zeal in all my works. Through my efforts,
  The population has been doubled—nay, indeed,
  Wellnigh tripled—because I have assured
  A source of livelihood for everyone. We have forged ahead
  As if driven by a veritable steam-engine progress
  In our unremitting battle against hostile nature.
  We have built roads. We have built bridges . . .

BRAND. But not between life and faith.

MAYOR. No. Between fjord and snowfield.

BRAND. But not between action and idea.

MAYOR. First things first! A highway
  Was needed to link our district with the next.
  Free communications between men and men
  Was what we first required. There were no
  Two opinions about *that*. At least,
  Not until you came here to serve the parish.
  Now you've got everything mixed up—
  Our street lamps and the Northern Lights
  Have nothing to do with one another, and this
  Has confused us all—we can't tell right from wrong
  In the puzzling glare of these opposing lights;
  We can't see what is help and what is hindrance.
  You've lumped all conditions of things together;
  And you've split into hostile camps the flock
  Which, united, would triumph over our adversities.

BRAND. I shall stay on here, despite of all you say.
One does not *choose* one's field of action.
The man who knows his goal, and strives to attain it,
Is one who beholds, in letters of fire,
The command of God, which is: 'Here you belong!'

MAYOR. If you must stay, you must. But do not overstep the mark!
I am gratified to see the efforts you are making
To cleanse the people here of all their sin and vice.
God knows such work is needed here!
But keep your efforts to Sundays! Don't go
Making holy days out of the other working six;
And don't keep bothering our seamen and fisherfolk
With your prayers and exhortations, as if Our Lord himself
Were on every ship and ferry crossing our fjord.

BRAND. For your advice to be of any good to me,
I should have to change my soul, and my convictions.
But this is my sacred Call: a man must be himself,
If he is to carry his own cause to victory. So I
Shall bear my cause aloft, so that it shines about
The place where I was born, like fire from Heaven!
These people, lulled asleep by you and your kind,
Shall be awakened! Too long you have tortured and confined
Their native mountain spirit in this petty cage!
You have broken their will, made each man
Sullen and disheartened, drained his life's blood,
Sucked dry the marrow of his courage!
The souls of men, which should endure like rock
And iron, you have smashed into a thousand
Little fragments. But beware! My call to action
Shall thunder in your ears! My word is 'War!'

MAYOR. War?

BRAND.   Yes, war!

MAYOR.   If you dare to give a call to arms,
You shall be the first to fall!

BRAND. One day, it shall be plain to all
That the greatest victory is in defeat!

MAYOR. I warn you, Brand! You stand at the crossroads.
Don't stake all on a single card!

BRAND. I will!

MAYOR.   But if you lose the game,
Your whole life will be as nothing.
You know the good things of this world,
You are the heir of a woman of property,
You have a child to live for,
A wife to love—the good things of this world,
Are yours as though handed to you on a platter!

BRAND. And what if I must turn my back
On what you call the good things of this world?
What then?

MAYOR.   If you declare war here,
Then everything you have is forfeit.
Here in this remote backwater of the world,
What would be the point of your crusade?
Go south, to richer and to kinder shores,
Where men can hold their heads up in the sun.
That's the place to hold your meetings,
And call upon the people's blood.
You can't squeeze blood from these hard stones
Of ours, only the sweat of fighting
For our daily bread among these rocky wastes.

BRAND. Here I stay. This is the place where I belong.
Here the flag of my crusade shall first be raised.

MAYOR. Remember what you stand to lose if you're defeated!
Above all, remember what you're throwing away with this!

BRAND. If I weaken, it is myself that I shall lose.

MAYOR. Brand, one man cannot fight alone.

BRAND. My flock is strong. I have the best men.

MAYOR [*smiles*]. That may be so. But *I* have the most. [*He goes.*]

BRAND [*watching him go*]. There goes your man-in-the-street . . .
Honest, sensible, well-meaning,
Competent up to a point, warm-hearted, fair . . .

And yet a menace to our country.
No landslide, flood or hurricane, no famine,
Frost or pestilence, wreaks half the havoc,
Over the years, as men like him.
A plague takes only *lives*. But he—!
How much thinking is destroyed,
How many vigorous minds are dulled,
How many brave songs are silenced
By such crippled, uninspired souls as his!
How many smiles upon the lips of passers-by,
How many raptures in the people's hearts,
How many passionate or joyful impulses
That might have fulfilled themselves in action
Has he not bloodlessly destroyed!

[*In sudden fear.*]

But the message!
The message! Why has no one brought the message?
Ah, yes . . . the doctor . . .

[*He hurries out to meet the* DOCTOR.]

What is it? Tell me! Is my mother . . .

DOCTOR. Gone to face her Judge.

BRAND.   Dead! But she repented?

DOCTOR. I would not say so. She clung to all her worldly goods
Till the last second, when death took them from her.

BRAND [*stares unseeingly, greatly moved*]. Is this the way it dies—the
human soul?

DOCTOR. Let us hope she will be lightly judged—not by the laws
Of God, but compassionately, according to her own lights.

BRAND [*in a low voice*]. What did she say?

DOCTOR.   She murmured: 'God is not as hard
As my own son!'

BRAND [*sinks down in anguish on the bench*]. In the final agony of guilt,
On the deathbed itself, the same lie cankers every soul!

[*He hides his face in his hands.*]

DOCTOR [*approaches, looks at him and shakes his head*].
    What you want can never be . . .
    To bring back to life an age long past.
    You believe that the ancient law
    Of God and man must still apply.
    But each generation has its different way.
    Ours cannot be cowed by threats of flaming scourges,
    Or old wives' tales of souls sold to the devil.
    Its first commandment is: 'Thou shalt be humane!'

BRAND [*looks up*]. Humane! That wishy-washy word has now
    Become the motto of the whole wide world!
    It is the pious slogan touted by every incompetent
    To conceal the fact that he cannot, *will* not act.
    It is the smug device paraded by every coward
    To conceal his shame—shame that he dare not
    Commit himself completely for an all-out victory!
    In the sheltering skirts of *that* despicable word,
    Every paltry promise is airily broken, cravenly betrayed.
    You lily-livered freaks will not be satisfied
    Till the day you have made all men humanists!
    Was God humane to Jesus Christ? If *your* God
    Had had his way, He would have come with mercy
    At the very hour of the Cross . . . and redemption
    Conveyed from Heaven by divine diplomacy!

        [*He hides his head and sits in quiet grief.*]

DOCTOR [*quietly*]. Let the tempest in your soul blow itself out.
    Let the tears flow. . . . You'll feel better then.

AGNES [*has come out on the steps; pale, terrified, she whispers to the* DOCTOR].
    Come here, quickly . . . come inside . . .

DOCTOR [*alarmed*].   You alarm me, child!
    What's the matter?

AGNES.   My heart is cold with fear!

DOCTOR [*going to her*]. What is it?

AGNES [*drawing him after her*].   Come quickly . . . Oh, dear God,
    help me . . .

        [*They go into the house.* BRAND *does not notice.*]

BRAND [*quietly, to himself*]. Died a sinner. Died unrepentant, as she lived.
This is the finger of God. Surely it is a sign?
Surely He has chosen me to be
The guardian of that treasure she destroyed!
If I should weaken now, I am damned for ever! [*Gets up.*]
Here, where I was born, like a dutiful son
I shall do battle, fight my crusade
For the victory of the soul and the subjugation of the flesh!
God has vouchsafed me the sword of His Word,
And kindled in my heart the fire of His wrath.
I stand strong in the armour of my will.
Now I dare all! I can crush mountains . . .

DOCTOR [*comes hurriedly out on the steps, followed by* AGNES, *and shouts*].
Shut your house up! You must leave at once!

BRAND. Come fire, flood or earthquake—I stay here!

DOCTOR. Then your child is doomed to die.

BRAND [*despairingly*]. My child? What shadows of terror are these!
My child!

[*He makes to go into the house.*]

DOCTOR [*restrains him*]. No, wait! And listen!
There is no sunshine in this gloomy fjord.
The winds from the Pole cut like a knife.
A clammy fog hangs round us like a shroud.
One winter more in this benighted place
Will be the death of him. But if you leave
Here now, he has a chance of life.
You must do it soon—tomorrow!

BRAND. Tonight, this afternoon, this minute!
Oh, he shall grow strong and healthy . . .
No icy blasts, no arctic gales
Shall ever freeze again that little breast.
Come, Agnes, lift him up gently, while he sleeps.
We must fly away, fly away to the South.
Oh, my dear, we must break the web
That death is spinning round our little boy.

AGNES. I half suspected this would happen. How blind I was!

BRAND [*to the* DOCTOR]. Our leaving will surely save him? You promise?

DOCTOR. The life a father watches over night and day
  Is sure to prosper. Be everything to him, and soon
  You'll see the bloom of health upon his cheeks. Believe me.

BRAND. I do believe you. [*To* AGNES.] Wrap him up tightly in his
  eiderdown.
  The evening wind is cutting sharply down the fjord.

[AGNES *goes into house.*]

DOCTOR [*silently watches* BRAND, *who stands motionless looking in through
  the door; then goes across to him, places a hand on his shoulder, and says*]:
  You, so implacable towards all your flock, but now
  So indulgent towards yourself. . . . For them, no question of
  Little or *much*—only the All or Nothing of your edict.
  But when it comes to the pinch—as soon as one's own
  Interest's at stake—what then? Ah, courage fails
  When the sacrificial lamb must be one's own!

BRAND. What are you saying?

DOCTOR.   You thundered
  At your dying mother with the hard words
  Of your implacable law: 'Unless you renounce
  All worldly things, unless you go naked to your grave,
  You are lost!' And how often the same cry thundered out
  At ordinary people, in their grave distress!
  Now you yourself are the one in distress;
  But like a castaway clinging to the keel
  Of his storm-toppled boat, you throw
  Into the raging waves all your fulminations
  And your threats of hellfire, throw away
  That heavy book of stern morality
  With which you beat your brothers' backs.
  All you look for now is to save
  Your child's life in this raging gale.
  Fly . . . fly away down the fjord and the bay,
  Fly from your own mother's corpse,
  Fly from your flock, and from your calling.
  The priest has cancelled evening prayers!

BRAND [*clutches despairingly at his head as though to collect his thoughts*].
Have I gone blind? Or was I blind before?

DOCTOR. You are behaving as a father should.
Do not think I blame you for your present stand.
I think you are a bigger man now,
With your wings clipped, than you were before,
When you declared yourself the Voice of God.
Farewell! I have handed you a looking-glass—
See your true self reflected in it, and then sigh:
'Oh, God! So this is the face of an iconoclast!' [*He goes.*]

BRAND [*gazes a while unseeingly and suddenly bursts out*].
Where did I go wrong? Oh, was it then—or now?

[AGNES *comes through the door, with a cloak over her shoulders, and
the child in her arms.* BRAND *does not see her; she is about to speak,
but stops as though terror-stricken when she sees the expression on his
face. At that moment a man hurries in through the garden gate. The
sun is setting.*]

THE MAN. Sir, listen to me, sir! You have an enemy!

BRAND [*clenches his fist against his breast*].   Yes, here.

MAN. Be on your guard against the Mayor. The seed you sowed
Had started flourishing all through this land until
He killed it with the blight of rumour. He has already
Often hinted that this house would soon stand empty,
That once your mother died, leaving you her wealth,
You'd turn your back on us.

BRAND.   And if that were so?

MAN. Sir, I know you, and I know also
Why he spread these poisonous rumours.
You are opposed to him in everything, in all his ways.
He could never bend his pride to meet your will.
That is the real source of his false words. . . .

BRAND [*uncertain*]. Some might think . . . he was speaking the truth.

MAN. Then you have deceived us all disgracefully!

BRAND. I have . . . ?

MAN.   Haven't you often told us
God Himself had called you to the fray . . .
That your home is here with us,
That you are to do battle here,
And that no man must evade that call . . .
That he must fight, and never yield?
And you *have* that call! The fire you kindled
In many a breast still burns strong and fierce!

BRAND. But the people here are deaf, man!
Is there a single soul hasn't lost its fire?

MAN. You know better than to tell me that. Many a soul
Still shines with the radiance of eternal light.

BRAND. For ten times as many, darkness still prevails.

MAN. You are the beacon in our night.
In any case, there is no need to count heads.
Here I stand, one solitary man,
And say to you: 'Leave if you can!'
I, too, have a soul that I can call my own
As much as anyone. I cannot use the Book to help me.
It was *you* who raised me from the depths:
How can you dare let go of me! You cannot let me fall!
I will cling fast to you. My soul is lost for ever
If you let me go! . . . Farewell! I'm sure
My priest will not abandon God, nor me.

[*He goes.*]

AGNES [*timidly*]. Your face is white, your lips are pale.
You look to be in mortal agony.

BRAND. All those words I thundered now re-echo
Ten times as loudly from the mountain sides.

AGNES [*takes a step forward*]. I am ready.

BRAND.   Ready? Ready for what?

AGNES [*firmly*]. Ready for everything a mother should and must
do!

[GERD *runs by on the road and stops at the garden gate.*]

GERD [*claps her hands and calls out in wild delight*].
  Have you heard? The priest has flown! . . .
  From the mountains and from the hills
  The goblins and the trolls are swarming . . .
  Black ones, nasty ones, big ones, little ones . . .
  Aghh! What sharp claws they have . . . !
  Nearly scratched my eyes out.
  They've snatched away half my soul!
  Oh, I'll manage with what's left,
  There's still enough and to spare!

BRAND. Your words are wild. Look, child,
  Here I stand before your very eyes.

GERD. You? Yes, *you*! But not the priest!
  Down from Black Peak swooped my swift hawk,
  Bridled and saddled like a charger, wild and fierce,
  And he went screeching through the gusty dark.
  On his back there rode a man—the priest!
  It was our priest! Now the parish church
  Stands empty—locked, bolted, and barred.
  That ugly church's days are done. Now mine
  Shall come into its glory. In *my* church
  The priest stands tall and strong,
  In surplice white, woven from winter's ice and hail.
  If you want to join my church, come now!
  The parish church stands dead and empty.
  But *my* priest speaks words
  That echo far across the world!

BRAND. Poor demented soul! What power sent you
  To bewilder me with ravings about heathen idols?

GERD [*comes inside garden gate*].
  Idols? Idols? What are they?
  Idols? Ah, yes, now I know.
  Sometimes big, sometimes small,
  Always gilded and gaily coloured.
  Idols? Well, you see that woman?
  Can't you see beneath the shawl
  The shape of baby hands and feet,

The outline of a sleeping child
Within those gaily-coloured folds?
She draws back! Wraps it closer!
Idols! Idols! There is one!

AGNES [*to* BRAND]. Have you tears to shed, have you prayers to speak?
My own have been extinguished in the furnaces
Of fear!

BRAND.   Agnes, my dear. I am afraid
Some Greater Power has sent her to us.

GERD. Hark at the bells ringing all together
Over the wild mountain snows!
Look at the congregation
Flocking towards the church!
Can you see the thousand trolls
The parish priest drove into the sea?
Can you see the thousand dwarfs?
Before they were buried under the snow,
Their graves shut tight by his heavy seal.
But neither seal nor grave can hold them.
Forth they swarm, all clammy and cold. . . .
Troll children with grinning mouths,
Once thought to be dead, but now
They toss aside the landslide's rocks.
Listen! They're shrieking: 'Mother! Father!'
Men and women scream back at them.
A man from the village walks among them
Like a father among his sons.
A village woman takes up her dead son,
And starts to feed him at her breast.
At no time since his baptism
Did she bear the child so proudly.
Life flourished when the priest fled!

BRAND. Away from me! My own visions rise
From even darker hells . . . !

GERD.   Ha! He laughs,
That man sitting by the road up there
Where it goes twisting up the mountain.

L1

In his book he writes the names
Of all the souls that climb up there.
Hah! He's got them nearly all.
The parish church stands dead and empty,
Locked, bolted, and barred . . .
And the priest flew off on the hawk's back.

[*She springs over the garden fence and disappears among the rocks.
Silence.*]

AGNES [*approaches and says in a low voice*]: Let us go now. It's time we
went.

BRAND [*stares at her*]. What? Where? [*He points to gate, then to house
door.*]   That way? Or this way?

AGNES [*recoils aghast*]. Brand! your child!

BRAND [*follows her*].   Answer me! Was I not
A priest before I was a father?

AGNES [*recoils further*]. Though a voice of thunder asked me—I cannot
answer!

BRAND [*still following her*]. You *shall* answer! You are the mother!
You have the last word here!

AGNES.   I am your wife.
Command me. I shall obey.

BRAND [*tries to take hold of her arm*]. Let this cup pass from me!

AGNES [*retreats behind the tree*]. Then I should be no mother to my
child!

BRAND. There is judgement in that answer!

AGNES [*vehemently*]. Ask yourself whether you have a choice?

BRAND. And that was a confirmation of the judgement!

AGNES. You firmly believe that God has called you?

BRAND. Yes. [*He takes a firm grip of her hand.*]
Now you must say: is it life—or death?

AGNES. You must take the path your God has bidden you to take.
[*Pause.*]

BRAND. Then let us go . . . for now it is time.

AGNES [*tonelessly*]. Which way are we going?

[BRAND *is silent.*]

AGNES [*points to the gate and asks*].   That way?

BRAND [*points to the house door*].   No. This way!

AGNES [*lifting the child high in her arms*].
God on high! The sacrifice thou cravest
I dare raise up towards Thy Heaven!
Lead me through the terrors of this world!

[*She goes into the house.*]

BRAND [*stares unseeingly a short while, bursts into tears, clasps his hands
together over his head, throws himself down on the steps and shouts*]:
Jesus! Lord Jesus! Give me light!

ACT FOUR

*Christmas Eve at the Parsonage. It is dark in the room. On the back
wall, a door leading outside. On one side a window, on the other side
a door.* AGNES *stands dressed in mourning at the window and staring
out into the darkness.*

AGNES. Not yet! No sign of him yet!
　　How hard it is, to wait like this . . .
　　To utter cry after cry of longing . . .
　　And never to receive an answer.
　　The snow keeps falling, falling thick and fast,
　　And softly covering the roof of the old church
　　As with a hood of soft, white lambswool . . . [*Listens.*]
　　What's that? Did I hear the gate creak?
　　Footsteps . . . the firm footsteps of a man!

[*She hurries to the door and opens it.*]

　　Is that you, Brand? Oh, come in, come in!

[BRAND *comes in, covered with snow, dressed in his travelling clothes,
which he removes during* AGNES' *next speech.*]

AGNES [*throwing her arms about him*].
　　Oh how long it's been! Don't leave me
　　Alone like that again. Say you won't leave me!
　　When I'm here all alone, I cannot
　　Shake off the shadows of the night.
　　These last two days—what days they have been!
　　But this last night, alone—Oh, Brand!

BRAND. Well, my dear, now you have me back again.

[*He lights a single candle, which throws a faint light across the room.*]

　　How pale you are!

AGNES.　　　　　　　And weary and worn out
　　With longing, loneliness, watching and waiting . . .
　　I made up a little bit of green stuff . . .

Just a little . . . it was all I had,
Saved from the summer greenery,
To decorate the Christmas Tree.
I used to call it *his* little bush;
Well, now he has his Christmas decorations—
But in a wreath laid upon his grave. [*Bursts into tears.*]
Look, there it lies, half buried in snow . . . O, God!

BRAND. In our sad little churchyard.

AGNES.   Oh, that word!

BRAND. Come, dry your tears.

AGNES.   Yes. But please be patient.
The wound is so fresh and tender,
My soul still seems to bleed,
And all my strength to be flowing from me.
But soon it will be better;
Once I am through the next few days,
You will never hear me complain again.

BRAND. Is this how to celebrate the birthday of Our Lord?

AGNES. Yes, I know. But be patient with me!
To think, this day last year, he was
So healthy and strong! Now, only one year later,
Taken from me, taken away from me and laid . . . [*She shrinks
from the word.*]

BRAND [*sternly*]. In the churchyard.

AGNES [*screams*].   No! No! Don't say that word!

BRAND. It *must* be said, and said out loud
And clear, if you are frightened of it.
It *must* be said, and said again,
Till it re-echoes and resounds
Like stormy breakers plunging on the shore!

AGNES. You yourself find the word more painful than
You like to admit. On your brow, I can see
The trickles of sweat it cost you to say it.

BRAND. The drops of moisture on my brow
Are only spray from the fjord.

AGNES. And is that water trembling in your eyes
　　Only the melted snowflakes from the wintry sky?
　　No, oh no! It flows too warm for that . . .
　　It has sprung from your own heart!

BRAND. My dear, we must both try to be strong,
　　And brave. Let us help each other
　　To be strong, and go on bravely
　　Step by step together, side by side.
　　Oh, out there I was a man.
　　The sea went surging over the rocks.
　　The storm deadened even the screaming of the gulls.
　　The sharp hail drummed on the planks of my frail boat.
　　We lay in mid-fjord. The waters raged;
　　Mast and tackle creaked and groaned;
　　The sail, ripped to shreds, rattled
　　In the wind and driving spray,
　　And every rivet in the hull screeched as in pain.
　　From the cliffs and precipices to either side
　　Great boulders came thundering down.
　　My eight men were resting on their oars.
　　Like eight corpses on a ship of ghosts.
　　I stood exultant at the helm, and felt myself
　　Grow tall and strong, like the hero of a legend,
　　For I was the man who took command;
　　I knew within my bones that some great power
　　Had anointed me for my mysterious calling . . .
　　A calling dearly bought indeed!

AGNES. Oh, it is easy to stand against a storm,
　　Easy to live a life of action,
　　But what about me, left here all alone,
　　And sitting silently amid the memories of grief
　　And pain and death? What about me?
　　However much I want to, I cannot
　　Kill my time as men are able to do.
　　What about me, denied the thrill of battle,
　　Never warmed by the fire of action . . . ?
　　Think of me here, alone with my little daily tasks.
　　Think of me like that, alone at home,
　　When I dare not remember . . . and *cannot* forget!

BRAND. Your daily tasks are not so little.
    Never were they as great as now.
    Listen. I want to tell you something
    That has come to me during this time of sorrow.
    My eyes often fill with tears,
    And my heart seems to be melting
    With tender feelings, gentle thoughts.
    At such moments, I feel it would bring joy
    If I could only weep and weep.
    Agnes, it is then I see God near me,
    As I never saw Him in the past . . .
    Oh, so close to me, I feel
    I could put out my hand and touch Him.
    And then I long to throw myself
    Upon his bosom, like a lost child
    Who is at last enfolded
    In his strong, warm father's arms.

AGNES. I pray you may always see Him so, my dear . . .
    As a God you can reach out to and touch . . .
    More loving father than stern taskmaster!

BRAND. I dare not look on Him like that,
    Dare not stand in the way of His own great work.
    I must see Him great and very strong . . .
    As great as Heaven itself.
    Our times demand this vision,
    For our age is one lacking in grandeur.
    Oh, but *you* can see Him face to face,
    Can look upon him as a loving father,
    And lay your weary head within his arms,
    And rest. . . . You can come
    From his divine embrace refreshed and healed,
    With the radiance of his glory in your eyes,
    A radiance and a glory you can bring to me
    As I labour here in suffering and strife.
    You see, Agnes, to be able to share like this
    Is the very heart of marriage.
    One of us must labour to protect the other,
    In storm and strife. The other should be able
    To heal all mortal wounds. And only then

Can it be said that these two are one.
From the moment when you turned your back
Upon the pleasures of this world to be my wife,
And boldly cast the die that told your destiny,
This calling became also your concern.
I must fight on to victory or defeat,
Fight on in the heat of the day,
Stand guard in the frosts of night . . .
And your task is to hand to me
Your brimming cups of sweet, refreshing love,
And wrap the cloak of tenderness
To keep me warm beneath my breastplate of steel . . .
That is no little task, my love.

AGNES. Any task would now be too much for my strength.
The thousand branches of my thought twine
Into one. It all still seems unreal.
Let me go on mourning, weeping,
And so help me to find myself again,
And find the path of duty I must tread.
Oh, Brand, last night, while you were gone,
He came into my room, his cheeks
Aglow with health, and in his thin little shirt
He toddled with faltering baby steps
Towards me where I lay upon my bed . . .
Stretched out his arms, called for his mother,
And with a pleading smile seemed
To be asking me to warm him back to life!
Yes, I saw it! It sent shivers down my spine . . . !

BRAND. Agnes!

AGNES.   Yes. I tell you, the child was starved!
Oh, he must be frozen, out there,
Lying on that bed of pine-shavings
With which they lined his grave!

BRAND. Only the body lies beneath the snow.
The child himself has mounted into Heaven.

AGNES [*shrinks from him*]. Why do you tear my open wound
So horribly in my frightful agony of grief?

What you so unfeelingly call 'the body'
To me is still my little boy.
To me his soul and body will be always one.
I'm not like you—I cannot separate the two.
Both are still one—my little Alf
Beneath the snow, and my little Alf in Heaven!

BRAND. Many a wound must be kept open
Until its poisons all have drained away.

AGNES. Yes, but please be patient with me.
You can lead me by the hand
So easily—but I won't be driven!
Stand by me; give me strength;
Speak to me gently. At those moments when the soul
Is forced to choose between its warring destinies
To win the crown of life—at such moments
You can speak like storm and tempest,
With a voice of thunder and ice.
But have you no gentler note, to make
More bearable this wilderness of pain?
Have you no words of comfort, no thoughts
That may guide me back into the light of day?
The God you have taught me to know
Reigns like a conquering tyrant.
How can I dare to turn to Him
With *my* petty mother's griefs?

BRAND. Would it have been much easier to turn
To the God you knew before?

AGNES. No. I could never return to Him.
Yet sometimes I feel a yearning
To be with him once again—
Where there is light, and warmth, and sun!
What was that old saying?
'Light to lift, heavy to bear!'
Your kingdom is too great for me . . .
Everything here is too much for me . .
You, your calling, your aims, the lonely
Furrow you plough, your almighty will,
Each path and precipice in this benighted place,

The fjord that locks us in, the cold, the snow,
The dark, the grief, the memory, the struggle . . .
Only your church is too little.

BRAND [*struck*]. My church! Little? That word again!
Is it something in the air of this land?
Why little?

AGNES [*sorrowfully shakes her head*]. How can I explain it rationally?
Feelings are not fixed that way—they waft over us
Like the fragrance of blossom drifting on the breeze.
Where did it come from . . . where is it going . . . ?
All I know is what I apprehend this way—knowing
Without knowledge—knowing your church is too small for me.

BRAND. There is vision in the dreams the people dream.
The same thought has been expressed to me
By hundreds of souls I have met in my wanderings.
Even that poor, mad girl who stood
In rags upon the mountain-top, shrieking at me,
Had the same idea: 'It's too ugly! It's too small!'
Nor could she find reasonable explanation.
Since then women by the hundreds have said:
'Your parish church is far too small!'
This cry from the mouths of women
Shows a subconscious longing for a palace . . .
Oh, Agnes . . . I see it all so plainly now!
You are the woman whom the Lord has sent
To guide me like an angel on my path!
Surely, though blindly, instinctively, you
Could see just where the pathway led, while I
Would have passed by the turning heedlessly!
No jack-o'-lantern ever led *your* careful feet astray.
From the start you pointed in the right direction,
Straight to the realm of true creation . . .
Then stopped me as I began to spread
My wings towards the vault of Heaven,
Turned back my gaze upon myself, and inwards
Into the inmost secrets of my heart and soul. . . .
Now once again you have spoken words
That struck me with the blaze of lightning,

Led me where I trod with faltering steps,
And brought the light of day to bear upon my work.
Our Lord's church is too little!
Then it shall be builded great and mighty!
Never did I see as clearly as I do this moment
The great gift that my Creator gave me
When he gave me you. And so, as you do,
I too must plead: 'Have patience with me!
Do not leave me! Do not leave me!'

AGNES. I will put aside my grief,
And I will dry my tears.
I will bolt and bar the castle
Of my memories, as if it were a tomb.
Between the future and the past
I shall extend an ocean of forgetfulness.
From my little world of dreams I shall obliterate
All thoughts of fantasy and foolish hopes.
I shall be a real wife to you!

BRAND. Our path leads onward to the heights!

AGNES. But do not spur me on with harsh demands!

BRAND. Through me, a greater One commands!

AGNES. One of whom you have yourself remarked
That He does not reject the will, although
It lack the power to achieve its ends.

[*Is about to go.*]

BRAND. Where are you going, Agnes?

AGNES [*smiles*].   There is still
Housework to be done. It cannot be forgotten,
Least of all upon this night of nights.
Last Christmas, do you remember,
You said I had been too extravagant.
I had put candles in all the candlesticks;
There was green stuff and pretty baubles,
And toys upon the lighted Christmas tree.
There was singing, there was laughter . . .
And this year, too, all those candles

Shall be lit again, to mark this festival.
Let us put out all our joyful decorations
For this great festival of peace.
If God should look within this room,
May he behold a chastened daughter,
A chastened son, children properly chastised,
Who know and understand they are not
To cast away all hope of happiness
Because of their Father's righteous anger.
Look at me now! Can you see
Any trace of tears left upon these cheeks?

BRAND [*draws her close, then lets her go*].
My dear, light the candles. That is *your* task.

AGNES [*smiles sorrowfully*]. And *yours* to build your mighty church . . .
But let it be before the spring. [*She goes.*]

BRAND [*looks after her*]. In all her anguish, how willingly she works,
And bravely fights the flames of martyrdom!
If her spirit should falter, her powers fail,
It can never be for want of will,
Of willing self-sacrifice. Lord, give her Thy strength . . .
And take from me the cup, the bitterest dregs
That I have had to drink in all my mission,
The bitter cup of having to unleash upon her
The grim hawk and stern-eyed falcon of the law
To tear her full, warm flesh and drink her heart's blood!
I have the strength. I have the courage. Oh Lord,
Let a double burden of Thy wrath be laid upon my head.
Only—be merciful to her! Be merciful!

[*There is a knock at the door. The* MAYOR *comes in.*]

MAYOR. Well, sir, I confess you've got me beat.

BRAND. What do you mean?

MAYOR.   Just what I say.
You can't have forgotten that time last summer,
When I wanted to get you away from here.
I warned you then I wouldn't be bested
If it came to a fight between us . . .

BRAND.   Well?

MAYOR. I still believe I'm in the right.
  But I'm throwing in the sponge.

BRAND.   What for?

MAYOR. Because you've got them all on your side.

BRAND. Have I?

MAYOR.   You know you have. People
  Come from near and far for your advice.
  Lately, there's been a new spirit in this parish.
  God knows it did not come from me,
  And so I venture to conclude it comes from you.
  Give me your hand, man! Let's call it quits.

BRAND. A war like ours is never concluded, even though
  One of the sides finds his defences breached.

MAYOR. There's only one way to end a war . . .
  Through peaceful discussion and reconciliation.
  I'm not a man to kick against the pricks.
  I'm an ordinary man of flesh and blood,
  Constituted like the rest of folks.
  When one feels against one's throat
  The dagger of the foe, one admits defeat.
  If all you have against a lance
  Is the jawbone of an ass, you must leave
  The field with as good a grace as possible.
  When you're left to fight all on your own,
  The best thing to do is to pack it in.

BRAND. One might, I think, select for comment
  Two points in your discourse: the first,
  That you regard me as the stronger.
  I have the majority . . .

MAYOR.   That's plain to see!

BRAND. I have the majority *at this moment*. But . . .
  On that last solemn day of sacrifice and judgement . . .
  Who then will have the majority on his side?

MAYOR. The day of sacrifice? But, heavens above, man
    That day never comes! If the worst
    Comes to the worst, all that sacrifice means
    Is a loosening of people's purse-strings.
    Society today is more humane. We do not demand
    Any more drastic sacrifices. The pity of it is,
    I was one of the first to advocate this
    'Humane society' stuff, and thereby played a part
    In pigeonholing what you call the day of sacrifice.
    So that in one sense it may be posited
    That I have fallen victim to my own benevolence . . .
    Anyhow, I put a rod in pickle for my own back.

BRAND. That may well be so. But—to take my second point—
    I find it hard to comprehend why you dare
    Admit defeat. Whatever the eventual application
    Of the rod, a man is called to one task only.
    Its fulfilment is all we know of paradise.
    If an ocean surged between him and his goal,
    And he could save himself quite easily
    By putting into one of Satan's near-by ports,
    May he then merely cry: 'Why bother?
    This way—the way to Hell—is shorter!'

MAYOR. To these objections, sir, my answer
    Must be yes and no. A man has to cast his anchor
    Some day . . . and if he sees his efforts
    Get him nowhere, why go on smashing eggs with sticks?
    One thing is sure: whatever kind of work we do,
    We want to see our efforts bring in some return.
    If you can't win by fighting, then
    You must do it some other, easier way.

BRAND. But black is black, and white is white.

MAYOR. My dear boy, there's not much point
    In calling something 'white as snow',
    When everybody's shouting 'black as snow'.

BRAND. And so you howl along with the pack?

MAYOR. Well . . . yes, but I shout *grey*, not black.
    This is a humane society we live in;

People must meet each other half-way,
Not always be up in arms against each other.
Remember, sir, this is a free country.
So naturally every man has a right
To his own opinion, and must be heard.
How dare any *one* person hold out
Against the rest in questions of black and white?
Now *you* have the majority; so *your* opinion counts.
Like everyone else, I shall fall in step behind you.
I only hope no one will complain
That I did not battle to the bitter end.
Oh, I can see what people think of me:
They judge my work as something trivial and petty.
They now look for something more
Than making bigger profits every year.
They are no longer willing as once they were
To contribute their savings to a sensible fund . . .
No project succeeds when the heart isn't in it.
Believe me, I find it hard to abandon plans
For roads, bridges, draining fens, reclaiming land,
And many other projects in the public interest.
But Lord love us, what was I to do?
If one can't win the day, one must give in,
And possess one's soul in patience, hoping
For a turn in the tide, and prudently withdrawing.
Well . . . I have lost my voters' confidence
The same way as I gained it; so must find other ways
To retrieve and consolidate my scattered forces.

BRAND. So was it just to gain the favour of your voters
You exercised your wiles?

MAYOR.   Oh, no.
As God is my witness, it wasn't that.
I just wanted the general good . . .
What was best for the community at large.
Yet I would be the last one to deny
There was some modicum of hope behind it all
Of some small, modest recompense, the labourer's
Just reward, being worthy of his hire, at the end
Of a hard day's work. That's life, isn't it?

A hard-working man with skill and common sense
Wants to enjoy the fruits of his labours,
And not to go groaning and toiling all his days,
Giving of himself unstintingly for . . . some ideal?
With the best will in the world, a man
Can't neglect his own and give of his strength
And skill just to feather other nests.
I have a considerable family to support;
A wife and several daughters to provide for.
When you've a houseful of mouths to feed,
Your ideals don't butter any parsnips
Nor do they help much with a thirst.
And any man surprised at such an attitude
Must be an unnatural father. That's all I can say.

BRAND. And now—what plans have you in mind?

MAYOR. I'm going to build!

BRAND.   Build?

MAYOR. Yes . . . Build—in the interests of both myself
And the parish. The first thing will be to build up
Once again the reputation I enjoyed till recently.
Election time is near, so I must really pull off
Something big, start some new enterprise
If I'm to be cock of the walk as once I was,
And put a spoke in the wheels of the other candidates.
The way I saw it was this: no man
Of common sense ever swam against the stream.
These days, people want to be 'improved', as they say.
Well, I'm not much good at that. All I can do
Is help folks get back on their feet again.
But that needs goodwill, and every man's against me.
So what has been exercising my mind is this:
Whether some remedy might not be found
For the curse of poverty?

BRAND.   You want to stamp it out?

MAYOR. I wouldn't say that. The poor are always with us.
In all communities, it is a necessary evil.
Poverty is no disgrace. We have to put up with it.

But with a little contrivance it can be made
To take on other forms. In time,
If only the proper measures can be taken,
It can be strictly controlled. We all know, of course,
That poverty's the muck on which the country's vices thrive.
But the proper place for muck is in a midden.

BRAND. What do you mean?

MAYOR.   Don't you see?
It will meet a long-felt want, and greatly benefit
The district as a whole, if I can build
What I might call a 'pest-house' for the poor.
Yes, I call it pest-house and for good reason:
It would spare us the foul contagion of crime.
To which end, I fancy, this building
Could nicely be combined with a lock-up, so that
Cause and effect might be safely incarcerated
Behind the same strong bolts and bars,
With partitions for privacy between the cells.
We need not stop there: once I've started work,
I can envisage myself as building, under the same roof,
A grand wing which could be used for elections and receptions,
For solemn and particular occasions, a stage
And auditorium, and some guest accommodation.
In short, a magnificent political and social centre.

BRAND. A place like that is badly needed, certainly.
But I know one thing that is needed even more.

MAYOR. I know exactly what you're thinking of—a madhouse!
Oh, yes! That's badly needed here. To tell the truth,
That was what *I* thought of first; but after
Discussing the project with several interested persons
I abandoned the idea. For where would we find
The cash for a building as enormous as that?
Believe me, a madhouse would cost a pretty penny,
That is, if everyone in need of it or worthy of it
Is to find accommodation. We have to build
For the future, not only for ourselves.
Developments are proceeding with leaps and bounds . . .
Places that last year would have been big enough

Are already too small. This gives some idea of how
The public clamour for essential services has grown.
In any branch of life you care to mention,
All sorts of skills and talents now are flourishing
As if by magic. Costs have risen out of all proportion.
We cannot afford to build the proper accommodation
For the wives and children of this and the following generation.
So what I say is: 'If a tooth hurts, best yank it out!'

BRAND. And if someone's madness gets beyond control,
We can always let him loose in the auditorium.

MAYOR [*delighted*]. Yes! That place will be mostly empty,
Just going to waste. Ingenious! Build our building—
And we get our asylum thrown in free of charge!
Then shall we see, together under one great roof,
And under the protection of the selfsame flag,
All those essential elements that give
Our little town its own peculiar savour:
All our paupers, together with the main stream
Of our juvenile delinquents and other malefactors,
As well as the local lunatics, who until now
Have gone around without care or correction.
We shall also enjoy the fruits of freedom,
With regular elections and flights of oratory.
We shall have our council-chamber for debating
How best to benefit the community at large;
And our festival hall, where we can declare
Our intention to preserve the heritage of our past.
As long as this plan comes off, our rugged son of Norway
Will have everything he can fairly ask for
To help him live a full and virtuous life.
God knows, our district is not rich;
Yet once this community centre has been built,
I think that I can safely say my district
Will be well organized.

BRAND.   But the money . . .

MAYOR. Ah, that's the stumbling-block, in this as all things.
People have no great urge to contribute.
Now if I appeal to them without your support,

I know I must call the whole thing off.
But if you could lend your eloquence in the cause
Of my ideal, it will go forward smoothly.
And if I bring it to fulfilment,
Your kind help would not go unrewarded.

BRAND. You mean you want to buy me?

MAYOR. Let me call my plan by another name,
Thus bringing us mutual advantage in
The bridging of that abyss of disagreement
Which hitherto has always yawned between us,
To our common disadvantage.

BRAND. You've come at the wrong time . . .

MAYOR. Ah, yes, I know, I know . . . the great grief
Which has recently afflicted you and your wife.
I'm afraid your manly fortitude deceived me;
And with the welfare of the district so much at heart . . .

BRAND. I am ready to give my services whenever needed—
In times of grief as in times of joy.
It was for another and more pertinent reason
I said you had come to me too late.

MAYOR. Too late?

BRAND.   I intend to start building myself.

MAYOR. What? Steal a march on me, would you?

BRAND. Not quite that. [*Points out of the window.*] Mr. Mayor, you
    see . . . ?

MAYOR. Out there?

BRAND.   Yes.

MAYOR.   That big ugly wooden building?
That's the vicarage cowshed.

BRAND.   No, not that one.
The little ugly wooden building.

MAYOR.   Eh? The church?

BRAND [*nods*]. I'm going to rebuild it, and build it big.

MAYOR. No, the Devil you won't! No man's
    Going to touch that church! It would ruin my whole plan!
    My plan is all drawn up. It's an urgent matter!
    This plan of yours would spike my guns! *Two* plans!
    That's one too many. Call it off at once!

BRAND. Once I have decided, I do not alter.

MAYOR. But in this case, man, you must!
    If we build my lock-up, my pest-house
    And my political and social centre all in one—
    In short, my madhouse—no one will worry if the church
    Falls to pieces. And why should it come down?
    It was always good enough for us before.

BRAND. *Before*—possibly. Now it is too small.

MAYOR. And yet I've never seen it full!

BRAND. There is not room in there even
    For a single soul to spread its wings.

MAYOR [*shakes his head in bewilderment*].
    Any poor soul who feels like that
    Amply proves the necessity for my madhouse. [*Changes tone.*]
    Now this is my advice, sir. Let the old church stand.
    In its own way, it may well be called a relic
    Of our noble and heroic heritage—a *noble* relic;
    It must not be swept away by one man's whim!
    Even if my plans are disapproved,
    In the eyes of the public I shall rise in grandeur
    Like a phoenix from its nest of ashes!
    I shall emerge as the champion of the monument
    That graces our shores.—A heathen temple
    Once stood here, in the days of King Bele;
    Then in time the church was built,
    Financed by the loot of pious warriors.
    Reverent in its simple splendour,
    Venerable in its ancient style,
    It has proudly reared its head till now . . .

BRAND. But those heathen symbols of a former tyranny
    Were long since laid in their graves.
    Nothing remains of them today.

MAYOR. Exactly! It is all so ancient, it no longer exists.
    But in my grandfather's day there was still
    Something left—a hole in the wall.

BRAND.   A hole?

MAYOR. As big as a barrel!

BRAND.   But the wall itself . . . ?

MAYOR. Oh, that had gone. That's why I'm telling you
    The church itself must not be touched.
    It would be something unprecedented . . .
    A shameful, horrible, barbaric deed!
    And then the cash—where's that to come from?
    Do you think folks in these parts will freely
    Authorize expenditure for harebrained schemes like this
    When a few planks'll patch up the old place well enough—
    At least to keep it from tumbling down in our time?
    Well, go and spy out the lie of the land. . . .
    But I'll have you bested in the end!

BRAND. It is not my intention to extort
    A single penny from anyone. That's no way
    To build a mansion to the Lord.
    No, I shall build with my own money—
    My inheritance! I shall spend it all,
    To the last farthing, on this labour of love.
    Well, now, Mr. Mayor—are you still so bold
    As to think you can shake my resolution?

MAYOR [*with folded hands*]. Well! You could knock me down with a
    feather!
    The likes of *that* is hardly ever heard of,
    Even in big towns . . . and here in the back of beyond . . . !
    Where it's always been the thing
    To keep your moneybags well locked away
    When it came to contributing to the common weal . . .
    And here you are, promising to unleash

An avalanche of liberality—a rippling, glittering,
Splashing, effervescing torrent of munificence . . .
Well, really, Brand, I said it once and I'll say it again—
You could knock me down with a feather!

BRAND. I had long ago decided to give up all claims
To my inheritance. . . .

MAYOR.　　　　　　　Oo, yes! Now there's been
A lot of rumours hinting at something in that department,
But naturally *I* passed it all off as idle gossip.
After all, I ask you, who would sacrifice
A tidy sum like that—and for what? . . .
Nothing! I ask you! Anyhow, that's *your* affair.
Lead on, my friend! Yours truly will bring up the rear.
You bask in the people's favour; you can do things.
As for little me, I'll wiggle my way forward as best I can.
Yes, Brand, *we* shall build this glorious church
Together!

BRAND.　　What! And give up your own plan?

MAYOR. I will, so help me God! Why, man!
I'd be mad to let an opportunity like this pass by!
Whom do you think the masses flock to—
The one who wants to fatten, feed and fodder them, or
The extortionist who milks and shears and flays them?
Yes, devil take it, I'll be with you hand in glove!
The thought of it makes me feel quite feverish. . . .
My mind's ablaze—I'm moved, captivated, charmed . . .
Yes, almost touched—touched in my inmost heart . . .
Yea, verily, it was a lucky star that led
My steps this evening unto this the parsonage;
I venture to think that but for *my* plan,
Your own design would hardly have occurred to you,
And never been offered to the world's applause!
To build a new parish church!
Exactly what I had in mind myself!

BRAND. But remember, we'll not be able to preserve
That proud and ancient ruin!

MAYOR [*looks out*]. Oh, what of that?
  Clad in the spectral radiance of the moonlight
  On the newly-fallen snow, it does look pretty mouldy.

BRAND. Mr. Mayor! What is this you are saying?

MAYOR. My dear Brand, it's far too old. It beats me
  How I never saw it in this light until this evening . . .
  Why, that gable-end is all askew! It would be
  Utterly irresponsible to go on using such a firetrap!
  And when one examines the roof, the walls—my dear sir,
  What kind of architecture, what kind of style is that.
  Look at those arches—are they gothic, Greek, or what?
  Any expert would condemn them out of hand
  As hideous . . . and I should have to share that view!
  Those mossy tuffets on the roof . . . God bless my soul,
  They don't go back to the days of old King Bele!
  No! Piety can go too far! Any fool can see
  This old rotten junk-heap is just a pile of muck!

BRAND. But what if the public sentiment were
  To declare against its demolition . . . ?

MAYOR. If no one else will, I will tear it down
  With my own two hands, and the quicker the better!
  Leave it to me. I'll fix everything this weekend,
  Getting formal permission and all that, you know,
  And get the thing off to a good start.
  You may depend on me, I'll stir them up.
  I'll write, I'll get things moving . . .
  Between you and me, we know our Mayor. . . .
  And if I cannot get the hoi polloi
  To put their shoulders to the wheel
  And pull the whole place down, I'll tear
  It apart with my own hands, log by log.
  Even if it means bringing the wife
  And all the girls along to help,
  I'll get the job done, God damn me!

BRAND. You seem to have changed your tune
  Quite considerably.

MAYOR.   One of the things
  Culture and civilization teach us
  Is not to take one-sided views.
  And if what the poet tells us is true,
  There is something uncommonly fine and noble
  In a man's thoughts having wings . . .
  In other words, that thoughts can fly. . . .
  Well, goodbye. [*Picks up his hat.*]
                    I have to see to my little mob. . . .

BRAND. Your what?

MAYOR.   Well, I and one of my men
  Came on a pack of gypsies, black as sweeps
  They were, at the entrance to the village.
  I had them rounded up, and roped and chained.
  Now the whole lot are under lock and key
  At your neighbour's, to the north of here.
  But damn it all, two or three of them
  Managed to give me the slip . . .

BRAND. But the bells have just sounded the Christmas message:
  Peace on earth, goodwill to all men . . .

MAYOR. What brought that raggle-taggle here?
  Of course, in a sense they are the responsibility
  Of the parish. [*Laughs.*] And yours, too! Listen!
  I have a riddle for you—solve it if you can:
  Folk there are who do exist
  By virtue of her from whom you sprang,
  Yet why they exist is just because
  To different families they belong!

BRAND [*shakes his head*]. Dear God, what a mouthful! What a conun-
    drum!
  The kind you stare at and cannot answer.

MAYOR. Well, the answer's easy. Many's the time
  You must have heard folks tell in the village
  Of the poor lad who lived to the west of us
  Who knew more than four priests put together?
  He fell in love with your mother,
  And courted her . . .

BRAND. Well?

MAYOR. Just imagine,
A girl from a respectable landed family?
Of course, she sent him packing, as was only
To be expected. But then what does the poor lad
Go and do? Half daft with disappointment,
He finally takes up with another girl—
A gypsy trollop—and before he snuffed it
Left behind several additions to the tribe,
Which now roams destitute about the place.
Indeed, the parish was saddled permanently
With one of these bastard trolls . . . a nice souvenir
He left us of his goings-on . . .

BRAND. Who is it?

MAYOR. Gerd, the gypsy girl.

BRAND [*in a low voice*]. I see.

MAYOR [*gaily*]. Not bad, eh? His offspring thus exists
By virtue of her from whom you sprang—
For the real origin of all that brood
Lies in his unrequited love for your mother.

BRAND. Tell me, Mr. Mayor, is there anything
That can be done for these poor souls?

MAYOR. Huh! Clap 'em in irons is what I say!
They're damned to eternity, the lot of them.
Saving *them* would be like stealing
From the Devil—and he's got to have his share!
We don't want Old Nick to go bankrupt!

BRAND. You were thinking of building a large establishment
As a shelter from distress and poverty . . .

MAYOR. A proposal withdrawn by the proposer
As soon as it was made.

BRAND. And yet supposing . . .
It was a fine idea in its way . . .

MAYOR [*smiling*]. Now, *you* seem to have changed your tune
    Quite considerably! [*Slaps him on the shoulder.*] Let the dead
    Bury the dead, what's past is past!
    A man must be firm, and act with decision.
    Well, goodbye! I can't bide a minute longer.
    I must be off now to find out where
    Those raggle-taggle runaways have hid themselves.
    I'll be seeing you soon. Merry Christmas to you!
    Goodbye! My greetings to your good lady! [*He goes.*]

BRAND [*after a thoughtful silence*]. Oh, how endless is the burden of
    atonement!
    A thousand strands of destiny's dark threads
    Are tangled here in wild confusion . . .
    Guilt is interwoven with the consequences
    Of our guilt; the one infects the other.
    And no man's eye can any more distinguish
    The purest right from the bloodiest wrong.

[*He goes to the window and looks out a long time.*]

Oh, my little boy, my innocent lamb. . . .
Your death an atonement for my mother's deeds!
A brain distracted brought me word from Him
Who has His throne beyond the clouds, and bade
Me make a choice between my destinies.
And that same distracted brain was brought
Into this world because my mother chose wrong!
Even thus does the Lord above employ the fruits
Of guilt to feed the roots of sanity and justice.
Even thus does He hurl down upon us from on high
Retribution—unto the third generation.

[*He turns away in terror from the window.*]

Yes, the God of the almighty law
Has raised His hand against our people;
The main thing is to hold a balance
Between His wrath and our repentance.
The possibility of our redemption
Lies within our own self-sacrifice.

But in these times, this one truth is denied,
Because the people are afraid of knowing it.

[*He walks for some time up and down the room.*]

Prayer . . . prayer. . . . Hm . . . a word
That falls so glibly from the lips,
And senselessly parroted by high and low . . .
For them, prayer is a scream for mercy
Uttered at the tempest's height
To that great mystery of mysteries . . .
A plea to become a part of Christ's burden . . .
A lifting up of hands to Heaven, while they
Stand knee-deep in the middens of their unbelief!
Ha! ha! If things could be conveniently settled thus,
Then I, like any other man, might dare
To beat upon the portals of the Lord—
So swift to wrath, and terrible to praise!

[*He stops and ponders awhile in silence.*]

And yet . . . in the days of our most desperate anguish,
In the tremendous, overwhelming moment of our grief,
When the child was sleeping his final sleep,
And when none of his mother's kisses
Could restore that smile to his dear lips . . .
How was it then . . . ? Did I not pray then?
If not, whence came that gentle rapture,
That sweet stream of song, that melody
That wafted from afar, and floated me away
Upon the heights, high into freedom?
Did I pray then? Did my soul's refreshment
Come from prayer? Here in my inmost heart,
Did I hold converse with God?
And did He hear me? Did He look down upon
This house of sorrow, and take pity on my tears?
How can I tell? All now is barred and shuttered,
And darkness has once more descended over me . . .
No light, there is no light. . . . Yes, there is one . . .
She who can see within the deepest dark . . . !

[*Cries out in anguish.*]

Give me light! My dearest . . . Bring me light!

[AGNES *opens the door and steps in holding a candlestick with lighted candles; a clear radiance fills the room.*]

BRAND. Light!

AGNES.   Look, Brand! The Christmas candles!

BRAND [*in a low voice*]. Ah, yes, the Christmas candles.

AGNES [*placing the candlestick on the table*]. Was I long?

BRAND.   No, no!

AGNES. Oh, how cold it is in here! You must be freezing . . .

BRAND [*firmly*].   No.

AGNES [*smiling*]. This pride, as always! You *will* not admit
     You need light and warmth. [*She puts fuel on the stove.*]

BRAND [*walking up and down*].   Ah, yes . . . *will* not!

AGNES [*talking to herself in a low voice as she decorates the room*].
     The candlestick here. Last year at this time,
     How he reached out his little fingers
     Towards the bright light of the Christmas candles!
     He was so happy and healthy and clever.
     He leaned from his little chair and asked
     If it was the sun. [*Moves the candlestick a little.*]
                         Now the full radiance
     From the candles falls across that place where . . .
     Now, from where he sleeps,
     He can see the light from the window.
     Now he can come quietly and peep
     Into this bright, gay Christmas scene . . .
     But the window-pane is veiled in tears . . .
     But wait, wait . . . Soon it shall smile again . . . [*She wipes the
     window.*]

BRAND [*has been following her with his eyes, and speaks now in a low voice*].
     When will this sea of grief, so deep
     And turbulent, calm down and give her peace?
     It *must* calm down, or . . .

AGNES [*to herself*].   See, how clear!
It is as if the barrier were gone,
As if the room had widened out,
As if the grim, cold earth
Has suddenly become a fireside nook
Where my little boy can sleep sweet and sound.

BRAND. What are you doing, Agnes?

AGNES.   Hush! Be quiet!

BRAND [*goes closer*]. Why did you draw the curtain?

AGNES. Merely a dream. Now I am awake.

BRAND. Dreams are a snare and a delusion.
Close the shutters!

AGNES [*entreats*].   Brand!

BRAND.   Close them! Tight!

AGNES. Why are you so hard? It's not right!

BRAND. Tight shut!

AGNES [*closes the shutters*]. There, I've shut and barred them.
But all the same, I am sure that God is not offended
Even though for the space of a fleeting dream
I drank from a warm, deep well of comfort . . .

BRAND. Indeed, no. He is a mild indulgent judge.
You are still on good terms with Him,
Even though in your adoration there is
A touch of idolatry from time to time.

AGNES [*bursts into tears*]. Tell me how much more you expect?
My feet drag wearily . . . my wings droop . . .

BRAND. I shall tell you what I told you
Once before—that every sacrifice is but a drop
Of water in the ocean if it be not *All*.

AGNES. But mine *was* All! I have nothing left!

BRAND [*shakes his head*]. No. There is yet more to give.

AGNES [*smiles*]. Ask! I cannot give what I do not have!

BRAND. Give *All*!

AGNES.   Why don't you take it?
Ah, Brand, you will find nothing there!

BRAND. You have your grieving, and your memories . . .
You have your flood of sinful yearning . . .

AGNES [*in despair*]. Then tear my tormented heart out by the roots!
Tear it out!

BRAND.   If you weep and wail
About the loss, it is in vain you cast
Your sacrifice into the chasm of the abyss.

AGNES [*shudders*]. The way of your Lord is steep and narrow.

BRAND. It is the way of the Will. There is no other.

AGNES. But the way of *mercy* . . . ?

BRAND [*with a gesture of repudiation*]. That way
Is paved with sacrificial altars.

AGNES [*stares vacantly and says, shaken*]:
Now I behold before me, yawning
Beneath my feet like some great precipice,
Those words of the Scriptures which, until now,
I could never fathom.

BRAND.   Which words?

AGNES. He who sees Jehovah face to face
Shall surely die!

BRAND [*throws his arms round her, and presses her close to him*].
                    Oh, hide your face!
You must not see Him! Shut your eyes!

AGNES. Must I?

BRAND [*lets her go*]. No!

AGNES.   Your heart is troubled, Brand.

BRAND. Because I love you.

AGNES.   Your love is hard.

BRAND. Too hard?

AGNES.　　　　　Do not ask me that. Lead me,
And I shall follow wheresoever you may go.

BRAND. Do you imagine I would take you
From your dancing and your play
Quite thoughtlessly. . . . That I would impose
Upon your youth the role of willing sacrifice
In some half-thought-out plan?
If so, I grieve for both of us.
For then the sacrifice you are to make
Would be too great, too dearly bought.
You are my wife. I can demand
That you give your life entirely
To this calling. It is my right.

AGNES. Make your demand! Only do not leave me!

BRAND. I must leave you. I need quiet, peace.
Soon I must begin the building of my church.

AGNES. My little church is now in ruins.

BRAND. If it was a temple for the idols of your longing,
Then it had best be cast down in the storm.

[*He embraces her, as though in fear.*]

Peace be with you . . . and through you
With me and mine . . . the straight and narrow way!

[*He walks to the side door.*]

AGNES. Brand, may I move aside a little
This horrid barrier . . . this shutter,
Just a little? Just a little crack? May I, Brand?

BRAND [*at the door*]. No.

[*He goes into his room.*]

AGNES.　　　　　Shut. Tight shut . . . everything shut!
Even oblivion is shut from me.
Bolted and barred my grief, my sighs;

And locks on Heaven and on the grave!
I must get out! I cannot breathe
Here in this agony of loneliness!
Out? Where? Stern eye of God,
Do not look down upon me now!
If I fled this place, could I take
My heart's most cherished treasures with me?
Even if I wanted to, could I fly for ever
From the blank numbness of my terror?

[*She listens at the door of* BRAND'*s room.*]

He is reading aloud. My voice
Could never reach him. No helping hand
For me, and no advice, no comfort!
The God of Christmas has enough to do,
Listening to prayers of thanks, and songs
And games and dances of those happy people
Blessed with children and good fortune.
Christmas is the time of joy.
It is His time, but he does not see me,
Does not hear the cries of lonely mothers.

[*She stealthily approaches the window.*]

Shall I slide apart these shutters,
So that the full, clear light
May drive away the terrors of the night
From my little one's dark bedchamber?
No, he cannot be down there!
Christmas is the children's time.
Surely they'll let him come for that?
Perhaps he's standing outside now,
Stretching up his arms to knock
Upon the window that his mother closed.
Was that a child I heard crying?
Oh, I don't know what to do, to say!
It is shut. . . . Your father made me shut it . . .
Alf, I dare not open now!
There's a good little boy!
We never made him cross before,
Oh, fly home again to Heaven.

There's light and happiness up there,
And crowds of little children playing.
But do not let them see you crying . . .
Do not tell them your father shut
The door against you when you knocked.
A little boy like you still does not
Understand the things we grown-ups do.
Say he was sad . . . tell them he sighed.
Tell them it was *he* who picked
Those pretty leaves to make your wreath.
Do you see it? He made it!

[*She listens, comes to her senses and shakes her head.*]

Ah, I am dreaming! Something more
Than this shutter stands between us.
Only the flames of purifying fire
Can destroy the hateful barrier,
Tear down the vault and burst the bolts,
Throw open the creaking prison gates
And smash the enormous lock!
There is much, much to be done down here
Before we two can be brought together.
I must work, and strive in silence
To fulfil his terrible commandments.
I must steel myself, steel my *will*.
But this is a time of festival.
How very different from last year . . . !
But we shall celebrate it!
I shall bring out all my treasures . . .
Which, since the shipwreck of my joy,
Have become things of infinite value
To my sorrowing mother's heart.

[*She kneels down by the chest of drawers, opens a drawer and takes out various things. At the same moment,* BRAND *opens the door, and is about to speak to her. But when he sees what she is doing he stops and remains standing there.* AGNES *does not see him.*]

BRAND [*in a low voice*]. Always her thoughts on that grave outside.
Always these same games in the garden of the dead.

N1

AGNES. Here is the veil. Here the little mantle
He was wrapped in for his christening.
Here in this bundle I have the dress . . .

[*Holds it up, looks at it and laughs.*]

Dear God, how pretty it is, how sweet!
How smart my little boy looked
When he sat in the pew in church.
Here is the scarf he used to wear.
Here is his jersey: he wore it
The very first time we took him out.
It was far too long for him then,
But it soon became too small for him.
We'll lay that here on one side.
Mittens, stockings . . . what sturdy legs!
And here we have his new silk bonnet . . .
I made it to keep off the draughts . . .
It's still unused, lovely and clean.
Oh, here are his travelling clothes;
He was always wrapped up warm and snug
To be nice and cosy on our travels.
When for the last time I put them
Away, I felt weary unto death.

BRAND [*clenches his fists in pain*].
Have pity, God! I cannot destroy
These last vestiges of her idolatry.
If, Lord, it has to be,
Let it be done by other hands than mine!

AGNES. Why, it's wet. Have I been weeping?
What riches there are here!
Embroidered with the pearls of tears,
Dyed with my anguish, stitched
With the dreadful threads of destiny and terror!
Oh, holy! This is the coronation robe
He wore to his sacrificial baptism!
Oh, what riches still are mine!

[*There is a sharp knocking at the door.* AGNES *turns round with a cry
and sees* BRAND *at the same moment. The door bursts open and a*
WOMAN, *clad in rags, comes rushing in with a child in her arms.*]

WOMAN [*sees the child's clothing and cries to* AGNES].
Share them with me! You are rich!

AGNES. You are ten times richer than I!

WOMAN. Oh, you're just like all the rest.
Full of words and nothing else.

BRAND [*approaches*]. Tell me what you are doing here.

WOMAN. I don't want you . . . you're the priest!
I'd rather go back out into the storm
Than listen to your preaching about sin.
Rather go to my death I would,
And drown, be tossed up on the rocks,
Than stand before a man in black
Who knows the road to hellfire!
In the Devil's name, can I help
Being what I am?

BRAND [*in a low voice*]. This voice
And these wild features fill me with dread,
And chill me with a strange foreboding.

AGNES. Come, rest and warm yourself beside the fire.
If your baby's hungry, we shall feed him . . .

WOMAN. A gypsy's child must not be laid
Where there's warmth and light. Our home
Is on the country lanes, among the rocks,
The woods, the mountains and the moors. . . .
We're wanderers, and always on the move.
House and home—that's for *your* sort.
I can't stay here. I must be off.
They're after me, like a pack of hounds!
The mayor, the constable, the men of the law. . . .
They'd have me in chains if they had their way.

BRAND. No one shall lay a finger on you here.

WOMAN. Here? Between four walls, with a roof
Over my head? No, thank you. For us two
The snowy winter night's a healthier place.
But give us some rags to wrap the baby in!

His big brother, the rotten villain,
Pinched the blanket I'd wrapped him in.
Look, the poor mite's half naked,
Blue with cold, half frozen by the wind . . .
It's as raw as ice outside!

BRAND. Woman, set your child free
From this unholy way of life.
Let him be comforted . . . raised up.
The brand can be washed away . . .

WOMAN. Yes, you know all about that kind of thing!
No man alive can work that wonder. . . .
And if there was, I wouldn't let him!
Cursed be all you who cast him out!
Do you know where his mother gave him birth?
By the side of a foul ditch, and everybody drinking,
Gambling, singing, dancing all around.
He was christened in the muddy slush,
Crossed with a stick of charcoal,
Reared on a swig from the bottle.
No sooner did he see the light of day,
He heard the filthy curses of the tribe.
You know who they belonged to, those voices?
God help me . . . the baby's father himself,
And the baby's fathers . . . !

BRAND. Agnes!

AGNES.   Yes.

BRAND.   Your duty is plain to see.

AGNES [*in terror*]. Brand! Not to her! No, never!

WOMAN. Give me! Give it all to me!
Finest silks or worn-out rags!
Nothing's too poor or too good,
As long as it's something soft and warm.
He's not going to live much longer.
I want him to die in comfort.

BRAND [*to* AGNES]. This is the moment you must make the Choice.

WOMAN. You've more than enough for your own child.
  What about mine? Haven't you a rag
  For him while he's still alive,
  And a shroud for him when he's dead?

BRAND. Do you not hear the warning
  In her voice, the omen on her lips?

WOMAN. Give me!

AGNES.   This is sacrilege.
  A crime against my dead child.

BRAND. His departure to his death is meaningless
  If the road ends on the threshold here.

AGNES [*crushed*]. Your will be done, then. I must trample
  Underfoot the deepest promptings of my heart.
  Come, take them. I shall share with you.

WOMAN. Let me have them!

BRAND.   Share, Agnes . . . *share*?

AGNES [*with passionate intensity*].
  I'd rather die, than be robbed of everything!
  Look, how I have yielded to you
  Inch by inch! I can go no further!
  Half is enough. Her need is not so great.

BRAND. When you bought it for your child,
  Was it too much then?

AGNES [*giving*].   Here, then, take
  The mantle my own child wore to his baptism.
  Here are the dress, the scarf, the jersey;
  That will keep him warm in the bitter
  Air of night. Here is a little silken hood;
  That will shield him from the cold.
  Take it! Take every stitch . . .

WOMAN. Give it me!

BRAND.   Agnes, have you given *all*?

AGNES [*gives again*]. Here is the coronation robe
  He wore to his sacrificial baptism!

WOMAN. Well, that's the lot, I see!
  Now I've got to get away from here!
  I'll bundle him up on the steps outside . . .
  Then quickly off and away with him. [*Goes.*]

AGNES [*struggling inwardly, finally asks*].
  Tell me Brand, are you satisfied now?
  Can you ask any more of me?

BRAND. First tell me this: did you accept *willingly*
  The pain of giving?

AGNES.   No! I did not.

BRAND. Then your gift is cast away into the sea.
  You still have not surrendered all to my demand. [*He makes to go.*]

AGNES [*remains silent until he nears the doorway, then cries*].
  Brand!

BRAND.   What is it?

AGNES.   I lied . . .
  See, I am repentant. I submit.
  You did not know, could not suspect,
  That I had not given everything away.

BRAND. Well?

AGNES [*takes a child's cap, folded, from her bosom*]. You see, I kept this
  back.

BRAND. His cap?

AGNES.   Yes, wet with tears.
  As with the cold sweat of death . . .
  Since then, I've worn it next my heart!

BRAND. Stay in the power of your idols! [*Is about to go.*]

AGNES. Stop.

BRAND.   What is it now?

AGNES.   Oh, you know! [*She holds the cap out to
  him.*]

BRAND [*approaching but not taking the cap*].
  Willingly?

AGNES.   Willingly!

BRAND.   Give it to me.
The woman is sitting outside on the steps. [*He goes.*]

AGNES. Robbed . . . stripped of everything . . .
The last tie that bound me to the dust!

[*She stands motionless for a moment; little by little the expression on
her face changes to radiant joy,* BRAND *comes back; she rushes joyfully
to meet him, throws her arms about his neck and cries:*]

I am free, Brand! I am free!

BRAND.   Agnes!

AGNES. The darkness has gone. All the terrors
That weighed like a nightmare on my mind
Have now been cast out into the abyss!
I have won the battle of the Will!
All the mists have cleared away,
All the clouds are swept away;
Beyond the night, beyond the dark of death,
I see the radiance of a rosy dawn!
Let me say that word—the churchyard—
The churchyard—no, it brings no tears now.
It does not open up my wound again . . .
Our child has ascended into Heaven!

BRAND. Yes! Now you have truly conquered.

AGNES. I have conquered . . . conquered
Terror and the grave! Look up!
Look there, on high!
Do you see him, standing
In the radiance of the throne,
Carefree as he was in life, and
Holding out his arms to us?
If I had a thousand voices,
If I dared to, if I could,
I should not raise one whisper
To beg him back again.
Oh, how great, how rich is God

In all his ways and wonders!
My child's own sacrifice,
A sacrifice for guilt,
Has freed my soul from death.
He was born that I might lose him;
I had to be led on thus to victory!
Thank you for your guiding hand:
How faithfully you strove for me.
I knew the anguish in your heart.
Now *you* stand in the valley of the Choice.
On *you* now falls the burden
Of this 'All or Nothing'!

BRAND. Your words are wild. All the torment
Of your struggle now is over.

AGNES. Have you forgotten what I said:
'He who sees Jehovah face to face
Shall surely die'?

BRAND [*shrinks back*]. Oh, what fateful
Fire is this you kindle? No!
It shall never, never be!
In my hands a giant's strength.
You must not, shall not leave me!
Let all else on earth be swept away,
I can do without it all . . .
But never, never without you!

AGNES. Choose, at this crossroads in your life!
Quench the light that burns within me.
Dam the fresh spring of my Christmas joy.
Give me back those garments of idolatry—
The woman still is sitting there outside—
Let me once again return
To those fair, heaven-blinded days,
Lower me again into the mire
Of my sloth and my sinfulness . . .
You may do everything, are free to choose.
Compared with you, I have no strength.
So clip my wings, lock up my soul,
Impose the leaden burden of the daily round!

Bind me in chains! Drag me down again
To that mire from which you raised me!
Let me live as I lived when I writhed in darkness!
If you dare do this, and will,
I am your wife as I was before.
Choose, at this crossroads in your life!

BRAND. Heaven help me if I should do so!
Ah, but far from this place, and far
From all memories of grief, you'll find
That life and light are *one*!

AGNES. Are you forgetting that the baptism
Of your calling binds you *here* . . .
And of your sacrifice as well?
Are you forgetting the thousand souls
It is your mission to redeem right *here* . . .
Those whom the Lord bade you to lead
Onward to the springs of their salvation?
Choose, at this crossroads in your life!

BRAND. I have no choice.

AGNES [*throws her arms around his neck*]. Thank you
For all you have given me.
And thank you especially for this!
How faithfully you guided me, weary as I was!
The mists of despair still hang above me . . .
Keep watch faithfully beside my bed.

BRAND. Sleep! Your day's work is ended now.

AGNES. Ended, and the candle lit for the night.
My victory has taken all my strength.
I am faint, and I am weary.
Oh, how easy to offer praise to God!
Goodnight, Brand.

BRAND.   Goodnight.

AGNES.   And again goodnight.
Thank you for *All*. Now I can sleep. [*She goes.*]

BRAND [*clenches his fists against his breast*].
    My soul, be steadfast to the end!
    The victory of victories is to lose all.
    The loss of *All* brought everything to you . . .
    Only what is lost can be possessed for ever!

ACT FIVE

Eighteen months later. The new church stands completed and decorated for the consecration. The river runs close by. It is early morning, and misty. THE SEXTON *is busy hanging up garlands outside the church. A little later* THE SCHOOLMASTER *arrives.*

SCHOOLMASTER. On the job already?

SEXTON.   Somebody's got to do it.
  Give us a hand, this greenery
  Has to be looped from post to post
  To mark off the route of the procession.

SCHOOLMASTER. They're putting up something at the parsonage
  With a round opening at one end . . .

SEXTON.   Are they, now!

SCHOOLMASTER. What can it be, I wonder?

SEXTON.   What they call a plaque
  In honour of the priest, with his name in gilt.

SCHOOLMASTER. My word! What goings-on in the parish today!
  People are streaming in from near and far.
  Look! The whole fjord is flocked with sails!

SEXTON. Yes, the parish is on the move now. Before he came,
  Nobody ever heard tell of struggle and strife.
  We slept the sleep of the just, minding our own business.
  I don't know which was the better—then or now.

SCHOOLMASTER. That's life, sexton, that's life!

SEXTON.   But you and I
  Are hardly touched by this new life. How's that?

SCHOOLMASTER. We worked while others slept; and when they woke
  We fell asleep . . . for then there was no need for us.

SEXTON. But you did say that life's the thing?

SCHOOLMASTER. That's what the dean and the parson tell us;
   Not that I have anything against it, mind you . . .
   But between you and me, such opinions are
   For the common mass of the people.
   We are subject to a law quite different
   From the one prevailing in these hills.
   We are the district's public officials.
   Our duty is to preserve the status quo,
   To foster church discipline, instruct the young,
   And not concern ourselves with vulgar human passions.
   In short, to keep aloof from all controversy.

SEXTON. But he himself is the driving power.

SCHOOLMASTER. And that is precisely what he should *not* be.
   It has come to my ears that among his superiors
   There is much dissatisfaction with his doings,
   And if only they dared stand up to the people
   They would have had him out of office long ago.
   But he has a clever way with him; he knows
   What makes these people tick. So he builds this church.
   In these parts, when anything is 'doing'
   People lose their common sense. *What* is being done,
   Nobody cares; all that matters is that something is *done*.
   We might all indeed, leaders and flock alike,
   Be called a generation of 'doers'.

SEXTON. Of course, you have sat in Parliament,
   So you must know the country and the people.
   But one chap who passed through this parish
   Shortly after the awakening declared
   That whereas formerly we had just been sleepers,
   When we awoke . . . we became men of promise.

SCHOOLMASTER. Yes, our people are promising, all right . . .
   A people that proclaims enormous promise,
   A people that's made such rapid advance
   That each man now interprets that promise himself.

SEXTON. One thing I've never been quite clear about.
   You who have studied these things can tell me:
   What is this so-called 'people's promise'?

SCHOOLMASTER. A 'people's promise', my dear man, is
    Too complicated to discuss right now.
    But it is something everybody looks to,
    Because they're attracted by some grand idea—
    Some great thing about to happen to them . . .
    In the people's *future*, you will observe.

SEXTON. Thank you! That's one thing I've got clear at last.
    But there's something else I can't get straight.

SCHOOLMASTER. What's that?

SEXTON.   Tell me, what is this great future
    They talk about? And *when* is it?

SCHOOLMASTER. Ah-ha, the future never comes!

SEXTON.   Never?

SCHOOLMASTER. It stands to reason . . . it's the natural order.
    For when what we call the future arrives,
    It's become the *present*—is no longer the future.

SEXTON. Yes, I can see that's fair enough.
    I have no quarrel with you there.
    But when is this promise to be kept?

SCHOOLMASTER. Haven't I just told you that a promise
    Is a form of compact with the future?
    It will be honoured in the future.

SEXTON. But tell me when this future will be here!

SCHOOLMASTER [*in a low voice*]. How like a sexton! Always tolling the
    same bell!
    [*Aloud.*] My dear man, have I to go over the whole thing again?
    The future cannot possibly come, because
    As soon as it's present it's already past.

SEXTON. I see.

SCHOOLMASTER. Every concept is based in something
    That seems like a trick, but is quite straightforward—
    At least, for anyone who is capable
    Of putting two and two together.
    In the final analysis, to *promise* is

To *prevaricate*, though anyone who makes
A promise is still an honourable man.
To keep a promise is thought to be difficult;
But it would be considered quite impossible
If one were to examine the concept of 'promise'
In the light of logic. . . . Now shall we drop
This promise business. Tell me . . .

SEXTON.   Hush!

SCHOOLMASTER.   Eh?

SEXTON.   Quiet!

SCHOOLMASTER. Well I never! I can hear someone playing the organ.

SEXTON. It's him.

SCHOOLMASTER. Who? Not *him*!

SEXTON.   Yes, him.

SCHOOLMASTER. Heavens! He's up with the lark, isn't he?

SEXTON. I'd be prepared to wager that his head
Didn't touch his pillow last night.

SCHOOLMASTER.   Really?

SEXTON. Things never go right with him these days.
Some secret grief's been gnawing at him
Ever since he lost his wife. He tries
To hide it, but it keeps breaking out.
It's as if his heart were too full . . .
A bitter cup, that keeps running over.
So he plays the organ. Listen! Every note
Sounds like a tear shed for his wife and child.

SCHOOLMASTER. As if they were talking with one another . . .

SEXTON. Yes, one of them comforting the one who weeps . . .

SCHOOLMASTER. Hm! One could feel quite emotional oneself!

SEXTON. Yes, if one were not a public official!

SCHOOLMASTER. Yes, anyone who wasn't bound hand and foot
By many considerations, his duty, his position!

SEXTON. Anyone who could send his clerking to the Devil!

SCHOOLMASTER. Anyone who didn't have to be so clever.
Indeed, anyone who dared to—*have feelings*!

SEXTON. Well, there's nobody looking . . . shall we—*have feelings*?

SCHOOLMASTER. It would be highly improper and, indeed, disreputable
To descend to the level of mortal matters.
As the priest has taught us, no man
Can be two things at one and the same time.
No man, even should he desire such a thing,
Can be both a human being and an official.
In this, as in all things, one should strive
To emulate his Worship, the Mayor.

SEXTON. Why him, of all people?

SCHOOLMASTER.   Surely you
Remember the great fire at his house
When the treasured archives of our people
Were rescued from the conflagration?

SEXTON. Oh, yes. It was an evening in . . .

SCHOOLMASTER. A stormy night it was, and our good Mayor
Worked as if he had the strength of twenty men.
But the Devil was standing there inside,
Laughing. As soon as the Mayor's good lady saw him,
She cried: 'Oh, my dear, look out for your soul . . .
Beelzebub himself is after you!' Then through the smoke
And flames he shouted: 'My soul? To Hell with that . . . !
Give me a hand to get these archives out!' You see,
He is a Mayor through and through, body and soul,
From top to toe; so I'm sure he will be elevated
Where his devotion to work will be rewarded.

SEXTON. And where might that be?

SCHOOLMASTER.   Naturally,
The paradise where all good mayors go.

SEXTON. My learned friend . . .

SCHOOLMASTER.   My dear sexton . . .

SEXTON. I have a notion that behind your words
    I detect some hint of the current unrest.
    For unrest there is, without a doubt.
    It shows itself in the common disrespect
    For old-established ways and customs.

SCHOOLMASTER. Things grown mouldy must be cast on the midden.
    New growth feeds on what is rotten and corrupt.
    Our people's lungs are choked with foul disease,
    And if they cannot cough up the contamination,
    They'll be so much graveyard fodder. Yes, unrest
    Is all around us, you can feel it in the air.
    The day the old church fell, it seemed
    To take with it everything that until then
    Our lives had sunk their roots in.

SEXTON. The people stood nonplussed, after all their shouts
    To 'tear it down, tear it down!' But the shouts
    Soon died out, and many's the man grew pink about the ears
    And looked askance and stood there at a loss
    When our old village House of God
    Was actually going to be pulled down at last . . .
    And there were many thought it sinful
    To lay hands upon the place.

SCHOOLMASTER. But the general consensus of opinion
    Was that a thousand ties still bound them
    To the ancient ways—so long as the new edifice
    Was still not well and truly consecrated.
    That is why, uneasy and afraid, they viewed
    The progress of the thing with growing doubts.
    And now that day has come—the great day
    When the tattered flag will be hauled down
    And new colours flutter free and brave.
    Yet as the spire grew and grew, the people
    Turned more silent, pale with grim foreboding . . .
    And now . . . well, now the time has come.

SEXTON [*pointing off-stage*]. Look at the crowds! Old, young, babes in
    arms . . .

SCHOOLMASTER. Thousands of them. How quiet it is up here!

SEXTON. And yet . . . there is a far-off sound,
    As of a swelling sea under a rising wind.

SCHOOLMASTER. It is the keening of the people's hearts . . .
    They seem to realize that these are stirring times . . .
    As if they had been summoned to a great assembly
    Convened to elect another God. But where is the priest?
    I feel uneasy. I wish I hadn't come here!

SEXTON. I feel the same!

SCHOOLMASTER.   In moments
    Like the present, no man can plumb
    The chasm of his soul. Below each deep abyss
    A deeper something lies. First one makes an act
    Of will, one retreats, and finally—prevaricates!

SEXTON. My friend . . .

SCHOOLMASTER.   Yes, my friend?

SEXTON.   Er . . .

SCHOOLMASTER.   Come, out with it!

SEXTON. I do believe we are actually—*having feelings*!

SCHOOLMASTER. What! Not I!

SEXTON.   Nor me, neither!
    A man is innocent until he's proven guilty!

SCHOOLMASTER. We are grown men . . . not a pair of giddy girls.
    Good day to you! I am awaited in the schoolhouse
    By the rising generation. [*He goes.*]

SEXTON.   I get
    Some funny notions in my head sometimes!
    But now I'm cool, calm and collected.
    My lips are sealed. And now to work.
    No more of this nonsense. Or the Devil
    Will find mischief for these idle hands!

[*He goes out on the other side. The organ, the subdued sound of which
has been heard during the foregoing, becomes loud, and ends with a
gruelling discord. Shortly afterwards,* BRAND *comes out of the church.*]

O1

BRAND. No. I cannot coax the keys to sing in harmony.
Always the organ's voices rise into a scream.
The vaulted roof, the arches and the walls
All seem to weigh down heavily upon me,
Seem in some inflexible and unrelenting way
To batten down the melody, as a coffin-lid
Upon its corpse! I have tried, I have striven!
But the organ has lost its tongue.
I lifted up its voice in prayer,
But it sounded cracked and broken . . .
A hollow, wheezing groan was all it gave,
Like a rusty, cracked, discordant ring of bells.
It was as if the Lord my God did sit
Enthroned high in the choir, and with one wave
Of his hands angrily rejected my petition . . . !
The House of the Lord shall be builded great
And mighty—this was the promise I confidently made.
I ventured resolutely to tear down, clear,
Level, sweep away. Now my labours are completed.
When they beheld it, they all crossed themselves
And cried: 'Lord, how great, how great!'
What did they see that my own eyes cannot behold?
Is it truly great? Is this the house I wanted?
Have those passionate emotions that first
Gave a promise of its birth been stilled?
Is it that temple of the spirit I beheld,
Sheltering within its walls the whole world's anguish?
If only Agnes had lived, how different it had been!
She could see great things in small; she alone
Could free me from the pain of doubt,
Could marry earth and heaven for me,
As a tree roofs itself in its own leaves.

[*He notices the preparations for the festival.*]

Leaves and garlands, wreaths and flags,
And the whole school practising its hymn.
All the people come to greet me . . .
They have set up my name in letters of gold
Oh God, give me light . . . or cast me
A thousand leagues beneath the ground!

The ceremonies begin an hour from now;
The thoughts of all are with their priest.
His name is on the lips of everyone!
What their thoughts are I can guess;
I can feel their words making my cheeks burn.
Compliments and praise will eddy
Round my head like rivulets of ice
Borne through the air by troops of trolls!
Oh, if only I could take upon myself
The cloak of invisibility, or hide
My shame in some wild creature's lair!

MAYOR [*enters in full fig and greets him with a beaming face*].
 The great day now has come at last, a Sabbath
 After six long days of labour. We furl our sails,
 And hoist aloft our Sunday flag, and drift
 Lazily along upon the gliding waters, enjoying
 The goodly fruits of our exertions!
 You great and noble man, whose high renown
 Will soon be spread like wildfire through the land,
 Congratulations and felicitations! I feel
 Quite moved, and at the same time highly delighted.
 Don't you?

BRAND.   I feel suffocated!

MAYOR. Well, now, we can't have that!
 You've to preach a thundering great sermon!
 Give it plenty of punch! Let them have it
 Right between the eyes! Everyone I've spoken to
 Is utterly amazed by the acoustics . . .

BRAND.   Oh?

MAYOR. Yes, even the Dean was thunderstruck,
 And praised it highly. And what a noble style
 Of architecture! How strikingly designed!

BRAND. You felt that, did you?

MAYOR.   Felt what?

BRAND. That it gives an impression of greatness?

MAYOR. Not just an impression. . . . No, it *is* great,
    Whether seen from a distance or close at hand.

BRAND. Is it really? You really do think . . .

MAYOR. Death and damnation, of course it's great . . .
    Too great for people buried so far up north.
    I am aware, of course, that in other lands
    Even grander proportions than these are used.
    But for us up here, scratching a bare existence
    On bare fields and barren slopes on a wretched
    Strip of soil between the mountains and the fjord . . .
    Well, it's overwhelming in its greatness!

BRAND. In that case, we have simply exchanged
    An old lie for a new one.

MAYOR. What do you mean?

BRAND.   We have turned
    The people's minds from mouldering ruins
    To this contemporary spire in the sky.
    Before, their cry was: 'How venerable!'
    But now the cry goes up: 'How great!
    There is nothing to match it in the world!'

MAYOR. My dear sir, quite frankly, if anyone were to demand
    A larger edifice, I should have to classify him
    As a model of unspeakable vulgarity.

BRAND. But it must be made quite clear to everyone
    That the church as it stands is much too small.
    To conceal this would be to countenance a lie.

MAYOR. Now listen here. . . . Let's have no more of this.
    Here's something that has cost much pain to build:
    What's the point of telling people it's no good?
    People are really and truly satisfied with it;
    They think it's grand, they've never seen anything
    Like it before! Well, let them go on thinking so!
    Why should we confuse them, and bother their poor brains
    With dazzling insights they can have no use for?
    Everything rests upon the verdict faith pronounces.
    It matters not a jot in any case

Even if the church should be no more
Than a common dog-kennel, just as long as you let
People go on thinking it's tremendous.

BRAND. Always the same story!

MAYOR.   In any case,
This is a day of celebration. Each soul
Is, in a sense, our guest. It would be unpardonable
If we did not put the best face on everything.
And particularly for your own sake it would be inadvisable
To press this myth of 'littleness'.

BRAND. How so?

MAYOR.   Now listen to me!
In the first place, our committee has decided
To present you with a silver loving-cup.
The inscription on it would be nonsense
If we start dickering about the size of the church.
And the triumphal hymn that has been specially
Composed for the occasion, not to mention
The address which I intend to make myself—
These too would be just nonsense. So you see
You must give way, and face the music as best you can.

BRAND. I shall face what I have always loathed to see:
A festival of liars celebrating lies.

MAYOR. God bless my soul, my dear man,
These are strong words! Whatever's got into you?
Anyhow—to get this matter settled . . .
Listen please to my second point:
If the first was silver, then this is gold!
You must realize that in all this business
You are a favoured child, to whom all honour
And esteem are due. To keep it brief,
You have been awarded—a knighthood!
Today you will receive the ribbon of the order,
And wear its cross right proudly on your breast.

BRAND. I am already crushed beneath a heavier cross.
No man can take that cross away from me.

MAYOR. What's the matter? Don't you feel excited
　　To be receiving this high honour?
　　You're a mystery, and that's a fact!
　　But for God's sake consider whether . . .

BRAND [*stamps his foot*]. Stop! Your words mean nothing to me.
　　I am no wiser now than when I met you,
　　You don't understand a single word I say . . .
　　Nothing enters that thick head of yours.
　　I was not referring to a greatness
　　To be measured in yards, feet, and inches;
　　But rather to that power which quietly irradiates,
　　Which chills and also fires the soul,
　　Which beckons us towards the realms
　　Of dreams and wonders; which towers
　　Over us like Heaven ablaze with stars, which . . .
　　Oh, get away! Leave me alone! I am weary of it all!
　　Go and give them some explanation . . . tell them something. . . .

　　　　　　[*He walks over towards the church.*]

MAYOR [*to himself*]. Who on earth could make head or tail
　　Of such a rigmarole? 'Greatness' is something
　　Or other that 'quietly irradiates', that cannot
　　Be measured in yards, feet, and inches?
　　And that about a Heaven ablaze with stars?
　　What a cantata! Has he been at the punch-bowl? [*He goes.*]

BRAND [*crosses the open stage*]. Up on that bare mountain-top
　　I was never as lonely as I am now.
　　They chatter and cackle so . . . such is
　　Their one wretched response to all my questionings.

　　　　　　[*He looks after the retreating* MAYOR.]

I'd like to stamp him underfoot!
Each time I try to raise his vision
Away from falsehoods and deceit,
He spits out gobbets of his putrid soul,
Quite shamelessly, before my very eyes!
Oh, Agnes, how could you fail me so?
I am sick and weary of this pointless contest
That can be neither won nor lost by anyone.
There is no hope for one who fights alone!

DEAN [*enters*]. And so, my children, my little lambs . . .
    Oh! what am I saying? I mean, dear colleagues . . .
    These festival performances . . . my sermon . . .
    So much on my mind. I rehearsed it
    All day yesterday, so that it may seem
    To spring fresh from my lips. Well,
    Enough of that. Dear sir, accept my thanks . . .
    It was you who so manfully broke the ice,
    Who breasted his way through all the talk and uproar,
    Who removed that old, dilapidated pile, and built
    It up in this great and worthy modern form!

BRAND. It's far from that.

DEAN.   What's that, my friend?
    There's nothing more to be done, is there?
    Apart from the dedication, naturally . . .

BRAND. A new building must be possessed
    By a regenerating spirit and a purified soul.

DEAN. These things come in their own good time.
    This vast and finely-panelled vaulting,
    This splendid body of the church
    Will in themselves persuade our congregations
    To see themselves as fully purified.
    These magnificent acoustics with their resonant echo
    Of the preacher's every word must certainly
    Increase our congregation's faith
    One hundred per cent in every case.
    Verily, these are achievements which even
    The greatest nations will not be able to surpass.
    All this is due to you alone.
    Accept therefore from your colleague
    His heartfelt expression of thanks, which,
    I have no doubt, at the groaning banquet board
    Will be brilliantly reinforced, on this your day of honour,
    By many eloquent speeches from the younger limbs
    Of all the clergy in the ministry.
    But my dear Brand, you look so pale . . .

BRAND. Strength and courage failed me long ago.

DEAN. Very understandable! So much to see to,
  And all without help or encouragement.
  But now of course the worst is over.
  And all's set fair for a tremendous day.
  So keep your spirits up! Everything will be all right!
  A crowd of several thousand has assembled,
  And some have come from very distant parishes.
  Be honest with yourself. . . . Who can rival
  You in eloquence? Behold, a solemn body
  Of your colleagues approaches you with open arms!
  The congregation's hearts are filled
  With gratitude and warmth towards you!
  And your building! What a success!
  And everything so elegantly decorated!
  And the text for the day: 'How tall, how great!'
  And then, this incomparable banquet!
  I've just come from the parsonage,
  Where they were carving the fatted calf.
  I think I never saw a lovelier piece of meat!
  I declare it must have been a problem
  To rustle up such a delicious specimen
  In these hard times, when meat costs
  Up to nine marks and more a pound.
  But let us not dwell too much on this.
  I came here on quite a different errand.

BRAND. Out with it! Slash away! Stab, cut, thrust!

DEAN. Gently, my friend. That is not my way of doing things.
  But I'll be brief, for time is running out.
  There is one tiny little point which from now on
  We feel we ought to try to—to correct,
  And, oh, I'm sure it won't be difficult.
  I take it you can more or less discern
  What I am referring to? It concerns
  Your duties—your official duties.
  Hitherto you have at times, I fear, laid
  Too little stress on precedent and custom;
  Yet precedent and custom are of prime concern,
  If not the most important aspects of our calling.
  Pray do not imagine that I mean any rebuke.

You are of course young, and inexperienced,
And have come straight from the big city,
Knowing very little of country ways.
But *now*, my friend, now it is important
To take a firmer grip on your demeanour.
Hitherto you put a little too much emphasis
Upon the special needs of individuals . . .
Between ourselves, that was a grave error.
They should be dealt with in the mass.
Look upon all alike as grist to your mill.
Believe me, you'll never regret it.

BRAND. Explain yourself!

DEAN.   Well, it's this way.
You have now built a church for the good
Of the parish. This fabric is a garment
Enfolding the spirit of peace and law;
For the State sees in religion a force
For uplifting the country's moral tone . . .
A bulwark against radical unrest . . .
In brief, a guide to virtuous behaviour.
The resources of the State are slender;
And it wants full value for its money.
'Good Christians make good citizens', they say.
But do you think the State pours out its money
To the glory of God and the people's comfort
Simply to stir up trouble for itself?
No, my dear man, the State isn't mad;
And people soon would find themselves to be
In sorry straits if the State did not, carefully and strictly,
Keep this design in mind. But, my friend,
This objective of the State can be achieved
Only through its official representatives,
Which in this case means its priests . . .

BRAND. What words of wisdom! Do go on!

DEAN.   There is
Little more to add. You have now contributed
This church towards the well-being of the State,
And consequently your activities must be directed

To the State's support. It is in this spirit
That I view the festival which we shall begin
To celebrate during these next few hours. . . .
The spirit that shall be rung out by the bells,
And in which the deed of gift shall be conveyed.
But that gift then entails a promise,
An obligation you must consider carefully . . .

BRAND. My God, I never wanted it to be like this!

DEAN. Well, now, my friend, it is a bit too late . . .

BRAND. Too late? Too late? We'll see about that!

DEAN. Be sensible. Really, it's almost laughable!
What have you got to moan about?
You don't have to promise anything wrong.
You can just as well take care of every
Individual soul *and* serve the State
Into the bargain. If only you'd be sensible,
You could easily accommodate two masters.
Your calling to the ministry was not to save
Every Tom, Dick and Harry from the flames of Hell,
But rather to provide a well of grace
On which the congregation as a whole
Could draw for spiritual refreshment.
Then, if the entire parish is saved,
It stands to reason that each individual
Receives his portion of salvation.
I don't think you realize it, but
The State is only *one half* Republican,
Hating freedom like the plague, but
Being terribly fond of equality for all.
But equality can never be achieved
Until each inequality is first levelled out . . .
And *this* is what you do not do!
On the contrary, you have considerably increased
An inequality of attitude, one
That had never been revealed before.
Formerly, each man was a member of the church;
Now he is a personality in his own right.
And the State is not very pleased about that.

This is why it proves so difficult
To scrape together the equity taxes,
As well as the other social benefits.
For the church is no longer the cloth
That can be cut to fit all shapes and sizes.

BRAND. A frightful spectre now begins to haunt my life!

DEAN. Don't be downhearted—there's no sense
In letting yourself go. But I agree. . . .
One shudders at the confusion that prevails.
However, where there's life, there's hope;
And you, by your gift of this great church,
Have increased your obligations to serve,
Through its church, the purposes of State.
In all things there must be some regulation,
Otherwise the operation of divergent forces
Will, like some wanton, untamed colt's
Distracted galoppades, make havoc of fence and hedge
And all the many boundaries of convention.
In all estates of order, there is in evidence
One law alone, though called by various names.
In the arts, that discipline is called a school;
And in the army—if memory serves me right—
It is known as 'keeping in step'.
Yes, that is the proper term, my friend!
That is the State's objective! Marching
At the double is rather too impetuous;
But running on the spot is not enough.
But when each man steps out beside his fellows
With the same length of stride as all the rest,
Each marching with the selfsame regulated rhythm—
That, my friend, is the supreme example of method!

BRAND. So the eagle must be relegated to the gutter,
And the goose must be made familiar
With the towering thunderheads above the mountain!

DEAN. We humans are, I am glad to say, not beasts.
But if we must resort to artifice and fable,
It's best we turn our eyes upon the Scriptures.
They have an answer to everything.

From Genesis to Revelations they abound
With every variety of striking parable.
Let me just remind you of the Tower of Babel.
Tell me—how far did those good people progress?
And why? The reason's very plain:
They did not keep their ranks;
They all spoke their own tongues,
They did not pull together under one yoke . . .
In short, they developed personalities.
That is only half the double kernel
That is hidden in the fable's shell—
That no one man can fight alone,
And that divided we fall. That man whom God
Intends to slay in life's long clash of arms,
He makes of him at first an individual.
Among the Romans, it was said the gods
First took away his reason. But being mad
And being isolated are the same; therefore
Each man who goes his way in solitude
Must be prepared to meet the selfsame fate
As when David sent Uriah to the front.

BRAND. Yes, that may well be. But what then?
I do not look on death as a defeat.
And are you absolutely sure those builders
Would eventually have raised the Tower of Babel
Unto Heaven, if only they had used
One language, and had one fixed idea?

DEAN. Unto Heaven? No, that's just the point.
No one can get quite to Heaven.
That is the kernel's other segment,
Hidden in the fable's shell—
That every edifice that strives to reach
The stars of Heaven must be bound to fall.

BRAND. Yet Jacob's ladder reached to Heaven.
A yearning soul may raise itself to Heaven.

DEAN. In that sense, yes. Good heavens, yes!
That point requires no further discussion.
Naturally Heaven is the just reward

Of well-spent lives of faith and prayer.
But life is one thing, faith another.
When they are mixed, both of them suffer.
Man is assigned six days for labour;
The seventh is the day prescribed
For movements of the heart.
If the church stood open seven days a week,
The tradition of the Sabbath would be gone.
You dissipate the purifying inspiration of the Word
Unless you husband it in this prudent way;
For religion, like art, should never be permitted
To waste its breath on the desert air.
From the sacred lookout of the pulpit
You may with confidence examine your ideals . . .
But hang them in the vestry with your surplice
As soon as you step down into the world.
As I have said, there is a law in all things,
A law that everywhere imposes severe
And rigid circumscriptions. I told you this
Because I thought some explanation
Of this point might be in order.

BRAND. To me one thing is clear: this pigeonholing
Of the human soul does not appeal to me.

DEAN. Why, yes, my friend . . . don't worry, we shall
Fit you into one most admirably . . . but naturally
On the highest level . . . you must rise to greater heights.

BRAND. Not by my wallowing in the mire.

DEAN. He that abases himself shall be exalted.
If the hook is to catch, it must be bent.

BRAND. If the man is to serve, he must be expunged!

DEAN. Heaven help us! How could you imagine I meant
Such a thing?

BRAND.   It's the truth! It must be so!
The first step is to bleed him to death!
Only when he's rigid as a sheet of leather
Or a barren bone can a man be fitted
To your impotent and stagnant way of life!

DEAN. God knows, I would not let the blood
    Of a cat, let alone yours!
    I just thought there could be no objection
    To my leaving the gate slightly ajar
    On the path I have myself pursued.

BRAND. Do you realize what you are asking of me?
    That at the cock-crow of the State
    I should deny the great ideal
    I have lived for until this day!

DEAN. Deny a great ideal? My dear Brand,
    Did I ever ask you to do that? All I did
    Was indicate your path of duty. All I request
    Is that you husband for yourself those things
    That are of no utility to the community.
    Conserve the whole lot, if you so wish . . .
    But see you keep it under lock and key.
    For God's sake, soar, enthuse . . . but inwardly,
    Not openly in front of everybody's nose.
    Believe me, Brand. It would only do you harm
    To go on acting stubbornly and wilfully.

BRAND. Ah, fear of retribution and love of gain
    Have laid their mark of Cain upon your brow.
    This tells me you have slain that pure
    And innocent brother, Abel, who was your heart!

DEAN [*in a low voice*]. To berate me in this familiar way
    Is quite unpardonable! [*Aloud.*] It is not my intention
    To protract this long discussion, but I implore you
    Once again to understand that if you wish
    Advancement you must realize the nature of the land
    In which you live, and of the age you serve in.
    No one triumphs in the lists of life
    If time itself is not upon his side.
    Look at the example of the artists, of the poets!
    Dare they despise their duties to society?
    Look at our warriors! The blade of heroes
    Is something only met in legends. Why?
    Because there is a law that admonishes:

'Take thought only for your country's needs.'
Each man must subjugate his own peculiar gifts,
Neither advancing nor raising himself unduly,
But humbly hiding himself among the masses.
'We live in a humane society', the Mayor declares;
And if you could only accept it as humane,
You too could make something of yourself.
But all the rough edges must be filed,
And all the adventitious branches lopped;
Like other men, you must be smooth,
And never follow any solitary path
If you would master anything with permanence.

BRAND. Out of my sight!

DEAN.   Yes, indeed.
A man like you must in the end
Map out a field of action more befitting.
But if you seek to find contentment—
In great things as in small—you must
Put on the uniform that fits our age today.
With rod in hand, the corporal must drill
The people till they march along in step;
For in this country the ideal of a leader
Now most current is that of corporal.
As the corporal marshals his church parade in squads,
The man of God must lead his flock to Heaven—
Parish by parish. It is all so simple:
As a basis for the faith you have authority;
And since this is built on learning,
It can be followed blindly and with confidence.
Then the manner wherein this faith is manifest
Is taught by rule and ritual. So brother,
Do not be downhearted! Take time for reflection.
Examine your position; do not be dismayed!
In this church I must test carefully to see
If I should give my voice a higher pitch.
One is not used to such remarkable acoustics—
Something never met with in these parts.
Well, goodbye for now. I am to preach a sermon
On the duality of human nature and why we should eschew

The obfuscation of the image of the Lord.
But first I think I might be tempted to partake
Of a little light refreshment—a small decoction. [*He goes.*]

BRAND [*stands a moment as if petrified by his thoughts*].
Everything I have sacrificed unto my call,
To God's call, as in my blindness I had thought it.
Then came the blast of the trumpet-mouths of doom,
Revealing unto me what spirit I served.
No, not yet! They have not got me yet!
I gave my blood to drink to this ground
I built my church on! My light,
My life, lie buried here. But they . . .
They shall not get my soul to join them!
It is terrible to have to stand alone . . .
Wherever I turn it is death I see.
Terrible to hand me stones
When what I am starving for is bread.
How truly, yes, how horribly true he spoke . . .
And yet with what an empty, hollow voice.
The precious dove of God's keen clarity
Is perched upon a hidden bough;
Alas, it never did descend on me.
Oh, if I could meet but one in faith . . .
Who gave me confidence again, and gave me peace!

[EINAR, *pale and emaciated, dressed in black, comes along the road and
halts at the sight of* BRAND.]

BRAND [*cries out*]. Einar! Is it you?

EINAR.   Yes, that is my name.

BRAND. At this very moment I was thirsting for one
    Whose heart was not of wood or stone.
    Oh, come, let me take you in my arms . . .

EINAR. I do not need them. I have reached my haven.

BRAND. You bear me a grudge for what happened
    Last time we met. . . .

EINAR. No, you are not to blame.
In you I see the blind instrument
The Lord sent to me when I went astray
Upon the sinful pathways of the world.

BRAND [*shrinks back*]. What language is this?

EINAR. The language of peace ...
The language a man learns when wakened
From the sleep of sin, and is born again.

BRAND. Strange! I heard that you had started off
On quite a different path ...

EINAR. I was seduced
By pride, by a rash confidence in my own strength.
Those gods the world is drawn to worship,
Those talents I was told that I possessed,
My singing voice, were merely wiles
To tempt me into Satan's snares.
But God be praised! The Lord was good!
He did not forsake me, the lamb who strayed.
When I needed Him, He tended me.

BRAND. In what way?

EINAR. I had fallen.

BRAND. Fallen? How?

EINAR. Drinking, gambling.
He gave me a taste for cards and dice ...

BRAND. And you call *this* the Lord's work?

EINAR. It was the first step towards salvation.
Thereupon He took away my health.
I lost my talents, utterly.
My love of gaiety was gone.
I entered hospital, lay a long time sick ...
Lay as though on coals of fire ...
I thought I saw in all the wards
Thousands of enormous flies ...
Finally I came out, and made
The acquaintance of three sisters who

P1

Had enlisted in the ranks of Heaven's army;
And they, and a student of theology,
Freed me entirely from this world's yoke,
Released me from the snares of sin. And so
I became a child of our Lord in Heaven.

BRAND. I see.

EINAR.   The paths are many . . .
One in the valley, another on the hill.

BRAND. And then?

EINAR.   Then I became a preacher
Advocating total abstinence. But sometimes
There are temptations in that kind of work,
So I took to something else, and now I am
A travelling missionary. . . .

BRAND.   Travelling where?

EINAR. To black Africa. Now I think I'd best be going.
I have so little time.

BRAND.   You'll not stay awhile?
Look, we have a festival today.

EINAR.   Thank you, no.
My place is with the souls of black men.
So goodbye.

               [*He is about to go.*]

BRAND.   Are there no glimmerings
Of memory to hold you here?
No curiosity to know . . . ?

EINAR.   Know what?

BRAND. Something of one who would be grieving
At the chasm between now and then . . .

EINAR. I begin to follow you. I suppose
That you are thinking of that young girl
Who held me in the toils of lust
Before my sins were washed by faith.
Well, how are things with her?

BRAND. The next year she became my wife.

EINAR. That is of no significance to me. I do not
Concern myself with matters of that kind.
I only want to know *important* things.

BRAND. Our life together was richly blessed with joy.
With sorrow too. Our little baby died . . .

EINAR. That is of no importance.

BRAND.   Ah, well,
He came to us on loan, not as a gift,
And some day we shall meet again.
But afterwards, she herself departed from me.
There you see the green grass on their graves.

EINAR. That too is of no importance.

BRAND.   Even that?

EINAR. These are not the things I wish to know.
I want to know one thing—*how* she died.

BRAND. In full hope of a new dawning,
Her heart's rich treasure still intact,
And steadfast of will to the very end . . .
With gratitude for all that life had given her
And was to take away, she went to her grave . . .

EINAR. All this is but a sham and a delusion.
All vanity! Tell me—how was her faith?

BRAND. Unshakeable.

EINAR.   In whom?

BRAND.   In her God!

EINAR. Ah, only in Him. Then she is doomed.

BRAND. What are you saying?

EINAR.   Damned to perdition.

BRAND [*quietly*]. Get away from me, you blackguard!

EINAR. The Lord of Hell will seize
You in his clutches, too! Like her,
You too shall burn in everlasting fires!

BRAND. You viper! You condemn us to the pit,
When only lately you wallowed in sin. . . .

EINAR. There is no stain on me. My faith
Has washed me clean. Every foul speck of dirt
Has been scrubbed away upon the stones of sanctity.
I have thrashed my Adam's linen clean
Upon the river rocks of vigilance.
I am as unspotted as a perfect altar-cloth
Starched and laundered with the irons of prayer.

BRAND. Abomination!

EINAR.   *You* are the abomination!
I smell sulphur here, and on your brow
I glimpse the Devil's horns. But I am
A grain of God's immortal wheat, and you
Are chaff upon the threshing-floor of doom. [*He goes.*]

BRAND [*looks after him for a while, then suddenly his eyes flash, and he
     bursts out*].
That was the man I needed!
Now all my bonds are burst; now
I shall fly a banner with my own device,
Though not *one* man follow it or me!

MAYOR [*enters hurriedly*]. My dear pastor, please do hurry!
The procession to the church is drawn up
In order now and ready to depart . . .

BRAND. Well, let them depart.

MAYOR.   Without *you*?
Pull yourself together and hurry back home!
The people will not wait much longer.
The entire congregation is surging on
Towards the parsonage like a swollen torrent
In the Spring, and shouting for their priest.
Just listen! Shouting even louder for you now!
Hurry! I'm afraid they may behave
Somewhat indecorously if you don't.

BRAND. You shall never see my face again
Among my flock, among your followers.
I shall not move.

MAYOR.   Are you mad?

BRAND. The path you follow is too narrow for me.

MAYOR. The more the congregation presses on,
The narrower it becomes. Merciful heaven!
Look at the way they're surging through!
Dean and priests and other officials
Being shoved without ceremony into the ditches . . .
Please, my good friend, please come, and wield
The eloquent whip of your great influence!
Too late! They're breaking down the barriers!
The procession itself is being disbanded!

[*The crowd streams in and forces its way in wild disorder through the
procession towards the church.*]

VOICES. Priest!

OTHERS [*pointing up towards the church steps, where* BRAND *stands, and
shouting*].
                There!

STILL OTHERS.   Give the opening signal!

DEAN [*caught in the crowd*]. Mr. Mayor, why don't you control them!

MAYOR. They pay no heed to authority!

SCHOOLMASTER [*to* BRAND]. Speak to them! Bring illumination
To their darkened minds! Is this great occasion
To be turned into a shambles?

BRAND.   Something is stirring
The lethargy of the people's stagnant spirit!
Men, you stand at a crossroads in your lives!
You must *will* yourselves to be entirely new . . .
Sweep away all rottenness before . . .
The great temple can be built
As it should be—as it *shall* be built!

OFFICIALS. The priest is raving!

CLERGY.   The man is mad.

BRAND. Yes, I was mad indeed to think that you,
In one way or another, were serving Him

Who stood for the spirit and the truth! . . .
Mad to believe I could guide Him to you
By trifling and fiddling round the problem!
The old church was small; and, coward that I was,
I could only cry: 'Double it . . . that will do!
Five times greater . . . surely that will do it!'
Oh, I did not see only one decision
Was to be made—between All or Nothing.
I followed the easy path of compromise.
But today the Lord has spoken.
This very hour the trumpet-mouths of doom
Have sounded above this house . . .
And I hearkened in a hurricane of fear,
Crushed, as when David stood before Nathan,
Defeated and carried away by terror . . .
Now doubt is gone. You people all!
The spirit of compromise is the path to Hell!

THE CROWD [*in growing agitation*]. Away with those who blinded and
  misled us!
Down with those who sucked marrow from our bones!

BRAND. The foul fiend who cunningly has bound you
Dwells within your hearts. You have wasted
All your natural strength, and cleft yourselves
In two. All that remains to you,
In all its horrid emptiness, is dissipation.
What need have you now of churches?
Pomp and show is what attracts you,
The pealing organ, the ringing of bells,
The thrill of being moved and fired
By high-sounding rhetoric . . . whispering and sighing,
Its flood of thundering, tempestuous declamation,
All, all regulated by the rules of art!

DEAN [*in a low voice*]. He means the way the Mayor goes on!

MAYOR [*in a similar tone*]. *That's* a dig at the Dean's twaddle!

BRAND. Yes, all you desire is the outward show
Of reverence . . . the lamps, the lighted tapers.
Then you trail back home again . . .

To sloth, to the deadly daily round,
Your soul dressed in its working breeches
While the Book of Life lies buried there,
Neglected at the bottom of a chest
Until the next Sunday comes around.
Oh, *this* was not what I dreamed of
When I drained the cup of sacrifice!
I wanted to build a church that was great,
Its vaulted roof sheltering something
More than simply faith and dogma. . . .
It was to be the shrine of All in life
That has its being from our God on high . . .
The temple of our daily toil,
Of rest at evening, of the sorrows of night,
And of the fresh delights of springtime
In the veins of youth. . . . All things
Which, rich or mean, the heart makes its own.
That river foaming down below,
That waterfall upon the heights,
Suspended in its rocky cleft,
The music borne towards us in
The living voices of the storm,
The legends singing from the sea,
All to be incorporated by the soul,
Embracing both the organ's notes
And all the songs the people sing.
Away with the labour completed here!
Great? It is nothing but one great lie!
Already in the spirit it is derelict,
An expression of your wretched lack of will.
You conspire to stifle all that is new
In our creation, all fresh growth
By rigid assignments and division of labour;
For six days in the week you haul
God's flag down to the deck,
And only on the seventh day
Does it fly among the masts of Heaven!

CROWD VOICES. Lead us! There is a tempest in the air!
Lead us! You can lead us on to victory!

DEAN. Do not listen to him! He has not the faith
    Befitting true and Christian believers!

BRAND. You're right. You put your finger on the fault . . .
    The flaw there is in both of us, the flaw
    That splinters the entire contrivance!
    Faith can be possessed only by *souls*;
    What one man among you has a soul?
    Show me *one* who has not cast away
    His inmost being in his fumbling haste
    To grub a living, to enjoy!
    Through the tricks and thrills of pleasure,
    And the strains of lust's bewitching drums
    And pipes, your senses all are blunted
    To the real ecstasies of life.
    Only when they are crabbed and cankered
    Do your souls dance before the Ark!
    Once the sparkling glass is finished
    To the final drop by dolts and cripples . . .
    Then you find the time to hope,
    Time for prayer and supplication.
    First you abuse the image God Himself
    Did make you in, reduce yourselves
    To nothing but a poor, forked animal . . .
    Then you stampede to the gate of mercy,
    Seeking God . . . but coming as men diseased.
    How can His kingdom do anything but fall?
    He has no need of senile souls, gathered
    About His footstool. Did He not proclaim,
    With ringing voice, that He would choose
    Among you only those with fresh blood pulsing
    Through hearts and minds as His inheritors?
    Only if you become as little children
    Can you enter into the kingdom of Heaven!
    No one enters grovelling on hands and knees.
    Come then, men and women all . . . let us meet
    With souls renewed in life's great church!

MAYOR. Then why not open it?

CROWD [*shouting as though in terror*]. No! Not this one!

BRAND. The church is infinite and without end.
  Its floor is the green earth,
  Mountain, meadow, sea and fjord;
  The Heavens alone are vast enough
  To span its great and vaulted roof.
  There you shall live your active faith
  That its perfection may be sung
  As in a choir of daily song;
  Face your daily tasks with cheerfulness,
  And yet commit no sacrilege.
  It shall embrace All, and hold us closely,
  As the tree's bark holds the trunk's completeness.
  Life and faith shall be fused together.
  There the ordinary daily toil
  Shall be as one with law and dogma.
  The daily task shall be as one
  With the flight among the undiscovered stars,
  With the children's games round the Christmas tree,
  One with the dance of David before the Ark!

  [*A gale seems to pass through the crowd; some shrink back; but most
  gather round* BRAND.]

THOUSANDS OF VOICES. Now illumination shines
                Where before was deepest dark!
                Our daily lives shall be
                One with adoration and
                Worship of the Lord our God!

DEAN. He is beguiling our flock away from us!
  Mayor! Judge! Constable! Sexton!

MAYOR [*in a low voice*]. Damn it, man, don't shout like that!
  It's like a red rag to a bull!
  Let him tire himself out first.

BRAND [*to the crowd*]. Away from here! God is not here!
  He *cannot* be among such men as these.
  His kingdom flies the flags of freedom.
  [*He locks the door of the church and takes the key in his hands.*]
  I am no longer minister of this church.
  I herewith take back my gift . . .

From these hands, no man shall take
The keys to your infernal celebrations!

[*Throws keys in river.*]

If you want to enter, you grovelling slaves,
Crawl in through the cellar hole.
Your spines are soft—so bend and crawl!
Your tainted poisoned breath shall swell
Like clouds amid the pestilential pit,
Panting in sick, consumptive vapours!

MAYOR [*in a low voice, relieved*]. There goes his knighthood up in smoke!

DEAN [*similarly*]. Ah, after that, he'll never be bishop!

BRAND. Come, all who are young, all who are strong!
Bring back the sweet breath of living air
To blow the dust from this grim graveyard!
Follow me upon the way to victory!
One day, one day soon ye *must* awaken!
Ye *must* lift up your heads, and with a noble will,
Shatter the prison chains of compromise!
Out of these miserable bonds . . . Away
From this mediocrity and muddling indecision . . .
Strike your enemy full in the face . . .
Declare war upon him to the death!

MAYOR. Stop, or I read the riot act!

BRAND. Read it! My pact with you is broken!

CROWD. Show us the way! We will follow you!

BRAND. Over the frozen mountain heaths,
Over the wasteland we shall go,
Freeing from traps and snares
The people's captive souls!
Cleansing, liberating, bringing
A newer air, destroying deadly sloth!
We shall be both men and priests,
We shall set God's image up anew,
And make our land a mighty temple!

[THE CROWD, *among them* THE SEXTON *and* THE SCHOOLMASTER, *surges round him. The men raise up* BRAND *upon their shoulders.*]

MANY VOICES. Great is this new age of ours!
     Great the visions now that flash
     Their starry lightnings in the brightest day!

[*The mass of people streams up through the valley; a few remain behind.*]

DEAN [*to those who are departing*]. You blind fools! Where are you
    going?
Don't you see that Satan's wiles
Are in every word he speaks?

MAYOR. Hey, there! Turn back! Your path lies rather
With the quiet waters of your village stream.
Good people, stop! You are heading for destruction!
They do not listen, the silly curs.

DEAN. Remember your hearth, your house and home!

VOICES FROM THE CROWD. We shall build a greater house!

MAYOR. Think of your meadows, moors and fields!
Think of all your sheep and cattle!

VOICES. When the chosen people hungered in the wilderness,
The dew of Heaven fell like manna on them.

DEAN. The women you leave behind are weeping!

VOICES [*far away*]. We are not responsible for those who fail us!

DEAN. Your children cry: 'Our fathers have left us.'

THE CROWD. Who is not for us is against us.

DEAN [*with folded hands, watches them depart, then says dejectedly*]:
Without his flock, bereft of all,
Here the venerable shepherd stands—
And nothing left him but his shirt.

MAYOR [*shaking his fist after* BRAND]. He'll pay for this with shame and
    disgrace.
The final victory will soon be ours!

DEAN [*on the point of weeping*]. Victory? They have all abandoned us!

MAYOR. Yes, but we are not beaten yet.
This old shepherd knows his flock!

[*He follows after the crowd.*]

DEAN. I wonder where the Mayor is going?
　　He's following them, I do declare!
　　Ah, my spirits begin to rise again!
　　I too shall follow them up there . . .
　　I shall take my crook and bring
　　Some lost sheep to the fold again!
　　Saddle me my noble charger . . . Well, some nice
　　Safe mare, accustomed to the mountain heights!

[They go.]

---

*[The village's highest mountain pasture. The landscape rises in the
background, and gives way to great bare mountain wastes in the distance.
It is raining.* BRAND, *followed by the crowd*—MEN, WOMEN *and*
CHILDREN—*is coming up the hillside.]*

BRAND. Onward and upward! This is our flight to victory!
　　Far below us lies the landlocked village,
　　And over it from peak to peak
　　The rain has spread its misty canopy.
　　Forget the dull life of that gloomy place.
　　Fly free, fly high, ye men of God!

A MAN. Halt a moment. My old father is weary.

ANOTHER. I haven't had a bite since yesterday . . .

SEVERAL. Yes, still our hunger, quench our thirst!

BRAND. First, onward and upward, over the mountain!

SCHOOLMASTER. Which path?

BRAND.　　　　　　　　　　　　Any path is good
　　That leads us on towards our goal.
　　Follow me!

A MAN.　　　　　No. It is too steep.
　　Night will fall before we get there!

SEXTON. The Ice Church also lies up there.

BRAND. The steepest is the shortest path.

A WOMAN. My child is sick!

ANOTHER.　　　　　　　My feet are sore!

A THIRD. Water! There's not a drop to drink.

SCHOOLMASTER. Satisfy the people, Brand.
　You see their courage starts to waver.

MANY VOICES. A miracle, priest. Work us a miracle!

BRAND. Your years of servitude have left an ugly mark.
　You cry for your reward before you work.
　Shake off this deadly sloth, or go
　Back to that grave down there again!

SCHOOLMASTER. Yes, he is right. First the struggle.
　We know our just reward will follow.

BRAND. My people, I promise that it shall,
　As true as God's in his Heaven above!

MANY VOICES. He is a prophet! He is a prophet!

SEVERAL VOICES AMONG THE CROWD.
　Tell us, priest . . . will the struggle be severe?

OTHERS. And will it be long? Will it be bloody?

A MAN. Tell me, priest, will courage be needed?

SCHOOLMASTER [*in a low voice*]. I trust there's no fear of loss of life?

ANOTHER MAN. What is *my* share of the fruits of victory?

A WOMAN. Can I be sure I'll not lose my son?

SEXTON. Will the victory be won come Tuesday?

BRAND [*looks round the crowd, bewildered*]. What is this you are asking
　me?
　What are these things you wish to know?

SEXTON. First, how long the fight will be.
　Next, what our battle losses may amount to.
　And finally . . . the prize of victory!

BRAND. Is that all you want to know?

SCHOOLMASTER. Of course. Down there, you didn't tell us
　Properly about it.

BRAND [*incensed*].　Then you'll hear it now.

THE CROWD [*crowding closer together round him*]. Speak! Tell us all!
　Speak now!

BRAND. How long shall the struggle last?
　It shall last until your life's end,
　Till you have sacrificed your All,
　And freed your spirits from the bonds
　Of compromise . . . until you hold
　Your whole Will in your hands,
　Until fainthearted doubts have fled away
　Before the stern command: 'All or Nothing!'
　And the battle losses, what shall they be?
　Those idols, those ornaments of selfish greed,
　Those gleaming golden chains of thraldom,
　Those feather beds of apathy and sloth!
　And what shall be the prize of victory?
　The Will, purged clean and pure, a soaring
　Faith, a new integrity of soul . . .
　A willingness to sacrifice so great,
　That you would give yourselves with joy
　Even unto death, unto the grave . . .
　The prize of victory shall be a crown
　Of thorns round each man's and woman's head . . .
　These are the prizes you would win!

THE CROWD [*amid angry cries*].
　Betrayed! Betrayed! You deceive, you trick us!

BRAND. I have simply kept my word.

INDIVIDUAL VOICES. You promised us victory in our grasp . . .
　Now you change it to sacrifice!

BRAND. Yes, I promised victory . . . And I swear
　It shall be won through you alone.
　But he who marches in the foremost ranks
　Must fall in battle for the cause he serves.
　If he dare not, let him lay
　His arms down now, before the battle.
　A flag defended by a wavering will
　Is doomed to be captured by the foe.
　If fear of sacrifice strikes your hearts,
　You are marked for death before the fight!

THE CROWD. He dares demand our own destruction
  For the sake of generations yet unborn!

BRAND. On through the barren wastes of sacrifice
  Our path will lead us into Canaan.
  The only victory is found in death!
  I call upon each one of you
  To go to battle as champion of the Lord!

SEXTON. Well, now we've landed in a pretty mess!
  We are outlaws from the village . . .

SCHOOLMASTER. We can never go back there.

SEXTON. And no one . . . no one dares go on!

SOME VOICES. Kill him! Kill him! Put him to death!

SCHOOLMASTER. No, that would only make things worse.
  We need a leader!

WOMEN [*pointing in terror down the path*]. Here comes the Dean!

SCHOOLMASTER. Whatever you do, don't be afraid!

DEAN [*enters, accompanied by some of those who had remained behind*].
  Oh, my children! Oh, my beloved flock!
  Listen to the words of your old shepherd!

SCHOOLMASTER [*to the crowd*]. We no longer have a home in the village.
  Best we make a crossing of the mountain!

DEAN. Oh, that you could cause me so much grief
  And strike such daggers deep within my heart!

BRAND. For years and years, you have struck daggers
  Into people's souls!

DEAN.   Do not listen to him!
  He's stuffing you with empty promises.

SEVERAL VOICES. That's a fact.

DEAN.   But we are merciful.
  Where there is genuine repentance,
  We surely find we can forgive.
  Oh, look into your hearts, and see
  With how much black and hellish cunning
  He has gathered you about him!

MANY VOICES. Yes, that's right! He cast a spell on us!

DEAN. Oh, think again, my children! What can
　　You achieve up here, so far away
　　From everything, a little band like you?
　　Have *you* been chosen for some great cause?
　　Can *you* set free those who are oppressed?
　　You have your appointed daily tasks;
　　Anything beyond that daily round is evil.
　　What use are *your* arms on a field of battle?
　　It is your own small, simple homes
　　You must defend. What place have *you*
　　Among eagles and falcons on the peaks?
　　How can *you* live among wolves and bears?
　　You can only fall victim to the elements,
　　Oh, my little flock, my little children!

THE CROWD. Oh, misfortune. . . . He speaks the truth!

SEXTON. But when we left the village, we shut
　　Behind us, as if for ever, our cottage doors . . .
　　They can never be our homes as once they were.

SCHOOLMASTER. No. He has opened the eyes of the people,
　　Has pointed out failings, corruption, lies.
　　Our small society is no longer sleeping.
　　The life that was enough for us before
　　Is now a mockery, now our eyes are open.

DEAN. Believe me, that will all soon pass away.
　　Things will settle into the same old grooves,
　　If only you will take things easy a while.
　　I guarantee that our community
　　Will soon regain its past contentment.

BRAND. Choose, men and women!

SOME VOICES.　　　　　　　　　　We want to go home!

OTHERS. Too late, too late! We must cross the mountain!

MAYOR [*arriving in haste*]. What great good fortune I could find you!

WOMEN. Mr. Mayor, be kind! Do not be angry!

MAYOR. No, no, of course not! Just follow me!
A new day is dawning for our village . . .
If you'll be sensible and listen to me,
Every man among you will be rich tonight!

SEVERAL VOICES. Every man? How?

MAYOR.   A gigantic shoal . . .
Fish by the million . . . in the fjord!

THE CROWD. What is he saying?

MAYOR.   Come to your senses!
Come down, out of this sleet and frost,
Leave behind these mountain storms!
Such mighty shoals have never come
This way before. . . . *Now*, friends, better times
Are promised for our northern shores!

BRAND. Choose between *his* call and—the Lord's!

MAYOR. Use common sense!

DEAN.   This is a miracle!
A sign sent down to us from Heaven!
Something I have often dreamed of,
But always dismissed as sheer fantasy . . .
We can clearly see what this sign means!

BRAND. You are lost, lost, if you give way!

MANY VOICES. A shoal of fish!

MAYOR.   Millions of them!

DEAN. Food, and money for your wives and children!

MAYOR. Surely you can see this is no time
To squander all your strength in conflict,
Especially against an evil force
That even makes our Dean despair?
Now you have other ends in view
Than vaguely aspiring after higher things.
Our Lord can take good care of Himself;
The fortresses of paradise are builded strong.
Do not involve yourselves in others' troubles,

Q1

But make haste and sweep the ocean of its treasure.
That's a job requiring neither blood nor steel;
Something that will fill your pockets
But demands no personal sacrifice!

BRAND. That sacrifice is written as the Lord's command,
Beyond the clouds, a fiery superscription!

DEAN. If you really feel the need for sacrifice,
You can safely come and see me, any day . . .
Next Sunday, for example. I shall certainly . . .

MAYOR [*interrupting*].   Yes, yes!

SEXTON [*in a low voice to the* DEAN]. Shall I keep my job as sexton?

SCHOOLMASTER [*similarly*]. Will I get my school back again?

DEAN [*in a low voice*]. If you were to prevail upon the obstinacy
Of the crowd, I'm sure some generous arrangement . . .

MAYOR. Come on, men! There's no time to waste!

SEXTON. To the boats! If you've any sense, man the boats!

SOME VOICES. But the priest?

SEXTON.   Take no notice of that madman!

SCHOOLMASTER. You behold here the writing of our Lord
As in an open book.

MAYOR.   Let the priest
Go to Hell! You owe it to yourselves!
He led you a dance with fancy tales . . .

SEVERAL VOICES. He lied to us!

DEAN.   His faith is false.
And . . . you know . . . he hasn't even an honours degree!

SOME VOICES. What did he get?

MAYOR.   Nothing but a pass degree.

SEXTON. Yes, that's true enough. It's obvious now.

DEAN. His dying mother waited for him in vain.
He even refused her the sacraments!

MAYOR. He as good as murdered his own child!

SEXTON. And his wife, too!

WOMEN.   For shame, the villain!

DEAN. A bad son, a bad father, and a bad husband!
  Could you find a Christian worse than that?

MANY VOICES. He went and pulled down our old church!

OTHERS. And locked us out of the new one!

YET OTHERS. He cast us adrift on a sinking raft!

MAYOR. He stole my plan for a madhouse!

BRAND. I see the mark of Cain on each man's brow.
  I see now what they all will come to.

THE WHOLE CROWD [*roars*]. No! Don't listen to him! Drive this hell-
  brand
  From out our midst with stones and knives!

    [*They throw stones at* BRAND *and drive him towards the barren wastes.
    His pursuers gradually turn back.*]

DEAN. Well done, my children! Well done, my flock!
  Return now to your hearth and home.
  Let repentance light your eyes,
  And you shall see, all will go well.
  We know our Lord is good; He does
  Not crave the blood of the innocent lamb.
  And similarly our government is lenient—
  Far more than in almost any other land.
  Nor will the authorities . . . Magistrate, Mayor . . .
  Be in any wise too hard upon you!
  And be assured, I myself am filled
  As full of the milk of loving-kindness
  As the humane Christian society of our age.
  Your superiors all will dwell with you
  Henceforth in prosperity and peace.

MAYOR. But if we *should* find any faults,
  They must, of course, be rectified.
  Once we have settled down again,

We shall elect a commission of inquiry
Into the ways our understanding
And our faith are to be improved.
It should be composed of a number of priests
Nominated by the Dean and, of course, by me.
In addition, if such be your general desire,
Our sexton and our schoolmaster here,
And other public men might serve . . .
So you can rest your souls in peace.

DEAN. We shall strive to lighten your burdens,
Just as today you have lifted a great weight
From off your old shepherd's mind.
Let every man take courage from the thought
That here a miracle has happened.
Fare ye well! And good luck in the fishing!

SEXTON. Now *there's* a man who's really full
Of the milk of Christian loving-kindness!

SCHOOLMASTER. There they go their ways in peace.

SOME WOMEN. What nice, kind men they really are!

OTHER WOMEN. With just enough of the right common touch!

SEXTON. *They* don't make harsh demands upon us.

SCHOOLMASTER. *Those* men know more than the Lord's Prayer!

[*The crowd moves off downhill.*]

DEAN [*to* MAYOR]. There now, that will clear the air a bit.
The general attitude seems ripe for change;
Thank God there's something called reaction.

MAYOR. I think I can pat myself upon the back
For having smothered the affair at birth.

DEAN. But most we owe it to God's miracle . . .

MAYOR. What miracle?

DEAN.   Why, the shoal of fish.

MAYOR [*blusters*]. That was a trumped-up tale, of course.

DEAN. Indeed? A lie?

MAYOR. I've quite a gift
For telling the tale, once I get started . . .
But can I really be blamed, when such
An important issue is at stake?

DEAN. Heavens, no!
Lies are quite defensible in an emergency.

MAYOR. And besides, in a day or two,
When the people have come to their senses,
What will it matter whether our victory
Was won by the truth or by a lie?

DEAN. Friend, I'm no stickler in these matters.

[*Looks out over the barren wastes.*]

But isn't that Brand, struggling onward
Over there?

MAYOR. It is, you know!
A solitary warrior marching alone!

DEAN. No, wait! I can see someone else as well! . . .
A long way behind him!

MAYOR. Why . . . ! It's *Gerd*!
He well deserves such a mad disciple!

DEAN [*lightly*]. When his urge to sacrifice is finally satisfied,
We must write him an epitaph . . . something like this:
Here lieth Brand.
No victory he had.
One soul he won,
And she was mad!

MAYOR [*scratching his nose*]. Though when I come to think about it,
It does seem to me as if their treatment
Of him was a little inhumane . . .

DEAN [*shrugs his shoulders*]. Vox populi, vox dei, Mr. Mayor! Come!

[*They leave.*]

———————————

[*Deep within the great mountain wastes. A storm is gathering and driving heavy clouds over the snowfields; black peaks and snowy summits appear here and there, and then are once more veiled in mist.* BRAND, *bruised and bleeding, makes his way across the mountain.*]

BRAND [*stops and looks back*]. Thousands followed me from the village;
Not *one* of them won his way to the top.
In all hearts there is the cry
Of yearning for a nobler age;
And in every soul, the challenge
Beckons to sublimer combats.
Ah, but the thought of sacrifice
Strikes sharp terror in the mind;
Enfeebled, timorous, the will
Shrinks from the light of life.
Did not *One* die for all of them . . . ?
So now they think that cowardice
Counts no longer as a crime.

[*He sinks down on a stone and looks round cautiously.*]

Many a time, I have known fear.
My hair would stand on end with terror
When, as children will, I wandered
Through dark-curtained, haunted chambers,
While the dogs howled and whined . . .
But I composed my heart's beating
And comforted myself by thinking:
'There is bright day outside;
This dark is not night, nor even twilight . . .
It is only the shutters on the windows.'
I would tell myself the light of day
And the bright gleam of summer sun
Would soon strike full and fair across
The opened door, and stream all gold
Into the dark and haunted room.
Oh, how bitter that delusion was!
I encountered pitch black night . . .
Outside there sat dejected men,
Dispersed along the bays and fjords,
Clinging, spiritless, to their memories,
Hoarding memories of happiness gone by

As that king of old kept hoarding,
Year after year, the corpse of Snefrid
His beloved, every day undoing
The patchwork linen of the shroud,
Putting his ear against the heart,
And seizing pitiful crumbs of hope
That life might come again; imagining
Life's blood-red roses bloomed again
Upon that clammy form. Like him,
They sat, none willing to rise
And give the grave what was its due.
Not one among them down there knows
A corpse is never revived by dreams,
That it must go back to dust and ashes,
There to perform its one purpose . . .
Which is but to nourish seed new-sown.
Night! Night, nothing but night
Hangs over women, children, men!
Could I hurl lightning from these hands,
I might save them from a pauper's grave! [*Leaps up.*]
Black visions come of shadowy shapes
Charging from Hades through the night!
The times, like rocks against impending storms,
Challenge us to mortal deeds,
Cry out for the clash of steel on stone,
Crave the drawing of the sword!
I see my kinsmen departing unto war . . .
See my brothers meekly cringing, squatting
On their heels, in hopes of being overlooked.
And there is even more . . . my visions show me
All the misery, the horror of it all . . .
The whimpering of women, and the horrid yells
Of men whose ears are deaf to prayer and plea . . .
I see them scratching on their brows the brand
Of poor seafolk, the small change of God's creation.
White-faced, they listen to the tumult, thinking
A self-inflicted powerlessness will protect them.
Oh, flag, rainbow stretched across a field in May,
Where are you now? Where are those colours now
That whipped and clamoured round the mast,

Accompanied by roared songs of ecstasy,
Until a zealot king with flashing sword
Slashed in the fluttering flag a pointed tongue?
That tongue you used for idle boasting;
For if the dragon cannot bare his fangs,
A speaking flag is useless. The people
Might as well have held their tongues,
The king might well have left the flag alone;
A flag with the four corners of indifference
Serves adequately as a distress signal
When a ship's capsizing on the rocks!
—More evil times, more evil visions
Illuminate the dark midnight of the future!
A heavy pall of coal-smoke falls black
Across the countryside, its British blackness
Besmirching all the fresh green growth,
And stifling all the fair new shoots!
It swirls low, mixed with poisons,
Robbing our fields of sun and daylight,
Sifting down like rains of ash
Upon that doomed and ancient city.
Mankind grows ugly. In the crooked galleries
Of the mines, the dripping waters moan their songs,
While tiny, busy creatures, men,
Blast out the caverned ore's imprisoned strength;
They creep with hunchback bodies, crippled souls,
Like dwarfs whose gleaming, greedy eyes
Spy out the glitter of delusive gold.
No soul sighs, no lips laugh.
A brother's fall will never rend one heart,
Their own fall cannot touch a human mind . . .
The masses hammer, smithy, forge,
File—and mint their filthy lucre.
The last prophet of the light is fled.
Now they have become a people who
Have long forgotten that when powers fail
The duties of the will are still not ended!
—More evil times, more evil visions
Illuminate the dark midnight of the future!
The wolf of cunning, with hideous yelps,

Bays at the sun of learning here on earth.
Cries of distress ring out from the North,
Rallying to arms out along the fjords.
The sulking dwarf crouches, spitting hatred—
This matter is of no concern to *him*.
Let great powers manifest their mighty fire;
Let others march out to join the battle. . . .
We cannot afford to bleed. . . . We are small,
We lack resources to fight for truth;
Our people's welfare cannot be sacrificed
For *our* poor share of the world's salvation.
Not for us was the bitter chalice drained!
Not for us the crown of thorns
Did pierce His brow with bloody spikes!
Not for us the Roman lance
Thrust into His side, as He hung dying!
Not for us the searing nails
Burning like fire through His feet and hands.
For we are small, the last in line,
We can reject the call to arms.
No! Not for us the Cross was borne!
The blow from Ahasuerus' whip,
The purple weal on the doomed man's shoulder . . .
That fragment of the Passion suffices for us!

[*He throws himself down in the snow and covers his face; after a while,
    he looks up.*]

Have I been dreaming. Am I now awake?
All is grey and lost in mist.
Were they but a sick man's fancies,
The things that I have seen till now?
Is the image in which man's soul was made
Now utterly forgotten and forlorn?
Has the spirit of the origins
From whence we sprang been killed for ever? [*Listens.*]
Ah, a sound like singing on the air!

THE CHOIR INVISIBLE [*through the roaring of the storm*].
    Never, never will you be like Him . . .
    For of flesh are you created;
    Serve Him true, or serve Him false,
    You are lost *both* ways, you are lost!

BRAND [*repeats the words and says in a low voice*].
  I am lost! I am lost!
  I am beginning to believe that now.
  Did He not stand within the choir of the church,
  Angrily repudiating all my words?
  Did he not take from me all that I possessed?
  Barred now are all my pathways to the light!
  He let me do battle to the very end!
  And let me suffer a last defeat!

CHORUS [*sounding louder above him*].
  Worm! You can never be like Him!
  The cup of death is drained.
  Follow Him, or let Him go,
  You are doomed *both* ways, you are doomed!

BRAND [*quietly*]. My wife! My little boy! Happy, carefree days!
  These I exchanged for conflict and grief.
  I tore my heart with the claws of sacrifice . . .
  Yet failed to slay the people's dragon.

CHORUS [*gently and appealingly*]. Never, dreamer, will you be like Him.
               Your heritage is lost;
               All your sacrifice
               Can never make Him rich . . .
               For earthly life
               You were created!

BRAND [*breaks into quiet weeping*]. My little boy, my wife, come back!
  All alone I sit on this mountain peak,
  My body pierced by the cold North wind,
  Haunted by spectres, soft and clammy . . . !

  [*He looks up; a spotlight opens and spreads in the mist; the figure of a woman stands there, brightly dressed, a cloak over her shoulders. It is* AGNES.]

THE FIGURE [*smiles and stretches out its arms towards him*].
  Now, Brand . . . here you have me back again!

BRAND [*starts up bewildered*]. My dearest! What is this?

THE FIGURE.   It was
  Only a fevered dream, my dear! Now the mists
  Of sickness will begin to lift!

BRAND. Oh, Agnes! Dear one!

[*He is about to run across to her.*]

THE FIGURE [*screams*].   No! Do not cross!
Don't you see the chasm that lies between us?
Not hear the roaring mountain waterfalls? [*Gently.*]
You are not dreaming, you are not asleep,
You are no longer struggling with visions.
You have been sick, my dearest one . . .
Have drunk the bitter cup of madness,
Have dreamt your wife had left you . . .

BRAND. Oh! You are alive! Praise be to . . . !

THE FIGURE [*hastily*]. Hush, now! Later we can speak of that.
Follow me! Follow me! The time is running out.

BRAND. And our little boy?

THE FIGURE.   He is not dead.

BRAND. He is alive?

THE FIGURE.   Yes, strong and healthy!
All your sorrows were only dreams.
All your battles mere illusions.
Our little boy is with your mother;
She is well, and he has grown tall.
The village church still stands down there;
It can be pulled down, if you so wish.
The village folk still toil away
As steadily as in the good old days.

BRAND. *Good* old days?

THE FIGURE.   Yes . . . when there was peace.

BRAND. Peace?

THE FIGURE.   Oh, hurry, Brand! Come with me!

BRAND. I fear I am dreaming.

THE FIGURE.   Not any longer.
But you need care and shelter . . .

BRAND. I am strong.

THE FIGURE.   No, not yet. Behind you
  Lurks the horror of the dream.
  With your brain bewildered and bemisted,
  You'll slip away from the child and me,
  Your mind will once again be dulled . . .
  Unless you try this remedy.

BRAND. Oh, let me try it!

THE FIGURE.   You alone
  Can cure yourself. No one but you.

BRAND. Name it then!

THE FIGURE.   Our old doctor . . .
  He who has read so many books,
  Whose cleverness is without end,
  Has tracked your sickness to its source.
  All those horrid, harried visions
  Are evoked by *three words* only.
  These three you must now boldly
  Scratch out from the page of memory,
  Expunge from the tables of the law.
  It is *they* have caused this dread sickness
  To fall upon you like a shower of madness.
  Forget them! Forget these words, if you would
  Cleanse yourself of sickness and disease!

BRAND. Speak them!

THE FIGURE.   'All—or—Nothing!'

BRAND [*shrinks back*]. Ah—so that's it?

THE FIGURE.   As sure as I live,
  As sure as you will one day die!

BRAND. We are both lost! The drawn sword
  Hangs over us as it did before!

THE FIGURE. Brand, be kind! My flesh is warm.
  Your arms are strong . . . hold me again . . .
  Let us seek the sunlight and summer lands. . . .

BRAND. The sickness will not come again.

THE FIGURE. Oh, but it will, Brand, it surely will.

BRAND [*shakes his head*]. I have put it all behind me now.
No more the terrors of disordered dreams!
It is the terrors of life that face me now!

THE FIGURE. Of life?

BRAND.   Come, follow me, my dear.

THE FIGURE.   Stop!
What are you doing?

BRAND.   What I *must* do.
Live what until now was only *dreamt* . . .
Make *true* all that is still *illusion*.

THE FIGURE. Ah! That is no longer possible.
Remember where *that* pathway led you!

BRAND. I shall travel it again!

THE FIGURE.   That terrifying
Gallop through the mists of dreams?
Will you ride once more—willingly, awake?

BRAND. Willingly—and awake!

THE FIGURE.   And lose your child?

BRAND. And lose my child.

THE FIGURE.   Brand!

BRAND.   I must!

THE FIGURE. And kill me too? Tear me
Bleeding from the trap? Flog me to death
With the scourge of sacrifice?

BRAND. I must.

THE FIGURE.   Plunge into darkness
All the lanterns of the night!
Banish the sun from Heaven's height?
Never pluck the golden fruits of life,
Never be transported by ecstatic songs?
Oh—and I know so many songs!

BRAND. I must. Your prayers leave me
Indifferent.

THE FIGURE. Are you forgetting what rewards
All those sacrifices brought you?
All your hopes of change utterly destroyed.
Everyone betrayed you, stoned you!

BRAND. It is not for personal reward I suffer;
Nor fight to win victory for myself . . .

THE FIGURE. For creatures grubbing coal and gold
In the poisoned galleries of the mines!

BRAND. *One* man may be a light unto many.

THE FIGURE. Whose coming generations are surely doomed!

BRAND. Great is the strength of *one* man's will.

THE FIGURE. Remember, *one* with flaming sword
Drove man out from Paradise!
Outside its gate he set a chasm . . .
Over *that* you will never leap!

BRAND. But he left open the path of *longing*!

THE FIGURE [*disappearing with a clap of thunder; the mist swirls over the place where it stood, and a shrill and piercing cry is heard, as from one fleeing*].
Then die! This world has no more use for you!

BRAND [*stands for a moment as though stunned*].
Away it fled in whirls of mist,
Winging on great, savage pinions
Like a hawk over the barren mountain-top!
Her demands were powerless to move me—
Mere crooked pins to catch a whale . . . !
That was the spirit of compromise!

GERD [*enters with a rifle*]. Did you see the hawk? Did you see the hawk?

BRAND. Yes, Gerd, I did. This time I saw him.

GERD. Quick, tell me which way he flew!
Let's after him! We'll get him this time!

BRAND. No human weapon can ever touch him.
    Sometimes his flight's uncertain, as if
    Death's bullet had shot him through the heart . . .
    But when you go to give the death-blow,
    He's behind you again, as swift as ever,
    Mocking and beckoning you on once more.

GERD. I stole the reindeer hunter's rifle,
    And loaded with silver bullets and steel.
    Believe me, I'm not nearly as crazy
    As they say!

BRAND.   Hit your target! [*Is about to go.*]

GERD. Priest, you are limping. What has happened?

BRAND. The people spurned me.

GERD [*comes closer*].   Your brow is bleeding . . .
    Stained red with your heart's blood.

BRAND. The people hunted me and stoned me.

GERD. Before, there was music in your voice.
    But now it sounds broken and forlorn,
    Like leaves in autumn!

BRAND.   All things
    And all men . . .

GERD.   Yes?

BRAND.   Deceived me and betrayed me!

GERD [*looks at him wide-eyed*]. Ha! . . . Now I know who you are! I
    thought
    You were the priest . . . let him be cursed,
    And cursed be all the rest of them!
    No . . . *you* are Man . . . the greatest of Men!

BRAND. In my folly, I used to think so.

GERD. Show me your hands.

BRAND.   My hands?

GERD. Here are the wounds left by the nails!
  In your hair I can see drops of blood . . .
  The thorns' sharp spikes have slashed savagely
  Across your brow. Oh, you have been hanging
  On a bitter tree—the tree of the Cross!
  My father told me, when I was little,
  That this thing was done long years ago,
  And far from here—to some other man.
  But now I see he tried to deceive me. . . .
  For you are that Man . . . you are the Saviour!

BRAND. Get away from me!

GERD.   Shall I fall
  Down at your feet and worship you?

BRAND. Get away!

GERD.   You shed the blood
  That has power to save us all!

BRAND. When I can find no scrap of wreckage
  To save my own shipwrecked soul!

GERD. Take my rifle! Let them all be killed!

BRAND [*shakes his head*]. He who falls can fight no more.

GERD. No, not you! You are above us all!
  In your hands are the holes of the nails . . .
  You are the Chosen One . . . the Greatest.

BRAND. I am the lowest creature of the dust.

GERD [*looks upwards; the clouds are lifting*].
  Do you know where you are standing now?

BRAND [*stares straight ahead*]. I stand on the lowest rung of the ladder,
  With a long way to climb, weary, footsore.

GERD [*wilder*]. Answer me! Do you know where you are standing?

BRAND. Yes. Now the veils of mist are parting.

GERD. Yes, the mist is lifting. Look!
  Black Peak points straight to Heaven!

BRAND [*looks up*]. Black Peak? The Ice Church?

GERD.   Yes!
  So you came to *my* church after all.

BRAND. I wish I were a thousand leagues from here . . .
  Oh, how I long, oh, how I yearn
  For light and sun and gentleness,
  For a tender and serene cathedral calm,
  For the summer kingdoms of this life! [*Bursts into tears.*]
  Oh, Jesus, I did call upon Thy name,
  But Thou never took me to Thy bosom.
  Thou passed close by me, like
  Some ancient word in a foreign tongue.
  Oh, let me now but reach the lowest hem
  Of Thy bright raiment of salvation,
  Stained with the wine and with the tears
  Of true repentance!

GERD [*pale*].   What is this?
  You're weeping . . . weeping hot tears
  That turn to smoke upon your cheeks . . .
  Scalding tears to make the glacier's shroud
  Melt and fall like dew from every peak . . .
  Warm tears to make my frozen memories
  Thaw to these salt water-drops within me . . .
  Warm tears to pull the snowy surplice
  From the shoulders of the glacier's priest! [*Trembles.*]
  Man, why have you never wept before?

BRAND [*serene, radiant and young again*].
  A path of iron ice led through
  The frozen tundras of the law!
  And then, a summer sun shone warm!
  Until this moment, what I wanted to be
  Was a tablet on which God might write.
  But from today, the poem of my life
  Shall surge and fountain warm and rich . . .
  The crust of ice is breaking now . . .
  I can weep . . . I can kneel . . . I can pray.

                [*He falls upon his knees.*]

R1

GERD [*looks upwards and says in a low and frightened voice*].
    Look, there he perches, the evil beast!
    There he flies, casting that great shadow,
    And battering the peak, the mountain flanks
    With his broad, iron-feathered wings . . .
    Now is the moment of salvation . . .
    Now deliverance is near . . . If only
    This silver bullet savages his heart!

> [*She raises the rifle to her cheek and shoots. A hollow roar, as of a roll of thunder, sounds high up on the mountain side.*]

BRAND [*starts up*]. What have you done?

GERD.   I got him!
    He's slipping down! Look there, he's falling!
    Listen to his screams—how he roars and rumbles!
    A thousand feathers from his icy plumage
    Come swirling down from the mountain ridge . . .
    Oh, look, how big and white he's growing . . . !
    See him rolling, ever bigger, ever nearer!

BRAND [*sinks to the ground*]. Condemned is every son of man
    To die the death for mankind's sins.

GERD. Now he is slain, the canopy of Heaven
    Rises ever higher . . . ten times as high!
    See him tumbling, see him rolling . . . !
    I need never be afraid again.
    See, he is as white as any dove . . . ! [*Cries out in terror.*]
    Oh, that tremendous, awful roaring! [*Throws herself down in the snow.*]

BRAND [*crushed beneath the onrushing avalanche, but still shouting to the heights*].
    Answer me, God, in the jaws of death:
    Is there no salvation for the Will of Man?
    No small measure of salvation . . . ?

> [*The avalanche buries him and fills the entire valley.*]

A VOICE [*sounding above the thunder*]. God is Love!

PEER GYNT
[Peer Gynt]

A DRAMATIC POEM
(1867)

English version by
Christopher Fry

based on a literal translation by
Johan Fillinger

AASE,[1] a farmer's widow

PEER GYNT, her son

TWO WOMEN with sacks of corn

ASLAK, a smith

WEDDING GUESTS. STEWARD. FIDDLER, etc.

A MAN and HIS WIFE newly arrived in the district

SOLVEIG and LITTLE HELGA, their daughters

THE FARMER at HAEGSTAD

INGRID, his daughter

THE BRIDEGROOM and HIS PARENTS

THREE HERDGIRLS

WOMAN IN GREEN

DOVRE-MASTER

TROLL COURTIERS. TROLL GIRLS and BOYS. WITCHES. GNOMES,
    GOBLINS and ELVES, etc.

AN UGLY CHILD

A VOICE IN THE DARK. BIRD CRIES

KARI, a cottager's wife

MR. COTTON, MONSIEUR BALLON, HERR VON EBERKOPF and HERR
    TRUMPETERSTRAALE, travellers. A THIEF and A FENCE

ANITRA, daughter of a Bedouin sheik

ARABS, SLAVE GIRLS, DANCING GIRLS, etc.

STATUE OF MEMNON (singing), SPHINX OF GIZEH (dumb)

BEGRIFFENFELDT, professor and director of the lunatic asylum in Cairo

[1] [pron. AW-SË.]

HUHU, a language fanatic from the Malabar coast. HUSSEIN, an oriental minister. A FELLAH with a mummy

SEVERAL LUNATICS with their WARDERS

NORWEGIAN CAPTAIN and his CREW. A STRANGE PASSENGER

A PRIEST. A FUNERAL PROCESSION. A BAILIFF. A BUTTONMOULDER. A THIN MAN

The action, which begins in the early part of this century and ends close to the present day [1867], takes place partly in Gudbrandsdal and in the surrounding mountains, partly on the coast of Morocco, partly in the Sahara Desert, in the lunatic asylum in Cairo, on the sea, etc.

ACT ONE

A slope of birch-trees near AASE's *farm. A stream dashes over rocks; an old mill-house on the far side. A hot summer's day.*

PEER GYNT, *a sturdy twenty-year-old, comes down the path, followed by* AASE, *his mother, a short, slightly built woman, who scolds him angrily.*

AASE. Peer, you're a liar!

PEER [*without stopping*]. No, I'm not!

AASE. Well, swear it's true, then.

PEER.   Why should I swear?

AASE. You see, you daren't! I never heard
Such a pack of lies.

PEER [*stops*].   The whole thing's true!

AASE [*facing him*]. Would you even try and cheat your mother?
First you slope off into the mountains
For weeks when we're busy haymaking
And go chasing reindeer over the snow;
Then you come home, a mass of scratches,
Without your gun or as much as a rabbit;
And now you stare me in the face
And think I'll believe this stuff about *hunting*!
Where did you say you found this buck?

PEER. West, by Gjendin.

AASE [*laughs scornfully*]. Oh, yes, of course!

PEER. I was down-wind of him, frozen stiff;
I could hear him scraping away the snow
Behind some trees to get at the moss.

AASE [*as before*]. Of course!

PEER.   I stood, not daring to breathe,
Heard his crunching hooves, and suddenly
Saw his antlers. Then I wriggled

Along on my belly into a gully
To get a look;—what a buck he was!
So fat and sleek, you couldn't imagine!

AASE. I'm sure I couldn't!

PEER.   Bang! I shot him!
He dropped like thunder on the snow.
The moment he fell I got astride him,
Gripped his left ear, my knife at the ready
To sink in the neck behind the skull;—
Hey! He screamed like a lunatic,
The brute, and in a flash he had scrambled
On to his feet, with a toss of the head
That sent my knife and the sheath flying,
Pinned me round the loins, and locked
His horns against my buttocks: had me
Clamped in a vice; and then we bounded
Off along the Gjendin ridge!

AASE [*involuntarily*]. Jesus help us!

PEER.   Have you seen
That Gjendin ridge? It cuts along
With an edge like a scythe for miles and miles.
You're able to look from that height of snows
And scars and glaciers sheer down
The precipice to the glassy lakes
Sixteen hundred feet below
On either side.—We tore along
The ridge together through the wind.
I've never ridden such a pony!
It seemed as if suns were exploding
Right in my face. Brown-backed eagles
Swam in that vertigo of space
Half-way between us and the lakes,
And dropped away like whirling fluff.
The ice below was crashing and splitting
On shore, but I couldn't hear a sound—
Just the rush of spinning shapes,
A dance of mist that swung and sang
In a frenzy round my ears and eyes!

AASE [*giddy*]. Ah, God help us!

PEER.   Suddenly
  When we reached a vicious, break-neck place,
  A cock-ptarmigan shot up, scared,
  Flapping and cackling, out of the rock
  Where he was hiding, almost under
  The buck's foot on the ridge. The buck
  Shied half-round and jumped sky-high
  Out into space with both of us!

    [AASE *totters and reaches for a tree-trunk.* PEER GYNT *continues:*]

  Behind us, the black wall of mountain,
  Below us, the bottomless ravine!
  First we bored through layers of fog,
  Then sliced across a flock of seagulls,
  Sent them screaming in all directions.
  And down and down and down we went
  Until I saw straight underneath me
  A gleam, as white as the buck's belly.—
  Mother! It was our own reflection
  Hurtling up towards the lake's
  Glassy surface, as fast as we
  Were both careering down to meet it.

AASE [*gasping for breath*]. Peer! God keep me! Be quick, tell me—

PEER. Buck from above, and buck from below,
  Collided in a volley of foam.
  And there we splashed about for hours
  Before we somehow got to shore
  On the north side: the buck swimming,
  Me hanging on. And I came home.

AASE. And the buck, what happened to the buck, Peer?

PEER. Eh? He's probably still there.

    [*Snaps his fingers, turns on his heel, and adds:*]

  If you can find him, you can have him.

AASE. And your neck's not broken? No fractured ribs
  Or splintered shin? Not a crack to your spine?
  O merciful God! What thanks I owe you

For lending my boy such a helping hand!—
You've torn your breeches, but, heaven's above,
That needn't bother us, when I think
What might have happened in a plunge like that!

[*She suddenly stops, with open mouth and eyes, speechless.
Then she turns on him.*]

Ah, it's all a damned rigmarole!
Suffering Christ, you tell such lies!
I remember now this whole concoction;
I heard it all when I was twenty.
It was Gudbrand Glesne it happened to,
Not you, you—

PEER.   Why not me as well?
Things can happen more than once.

AASE [*angry*]. Yes, you can turn a tale inside out,
Polish it up with a lot of swagger,
Disguise it with your fancy feathers
So no one can see the scrawny old carcass.
That's exactly what you've done—
Made it so marvellous and frightful
With twaddle about 'eagles' backs'
And all the rest of the horrible business,
Piling your lies on top of each other
Until in the end I couldn't recognize
A tale I've known the whole of my life.

PEER. If anyone else said that to me
I'd knock him into the middle of next week.

AASE [*weeping*]. Ah, dear God, I wish I was dead:
Sleeping down in the black earth.
Tears and prayers don't touch him at all.—
Peer, you'll be damned, if you aren't already!

PEER. Dear little angel of a mother,
You're right in every word you say.
Come on, be cheerful.

AASE.   Shut your mouth!
How *can* I, even if I wanted,

Cursed with a pig of a son like you?
You never can see how hard it is
For me, a poor unwanted widow,
To get nothing out of life but shame.

[*She cries again.*]

What's become of the proud days
Of your grandpa's time, those bags of money
Old Rasmus Gynt left behind him?
Your father certainly knew how to spend it;
Scattered it everywhere like sand,
Bought up land in every parish,
Rode about in gilded carriages—
Where is it now, the fortune he wasted
On that great winter feast he gave,
When the guests hurled all the glasses and bottles
Against the wall—where is it, eh?

PEER. Where are the snows of yesterday?

AASE. Give your mother a chance to speak!
Look at this farmhouse! Every second
Window-pane is stuffed with rags.
Every fence and hedge is down,
Nowhere for the cows to shelter,
All the meadows lying fallow,
And, on top of that, the bailiff
Coming round here every month—

PEER. For goodness' sake stop whimpering!
Our luck has often given out
And sprung up just as high as ever!

AASE. Watered with enough salt tears!
Oh Lord, what a boy you are,
The clever-dick you've always been,
As cocky as you were that day
The pastor came from Copenhagen,
Called you by your Christian name
And swore that even Danish princes
Hadn't as much intelligence.
And your father gave him a horse and sledge

For being so friendly. Ah, dear me,
Life in those days was worth living!
Not a day passed without the captain,
The rural dean and the rest of them
Coming round to eat and drink
Till I thought they'd burst. But when misfortune
Comes you get to know your neighbours.
The house soon emptied and went quiet,
When our Jon-the-money-bag took to the road
With his pedlar's pack.

[*She wipes her eyes on her apron.*]

             God knows, you're tall
And strong enough, you should be a help
To your poor old mother. You ought to do
Your duty by the farm, and cherish
What little is left of what we had.

[*She cries again.*]

Heaven help me, little use
You've ever been to me, you lout!
At home you slop about by the fire
Raking the ashes with a poker:
Or else you're round the countryside
Frightening girls away from the parties,
Shaming me whatever you do,
And fighting every oaf you meet.—

PEER [*turning away*]. Let me alone.

AASE [*following him*].   Can you deny
You weren't the cause of all the trouble
In that brawl over at Lunde,
All of you fighting like mad dogs?
Don't say it wasn't you who broke
Blacksmith Aslak's arm, or anyhow
Twisted his finger out of joint?

PEER. Who's been stuffing you with such nonsense?

AASE [*hotly*]. The carter's wife; she heard the yelling!

PEER [*rubbing his elbow*]. So she might. The yells were mine.

AASE. Yours?

PEER.   Yes, mother. *I* got the thrashing.

AASE. What do you mean?

PEER.   He's a hefty chap.

AASE. Who is?

PEER.   Aslak. I ought to know.

AASE. Fiddle-faddle; you make me spit!
   That loafing sot, that good-for-nothing
   Schnaps-gulper—beaten *you*?

                    [*Weeping again.*]

I've stood years of humiliation
But for *this* to happen to me
Is the worst disgrace I ever knew.
Suppose he is a hefty chap—
Does it mean you have to be a milksop?

PEER. You moan if I win and moan if I lose.
   [*Laughing.*] You needn't worry—

AASE.   What? Don't say
   You're lying again!

PEER.   I am, for once,
   As a matter of fact; so dry your eyes.

                [*Clenching his left fist.*]

I took the blacksmith with these tongs,
Bent him in half, and used my right
For a sledge-hammer—

AASE.   You big bully!
   You'll dig my grave, the way you go on!

PEER. I'll give you a better fate than that,
   Twenty thousand times as good.
   Kind little walnut of a mother,
   You can take my word for it,
   One of these days the whole parish
   Is going to sing your praises—just

Wait until I accomplish something—
Something absolutely tremendous!

AASE [*with a snort*]. You!

PEER.   Who knows what's round the corner?

AASE. I'd be satisfied if you could manage
To mend the skag in your own breeches!

PEER [*excited*]. I'll be a King—an Emperor!

AASE. O God, just listen!—now he has lost
The final remnants of his wits.

PEER. Oh yes, I will! Just give me time!

AASE. 'Give me time and I'll crow on a dunghill'—
That's what they say, as I remember.

PEER. Well, you wait!

AASE.   You hold your tongue!
You're as stark mad as a man can get.—
And yet we might have made something of you
If you hadn't gone and lost yourself
In a never-ending maze of lies.
Haegstad's daughter had a fancy for you,
You could have had her for the asking
If you had gone about it properly.

PEER. You think so, do you?

AASE.   Yes, I do.
The old man hasn't the strength to argue.
Up to a point he's pig-headed,
But Ingrid gets her way in the end:
She goes ahead, and the old fossil
Tags after, grumbling every step.

                    [*She starts to weep again.*]

Oh, Peer, Peer—all that money—
An heiress! I mustn't think about it.
If only you had put your mind to it
You'd be a splendid bridegroom now—
Instead of a filthy ragamuffin!

PEER [*quickly*]. All right, let's both go courting, then!

AASE. Where?

PEER.   To Haegstad!

AASE.   You poor boy;
   Nobody has a chance with her now!

PEER. Why not?

AASE.   Alas, I have to sigh!
   Time lost is chances lost.

PEER. Why?

AASE [*sobbing*]. While you were busy riding
   Up in the air on a buck's back
   She got engaged to Matt Moen!

PEER. What! That jelly-fish? To him?

AASE. Yes, he's the man she's going to marry.

PEER. Wait while I harness the horse and cart.

[*He starts to go.*]

AASE. You needn't trouble. The wedding's tomorrow.

PEER. Who cares? I shall be there tonight.

AASE. Fool! Do you want to shame us worse
   By giving them the chance to mock us?

PEER. Don't you fret. It will all be fine!

[*Shouting and laughing.*]

   Get a move on! We'll leave the cart;
   It would take too long to bridle the nag.

[*He picks her up.*]

AASE. Put me down!

PEER.   Not me, I'll carry you
   All the way to the wedding-feast!

[*He wades into the stream.*]

AASE. Help! God Almighty preserve us!
   Peer! We're drowning—

PEER.   I was born
  For a more glorious end than that.

AASE. Yes—cooling your heels from a gibbet.

                 [*Pulling his hair.*]

  Oh, you brute!

PEER.   Stop winnicking!
  The bottom is slippery here with slime.

AASE. Mutton-head!

PEER.   That's it, keep swearing;
  That doesn't hurt me!—Ah, you see,
  The ground is shelving up again.

AASE. You dare to drop me!

PEER.   Jiggetty-jig!
  I'll give you a game of Peer and the buck;

                 [*Curvetting.*]

  I'll be the buck and you can be Peer!

AASE. Oh! I'm going out of my mind!

PEER. There you are, we've got across.

                 [*He climbs the bank.*]

  Be a good girl, and kiss the buck
  For giving you such a nice ride.

AASE [*boxing his ears*]. There's all the thanks you're going to get!

PEER. Ow! That's a stingy payment!

AASE. Put me down!

PEER.   We're off to Haegstad.
  You're clever: you can argue for me.
  Talk the old curmudgeon round,
  Tell him Matt Moen is a drip—

AASE. Down!

PEER.   And let him know the bargain
  He'll be getting in Peer Gynt.

AASE. Oh yes, you take your oath on that!
   A pretty character I'll give you,
   A lifelike picture, warts and all.
   I'll come straight out with every single
   Devil's trick you ever played—

PEER. You will, will you?

AASE [*kicking with rage*]. I won't draw breath
   Until the old man sets his dog on you
   For the tramp you are!

PEER.   Hm; I'd better
   Go on my own, then.

AASE.   Please yourself,
   I'll follow behind.

PEER.   My dear old mother,
   You haven't the strength.

AASE.   Oh, haven't I?
   I could smash rocks, I'm so angry!
   I could eat flints, I'll tell you that!
   Put me down!

PEER.   Only if you promise—

AASE. Nothing! I'll go to Haegstad with you.
   I'll see they know everything about you!

PEER. If that's the case, you can stay here.

AASE. Never! I'm going to the wedding feast.

PEER. Not on your life.

AASE.   How can you stop me?

PEER. Put you up on the mill-house roof.

        [*He puts her there.* AASE *screams.*]

AASE. Take me down!

PEER.   Well, will you listen?

AASE. Rubbish!

PEER.   Please be sensible—

S1

AASE [*throwing a clod of turf at him*].
Lift me down off this roof this instant!

PEER. If I dared to, of course I would.

[*Coming closer.*]

Try and remember to sit still.
Don't stamp, or kick your legs about;
Or start lugging the stones away—
Otherwise you won't enjoy it;
You might fall down.

AASE.   Beast, beast!

PEER. Don't get excited.

AASE.   I only wish
You'd gone up the chimney like a changeling!

PEER. Tut tut!

AASE.   Twee!

[*She spits.*]

PEER.   You ought to give me
A mother's blessing on my courtship.
Do! Will you?

AASE.   I'll give you a thrashing,
Big as you are!

PEER.   Goodbye, then, mother.
Have patience. I won't be away too long.

[*He starts to go but turns to lift a warning finger.*]

Remember: don't get over-excited.

[*He goes.*]

AASE. Peer!—God help me, he's really going!
Stag-straddler! Liar! Hey!
Are you listening to me?—No, he's off
Across the fields—! [*She screams.*] Help! I'm giddy!

[TWO OLD WOMEN *with sacks on their backs approach the mill.*]

1ST WOMAN. Lord! Who's screaming?

AASE. Here, it's me!

2ND WOMAN. Aase! Well, you've gone up in the world!

AASE. This much isn't going to help;
Soon, dear God, I'll be in heaven!

1ST WOMAN. Pleasant journey!

AASE. Fetch a ladder;
I must get down! That devil Peer—

2ND WOMAN. Your son?

AASE. Now you can say you've seen
How he behaves.

1ST WOMAN. With our own eyes!

AASE. Just help me down; I've got to be
Away to Haegstad—

2ND WOMAN. He's there, is he?

1ST WOMAN. You'll get your own back on him all right;
The blacksmith's going to be at the feast.

AASE [*wringing her hands*]. Oh, God look after the wretched boy;
They'll end by killing him!

1ST WOMAN. Often enough
They've talked about it. Comfort yourself
That whatever happens was in the stars.

2ND WOMAN. She's properly gone off her rocker this time!

[*Calling up the hill.*]

Eivind, Anders! Hey, come here!

A MAN'S VOICE. Why, what's wrong?

2ND WOMAN. Peer Gynt has perched
His mother on the mill-house roof!

[*A small hill covered with bushes and heather. The main road runs behind it; a fence between.*

   PEER GYNT *comes along a footpath, hurries up to the fence and looks out at the view ahead of him.*]

PEER. There's Haegstad. I shall soon be there.

[*Puts a leg over the fence and hesitates.*]

I wonder if Ingrid will be alone.

[*He shades his eyes, looking down the hill.*]

No. The neighbours are swarming like gnats.
Hm, perhaps I ought to go home again.

[*He draws his leg back again.*]

They snigger at you behind your back,
Their whispering burns into your heart.

[*He goes a few steps away from the fence, and plucks leaves off a bush.*]

If I had a drink to start me off,
Or if I could walk about invisible,
Or if nobody knew me. A good strong drink's
The way to stop the laughter stinging.

[*He looks round, startled, and hides among the bushes. Some* GUESTS, *with wedding-presents, pass by on their way to the farm.*]

A MAN [*conversing*]. His father was a drunk, the mother's
An old crack-pot.

A WOMAN.   No wonder, then,
The boy turned out such a bad lot.

[*They pass by. In a moment* PEER GYNT *comes forward, hot with shame. He stares after them, and mutters:*]

PEER [*softly*]. Was it me they were talking about?

[*With a forced shrug.*] Well, let them!

I don't suppose slander's likely to kill me.

[*He throws himself down on the heather, and lies for some time on his back, his hands behind his neck, staring at the sky.*]

What an odd-shaped cloud! It looks like a horse.
With a man on its back—and a saddle and bridle.
And just behind, an old hag on a broomstick.

[*He laughs quietly to himself.*]

It's mother! She's cussing and carrying-on:
'You beast, you beast! Do you hear what I say, Peer?'

[*His eyes gradually close.*]

Well, she'll be in a fine state now! . . .
Peer Gynt at the head of a great procession,
His horse in a silver cap and gold shoes.
Himself with gauntlet, sabre and scabbard,
And a long cloak with a silk lining.
A glittering company ride behind him
But nobody sits his horse so well
Or sparkles quite like him in the sunlight.
Beside the road there are crowds of people
Lifting their hats and craning to see him.
The women are curtseying. Everyone knows
Emperor Peer Gynt and his thousands of courtiers.
He throws away handfuls of florins and sovereigns
To clink on the road. The whole of the parish
Before very long will be millionaires.
He rides right over the sea, Peer Gynt does;
The King of England waits on the beach.
And, with him, all of England's young women.
When Peer rides up, the English nobles
And the royal family stand to attention.
The King raises his crown, and says—

ASLAK THE SMITH [*to some others as they pass behind the fence*].
There's Peer Gynt, the drunken swine!

PEER [*startled*]. Eh, what, Your Majesty?

ASLAK [*grinning over the fence*].   On your feet
Fellow-my-lad!

PEER.   What the devil—? The blacksmith!
Well, what's on your mind?

ASLAK [*to the others*].   He hasn't got over
That little incident at Lunde!

PEER [*jumping up*]. Are you going, or do I have to make you?

ASLAK. I'm going—but where have you hidden yourself
These last six weeks? Did the fairies get you?

PEER. I've been doing strange things, one way and another.

ASLAK [*winking at the others*]. Go on? Tell us!

PEER.   It's none of your business.

ASLAK [*after a pause*]. Are you going to Haegstad?

PEER.   No.

ASLAK.   At one time
They said it was you that girl was after.

PEER. You black bastard—

ASLAK [*backing away*].   Keep your shirt on!
If you can't have her, there are plenty of others:
Think, the son of Jon Gynt, what a prize!
Lush widows as well as the girls are there.

PEER. Go to hell!

ASLAK.   I daresay someone would have you.
Good evening! I'll give your regards to the bride.

[*They go off, whispering and laughing.*]

PEER [*looks after them, shrugs, and turns away*].
For all I care the Haegstad girl
Can marry anybody she likes.
No skin off my nose.

[*He looks down at himself.*]

                    My breeches are torn.
I'm a grim sight. If I'd only got
Something new to put on. [*He stamps his foot.*] If only
I had the knack of a butcher—to chop
The contempt completely out of their innards.

[*Looking suddenly round.*]

What's that? Who sniggered behind my back?
I was sure I heard—No, it was nothing.
I reckon I'll go home to mother.

[*He starts to go up the hill, but pauses again to listen to the sounds from the farm.*]

The dancing has started!

[*He listens, and stares down the hill, gradually descending. His eyes shine and he rubs his hands down his thighs.*]

The place is seething
With girls—seven or eight to a man!
Oh, perishing death—I've got to be there!—
But how about mother, stuck up on the roof—

[*His eyes stray back to the farm; he jumps up and down, laughing.*]

Hey, look at that! They're dancing the Halling.
Guttorm's a really marvellous fiddler!
It twinkles and leaps like a waterfall.
And all that sparkling flock of girls!—
Yes, perishing death, I've got to be there!

[*He leaps over the fence and is off down the road.*]

———

[*The courtyard of Haegstad Farm, the house at the back. Many guests; a lively dance going on on the grass. The* FIDDLER *is sitting on a table. The* STEWARD *stands in a doorway.* SERVANTS *move between the house and out-buildings;* OLDER PEOPLE *sit about talking.*]

A WOMAN [*joining a group sitting on a pile of logs*].
The bride? Yes, of course, she's crying a bit.
There's no need to take any notice of that.

STEWARD [*in another group*]. Come on, now, friends, empty the jug.

A MAN. Thanks, but you fill it up too fast.

A BOY [*to the* FIDDLER, *as he dances past with a girl*].
Go it, Guttorm, punish those strings!

GIRL. Fiddle away, drown the valley in it!

GIRLS [*in a ring round a dancing* BOY].
Whee, what a leap!

A GIRL.   His legs are like springs!

THE BOY [*dancing*]. The roof's high out here, and the walls are nowhere!

[*The* BRIDEGROOM *comes whimpering to his* FATHER, *who is talking to one or two others, and pulls at his sleeve.*]

BRIDEGROOM. Father, she won't; she's so obstinate.

FATHER. Won't what?

BRIDEGROOM.   She has locked herself in.

FATHER. Well, find the key.

BRIDEGROOM.   I don't know where it is.

FATHER. You're an ass!

[*He turns back to the others. The* BRIDEGROOM *drifts across the yard.*]

A BOY [*from round the house*]. *Now* there's going to be fun, girls!
Peer Gynt has turned up.

ASLAK [*who has just appeared*]. Who invited him?

STEWARD [*going towards the house*]. Nobody.

ASLAK [*to the girls*].   If he tries to talk to you
Take no notice.

A GIRL [*to the others*]. No, we'll pretend
He doesn't exist.

[PEER GYNT *enters, excited and eager. He stops in front of the girls,
rubbing his hands.*]

PEER.   Who is the gamest
Girl in this bunch?

A GIRL [*as he comes to her*]. I'm not, for one.

ANOTHER [*similarly*]. I'm not, either.

A THIRD.   No, nor me.

PEER [*to a fourth*]. I'll settle for you, till a better turns up.

THE GIRL [*turns away*]. I haven't the time.

PEER [*to a fifth*].   What about you, then?

GIRL [*going*]. I'm just off home.

PEER.   Tonight? Are you mad?

ASLAK [*after a moment, in a low voice*].
You see, she prefers to dance with an old 'un.

PEER [*turning quickly to an* OLDER MAN].
Any spare girls around?

THE MAN. Find out for yourself.

[*He moves away.* PEER GYNT *is suddenly subdued. He glances shyly and surreptitiously at the crowd. They stare at him, but no one speaks. He goes to other groups. Wherever he turns there is silence. When he moves away they look after him, smiling.*]

PEER [*to himself*]. To be mocked, and whispered about, and grinned at.
It rasps like a sawblade under the file!

[*He slinks along the fence.* SOLVEIG, *holding little* HELGA *by the hand, comes into the yard with their* PARENTS.]

MAN [*to another standing near* PEER].
Here's that new family.

ANOTHER. The ones from the west?

1ST MAN. Yes, from Hedale.

THE OTHER. Ah, that's who they are.

PEER [*stepping in front of them, pointing to* SOLVEIG *and addressing the* FATHER].
May I dance with your daughter?

FATHER [*quietly*]. Certainly,
After we've paid our respects to the family.

[*They go in.*]

STEWARD [*offering* PEER *a drink*].
As you're here you might as well have a drink.

PEER [*staring after them*].
Thanks, I'm not thirsty. I'm waiting to dance.

[*The* STEWARD *moves on.* PEER, *smiling, looks towards the house.*]

Lovely! Who ever saw anything like it?
She kept looking down at her shoes and her apron!
She held shyly on to her mother's skirt,
And carried a prayer-book wrapped in a handkerchief!
I must look at that girl.

[*He goes towards the house.*]

BOY [*coming out with others*]. Have you given up dancing?

PEER. No.

BOY [*takes him by the shoulder to turn him round*].
            Then you're off in the wrong direction.

PEER. Let me get past!

BOY.   Are you scared of the blacksmith?

PEER. Scared?

BOY.   Are you thinking what happened at Lunde?

[*They go laughing towards the dancers.* SOLVEIG *comes into the doorway*.]

SOLVEIG [*in the doorway*]. Are you the boy who wanted to dance with
    me?

PEER. Yes, yes, yes! Do you have to ask?

                    [*He takes her hand.*]

    Come along!

SOLVEIG.   I mustn't go far, mother said.

PEER. Mother said! Mother said! Were you born last year?

SOLVEIG. Now you're laughing at me!

PEER.   You're such an infant.
    Aren't you grown up yet?

SOLVEIG.   I took my first
    Communion last spring.

PEER.   Well, what's your name?
    It's easier to talk if I know what it is.

SOLVEIG. I'm called Solveig. What are you called?

PEER. Peer Gynt.

SOLVEIG [*withdrawing her hand*]. Oh, goodness!

PEER.   Why, what's wrong?

SOLVEIG. My stocking's untied; I must go and see to it.

                    [*She leaves him.*]

BRIDEGROOM [*tugging at his mother*].
  Mother, she won't!

MOTHER.   Won't? Won't what?

BRIDEGROOM. She won't, mother!

MOTHER.   What?

BRIDEGROOM.   Unlock the door!

FATHER [*angrily, under his breath*].
  Ah, you're only fit to be tied up
  With the calves in a barn!

MOTHER.   Now don't scold him.
  Poor lad, he'll do well enough in time.

              [*They move away.*]

A BOY [*coming with a crowd of others from the dancing*].
  How about a drink, Peer?

PEER.   No.

A BOY.   Just a drop?

PEER [*looking at him gloomily*].
  Have you any?

BOY.   What do you think?

          [*He pulls a flask out of his pocket and drinks.*]

  Ah!—that singes your stomach!—Want some?

PEER. Let me try it. [*He drinks.*]

2ND BOY.   Now taste some of mine.

PEER. No, thanks.

2ND BOY.   Come on, don't be an idiot;
  Drink up, Peer!

PEER.   Give me a swig, then. [*Drinks again.*]

A GIRL [*quietly*]. Let's be going.

PEER.   Afraid of me, lass?

3RD BOY. Everyone is.

4TH BOY.   You showed us all
At Lunde what sort of games you get up to.

PEER. I do even better once I get going!

1ST BOY [*whispering*]. Now he's warming up!

SEVERAL [*in a ring round* PEER].   Tell us, do tell us!
What can you do?

PEER.   I'll show you tomorrow.

BOYS. Show us now!

GIRL.   Honestly, Peer, can you make
Magic?

PEER.   I can call up the Devil!

A MAN. My grandmother did that before I was born.

PEER. Liar! I do what nobody else can.
I ordered him once to go into a nut.
A worm-eaten nut, it was.

SEVERAL [*laughing*].   Oh, yes!

PEER. He cursed and cried, and tried to bribe me
With this and that—

ONE IN THE CROWD.   But he had to get into it!

PEER. Sure. Then I blocked up the hole with a spigot.
You should have heard the row he kicked up!

A GIRL. I bet he did!

PEER.   Like a furious bumble-bee.

THE GIRL. Have you still got him inside the nut?

PEER. No, I haven't; he escaped in the end.
But it's all his fault the blacksmith hates me.

A BOY. Why?

PEER.   Well, I went to the smithy to ask him
To crack that nut-skull; he said yes, he would.

He put it on the anvil—but you know Aslak,
He can't help being heavy-handed,
Hitting everything with a sledge-hammer—

VOICE. Did he smash the Devil?

PEER. He came down hard,
But the Devil was quicker, shot up like a spark
Right through the ceiling, splitting the wall.

SEVERAL. What about the blacksmith?

PEER. Left standing there
With his fingers burnt. We've never been friends
From that day to this.

[*General laughter.*]

SOMEONE. That's a good story!

ANOTHER. Just about his best!

PEER. Do you think I invented it?

A MAN. You didn't need to. I heard most of it
From my grandfather.

PEER. Liar! It happened to me.

A MAN. What is there that didn't?

PEER [*throwing up his head*]. I'm able to ride
Clean through the air on marvellous horses!
And that's not all I can do, let me say!

[*A roar of laughter again.*]

VOICE. Take a ride in the air, then!

SEVERAL. Yes, go on,
Dear Peer Gynt!

PEER. You don't have to beg me.
I'll ride like a hurricane over you lot!
The whole of the parish will fall at my feet!

OLDER MAN. He's out of his mind!

ANOTHER. Raving, raving!

A THIRD. Big mouth!

A FOURTH.   Liar!

PEER [*threatening*].   You wait and see!

A MAN [*half drunk*].
You wait, and your shirt'll be over your head!

OTHERS. Welts on your back, and two black eyes!

[*The* CROWD *disperses, the older ones angrily, the younger laughing and mocking.*]

BRIDEGROOM [*close to* PEER]. Peer, can you really ride through the air?

PEER [*shortly*]. If I want to, Matt; I can do anything.

BRIDEGROOM. Have you got the Invisible Cloak, as well?

PEER. The hat, you mean; yes, of course I've got it.

[*He turns away.* SOLVEIG *crosses the yard, leading* HELGA *by the hand.*]

PEER [*going happily towards them*].
Solveig! I'm so glad you have come!

[*He grasps her by the wrists.*]

I'll whirl you round, like the world spinning!

SOLVEIG. Let me go!

PEER.   Why should I?

SOLVEIG.   You're such a wild one.

PEER. So is a reindeer when summer's beginning.
Come on, girl; don't be so grudging!

SOLVEIG [*withdrawing her arm*].
I daren't.

PEER.   Why not?

SOLVEIG.   No, you've been drinking.

[*She moves away with* HELGA.]

PEER. If I'd only stuck my knife through them all!

BRIDEGROOM [*nudging him*].
Could you help me, do you think, to get at the bride?

PEER [*absently*]. The bride? Where is she?

BRIDEGROOM.   Locked in the store-room.

PEER. I see.

BRIDEGROOM. So, please, Peer Gynt, will you try?

PEER. No, you'll have to manage without me.

          [*A thought strikes him. Softly but sharply.*]

Ingrid—in the store-room!
                [*Crosses to* SOLVEIG.] Well,
Have you had second thoughts?

            [SOLVEIG *tries to leave. He bars her way.*]

                      I embarrass you
Because you think I look like a tramp.

SOLVEIG [*hastily*]. I don't think that; that isn't true!

PEER. Oh, yes! What's more, I'm slightly drunk;
I did that on purpose because you offended me.
Come on!

SOLVEIG.   I daren't now, even if I'd like to.

PEER. Who are you afraid of?

SOLVEIG.   My father, mostly.

PEER. Your father? I get it; he's a devout one,
Holier-than-thou, eh? Come on, answer!

SOLVEIG. Answer what?

PEER.   Isn't your father
Pious, and you and your mother as well?
Tell me the truth.

SOLVEIG.   Let me go in peace.

PEER. No!

               [*Quietly, but still bullying.*]

I can turn myself into a troll!
At midnight I'll come and stand by your bed.
If you hear something hissing and spitting
Don't comfort yourself it's only a cat.
It will be me! I'll drain your blood
Into a cup, and as for your sister—
I'll gobble her up; I will, because
At night I'm a werewolf; I shall bite
Your loins, and down each side of your spine—

[*Suddenly changing tone and entreating her.*]

Solveig, do dance with me!

SOLVEIG [*looking at him gravely*]. You were horrible.

[*She goes indoors.*]

BRIDEGROOM [*drifting across the yard*].
If you'll help, I'll give you a bullock.

PEER.   Come on, then!

[*They go behind the house. Meanwhile a large crowd, most of them
drunk, arrive from the dancing. Noise and confusion.* SOLVEIG, HELGA,
and their PARENTS *come into the doorway with some older people.*]

STEWARD [*to the* BLACKSMITH *who is in the forefront*].
Calm down, will you?

ASLAK [*taking off his jacket*]. It's the day of reckoning.
Either me or Gynt must bite the dust.

SOMEONE. Let them have a fight!

OTHERS.   No, keep it to argument.

ASLAK. Fists it has to be; words are punk.

SOLVEIG'S FATHER. Control yourself, man!

HELGA.   Will they beat him, mother?

A BOY. Chivvy him about the lies he tells!

ANOTHER. Kick him off the premises!

A THIRD.   Spit in his eye!

A FOURTH [*to* ASLAK]. Are you backing out?

ASLAK [*throwing down his jacket*].   I'll kill the bleeder!

SOLVEIG'S MOTHER [*to* SOLVEIG].
Now you see what they think of that foolish boy.

[*Enter* AASE, *with a stick in her hand.*]

AASE. Is my son here? He's got a good thrashing
Coming to him! I'll teach him a lesson!

ASLAK [*rolling up his sleeves*].
That stick's no good on a body like his!

SOMEBODY. The smith will deal with him!

OTHERS.   He'll flay him!

ASLAK [*spitting on his hands and nodding to* AASE].
I'll hang, draw, and quarter him!

AASE.   What?
Hang my Peer? You try and do it;
He's got a mother with teeth and claws!
Where is he? [*Calls.*] Peer!

BRIDEGROOM [*running in*].   Oh, it's terrible!
Father! Mother! Look!

FATHER.   What's happened?

BRIDEGROOM. I can't believe it!—Peer Gynt—

AASE [*shrieking*].   Have they killed him?

BRIDEGROOM. No—Peer Gynt—look up there, on the slopes—

CROWD. He's gone off with the bride!

AASE [*lowering her stick*].   The brute!

ASLAK [*thunderstruck*]. Up the steepest face of the mountain,
My God!—scrambling like a goat.

BRIDEGROOM [*weeping*]. Carrying her like a pig on his back!
T1

AASE [*shaking her fist towards* PEER].
Well, I hope you fall—
[*Screams in terror.*]   Take care what you're doing!

INGRID'S FATHER [*entering bareheaded and white with fury*].
I'll kill him for this, the ravishing thief!

AASE. God curse me for ever, if I let you!

ACT TWO

A high narrow mountain track. It is early morning, PEER GYNT *hurries sullenly along the path.* INGRID, *still wearing what is left of her wedding finery, tries to hold him back.*

PEER. Get away from me!

INGRID [*crying*]. After this?
　Where can I go?

PEER. The further the better.

INGRID [*wringing her hands*]. What lies you've told!

PEER. Don't start a row—
　From here we go our different ways.

INGRID. We've sinned, and that binds us together
　For good and all.

PEER. The Devil take
　All memories, and all women, too—
　Except for one—!

INGRID. What one?

PEER. Not you.

INGRID. Who is she, then?

PEER. Will you go away?
　Where you came from! Back to your father!

INGRID. Dear heart—!

PEER. Shut up, will you?

INGRID. You can't
　Mean what you say.

PEER. I can, and do.

INGRID. To tempt me away, and then disown me!

PEER. What have you to offer, tell me that?

INGRID. The Haegstad farm, and more.

PEER.   But have you
  A prayer-book wrapped in a handkerchief?
  Golden hair over your shoulders?
  Do you look shyly down at your dress
  Your fingers holding your mother's skirt?
  Answer me!

INGRID.   No, but—

PEER.   Did you make
  Your first communion in the spring?

INGRID. No, but, Peer—

PEER.   Are your eyes innocent,
  Can you say No when I ask?

INGRID.   Dear heaven,
  I think he's going out of his mind!

PEER. Does each day I see you become blest?
  Tell me!

INGRID.   No, but—!

PEER [*turning to go*].   What else matters?

INGRID [*intercepting him*].
  You can be hanged if you leave me now;
  Have you realized that?

PEER.   So be it.

INGRID. You can be wealthy and respected
  If you stay with me—

PEER.   I can't afford it.

INGRID [*in tears*]. You persuaded me!

PEER.   You were willing enough!

INGRID. I was desperate!

PEER.   I was hot for a girl.

INGRID [*threatening*].
 Yes, but you're going to pay dearly for it!

PEER. Any price would be cheap to me.

INGRID. Will nothing shake you?

PEER. No.

INGRID. We shall see
 Who wins in the end!

 [*She goes down the hill.* PEER *is silent for a moment, then suddenly cries out.*]

PEER. The Devil take
 All memories, and all women, too!

INGRID [*turning and calling back mockingly*].
 Except for one.

PEER. Yes; except for one.

 [*They go their opposite ways.*]

———

 [*Near a mountain lake in soggy moorland. A storm is coming up.* AASE *enters, calling and searching desperately.* SOLVEIG *has difficulty in keeping up with her. Her* FATHER, MOTHER *and* HELGA *follow at a little distance.*]

AASE [*tossing her arms and tearing her hair*].
 The world's fury is all against me!
 Heaven, the lakes and the awful mountains!
 Heaven coughs out fog to muddle him!
 Treacherous water is waiting to drown him!
 The mountains mean to slide and bury him!
 And the people are out to kill him, too!
 But, by God, they shan't—I can't do without him!
 The dunce, to let the Devil tempt him!

 [*Turning to* SOLVEIG.]

 Isn't it beyond belief?
 Him, who did nothing but make up tales,
 Whose tongue was the only strong thing in him,
 Who never did a decent day's work—

I don't know whether to laugh or cry!
But we've stuck together through thick and thin.
Ah yes, I don't mind telling you now,
My husband drank, and spent his time
Fooling and arguing all round the parish,
Throwing away our money like dirt,
While my little Peer and I sat at home.
The best we could do was try and forget it;
I never was good at standing firm.
It's frightful, looking life in the eye;
Better to shrug worry off if you can,
And try not to think too much about it.
So either you take to the bottle, or lies;
That's it: we made do with fairy stories
About princes and trolls and birds and beasts;
And bride-stealing, too. But who would have thought
Those infernal tales would have clung to him so?

[*With renewed anxiety.*]

What was that shriek? A nixie or demon?
Peer! Peer!—On the brow of the hill there!

[*She runs up the rise, looks out over the water as the others join her.*]

Not a thing to be seen!

FATHER [*quietly*].   It's worse for him.

AASE [*crying*]. Oh, my Peer! My poor lost lamb!

FATHER [*nodding gently*]. You're right. He's lost.

AASE.   Don't say such things!
He's clever as paint; there's no one like him.

FATHER. You're a foolish woman.

AASE.   Oh, yes, yes,
I'm foolish, but my boy's a marvel.

FATHER [*always softly, his eyes kindly*].
He hardened his heart, and lost his soul.

AASE [*fearfully*]. Oh, no, not that! God isn't so cruel!

FATHER. Does he weep for his burden of sins?

AASE.   Ah, no;
  But he can ride through the air on a buck!

MOTHER. Are you mad?

FATHER.   Do you know what you're saying, woman?

AASE. I say there's no deed too difficult for him.
  He'll show you, if only he lives to do it.

FATHER. You'd do better to see him hang on the gallows.

AASE [*with a scream*]. In Jesus' name!

FATHER.   Perhaps in the hands
  Of the hangman his thoughts would turn to repentance.

AASE [*bewildered*]. Oh, your talk is making my head reel!
  We must find him!

FATHER.   To save his soul.

AASE.   And his body!
  If he's into the bog, we must drag him out.
  If the trolls have got him, we must ring the bells.

FATHER. H'm! Here's a sheep-track—

AASE.   Heaven reward you
  For all your help!

FATHER.   It's a Christian duty.

AASE. Then the rest of them are nothing but heathens!
  Not one among them was willing to come.

FATHER. They knew him too well.

AASE.   He was too good for them.

[*She wrings her hands.*]

  Just think, he's in danger of his life!

FATHER. Here's a man's footprint!

AASE.   Then that's the way.

FATHER. At the shepherd's hut we'll divide forces.

[*He walks ahead with his* WIFE.]

SOLVEIG [*to* AASE]. Tell me some more.

AASE [*drying her eyes*].   About my son?

SOLVEIG. Yes, all of it!

AASE [*smiling and lifting her chin*].
                         All? You would soon get tired.

SOLVEIG. You'll get tired of telling it long before
    I'm tired of listening.

———————

[*Low, treeless knolls just below the high mountain plateau. Towering peaks in the distance. The shadows are long; it is late in the
day.*
     PEER GYNT *comes leaping into view and halts on the slope.*]

PEER. The whole parish is out in a mob to get me!
    They've armed themselves with sticks and guns,
    With old man Haegstad howling ahead.
    Word's got about Peer Gynt's around somewhere.
    This isn't the same as a scrap with the blacksmith!
    It's life! It gives you the brawn of a bear.

[*He strikes out with his arms and leaps in the air.*]

You feel you can crush and overthrow,
Stem the torrent, and root up fir-trees!
It's life! It makes you iron and air.
To hell with all those crappy lies!

[THREE HERDGIRLS *run across the hillside, screaming and singing.*]

GIRLS. Trond of Valfjeld! Baard, Aabakken!
    Troll-pack, when the mountains blacken,
    When the sun has taken flight
    Sleep between our arms tonight!

PEER. Who is it you want?

GIRLS.   The trolls! The trolls!

1ST GIRL. Trond do it smoothly!

2ND GIRL.   Baard do it roughly!

3RD GIRL. Our beds are there and no one in them!

1ST GIRL. Roughness is smooth!

2ND GIRL.   Smoothness is rough!

3RD GIRL. With no boys to be had we play with trolls!

PEER. Where are the boys, then?

ALL THREE [*laughing*].   They can't be here!

1ST GIRL. Mine called me sweetheart, his own dear love.
Now he has married a middle-aged widow.

2ND GIRL. Mine found a girl among the gypsies.
Now they're tramping the roads together.

3RD GIRL. Mine murdered our bastard baby.
Now his head grins down from the top of a stake.

ALL THREE. Trond of Valfjeld! Baard, Aabakken!
Sleep in our arms when the mountains blacken!

PEER [*leaping into their midst*].
I'm a three-headed troll, and a three-girl man!

GIRLS. Such a fellow, are you?

PEER.   Judge for yourselves!

1ST GIRL. To the hut, to the hut!

2ND GIRL.   There's mead!

PEER.   We'll drink it!

3RD GIRL. Our beds won't be empty this Saturday night!

2ND GIRL [*kissing him*].
He glows and sizzles like a white-hot poker!

3RD GIRL [*likewise*].
Like a baby's eyes from a pitch-dark pool.

PEER [*dancing among them*].
Dread in the heart, but rutting thoughts.
The eyes laugh, and the throat is choking!

GIRLS [*thumbing noses at the mountains, screaming, singing*].
Trond of Valfjeld! Baard, Aabakken!

Troll-pack, when the mountains blacken,
When the sun has taken flight,
You're not going to sleep in our arms tonight!

[*They dance away across the hills with* PEER GYNT *in their midst.*]

———————

[*Among the Rondane mountains. Sunset. Shining snow-capped peaks on every side.* PEER GYNT *enters, wild and distraught.*]

PEER. One castle piled on another!
The door of that one is dazzling!
Stay! Will you stay? It's vanishing
Further and further away!
The weather-cock up on the vane
Is lifting its wings to fly;
Everything goes into shadow,
The mountain is shut and fastened.
What are they, the branches and roots
Growing out of the crack on the hill?
Giants with herons' feet—
And now they are vanishing, too.
Bright wires, like shreds of a rainbow,
Bore through my eyes to my brain.
What bells are those, far away?
And the strange weight on my brow?
Oh, the pain across my forehead—
The grip of a burning crown!
I can't remember what devil
Hammered it round my head.

[*He sinks down.*]

That ride on the Gjendin ridge,
Invention and damned lies!
Humping the bride up the steepest
Rock-face—and drunk all day;
Pursued by hawks and kites,
Threatened by trolls and suchlike,
Racketing with crazy wenches;—
Lies and damned invention!

[*He gazes into the sky for a long time.*]

Two brown eagles hovering.
The wild geese flying south.
And here am I, trudging and stumbling
Over my shins in muck.

[He leaps up.]

I'll be with you! I'll wash myself clean
In a bath of scouring wind!
I'll go up, and plunge right in
To that bright baptismal font!
Up and over the earth
I'll skim till my mind is serene,
Out and above the sea
Higher than England's king!
You girls can stare, if you like;
My journey's my own concern.
You'll be wasting your time if you wait!
Though I might decide to swoop down.
Where have those eagles got to?
The devil probably took them!
There's the shape of a roof building up,
The eaves, and an angle of wall;
A house growing out of nothing.
You see, the gate's wide open!
Of course, now I recognize it;
It's my grandfather's new farm!
No rags stuffed in the windows;
No fences falling down.
Every window shining;
They're having a feast in the hall.
—I can hear the parson clinking
His knife on the back of his glass;
And the Captain has hurled a bottle
And smashed the mirror to bits.
All right, then, squander the lot!
Quiet, mother, there's more where that came from!
The wealthy Jon Gynt gives a banquet,
Hooray for the family Gynt!
What's all the hubbub about?
Why the shouting and roaring?

They've called for the son of the house:
The parson's proposing my health.
Now—enter Peer Gynt to be valued:
The whole house shakes with his name:
Peer Gynt, born out of greatness,
For what great things you are heading!

[*He rushes forward and collides with a rock. He falls and lies on the ground motionless.*]

———————

[*A meadow with tall swaying birchtrees. Stars wink through the leaves, and birds are singing.*
    A WOMAN IN GREEN *is walking in the meadow.* PEER GYNT *follows her, making amorous gestures.* THE WOMAN *stops and turns round.*]

WOMEN IN GREEN. Is it true?

PEER [*drawing his finger across his throat*].
                                As true as my name is Peer;
As true as you're a beautiful woman!
Will you have me? You'll see how well I turn out;
You needn't weave, you needn't spin,
You can eat so much you'll give at the seams.
What's more, I won't drag you about by the hair.

WOMAN IN GREEN. Nor beat me, either?

PEER.   Now is that likely?
    Kings' sons don't go around beating women.

WOMAN IN GREEN. Are you a king's son?

PEER.   Yes, I am.

WOMAN IN GREEN. And I am the King of the Dovre's daughter.

PEER. Really? Well, there's a happy coincidence.

WOMAN IN GREEN. His place is deep in the Ronde mountain.

PEER. My mother's is grander, I should say.

WOMAN IN GREEN. Do you know my father? King Brosse, his name is.

PEER. Do you know my mother? Her name's Queen Aase.

WOMAN IN GREEN. When father's angry, the mountains crack open.

PEER. They belch if my mother so much as grumbles.

WOMAN IN GREEN. My father can kick to the top of the roof-tree.

PEER. My mother can ride through a river in flood.

WOMAN IN GREEN. Are those rags the only clothes you've got?

PEER. Ah, you should see my Sunday outfit!

WOMAN IN GREEN. I wear silk and gold every day of the week.

PEER. It looks to me like shoddy and straw.

WOMAN IN GREEN. Yes, but you've got to bear in mind
   In my country everything we own
   Has two different ways of being looked at.
   If ever you visit my father's house
   At first you might believe you stood
   In a wilderness of scattered stones.

PEER. Extraordinary; it's the same with us.
   You'll think our gold is dirt and trash;
   You may even imagine the sparkling windows
   Are stuffed up with old stockings and rags.

WOMAN IN GREEN. Black can be white, and the ugly beautiful.

PEER. Big can seem little, and filth seem clean.

WOMAN IN GREEN [*throwing her arms round his neck*].
   Oh, Peer, I can see we were made for each other.

PEER. Like a leg and breeches, like faggots and peas.

WOMAN IN GREEN [*calling across the meadow*].
   Wedding-day horse! Wedding-day horse!
   Come at the call, my wedding-day horse!

   [*A gigantic pig comes running in, with a rope's end for a bridle, an old
   sack for a saddle.* PEER GYNT *vaults on to its back and lifts the* WOMAN
   up in front of him.]

PEER. Yoicks! We'll streak through the gates of Ronde!
   Gee-up, gee-up, my galloping grey!

WOMAN IN GREEN [*lovingly*].
And I've been so dull and moody lately—
You never know what will happen to you!

PEER [*whipping the pig as they trot off*].
You can tell who's well-born by the bloodstock they ride!

———————

[*The Throne Room of the* DOVRE-MASTER. *A great crowd of* TROLL
COURTIERS, GNOMES *and* GOBLINS. *The* DOVRE-MASTER *on the
throne, crowned, and holding a sceptre. His* CHILDREN *and*
RELATIVES *on either side of him.* PEER GYNT *stands before him.
Much commotion.*]

TROLLS. Kill him! The son of a Christian has raped
The heart of the Dovre-Master's daughter!

TROLL CHILD. Can I cut one of his fingers off?

2ND CHILD. Can I pull his hair?

TROLL GIRL.   Let me bite his crutch!

WITCH [*with a ladle*]. Render him down to make a soup!

2ND WITCH [*with a chopper*].
A roast on a spit, or stew in a pot!

DOVRE-MASTER. Cool down!
                    [*Beckoning his* COUNSELLORS:]
                              We don't want to have any bragging.
We've been losing ground these last few years;
It's a question whether we'll stand or fall,
Human help could be very useful.
Besides, he's almost without a blemish,
And well-built, too, by the look of him.
It's true he has only got one head,
But, then, my daughter's no better off.
Three-headed trolls have gone out of fashion;
Even two-headed ones aren't seen very often,
And the heads of those are pretty inferior.

                    [*To* PEER GYNT.]

So you want my daughter?

PEER. I do: and also
Your kingdom as dowry.

DOVRE-MASTER. You shall be given
Half when you marry, the rest when I'm dead.

PEER. That's fair enough.

DOVRE-MASTER. Yes, but not so fast;
We haven't settled your part of the bargain.
Promises have to be made on your side.
If you break even one the contract's void.
You'll never get out of here alive.
First, you must banish from your mind
Everything outside this kingdom;
Day must be shunned, and all its deeds,
And any place where the light gets in.

PEER. With a throne in prospect, that's no great drawback.

DOVRE-MASTER. Next—I must find out how clever you are.

[*He rises from his seat.*]

OLDEST COURTIER [*to* PEER GYNT].
Let's see how your wisdom-teeth can crack
The nutty problems he's going to propound.

DOVRE-MASTER. What's the difference between a troll and a human?

PEER. No difference at all, it seems to me.
Big trolls roast you, small trolls scratch you;
It's the same with us, when we're brave enough.

DOVRE-MASTER. You're right; we're alike in that and much else.
But morning is morning, and evening is evening,
So there is a difference, after all.
Allow me to tell you what it consists of:
Out there, under the radiant sky,
They say 'To thine own self be true.'
But here, in the world of trolls, we say
'To thine own self be—all-sufficient!'

TROLL COURTIER [*to* PEER GYNT].
Do you grasp his meaning?

PEER.   It seems—obscure.

DOVRE-MASTER. 'Sufficient', my son, that potent, thundering
Word you must bear on your coat-of-arms.

PEER [*scratching his head*].
Yes, but—

DOVRE-MASTER. *Must*, if you're going to rule here!

PEER. Yes, well, all right; it might be worse.

DOVRE-MASTER. And then you must learn to appreciate
Our simple, homely way of living.

[*He beckons; two* TROLLS *with pigs' heads, white nightcaps, etc.,
bring food and drink.*]

From the cow we get cake, from the bullock mead;
Don't ask if the taste is sweet or sour;
The main thing is, and don't you forget it,
It's all home-made.

PEER [*pushing it away*]. Home-made the devil!
I'll never get used to this country's habits.

DOVRE-MASTER. The bowl goes with it, it's made of gold.
Who has the bowl has my daughter, too.

PEER [*pondering*]. Well, it's said 'You must master your instincts';
I suppose in time it won't seem so sour.
Here goes!

[*He obeys.*]

DOVRE-MASTER. Very sensible. You spit?

PEER. I hope to get used to it after a while.

DOVRE-MASTER. You must now get out of your Christian clothes;
In Dovre we pride ourselves that nothing
Comes from the valley, all mountain-made,
Except the silk bow on the tip of the tail.

PEER [*indignant*]. I don't have a tail!

DOVRE-MASTER.   We'll get you one.
Steward, fetch my Sunday tail for him.

PEER. No fear! Are you trying to make a fool of me?

DOVRE-MASTER. You can't woo my daughter with a bare backside.

PEER. Turning men into beasts!

DOVRE-MASTER.   Not at all, my son;
I'm making you an acceptable suitor.
You will have a patriotic yellow
Bow to wave, to your lasting honour.

PEER [*thoughtfully*]. They say that a man is only dust.
One should make some concession to custom and fashion.
Tie away!

DOVRE-MASTER. You're a pleasant amenable fellow.

COURTIER. Now show us how well you can flourish and wag it!

PEER [*annoyed*]. Anything else you want me to do?
Do you ask me to give up my Christian faith?

DOVRE-MASTER. You're welcome to keep that undisturbed.
Belief is free; we don't tax that.
What makes a troll is the outward style.
So long as you match us in manner and dress
You can believe what horrifies *us*.

PEER. In spite of the many provisos, you seem
More reasonable than I thought you were.

DOVRE-MASTER. We trolls aren't as bad as we are made out.
That's one more distinction between you and us.—
Well, so much for the serious business.
Now we can gladden our ears and eyes.
Musicians, ripple the Dovrean harp!
Dancers, tap the Dovrean floor!

[*Music and a dance.*]

COURTIER. How do you like it?

PEER.   Like it? Well—

DOVRE-MASTER. Don't be afraid to speak your mind.
What do you see?

U1

PEER.   A hideosity.
A cow twangs a gutstring with its cloven hoof.
A sow in tights jigs to the strumming.

COURTIERS. Eat him!

DOVRE-MASTER.   Remember, his senses are human!

TROLL MAIDENS. Tear off his ears, rip out his eyes!

WOMAN IN GREEN [*weeping*]. To have to endure such things being said
When my sister and I are playing and dancing!

PEER. Oh, it was you? You mustn't take
A joke at a party for anything serious.

WOMAN IN GREEN. Do you *mean* that?

PEER.   I swear the dancing and music
Were both—quite good, or the cat can have me.

DOVRE-MASTER. A curious thing, this human nature.
It takes such a lot of getting rid of.
If it gets a gash from struggling with us
It may bear a scar, but the wound soon heals.
My son-in-law here is as docile as any:
Willing to take his Christian clothes off,
Willing to drink the home-made mead,
Willing to have a tail tied on him—
So willing, in fact, to do all we ask him
I took it for granted the old Adam
Had been shown the door once and for all.
But you see he's back in the saddle again.
Well, well, my son, you have to be cured
Of this tyrannical human nature.

PEER. What will you do?

DOVRE-MASTER.   I'll scratch the left eye
A little, to help you see obliquely;
But all that you see will be rich and strange.
Then I'll take the right one out completely—

PEER. Are you drunk?

DOVRE-MASTER [*placing some sharp instruments on the table*].
                    Here are the glazier's tools.
You must go in blinkers, like a dangerous bull.
Then you'll know how to value the charms of your bride—
And your eyes will never deceive you again
With dancing pigs and musical cows.

PEER. This is raving!

OLDEST COURTIER.   The thoughts of the Dovre-Master.
He has wisdom; it is you who are mad.

DOVRE-MASTER. Consider how much harm and anxiety
You will save yourself for the rest of your life.
Your eyes are the well-spring, don't forget,
Of tears, and their burning, bitter flow.

PEER. True enough; and the Bible says:
If thine eye offend thee, pluck it out.
But listen! When will the eyesight heal
And be human again?

DOVRE-MASTER.   Never, my friend.

PEER. Never? For ever, then, thanks very much.

DOVRE-MASTER. Where are you off to?

PEER.   I'll find my way.

DOVRE-MASTER. No, stop! The way in is easy enough,
But the gates aren't made to open outwards.

PEER. Do you think you're going to force me to stay here?

DOVRE-MASTER. Come, use your intelligence, Prince Peer!
You've a natural gift for being a troll.
Isn't he almost a troll already?
And surely that's what you want?

PEER.   God knows
I do. For a bride, and a well-run kingdom
Into the bargain, I realize
Something has got to be given up.
But there's a limit to everything.
I've accepted the tail, that's right enough;

But I guess I can slough what the steward tied on;
I've got out of my breeches, hardly worth wearing;
But it's easy enough to pull them on
And do up the buttons; and I dare say
I can also unburden myself
Of the habits you have here. I'm perfectly happy
To swear a cow is really a girl,
Later on I can always eat my words;—
But to know you can't ever free yourself,
Or die a respectable human death,
To be stuck as a troll for the rest of your days,
This thing of having no line of retreat,
As the text-book says, which you so insist on,
That's a condition I'll never give in to.

DOVRE-MASTER. Now, by corruption, I shall lose my temper.
You'll find I'm not someone to trifle with.
You sun-bleached ninny! Do you know who I am?
First you come and solicit my daughter—

PEER. A damnable lie!

DOVRE-MASTER.   You have to marry her.

PEER. Do you accuse me of—

DOVRE-MASTER.   What? You can't
Deny that you lusted after her?

PEER [*with a snort*]. If I did? Who cares a fig about that?

DOVRE-MASTER. You human beings are all alike.
Lip-service to your souls, but you worship
Only what you can grab with your fists.
So you really think lust doesn't matter?
Wait! You will soon have proof that it does—

PEER. You won't hook me with a bait of lies!

WOMAN IN GREEN. Peer, before the year's at an end,
You'll be a father.

PEER.   Open the doors!
Let me get out.

DOVRE-MASTER.   Your cub will come after you
  Wrapped in a buckskin.

PEER [*wiping his brow*].   Oh, let me wake!

DOVRE-MASTER. We should send him, no doubt, to your royal castle?

PEER. Who cares? You can put him on the parish!

DOVRE-MASTER. Very well, Prince Peer; it's just as you like.
  But one thing's certain, what's done is done,
  Which means your offspring is bound to grow.
  Mongrels mature at a fearful rate.

PEER. Look, sir, you don't have to be so stubborn.
  Woman, be reasonable. Come to terms.
  As it happens I'm neither a prince nor rich;
  Whether you weigh me or measure me
  You'll find I'm simply not worth keeping.

  [*The* WOMAN IN GREEN *faints and is carried out by* TROLL MAIDENS.]

DOVRE-MASTER [*looking at him contemptuously before speaking*].
  Dash him to pulp against the rocks!

YOUNG TROLLS. Oh, father, can we play owls-and-eagles?
  The wolf-game! Grey mouse and green-eyed cat!

DOVRE-MASTER. Be quick, then. I'm vexed and sleepy. Goodnight.
                          [*He goes.*]

PEER [*chased by the* YOUNG TROLLS].
  Let me alone, you rags of hell!

                [*Tries to get up the chimney.*]

YOUNG TROLLS. Hobs and goblins! Bite his buttocks!

PEER [*trying to get through the trap-door to the cellar*].
  Ow!

YOUNG TROLLS. Close the hatches!

COURTIER.   What happiness
  For the youngsters!

PEER [*struggling with a* TROLL CHILD *who is biting his ear*].
  Will you get off me, you horror!

COURTIER [*rapping* PEER *over the knuckles*].
Ruffian, that's no way to treat a princeling!

PEER. A rat-hole! [*He runs to it.*]

YOUNG TROLL.   Brother gnomes, block it up!

PEER. The old one was bad, but the kids are worse!

YOUNG TROLL. Flay him!

PEER. If only I were the size of a mouse!

[*He runs around.*]

YOUNG TROLLS [*closing in on him*].
Fence him round! Fence him round!

PEER [*weeping*]. Oh, to be a bed-bug! [*He falls.*]

YOUNG TROLLS.   Now for his eyes!

PEER [*buried under the* TROLLS].
Help, mother, I'm dying!

[*Church bells ring in the distance.*]

YOUNG TROLLS. Bells in the mountains! The holy-man's cows!

[*The* TROLLS *fly shrieking in disorder. The Throne Room collapses; everything disappears.*]

_____

[*Pitch darkness.* PEER GYNT *is heard slashing and flailing about with a great bough.*]

PEER. Give an answer! Who are you?

VOICE [*in the dark*].   Myself.

PEER. Get out of my way!

VOICE.   Go round and about.
This heath is big enough.

[PEER GYNT *tries to get through at another place, but hits against something.*]

PEER.   Who are *you*?

VOICE. Myself. Are you able to say the same?

PEER. I can say what I like; and my sword can smite!
  Whee! Look out for the stroke! Saul slew
  His thousands, Gynt his tens of thousands!

[*Slashing about him.*]

  Who *are* you?

VOICE.   Myself.

PEER.   I've had enough
  Of that damnfool answer. It doesn't clear up
  Anything. *What* are you, then?

VOICE. The great Boyg.

PEER.   Oh, are you, indeed?
  At least what was black is becoming grey.
  Out of the way, Boyg!

VOICE.   Go round and about!

PEER. Straight on! [*Hacking and slashing.*]

  I felled him!

[*He tries to advance, but meets opposition.*]

              Is there more than one of you?

VOICE. The Boyg, Peer Gynt! The only one.
  The Boyg that's unharmed, and the Boyg that is wounded.
  The Boyg that is dead, and the Boyg that's alive.

PEER [*throwing away the branch*].
  Trolls blunted my sword, but I've got my fists!

[*Pummels his way forward.*]

VOICE. Yes, trust to your fists; trust to your body.
  Well done, Peer Gynt, you'll get to the top.

PEER [*retreating*]. Forward or back, it's the same distance;
  Out or in, it's equally narrow!
  He's here! and there! And round the corner!
  When I seem to get clear I'm surrounded again.—
  Let me see you! What kind of thing are you?

VOICE.   The Boyg.

PEER [*groping*]. Neither dead nor alive. A slime, a mist.
  Not even a shape! It's worse than fighting
  A horde of growling, sleep-sodden bears!
  [*Screaming.*] Hit back, can't you?

VOICE.   The Boyg isn't mad.

PEER. Hit me!

VOICE.   The Boyg hits at nothing.

PEER.   Give battle!
  I'll make you!

VOICE.   The great Boyg wins without battle.

PEER. If there was only a pinching goblin,
  Or even a year-old baby troll!
  Just something to fight with. But here there's nothing.
  He's begun to snore! Boyg!

VOICE.   What is it?

PEER. Use force!

VOICE.   The great Boyg conquers
  Everything without an effort.

PEER [*biting his own arms and hands*].
  Teeth and nails into the flesh!
  I have to feel the flow of my blood.

              [*A sound like the wing-beat of great birds.*]

BIRD-CRIES. Is he coming towards us, Boyg?

VOICE [*in the dark*]. Yes, inch by inch.

BIRD-CRIES.   Sister birds
  Flying far off, meet with us here!

PEER. Solveig, if you mean to save me
  Do it quickly! Don't stand staring
  Down at the ground. Hurl your prayer-book
  With the silver clasp straight at his head!

BIRD-CRIES. He's flagging!

VOICE.   We have got him.

BIRD-CRIES. Sisters! Hurry!

PEER. It's too high a price to pay for life,
To bear any more of this fearful game.

[*He sinks down.*]

BIRD-CRIES. Boyg, he's down! Take him! Take him!

[*Church bells and hymn-singing are heard in the distance.*]

VOICE [*shrinking away to nothingness with a gasp*].
He's too strong. There are women behind him.

[*Sunrise. The hillside outside* AASE'*s mountain hut. The door is shut; everything deserted and silent.* PEER GYNT *is asleep by the wall. He wakes up, looks round with heavy eyes. He spits.*]

PEER. I'd give anything for a pickled herring!

[*He spits again, and catches sight of* HELGA *who enters with a basket of food.*]

Hey, chick, it's you! What are you here for?

HELGA. Because Solveig—

PEER [*jumping up*]. Where is she?

HELGA. Behind the hut.

SOLVEIG [*hidden*]. If you come any nearer I'll run away.

PEER [*stopping*]. Afraid that I shall put my arms round you,
Is that the trouble?

SOLVEIG. Shame on you!

PEER. Guess
Where I was last night! The Dovre-Master's
Daughter is plaguing me like a horse-fly.

SOLVEIG. It was lucky, then, that we rang the bells.

PEER. Peer Gynt's not the boy to be seduced.
What do you say?

HELGA [*weeping*]. Oh, she's going! Wait for me!

[*She runs after* SOLVEIG.]

PEER [*catching her by the arm*].
  Look what I've got in my pocket for you!
  A silver button! You can have it to keep,
  But put in a good word for me, will you?

HELGA. Let go; don't hold me!

PEER.   Here it is.

HELGA. Let me go! The food's over there.

PEER. If you don't, God help you—

HELGA.   I'm frightened of you!

PEER [*meekly releasing her*].
  All I meant was, ask her not to forget me!

[HELGA *runs off*.]

ACT THREE

In the depth of the pine forest. A grey autumn day. Snow is falling.
PEER GYNT, *in his shirt sleeves, is felling timber for building.*

PEER [*hewing a big fir-tree with twisted branches*].
    Ah, yes, you are strong, you mindless giant,
    But that won't help, you've got to come down.

[*Chopping again.*]

I notice you're wearing your chain-mail,
But I'll hack through that, hard as it is.
Yes, you can shake your sinewy arm;
You're right to feel indignant and furious;
Even so, I must bring you to your knees!

[*He breaks off his work.*]

Lies! It's only an old tree.
Lies! It isn't a giant in armour;
It's a fir-tree with a craggy bark.
Cutting down trees is hard work,
And hell if you're dreaming while you do it.
It will have to stop—this wool-gathering
And floating away in broad daylight.—
You're outlawed, my boy, condemned to the forest.

[*He chops energetically for a bit.*]

Yes, you're an outlaw. You haven't a mother
To bring you food and lay the table.
If you're hungry you must help yourself,
Get it raw from the forest and river,
Split your logs and make your fire,
Busy about, set things to rights.
If you want clothes, you must kill a deer,
If you want a house, you must quarry the stone,

Cut the planks for the timber in it
And carry them to the building site.

[*He lowers his axe and stares in front of him.*]

It will be splendid. A tower and weather-cock
Soaring up above the roof.
And then I'll carve on the end of the gable
A mermaid, fish from the navel downwards.
Latches and weather-cock made of brass;
And I'll have to find some glass somewhere.
Passers-by will ask what it is
Shining out across the hillside.

[*He laughs contemptuously.*]

Bloody lies! There you go again.
You're an outlaw, idiot! [*Chopping fiercely.*]
                    All you need
To keep out the weather is a log cabin.

[*He looks up at the tree.*]

He's starting to rock. Only a kick!
There he goes, crashing down;—
The undergrowth sighing and shuddering!

[*He begins to lop off the low branches. Suddenly, with uplifted axe, he stops to listen.*]

There's someone after me!—That's your game,
Old man Haegstad—to creep up behind me.

[*He hides behind a tree and peeps out cautiously.*]

A boy! By himself. He's looking scared,
And keeping his eyes skinned. What's he hiding
Under his jacket? A sickle. He looks
Round, and puts a hand flat on the fence.
What's he up to? He seems to be bracing himself to—
Ach! He has cut his finger off!
The whole finger off! And bleeds like an ox.—
Now he has bound it up, and run off.

[*He gets to his feet.*]

What spunk! An irreplaceable finger!
Right off! And no one making him do it.
Ah, now I remember! It's the only way
To avoid being called up for the army.
That's it. They were going to send him to war;
And the boy, not surprisingly, objected.—
But to hack it off—part with it for ever?—
To consider it, yes; wish it; even
Prepare yourself for it; but to *do* it!
No; that's something I can't understand.

[*He shakes his head and goes on with his work.*]

[*A room in* AASE's *house. Everything is in disorder. Chests standing open, and clothes scattered about. A cat is on the bed.*
    AASE *and* KARI, *the cottager's wife, are packing and clearing up.*]

AASE [*crossing the room*].
    Kari, listen—

KARI.   What is it, love?

AASE [*crossing back*].
    Do you know—where is—what has become of—
    You can tell me—where *is* that—what am I looking for?
    I'm so befuddled. Where's the key to that chest?

KARI. In the keyhole.

AASE.   What's that clattering noise?

KARI. It's the last load on its way to Haegstad.

AASE [*weeping*]. I'd be glad if the load was me in my coffin!
    Ah, what we mortals have to suffer!
    God pity me! The whole house stripped bare!
    What old Haegstad left the bailiffs went off with.
    They haven't left me the clothes I stand up in.
    They should be ashamed of that cruel sentence!

[*She sits on the edge of the bed.*]

The farm and the land gone out of the family.
Old Haegstad was bad enough, but the law

Was worse; no help, and no sympathy,
And Peer gone away; no one to advise me.

KARI. You can sit tight here, in this house, till you die.

AASE. Yes, the cat and I, living on charity.

KARI. Poor soul, your boy has cost you dearly.

AASE. Peer? You're as soft-headed as I am!
Didn't Ingrid get safely home in the end?
They should have laid the blame on the Devil;
He was the sinner and no one else;
He tempted my boy, the ugly monster!

KARI. Hadn't we better send for the priest?
Maybe you're not as well as you think.

AASE. For the priest? Yes, perhaps we should.

[*She starts up.*]

No, my God, I can't! I'm the boy's mother;
I must help him; that's no more than my duty;
I must do my best, when the rest let him down.
They've left him this coat. I'd better mend it.
For two pins, I'd hang on to this fur-rug, too.
Where are the stockings?

KARI.   Over there
With the rest of the rubbish.

AASE [*rummaging around*].   What's this? Bless me,
It's the old casting-ladle, Kari!
He used to play being buttonmoulder
With this, melt and mould and stamp them.
He came in one day when we had company
And asked his father for a lump of tin.
Not tin, Jon said, but here's a real coin,
God forgive him; but he was drunk,
And, tin or gold, it was all the same to him.
Here are the stockings. Nothing but holes;
They'll take some darning.

KARI.   They certainly will.

AASE. When I've done that I'll go to bed;
I feel so poorly, and weak and shivery.

[*Joyfully.*]

Two wool shirts, Kari! They left them behind!

KARI. Yes, so they did.

AASE.   What a bit of luck!
You'd better put one of them aside.
No, wait, I think we should have them both;
The one he's wearing is almost threadbare.

KARI. That would be sinful, mother Aase!

AASE. May be; but the priest will absolve us of it,
Along with all the rest of our sins.

———

[*Outside a newly-built hut in the forest. Reindeer antlers over the door. Deep snow lying. It is dusk.*
PEER GYNT *is outside the door, fastening a large wooden bolt.*]

PEER [*with occasional chuckles*].
You must have a lock; a lock to secure
The door against trolls, and men and women.
You must have a lock; a lock to shut out
All the pestering hobgoblins.—
They come rattling and knocking after dark:
Open up, Peer Gynt, we're as cunning as thoughts!
We fuss under the bed, rake about in the ashes,
And flail in the chimney like fiery dragons.
Aha! Peer Gynt; how can planks and nails
Keep out the pestering goblin thoughts?

[SOLVEIG *enters on skis across the clearing. She has a shawl over her head and carries a bundle.*]

SOLVEIG. God speed your work. Don't send me away.
You brought me here, and must welcome me.

PEER. Solveig. It can't be—! Yet it is!
And you're not afraid to come so close.

SOLVEIG. One message you sent by little Helga;
Others came with the wind and silence.

More came with all your mother told me.
They grew and multiplied in my dreams.
The heavy nights and empty days
Insisted that I should come to find you.
Down there life seemed to have come to an end;
I hadn't the heart to laugh or cry.
I couldn't be sure what you were thinking,
I was only sure what I had to do.

PEER. But your father?

SOLVEIG.   In all God's universe
I have no one now to call father or mother.
I have left them.

PEER.   Solveig, my beautiful—
To come to me?

SOLVEIG.   Yes, you alone;
There's no one else to befriend and comfort me.

[*In tears.*]

Leaving my sister was the worst;
Or still worse, parting from my father;
Or worst of all, from my dearest mother;—
No, God forgive me, the hardest grief
Was leaving all of them—all of them!

PEER. And you know the sentence I got in the spring?
Farm, land, and inheritance confiscated.

SOLVEIG. It wasn't because of what you owned
That I came away from those I loved.

PEER. And you know the rest? They're free to kill me
Whenever they see me outside the woods.

SOLVEIG. Coming over the snow I asked my way.
When they wanted to know where I was going
I told them, 'Home'.

PEER.   Then away with hammer,
And nails and planks! I'm not going to need
Protecting now against goblin thoughts.

If you're ready to share an outlaw's life
A blessing will hover over this hut.
Solveig! Let me look at you!
Don't come too near! To look at you!
You are like light and the pure air.
Let me lift you! Like thistledown.
When I carry you I shall never be tired.
I won't muss you. With arms outstretched
I'll hold you out there, my lovely warm one!
How could I guess I could bring you to me?
But I have longed for it night and day.
You can see how I've been hewing and building;
It will have to come down; too bare to house you.

SOLVEIG. Bare or not, it's what I like.
It's so easy to breathe up here in the wind.
Down there it was stifling; it seemed to crush me;
That was partly what scared me into leaving.
But now I can hear the fir-trees soughing,
Great silence and singing! This is my home.

PEER. Are you certain of that? For the rest of your days?

SOLVEIG. The road I have taken doesn't lead back.

PEER. You're really mine! Come into the house!
Let me see you indoors. Go in! I'll fetch
Some wood for the fire, to light and warm you!
Then rest happy, and never be cold.

[*He opens the door.* SOLVEIG *goes in. He stands still for a moment. Then he laughs for joy and leaps in the air.*]

My king's-daughter! Found and won!
Now I shall build a palace on rock!

[*He picks up his axe and starts to go. An* ELDERLY WOMAN *in a green tattered dress steps out of the woods. An* UGLY CHILD, *carrying a jug of ale, limps after her, holding her skirt.*]

WOMAN. Good evening, slippery friend.

PEER.   Who are *you*?

WOMAN. An old acquaintance. I live near by.
We're neighbours.

WI

PEER.   Indeed? I don't know about that.

WOMAN. While you built your hut mine grew beside it.

PEER [*going*]. I'm in a hurry—

WOMAN.   As you always were;
    But I trudge behind, and I'll catch you at last.

PEER. You've made some mistake—

WOMAN.   I made a mistake
    Once, in the past, when you promised so much.

PEER. I promised? What are you talking about?

WOMAN. Have you forgotten? Forgotten the night
    You drank with my father—

PEER.   If so, I've forgotten
    What I never knew. What's all this nonsense
    You're talking? When did we last meet?

WOMAN. We last met when we first met. [*To the* CHILD.]
    Give your father a drink. I think he's thirsty.

PEER. His father? You're drunk. Are you meaning to say—

WOMAN. Can't you recognize a pig by its skin?
    Where are your eyes? Can't you see he's lame
    In the leg, just as you're lame in the mind?

PEER. You'd have me believe—

WOMAN.   Are you trying to deny it?

PEER. This long-legged runt—!

WOMAN.   He is growing up fast.

PEER. Hag-face, don't father him on me!

WOMAN. That's enough, Peer Gynt, you uncouth ox!

                    [*Weeping.*]
    Is it my fault that I'm not as pretty
    As when you made love in the fields and woods?
    When I was in labour in the autumn

The Devil supported my back for me;
Small wonder I've lost all the looks I had.
But if you would see me as I used to be
You have only to show that girl the door,
Pack her off out of sight and mind;
Do this, friend, and the hag-face will vanish.

PEER. Go away, troll-witch!

WOMAN.   You see if I do!

PEER. I'll smash your skull in!

WOMAN.   Dare to try!
Peer Gynt, I'm not so easily broken!
I shall come and visit you every day,
Push the door open and look inside.
When you're sitting with her beside the fire,
Fondling her, and kissing and loving,
I'll sit there, too, and claim my share.
She and I will take you in turns.
Farewell, dear friend; get married tomorrow!

PEER. You succubus!

WOMAN.   But I almost forgot!
You must bring up your child, you slippery rogue!—
Chip of the devil, will you go to your father?

CHILD [*spitting at him*]. I'll hack you with my axe: you wait!

WOMAN [*kissing the* CHILD]. What a head he has got on his shoulders!
You'll be just like your father when you grow up!

PEER [*stamping*]. I wish you as far away—

WOMAN.   As I'm near?

PEER [*wringing his hands*]. All of that!

WOMAN.   And it's all the result
Of dream and desire! I pity you.

PEER. It's still worse for another, for Solveig,
My pure gold Solveig!

WOMAN.   The innocent
  Suffer, the devil says! His mother
  Whacked him because his father was drunk!

[*She trudges off into the forest with the* CHILD, *who throws the ale-jug
at* PEER.]

PEER [*after a long pause*]. The Boyg said: Go round and about.
  It looks this time as though I shall have to.
  My castle, which so nearly held her,
  Has come crashing down, and suddenly
  My world is ugly, and happiness over.
  Round and about, boy! There's no way
  Straight through this from you to her.
  Straight through? There ought to be a way.
  Isn't there a text about repentance?
  But what, now? How does it go? I've got
  No Bible, and most of it I forget,
  And there's no advice to be had in the forest.
  Repentance? But it might take years
  To win through. What a waste of life!
  To break what's vibrating and marvellous
  And try to piece it together again!
  You might do it to a fiddle, but not a bell.
  If you want green grass don't trample it down.
  Hallucination, that troll-witch business.
  It has disappeared now, out of sight.—
  Well, out of sight, but not out of mind.
  Skulking thoughts keep after me.
  Ingrid! The dancing three on the hill!
  Would they be there, too? Spitefully claiming
  To be hugged and held, like her, or gently
  Lifted, or touched with outstretched arms?
  Round and about, boy; if my arms
  Were as long as a fir-root or a pine-tree,
  I believe I should hold her too close even then
  To set her down clean and unharmed.—
  I've got to get round this, some way or other,
  So that it's neither gain or loss.
  I must throw all this off, and try and forget it.

[*He goes a few steps towards the hut, but stops.*]

Go in now? So contaminated?
Go in with all this troll-dirt on me?
To speak, and say nothing: confess, yet conceal—?

[*He throws his axe aside.*]

It's Sunday evening. To go to her now,
In the state I am, would be sacrilege.

SOLVEIG [*in the doorway*]. Are you coming in?

PEER [*to himself*]. Round and about.

SOLVEIG. What did you say?

PEER. You will have to wait.
It's beginning to get dark out here,
And there's something heavy I have to fetch.

SOLVEIG. I'll help you; we can lift it together.

PEER. No, stay where you are! I must bear it alone.

SOLVEIG. Not too far, then!

PEER. You have to be patient;
Far or near, you must wait.

SOLVEIG [*nodding*]. I'll wait!

[PEER GYNT *goes down the forest path.* SOLVEIG *stands in the open half-door.*]

[AASE's *cabin. Evening. A log fire is burning, lighting the chimney breast. A cat is on a chair by the foot of the bed.*
AASE *is in bed, plucking restlessly at the coverlet.*]

AASE. Oh, God, is he never coming?
Time drags along so slowly.
There's no one to send with a message;
And I've so much I must tell him.
No time to be lost! It has been
So sudden and unexpected.
Oh, if only I could be sure
That I wasn't too hard on him.

PEER [*entering*]. Good evening!

AASE.   God be praised!
　You've got here, my dear, dear son!
　You shouldn't have made the journey.
　You risk your life coming here.

PEER. Ah, who cares about that?
　I had to come here and see you.

AASE. Well, that puts Kari to shame;
　Now I can go in peace.

PEER. Go? What nonsense is that?
　Where are you thinking of going?

AASE. Ach, Peer, I'm reaching the end;
　I haven't much longer now.

PEER [*turning awkwardly and crossing the room*].
　I was trying to get out of the dark;
　I thought I'd be free of it here—!
　Are your feet and hands very cold?

AASE. Yes, Peer; it will soon be done.—
　When you see my eyes cloud over
　Close them with gentle fingers.
　Remember to order a coffin,
　Only, make sure it's a fine one.
　Oh, but I had forgotten—

PEER.   Quiet, mother!
　Time enough to think about that.

AASE. Yes, yes. [*She looks restlessly about the room.*]
　　　　　　　You can see the little
　They left. As you might have expected.

PEER [*awkward again*]. There you go! [*Harshly.*] I know I'm to blame.
　But why do you have to remind me?

AASE. You! No, the cursed drink,
　That's what made the disaster!
　You had been drinking, my boy;
　You didn't know what you were doing;

And you'd had that ride on the buck;
It's no wonder you lost your head!

PEER. Yes, well, let's drop the subject,
Try and forget all about it.
We'll leave any gloomy matters
Till later—some other day.

[*He sits on the edge of the bed.*]

Now, mother, we'll have a gossip,
But not about anything serious,—
Forget what's unpleasant and vexing,
The things that bruise and hurt us.
Why, look: the same old cat;
She's still keeping alive, then?

AASE. She carries-on so at night;
You know what that foretells!

PEER [*changing the subject*]. What's the news in the parish?

AASE [*smiling*]. They say somewhere about
Is a girl who longs for the mountains—

PEER [*hastily*]. How is Matt Moen getting on?

AASE. They say she pays no attention
To her mother and father's tears.
You ought to look in and see them;
You might be able to help—

PEER. And how is the blacksmith doing?

AASE. Don't mention that man to me.
I would rather tell you the name
Of the girl I was talking about—

PEER. No, now we'll have a gossip,
But not about anything serious,
Forget what's unpleasant and vexing,
The things that bruise and hurt us.
Are you thirsty? I'll get you a drink.
Can you stretch out? The bed's a bit short.
Let me see—I believe it's the one

That I had when I was little!
Remember, you used to sit
In the evenings here beside me
And tuck the fur-rug round me,
And sing ballads and nursery-rhymes?

AASE. Yes, remember! Playing at sleigh-rides
When your father was off on his travels.
The coverlet was the sleigh-rug
And the floor a frozen fjord.

PEER. Yes, but the best thing about it—
Can you remember it, too?—
Was all those marvellous horses—

AASE. Do you think I shall ever forget them?
It was Kari's cat we had borrowed;
It sat on the big log chair—

PEER. To the castle west of the moon
And the castle east of the sun,
To the Soria-Moria Castle
The road going up and down.
You made a driving-whip
From a stick we found in the cupboard.

AASE. I sat in the driving seat—

PEER. That's it; you let go the reins
And kept turning round as we galloped
To ask me if I was cold.
God bless you, you old walnut,
You were a lovable soul!—
What are you groaning for?

AASE. My back; the planks feel hard.

PEER. Stretch out; I'll hold you up.
There now, isn't that easier?

AASE [uneasily]. No, Peer, I want to move on.

PEER. Move on?

AASE.　　　　　　Yes, to move on;
I want it all the time now.

PEER. Nonsense! Let's pull up the coverlet.
  I'll sit here, the way you used to.
  We'll while the evening away
  With ballads and nursery-rhymes.

AASE. You'll find a book of sermons
  In the cupboard. My mind isn't easy.

PEER. In Soria-Moria Castle
  The King and the Prince are feasting.
  Lie back on the sledge-cushions;
  I'll drive you there over the moor—

AASE. But, kind son, am I invited?

PEER. Why yes, they've asked us both.

[*He throws a cord round the chair where the cat is lying, takes a stick in his hand and sits at the foot of the bed.*]

  Gee-up! Get going, Black Beauty!
  You're not feeling cold, are you, mother?
  Gk, gk! What a speed we shall go
  When the grey gets into his stride!

AASE. Peer, what is it that's ringing?

PEER. The shining sleigh-bells, mother!

AASE. It seems such a hollow sound!

PEER. We're going over a fjord.

AASE. I'm afraid! A noise of rushing
  And sighing, a strange wild breath?

PEER. It's the pine-trees, mother, soughing
  In the meadows. You sit still.

AASE. That distant sparkle and flashing.
  All that light, where does it come from?

PEER. From the windows and doors of the castle.
  Can you hear them dancing?

AASE.   Yes.

PEER. St. Peter is standing outside
     Waiting to ask you in.

AASE. Is he greeting us?

PEER.   Very graciously,
     And pouring out sweet wine.

AASE. Wine? Are there cakes as well?

PEER. There are. A piled up plateful.
     And the dean's lamented wife
     Is preparing the coffee and afters.

AASE. Do you mean I'll be talking to her?

PEER. Just whenever you want to.

AASE. What a grand celebration to take
     A poor old creature like me to!

PEER [*cracking his whip*]. Gk, gk! Get a move on, Black Beauty!

AASE. Are you sure you're on the right road?

PEER [*cracking his whip again*]. The high road!

AASE.   The speed we're going
     Is beginning to make me tired.

PEER. I can see the castle ahead;
     We shall soon have finished the journey.

AASE. I'll lie back and close my eyes, then,
     And leave it to you, my son!

PEER. Come up, Greycoat, my spanker!
     There's a huge crowd. They're swarming
     Up to the gate of the castle.
     Here comes Peer Gynt with his mother!
     What's that, Mr. St. Peter?
     You won't let mother in?
     You would have to search for years
     To find someone as good.
     We won't talk about me;
     I'll turn back again at the gate.
     I'd welcome a drink, if you offered;

If not, I'll set off with pleasure.
I've invented as many fibs
As the devil up in a pulpit,
And called my mother a hen
For keeping up such a cackle.
But just you respect and honour her
And make her feel at home.—
You'll find nobody better
Anywhere in the district.
Aha, so here's God the Father!
Now you're for it, St. Peter!

[*In a deep voice.*]

'Stop playing the heavy official:
Mother Aase will be my guest!'

[*He laughs loudly and turns to his* MOTHER.]

You see, as I thought it would be.
That's made him alter his tune.
[*Uneasily.*] What has happened to your eyes?
Mother! Have you gone mad—!

[*He goes to the head of the bed.*]

You mustn't lie there staring!
Say something; it's me, your son!

[*He feels her hands and brow cautiously; then, throwing the cord back on the chair, he says quietly:*]

That's it!—You can rest now, Greycoat;
The journey has come to an end.

[*He closes her eyes, and bends over her.*]

Take thanks for all you gave me,
The beatings and cradlesongs!—
And now you must thank me back—

[*He puts his cheek against her lips.*]

There; that was thanks for the ride.

KARI [*entering*]. What? Peer! You've come! So the worst
  Of her grieving and longing is over!
  God bless her, how soundly she's sleeping—
  Or is she—

PEER.   Hush! she is dead.

[KARI *weeps beside the body.* PEER GYNT *paces up and down the room
for a time; at last he stops at the bedside.*]

PEER. Give my mother a decent burial.
  I'm going away from here.

KARI. Are you going far?

PEER.   To the sea.

KARI. So far?

PEER.   And further still.

[*He goes.*]

ACT FOUR

The south-west coast of Morocco. A palm-grove. Under an awning, and standing on rush-matting, is a dinner-table, laid for a meal. In the grove behind are hammocks. Off shore, a steam-yacht flying the Norwegian and American flags. On the beach a jolly-boat. It is just before sunset.

PEER GYNT, *a handsome, middle-aged gentleman in an elegant travelling-suit, with gold-rimmed spectacles hanging from his waistcoat, is presiding at the head of the table.* MR. COTTON, MONSIEUR BALLON, HERR VON EBERKOPF, *and* HERR TRUMPETERSTRAALE *are finishing their dinner.*

PEER. Drink, gentlemen! If man is made
To enjoy himself, enjoy yourselves.
As somebody said: 'Lost is lost,
And gone is gone.'—What can I pass you?

TRUMPETERSTRAALE. Dear Gynt, you're a superb host!

PEER. I divide the compliment between
My money, my butler, and my cook.

COTTON. Right! Let's drink to the four of you!

BALLON. Monsieur, you possess a *gout*, a *ton*,
Nowadays very seldom found
In men living *en garçon*—
A certain—how do you say?

VON EBERKOPF.   A touch
Of emancipated soul-scrutiny,
A cosmopolyjudicobestriding,
A vision breaching the cloud-barrier,
Undeterred by narrow conformity:
A characteristic of high discernment,
An *Ur-natur* with life experience,
Uniting the trilogy at the apex.
Isn't that what you meant, monsieur?

BALLON. Yes, very possibly. It doesn't
 Sound so eloquent in French.

VON EBERKOPF. Ach, nein! Your language is so stiff.
 But if we wish to find the reason
 For this phenomenon—

PEER.   It's been found!
 The reason is that I'm not married.
 Yes, gentlemen, as obvious
 As that. What ought a man to be?
 Himself; there's my simple answer.
 His duty is to himself and what
 Is his. And how is this possible
 If he makes a pack-horse of himself
 For another person's benefit?

VON EBERKOPF. This for-and-within-yourself existence
 Incurred some struggle, I imagine—

PEER. Ah yes, indeed so, in the past;
 But I always came out of it with honour.
 Though on one occasion I came close
 To being trapped against my will.
 I was a lively, handsome fellow;
 And the lady I was attracted to
 Was of royal blood—

BALLON.   Of royal blood?

PEER [*casually*]. One of the ancient families,
 You know their kind—

TRUMPETERSTRAALE [*thumping the table*]. Blue-blooded trolls!

PEER [*shrugging his shoulders*].
 Obsolete aristocrats whose pride
 Is to see that no plebeian blot
 Is allowed to mar the family scutcheon.

COTTON. So nothing came of the affair?

BALLON. The family were against the match?

PEER. On the contrary.

BALLON.   Ah!

PEER [*picking his words*].   You see,
  There were particular circumstances
  That made it advisable to marry
  As soon as we could. But, to be honest,
  I found the whole thing, from first to last,
  Very disagreeable. The truth is
  I'm fastidious about certain things;
  And I like to stand on my own feet.
  So when my father-in-law hinted
  That I'd have to change my name and status,
  And apply for a nobleman's licence,
  Together with other things I found
  Unpalatable, not to say
  Altogether unacceptable—
  I turned down his ultimatum,
  Surrendered up my young bride,
  And withdrew gracefully.

                [*He drums on the table portentously.*]

                          Ah, yes;
  A destiny rules over us!
  Humankind can depend on that,
  And what a comfort it is to know it.

BALLON. And that brought the matter to an end?

PEER. No, no, I soon found otherwise;
  Certain individuals
  Kicked up a tremendous fuss about it,
  The junior members of the family
  Particularly. Seven of them
  Challenged me to fight a duel.
  That was a time I won't forget,
  Though I came triumphantly out of it.
  It cost blood; but still, that blood
  Is evidence of my identity,
  And points encouragingly towards
  What I just now called the rule of destiny.

VON EBERKOPF. You have a view of life which puts you
  Into the category Thinker.
  Whereas the average intellect
  Separates the over-all scene
  Into detail, and ends in chaos,
  You manage to grasp the totality.
  You measure the whole by a single norm.
  You focus every random fact
  Until they become the radials
  Of a central life-philosophy.—
  And you've not been to a university?

PEER. No, as I believe I told you,
  I'm a plain, self-educated man.
  I've studied nothing methodically,
  But I have thought and speculated,
  And read, in a desultory way.
  I started somewhat late in life;
  When, as you know, it's rather a strain
  To plough through books, page after page,
  Trying to comprehend it all.
  I've a patchy knowledge of history,
  There's been no time for more than that.
  And as one needs something positive
  To depend on in times of stress,
  I've looked at religion from time to time.
  It goes down easier in small doses.
  A man shouldn't swallow all he reads,
  But rather choose what is useful to him.

COTTON. That's practical, I guess!

PEER [*lighting a cigar*].   Dear friends,
  Consider the rest of my career.
  What was I, when I came to the West?
  A poor boy, not a bean in the world.
  I had a struggle to keep alive;
  Believe me, I found it tough going.
  But life, my friends, is sweet, and death,
  As someone or other says, is bitter.
  Well! Luck, as you see, was on my side;

And our old friend Fate was accommodating.
I prospered. And, being adaptable,
I managed to get on better and better.
After ten years they nicknamed me
The Croesus of the Charleston traders.
My fame had spread from port to port;
And a fortune was piling up in the hold.

COTTON. What did you trade in?

PEER.   Very largely
In negro-slaves for Carolina
And heathen images for China.

BALLON. Fi donc!

TRUMPETERSTRAALE. Jesus, my dear Gynt!

PEER. It seems to you a market that hovers
On the border-line of the permissible?
I have felt the same myself, most keenly;
I found it even odious.
But, believe me, once begun
It's very hard to break loose.
And, of course, desperately complicated
In the case of such a huge concern
That gives employment to several thousands,
To wind it up once and for all.
Anyway, I don't really approve
Of burning one's boats. On the other hand
I've always had a great respect
For what are known as the consequences;
And the thought of overstepping the mark
Has always made me a bit cautious.
Besides, I'm not as young as I was,
I was already approaching fifty—
My hair was starting to turn grey;
And, even though my health was excellent,
The painful thought did occur to me:
Who knows how soon the hour will strike
When we shall have the jury's verdict
And the goats be divided from the sheep.
XI

What could I do? To close the trade
With China was impossible.
However, I found a way. I started
Additional trading with that country.
In the spring I exported idols,
And in the autumn—missionaries,
Fully equipped with what they needed,
Such as stockings, bibles, rice and rum—

COTTON. All at a profit?

PEER.   Naturally!
With great success. They threw themselves
Heart and soul into the work.
For each idol sold, they baptized a coolie,
So the effect was neutralized.
The mission-field wasn't fallow a moment,
The missionaries had to wrestle with
An inexhaustible supply of idols.

COTTON. And what about the African shipments?

PEER. My ethics triumphed on this point, too.
I realized the traffic was wrong
For someone not in the prime of life.
You don't know when you may have to go.
What's more, there were a thousand traps
Laid by the philanthropic societies,
Not to mention acts of piracy
And the risks incurred by wind and weather.
These things combined to win the day.
I thought: Peter, trim your sails;
Take good care to mend your ways!
I bought some land in the South, and kept
The last cargo of flesh for myself,
Which happened to be a specially good one.
They throve, and got so sleek and fat
It was nice for me, and nice for them.
Yes, without boasting I can say
I behaved like a father to them,
Which paid excellent dividends.
I built schools, so that their morals

Should be maintained at a general level,
And I took good care the thermometer
Was never allowed to drop below it.
But I've given up the whole thing now,
Sold the plantation and the livestock,
Hair and hide. On the day I left
I gave every man, woman, and child
Free grog, and all of them got pickled:
And the widows got a supply of snuff.
So I trust—if the maxim 'He who does
No ill does good' is valid—then
I can be sure, more than most people,
That my past mistakes will be overlooked
And my virtues be seen to outweigh my sins.

VON EBERKOPF [*clinking glasses with him*].
How invigorating it is to hear
Of a life-principle put into practice
Released from the dark night of theory,
Uninfluenced by external protest!

PEER [*who has been steadily drinking*].
We Northerners understand the need
To fight our way through! The key to life
Is a simple one: to shut one's ears
To the invitation of the serpent.

COTTON. What kind of serpent is that, dear friend?

PEER. A small one, but full of wiles
To make a man commit himself.

[*He drinks again.*]

The whole art of taking risks,
Of having the strength of mind to act,
Is this: to keep your freedom of choice
Whatever traps life puts in your way,—
To know that other days will come
When the day of battle's over—
To know that behind you there is always
A bridge, if you have to beat a retreat.
This theory has carried me along

And coloured everything I did;
A theory I inherited
From childhood in my family home.

BALLON. You are Norwegian?

PEER.   Yes, by birth.
But a world-citizen by nature.
For the good fortune I've enjoyed
I have to thank America.
I owe my well-stocked library
To the younger school of German writers.
From France I got my waistcoats, manners,
And what *esprit* I possess. From England
My industry, and a keen sense
Of what will be to my own advantage.
The Jew taught me how to wait.
A drop of *dolce far niente*
Was imported to me from Italy,—
And once, in a very dangerous corner,
I defended myself with Swedish steel.

TRUMPETERSTRAALE [*raising his glass*].
Ah, Swedish steel!

VON EBERKOPF.   First and foremost
We pay homage to the swordsman!

[*They clink glasses and drink with* PEER. *The drink is beginning to go to his head.*]

COTTON. All very good; but what I should like
To know, sir, is what you mean to do
With all your gold?

PEER [*smiling*].   Hm; do with it, eh?

ALL FOUR [*drawing closer*]. Yes, tell us!

PEER.   Well, now; in the first place,
To travel. That's why I took you aboard
At Gibraltar, as travelling-companions.
I wanted a *corps de ballet* of friends
To dance around my Golden Calf.

VON EBERKOPF. Wittily said!

COTTON.   But no one ever
   Hoisted sail for the sake of sailing.
   You have a purpose, it seems to me.
   What is it?

PEER.   To be an Emperor.

GENTLEMEN. What?

PEER [*nodding*].   Emperor.

ALL FOUR.   Where?

PEER.   Of the whole world!

BALLON. And how, my friend?

PEER.   By the power of gold!
   It isn't a new idea; it's been
   The motive behind whatever I did.
   In childhood, I used to dream I soared
   On a cloud over the high seas,
   In royal robes, with a golden sword;—
   Till I came down again with a bump.
   But the goal, my friends, never wavered.—
   There's a text, I think, or someone said
   Somewhere, I can't remember where,
   That if you gained the whole world
   And lost your*self*, the gain would be
   A wreath on the forehead of a skull.
   That's the phrase, or something like it,
   And it isn't a mere flight of fancy.

VON EBERKOPF. But what *is* this Gyntian 'Self', exactly?

PEER. The world behind the curve of my brow
   Which demonstrates that I'm no one else
   But Me, as God is not the Devil.

TRUMPETERSTRAALE. Now I see what you're getting at!

BALLON. Sublime thinking!

VON EBERKOPF.   Highly poetic.

PEER [*with rising excitement*].
  The Gyntian 'Self'—it's the regiment
  Of wishes, appetites and desires;—
  The Gyntian 'Self' is the sea of ambitions,
  Needs and demands; in fact, whatever
  Causes my breast to heave uniquely,
  And makes me exist as the 'I' that I am.
  But just as the Almighty needs
  The earth to make him omnipotent,
  So, for my part, I need the gold
  To make myself an Emperor.

BALLON. But you have the gold!

PEER.   Not enough.
  Yes, for two or three days, maybe,
  As Emperor *à la* Lippe-Detmold.
  But I have to be myself *en bloc*—
  Gynt of the entire globe,
  Root and branch the sovereign Gynt!

BALLON [*enraptured*]. Possessing the world's supreme beauty!

VON EBERKOPF. The entire Johannisberger brewery!

TRUMPETERSTRAALE. All Charles the Twelfth's collection of weapons!

COTTON. Above all, a rewarding opportunity
  For trade—

PEER.   I've discovered that already;
  The result of anchoring in this harbour.
  This evening we shall be sailing north.
  The newspapers that came aboard
  Brought us some very important news—!
                    [*He rises and lifts his glass.*]
  It seems good fortune never gives up
  Helping those with the will to take it—

GENTLEMEN. Well? Tell us!

PEER.   The Greeks are in revolt.

ALL FOUR [*springing to their feet*].
  What! The Greeks—?

PEER.   On their native soil.

ALL FOUR. Hurrah!

PEER.   And Turkey is in for trouble!

[*He empties his glass.*]

BALLON. To Greece! The path to glory's open!
   I'll come to their help with a French sword!

VON EBERKOPF. I'll shout encouragement—from a distance!

COTTON. I'll make a deal in armaments!

TRUMPETERSTRAALE. Lead on! I shall find the spur-buckles
   Charles the Twelfth tore the Vizier's robe with!

BALLON [*embracing* PEER]. Forgive me, my friend; it seems I have been
   Misjudging you.

VON EBERKOPF [*shaking* PEER'*s hand*]. Like a *dummkopf*
   I almost mistook you for a scoundrel!

COTTON. Too strong, that; merely for a fool!

TRUMPETERSTRAALE [*trying to kiss* PEER GYNT].
   I took you for a specimen
   Of the lowest kind of Yankee hoodlum!
   Forgive me!

VON EBERKOPF. We were all confused—

PEER. What's all this about?

VON EBERKOPF.   Now we see,
   Marshalled in splendour, the complete
   Gyntian army of wishes, appetites
   And desires—

BALLON [*admiringly*]. So this is what it is
   To be Monsieur Gynt!

VON EBERKOPF [*likewise*]. To be
   Gynt with honour!

PEER.   Will you explain—

BALLON. You don't understand?

PEER.   I'm hanged if I do!

BALLON. How can that be? Aren't you setting
   Sail for Greece with a ship and money—?

PEER [*with contempt*]. No, thanks! I support the stronger side;
   I shall lend my money to the Turks.

BALLON. Impossible!

VON EBERKOPF.   Witty, but a joke!

PEER [*pausing, and leaning with dignity on a chair*].
   Well, gentlemen, I think it's better
   That we should part, before the last
   Ties of friendship go up in smoke.
   Who owns nothing can take a chance.
   If a man possesses not much more
   Than the strip of earth his shadow covers
   He can afford to be cannon-fodder.
   But if he stands on an eminence
   As I do, the stake's far higher.
   You go to Greece. I'll put you ashore
   And provide you all with weapons, gratis.
   The more you fan the flame of rebellion
   The better it will be for me.
   Strike your blow for freedom and right!
   Hurl yourselves in! Give the Turks hell;—
   And end your days gloriously
   Stuck on a Janizary's spear.—
   But count me out. [*He pats his pocket.*]
                 I've got money,
   And I'm *myself*—Sir Peter Gynt.

   [*He puts up his sunshade and walks into the grove where the hammocks
   can be seen.*]

TRUMPETERSTRAALE. The filthy cur!

BALLON.   No sense of honour!

COTTON. Oh, honour, that's neither here nor there;
   But think of the enormous profits
   If the country **wins** its independence—

BALLON. I saw myself as a liberator
Surrounded by beautiful Greek women.

TRUMPETERSTRAALE. I saw, held in my Swedish hands,
Those legendary spur-buckles!

VON EBERKOPF. I saw the fatherland's vast culture
Spreading across earth and sea—!

COTTON. It's the financial loss that's worst.
Goddammit! I could cry my eyes out!
I saw myself owning Olympus.
If that mountain's like its reputation
There must be copper there, which ought
To be dug out. And furthermore,
There's this river Castalia
People talk so much about,
With one waterfall after another:
That, at the lowest estimate,
Should be good for more than a thousand horse-power—!

TRUMPETERSTRAALE. I shall still go! My Swedish sword
Has greater value than Yankee gold!

COTTON. Maybe; but crowded in the ranks
We'll be trampled underfoot by the mob;
And what profit do you see in that?

BALLON. *Merde!* So near the peak of success,
Only to have to watch it buried.

COTTON [*shaking his fist towards the yacht*].
Locked up there, in that black chest,
Is the nabob's nigger-sweating gold!

VON EBERKOPF. A masterly thought! Quick! Let's go!
His empire is about to fall!
Hurrah!

BALLON. What now?

VON EBERKOPF. We seize power!
The crew can easily be bribed.
Aboard! I'll commandeer the yacht!

COTTON. You'll—what?

VON EBERKOPF.   I'll grab the whole concern!

[*He goes down to the jolly-boat.*]

COTTON. My own interests seem to dictate
I should grab as well.

[*He follows.*]

TRUMPETERSTRAALE.   What a vulture!

BALLON. Villainous behaviour! Still—*enfin*!

[*He follows the others.*]

TRUMPETERSTRAALE. What else can I do but follow suit—
But I protest to all the world!

[*He goes after them.*]

[*Another part of the coast. Moonlight and drifting clouds. The
yacht is far out at sea, under full steam.*
      PEER GYNT *runs along the shore, now pinching himself awake,
now gazing out over the ocean.*]

PEER. Nightmare!—Illusion!—I'll wake up soon!
She's moving off shore! At the rate of knots!
Sheer illusion! I'm asleep, or delirious!

[*He wrings his hands.*]

It can't be that I'm going to die!

[*He tears his hair.*]

A dream! It has to be a dream!
Horrible! But obviously true!
My arse-licking friends! Hear me, God!
You're an all-wise and righteous judge!

[*With upstretched arms.*]

It's me, Peer Gynt! Protect me, God!
Take care of me, Father, or I shall perish!
Make them back the engine! And lower the boat!
Stop the thieves! Tangle the rigging!
Listen! Don't fret about other people!

The world can look after itself for a while!—
He's not hearing me! Stone deaf, as usual!
What a set-up! A God who's run out of advice!

[*He signals to the sky.*]

Pst! I've got rid of the nigger-plantation!
I've sent missionaries to Asia! Doesn't
One good turn deserve another?
Get me on that boat!

[*A sheet of flame shoots skywards from the yacht, followed by smoke and an explosion.* PEER GYNT *gives a cry and sinks on to the sand. Gradually the smoke clears; the ship has vanished.*]

PEER [*low-voiced and pale*]. The sword of the Lord!
Every man and mouse gone plumb to the bottom!
Thank God for a lucky accident!—
[*With emotion.*] Accident? No, it was more than that.
I was *meant* to be saved, and they to perish.
Thanks and praise that you kept me safe,
Preserved me in spite of all my faults—

[*He takes a deep breath.*]

What marvellous peace and consolation
To know you are personally looked after.
But in this desert! Where's food and water?
Oh, I'll find something. He will provide.
There's no danger.—[*Loudly and ingratiatingly.*]
                    He won't allow
A poor little sparrow like me to perish!
Practise humility. And give Him time.
Rest in the Lord, and don't be cast down.

[*With a leap of terror.*]

Was that a lion growling in the rushes?

[*His teeth chattering.*]

No, it wasn't a lion. [*Plucking up courage.*]
                    A lion; is it likely?
Wild animals like to stay at a distance.
Faced with their overlords they're wary.

It's instinctive; they feel, quite rightly,
It's risky to play with elephants.—
But still, I'd better look for a tree.
Here's a grove of acacias and palms;
If I climb up there I'll be safe and protected,—
Particularly if I can remember
A psalm or two—[*He climbs a tree.*]
                Morning is certainly
Different from evening. That text has given
Men food for thought often enough.

[*He settles himself comfortably.*]

How good to feel the spirit uplifted.
Virtuous thoughts are better than riches.
Simply trust in Him. He knows
Just how much of the cup of affliction
I have the stamina to drink.
He's paternally disposed towards me;—

[*He looks out to sea, and whispers with a sigh:*]

But economical—no, he's not that!

———————

[*Night. A Moorish camp on the edge of the desert.* SOLDIERS *resting round the camp fires.* A SLAVE *runs on, tearing his hair.*]

SLAVE. The Emperor's white charger has vanished!

[*A* SECOND SLAVE *runs on, tearing his clothes.*]

2ND SLAVE. The Emperor's sacred robes have been stolen!

GUARD [*entering*]. A hundred lashes on the soles of the feet
     For anyone failing to catch the thief!

[*The* SOLDIERS *mount their horses and gallop off in all directions.*]

———————

[*Dawn. The grove of acacias and palms.* PEER GYNT *in the tree with a broken branch in his hands, trying to beat off a horde of* MONKEYS.]

PEER. Disaster! A most unpleasant night. [*Swiping.*]
     Are you back again? This is bloody hell!
     Throwing fruit at me. No, something else!
     Your Barbary ape's a loathsome animal!

It's written: 'Watch and keep up the fight!'
I'm damned if I can. I'm shagged out.

[*They attack him again. Desperately.*]

I must put a stop to this persecution!
I must try and catch one of the brutes,
Hang him and skin him, and disguise
Myself, somehow, in his hairy coat.
And perhaps the others will think I'm genuine.—
What is a man? Only dust.
He has to make some concession to fashion.—
Another onslaught! They're swarming like bees.
Buzz off! Shoo! They're going berserk.
If I'd only got a false tail to wear,—
Or something to make me look like an animal—
What now? Something scrambling overhead—

[*He looks up.*]

The grandfather—with a paw full of filth—!

[*He crouches apprehensively, quite still for a moment. The ape moves.*
PEER *starts to wheedle and coax him as if he were a dog.*]

Hey, are you there, good old Buster?
There's a nice fellow. He wants to be friendly!
He won't throw anything; of course he won't—
This is me! Diggy-diggy! We're splendid friends!
Wough-wough! You see, I speak your language.
We both belong to the same family!—
Buster shall have some sugar presently!—
The beast! The whole load on top of me!
Ugh, this is disgusting!—Or was it
Food? The taste might have been anything;
With taste, it's a question of what you're used to.
What philosopher was it who said:
Spit, and hope to acquire the habit?—
Here are the young ones! [*Lashing out at them.*]
        It's monstrous
That a man, one of the Lords of Creation,
Should be compelled to—! Murder! Murder!
The old one was hideous, but these are worse!

[*Early morning. A stony place overlooking the desert. A cave and a ravine at one side.*

A THIEF *and* A FENCE *are in the ravine with the Emperor's horse and robes. The horse, richly caparisoned, is tied to a rock. Horsemen can be seen in the distance.*]

THIEF.   The tongues of the lances
                 Are licking, flickering,—
                 Watch out, watch out!

FENCE.   My noddle already
                 Is rolling in the sand,
                 Alas, alas!

THIEF [*folding his arms*].
                 My dad was a thief,
                 So his son has to be one.

FENCE.   Mine was a fence,
                 So I'm a fence, too.

THIEF.   You have to put up
                 With the person you are.

FENCE [*listening*].   Steps in the scrub!
                 We must fly! But where?

THIEF.   The cavern is deep
                 And the Prophet great!

[*They make off, leaving their booty behind. The horsemen in the distance disappear.*]

PEER [*enters, cutting a whistle from a reed*].
   What a miraculous hour of the morning!
   The dung-beetle trundles his ball in the dust;
   The snail has come to the door of his shell.
   First light; yes, it has gold in its mouth.—
   Nature gives an astonishing power
   To the light of day, there's no doubt of that.
   You feel so safe, your courage rising,
   Prepared to tackle a bull if you have to.
   Such quiet! The joy of the open country,—
   It's strange I have always despised it before;

And that men should crowd themselves in a city,
To be merely elbowed out of the door.—
Oh, look—there's a quicksilver lizard,
Snatching without a thought in its head.
What innocence, even in the animals.
Each obeys its Creator, unquestioning,
Keeping its own indelible character,
Playing or fighting, always itself,
As it was when God said 'Let there be life'.

[*He puts his spectacles on his nose.*]

A toad. In the middle of a block of sandstone.
In a fossil world. Just his head showing.
He sits and looks out at the world
As though through a window: himself—sufficient. [*Reflects.*]
Sufficient? Himself?—Where does that come from?
Something I read when I was a boy.
In the family prayer-book? Or the Wisdom of Solomon?
It's hopeless; I notice as time goes by
I'm losing my memory for dates and places.

[*He sits in the shade.*]

Here's a cool place, to stretch out and rest in.
Ferns; and these look like edible roots.

[*He tastes one.*]

More suitable for animal food.—
Well, they say 'You must master your instincts'!
And, furthermore, 'subdue your pride'.
Also, 'the humble shall be exalted'.

[*Uneasily.*]

Exalted? I'm sure that will happen to me;—
Anything else is unthinkable.
Fate will get me out of this place
And find me a way to begin again.
I'm being tried; salvation comes later,—
If only God will keep me healthy.

[*He shakes off these thoughts, lights a cigar, stretches himself, and stares out over the desert.*]

What a huge, limitless wilderness.—
Away over there, a striding ostrich.
What sense can you make of God's purpose
In all this emptiness and death?
There's nothing life-giving anywhere here,
A charred place, no good to anyone;—
A slice of world, eternally sterile;
A corpse that never, since earth was,
Gave a gesture of thanks to its maker,—
Why was it made?—Nature's prodigal.—
Is that the sea, glittering and flashing
Over in the east? Impossible!
It must be a mirage. The sea's to the west;
Higher up behind me, dammed
Off from the desert by a slope of dunes.

                [*A thought strikes him.*]

Dammed off?—Now, why couldn't I—
The slope is quite shallow. Dammed off!
It only needs one break, a canal,—
A flood of life would come cascading
Down through the gap, and fill the desert!
Soon the whole of this burning grave
Would be like a fresh, rippling sea.
Oases would lift from the water like islands,
Mount Atlas be green as the northern shore,
And ships would skim, like careening birds,
Southward along the caravan tracks.
A living air would scatter this torpid
Vapour, and the clouds drop dew;
Men would build city after city,
And grass grow under the waving palms.
The land south of the Sahara
Would be the shores of a new culture.
Steam would drive the factories
Of Timbuctoo, and Bornu would be
Colonized in a matter of weeks.
Archaeologists would drive their wagons
Safely through Habès to the Upper Nile.
On a plump oasis in the ocean

I would propagate the Norwegian race;
A dalesman's blood is almost royal,
And, crossed with an Arab, would do the trick.
Overlooking the bay on rising ground
I shall build the chief city, Peeropolis.
The world's outmoded! Now it's the turn
Of Gyntiana, my new young land!

[*He leaps up.*]

Given the capital, it's already done.—
A golden key to the gate of the ocean!
A crusade against Death! That old skinflint
Can open the sack he sits brooding over.
Because Freedom is the trumpet call
In every land; like Noah's donkey
I'll send a cry across the world,
Baptize the lands now under a yoke
In the name of freedom and the golden future.
I must forage east and west for the money!
My kingdom—half my kingdom for a horse!

[*The horse whinnies in the ravine.*]

A horse! And robes! And jewels—and weapons!

[*He goes closer.*]

Impossible! Yes, real! I've read
Somewhere that faith can move mountains;—
But fancy it shifting a horse as well—!
Absurd! But, no fooling, the horse is here;—
Ab esse ad posse, and all the rest of it—

[*He puts on the robes and looks down at himself.*]

Sir Peter,—and a Turk from top to toe!
Well, you never know what will happen to you.—
Gk, gk!—Come up, my galloping grey!

[*He climbs into the saddle.*]

Gold stirrups, too, for my feet to go in!—
You can tell who's well-born by the bloodstock they ride!

[*He gallops into the desert.*]

[*The tent of an Arab Sheik, standing alone in an oasis.* PEER GYNT, *in his eastern robes, reclines on cushions. He is drinking coffee and smoking a long pipe.* ANITRA *and a group of* GIRLS *are dancing and singing for him.*]

CHORUS OF GIRLS. The Prophet is come!
  The Prophet, the lord, the all-knowing,
  To us, to us he has come
  Riding over the sand!
  The Prophet, the lord, the infallible,
  To us, to us he has come
  Sailing over the sand.
  Sound the flute and drum;
  The Prophet, the Prophet is come!

ANITRA. His stallion is milk-white
  Like the rivers of Paradise.
  Bow, every knee and head!
  His eyes are dancing stars.
  No human can endure
  The glowing of that fire.
  Across the desert he came.
  From his breast sprang pearls and gold.
  The darkness of simoom
  And drought lay all behind him;
  Light was where he rode.
  He, the unexampled,
  Came across the desert
  Arrayed like a son of the earth.
  Kaba, Kaba stands empty;—
  He himself proclaims it!

GIRLS. Sound the flute and drum;
  The Prophet, the Prophet is come!

[*The* GIRLS *dance to soft music.*]

PEER. I have seen it in print—and it's very true—
  'No one's a prophet in his own country.'—
  It's certainly better being here
  Than back among those Charleston traders.
  There was something hollow in all that,

Something alien to me, something
Dubious lurking in the background.
I was never at home in such a set-up,
And never really the man for the job.
What was I doing in that galère?
Rummaging in the garbage of trade.
When I think of it now, I don't understand;—
It just happened; that's all there is to it.
To be yourself on the basis of gold
Is like trying to build a house on sand.
People go down on their knees in the dirt
When they see your rings and your gold watch;
They lift their hats to a diamond tie-pin;
But the rings and things aren't the man himself.—
A prophet; now there the position is clearer.
You know at least what footing you're on.
If you prosper, it's you—not your pounds,
Shillings and pence—that gets the applause.
You are what you are, and no nonsense;
You're not indebted to luck or chance,
You don't have to depend on orders and contracts.—
A prophet; yes, that's the thing for me.
And it caught me totally unaware—
Simply by loping across the desert
And coming across these children of nature.
The Prophet had come; they made that clear.
I didn't mean to deceive them;—answering
Prophetwise isn't really lying;
And, anyhow, I can always resign.
I'm not committed; it might have been worse;—
Just a private matter, you could call it;
I can go as I came; my horse stands ready;
In short, I'm master of the situation.

ANITRA [*approaching from the entrance*]. Prophet and master!

PEER. What would you have,
My slave?

ANITRA. Outside the sons of the desert
Are begging to look upon your face.

PEER. Tell them to go and stand at a distance;
　Tell them I hear prayers miles away.
　And add: I won't have men in here!
　Men are a worthless lot, my child,—
　Bad-tempered rascals, for the most part!
　Anitra, you can't think how vilely
　They have swind—I mean, have sinned, my child!
　Enough of that! Dance for me, women!
　The Prophet wants to forget the past.

GIRLS [*dancing*]. The Prophet is good; the Prophet is grieved
　For the evil done by the sons of dust!
　The Prophet is meek; praise to his meekness;
　He opens Paradise for sinners!

PEER [*his eyes following* ANITRA *during the dance*].
　Her feet move like the patter of drums.
　Hey! She is exquisite, this filly.
　Her build is on the generous side,
　Not what beauty normally measures;
　But what is beauty? A pure convention,—
　Value depends on where and when.
　The extravagance is very pleasing
　When you've had a bellyfull of the normal.
　The usual recipe has no kick.
　No: either very plump, or very skinny;
　Indecently young or incredibly old;—
　The in-between is a drag on the spirit.
　Her feet aren't altogether clean,—
　Nor her arms, either; especially one.
　But that isn't a serious drawback.
　I'd rather say it was in her favour—
　Anitra, listen!

ANITRA [*approaching*]. Your slave hears you!

PEER. You attract me, child! The Prophet is touched.
　If you don't believe me, I'll prove it to you;—
　I will make you a houri in Paradise!

ANITRA. Impossible, master!

PEER.　　　　　　　　　Do you think I'm joking?
　I'm perfectly serious, as I'm alive!

ANITRA. But I haven't a soul.

PEER.   Then you'll have to get one!

ANITRA. But how, master?

PEER.   Leave it to me;—
I shall take your education in hand.
No soul? I've noticed, to my regret,
You appear to be a bit dumb, as they say.
But, tush; there's always room for a soul.
Come here! Let me measure your cerebellum.—
There's room; there's room; I thought there was.
It's true, it will never go very deep;
You mustn't expect a *large* soul;—
But that's nothing to worry about;—
You will have enough not to feel embarrassed.

ANITRA. The Prophet is good—

PEER.   Are you hesitating?

ANITRA. I would rather—

PEER.   Don't be afraid to speak.

ANITRA. I don't mind about the soul so much;—
I'd rather have—

PEER.   What?

ANITRA [*pointing at his turban*]. That wonderful opal!

PEER [*enchanted, as he gives her the jewel*].
Anitra! You true daughter of Eve!
You affect me like a magnet.
I'm a man. To quote a famous author:
'Das ewig weibliche ziehet uns an!'

_____

[*A moonlit night. The palm-grove outside* ANITRA's *tent.*
    PEER GYNT, *with an Arabian lute in his hand, is sitting under a
tree. His beard and hair have been trimmed; he looks much younger.*]

PEER [*playing and singing*].
                I locked the gates of paradise
                    And took the key in my keeping.

And carried by the northern breeze
I sailed away across the seas
   And left the women weeping.

Southward, southward the keel cut
   The salt waves through like wire.
And where the palm-trees proudly sway
In a green garland round the bay
   I set my ship on fire.

I climbed aboard a desert ship,
   A four-legged ship was he.
It foamed under the lash's gird;—
   I am a migratory bird
   Carolling on a tree!

Anitra, nectar of the palm;
   This much I will allow!
Angora goatmilk cheese, or fish,
   Is not as edible a dish,
   Anitra dear, as thou!

[*He hangs the lute over his shoulder and moves towards the tent.*]

A silence! Is my charmer listening?
Has she heard my serenade?
Is she peering round the curtain,
Veil, and all the rest, abandoned?—
Hear that? A sound as though a cork
Had exploded from a bottle!
There it was again! And there!
Sighing of love? Surely, singing;—
No, unquestionably snoring.—
Sweet harmony! Anitra sleeps.
Nightingale, hold your tongue!
Woe betide you if you wake her
With your jug-tereu-tereu—
Ah well, forget it, as they say!
The nightingale is a born singer;
And so am I, if it comes to that.
He ensnares all hearts, as I do,
Tender, gentle hearts, with music.
This cool night was made for singing;

Song is the element we share;
We become ourselves in singing,
We, Peer Gynt, and the nightingale.
The simple fact of a girl sleeping
Is the climax of my passion;—
Touching with my parted lips
The rim of the glass, not drinking yet;—
But, by heaven, here she is!
After all, that's really better.

ANITRA [*from the tent*]. Master, do you call in the night?

PEER. Yes, indeed; the prophet calls.
I was awakened by the cat
Giving a wild hunting-cry—

ANITRA. Not a hunting-cry, my lord;
Far worse than that.

PEER.   What was it, then?

ANITRA. Have mercy—

PEER.   Tell me!

ANITRA.   It makes me blush—

PEER [*approaching her*].
Was it, perhaps, the same emotion
That completely overwhelmed me
When I gave my opal to you?

ANITRA [*horrified*]. Compare you, treasure of the world,
With a horrible old cat!

PEER.   My child,
Looked at from the point of view
Of love-making, tom-cat and prophet
In the end are much the same.

ANITRA. Master, the honey of a jest
Flows from your lips.

PEER.   My little friend,
You judge great men, as all girls do,
On appearances. Fundamentally

I'm a humorous chap, especially
In a duologue. But my position
Makes me assume a mask of gravity.
My official duties make me stern;
All the responsibility
Of coping with everybody's troubles
Turns me into a Jeremiah;
But it's only on the tongue.—
Enough of this! When we're together
I'm Peer—well, I am who I am.
Suppose we now forget the prophet;
You have me here, myself in person.

[*He sits under a tree and draws her to him.*]

Come, Anitra, we'll relax
Under the palm's green fan! And I
Will whisper while you smile, and then
Vice versa presently;
You will whisper words of love
To me, and I shall do the smiling.

ANITRA [*lying at his feet*].
Each word you say is like a song,
What I can understand of it.
Master, tell me, can a daughter
Get a soul by listening?

PEER. Soul, the intellect's light and reach,
You shall have all in good time.
When the east writes characters
Gold on rose to spell the day,
You shall have your first instruction
And see how well I educate you.
But in this magic mood of night
I should be certifiable
If I served up dreary scraps
Of knowledge like a schoolmaster.
Anyway, if you work it out,
The soul's not the important thing.
The heart is what concerns us most.

ANITRA. Speak, O master! When you speak
   I catch gleams of light, like opals!

PEER. Too much intelligence is folly;
   Coward blossoms into tyrant;
   The truth, when it's overdone,
   Is wisdom standing on its head.
   Yes,—I'd be a liar to say
   There aren't well-fed souls on earth
   Who're never going to get things clear.
   I once knew a man like that,
   One in a thousand; and even he
   Managed to mistake his way,
   Lost the meaning in the shouting.—
   You see the desert round this place?
   I only have to wave my turban,
   And I could force the entire ocean
   To tip over and fill the lot.
   But I'd be an idiot to start
   Creating seas and continents.
   D'you know what living is?

ANITRA.   Teach me.

PEER. To live is to be borne along
   Dryshod on the river of time
   Absolutely as yourself.
   Only as total man can I be
   What I really am, my sweet one!
   Old eagles drop their feathers,
   Old fogeys shuffle and stoop,
   Old crones lose their teeth,
   Old misers have shrivelled hands,—
   And all of them have withered souls.
   Youth! Youth! I mean to dominate
   Like a burning, absolute sultan,—
   Not on the shores of Gyntiana
   Under the vine-leaves and the palm-trees,—
   But in the fresh lap of the virgin
   Thoughts of a woman.—Do you see now,
   Little fish, why I've graciously
   Charmed you, chose *your* heart, established

There, if I may so describe it,
My whole nature's Caliphate?
All your desires belong to me.
I'm a demagogue in love!
You are going to be mine only.
I am what has to dazzle you
As if I were gold or precious stones.
If we part, life is over,—
Yours, at any rate, take note!
I must be sure that every inch
And fibre of you, without a will
For yea or nay, is full of me.
Your shadowy coils of midnight love,
All the charms that can be named,
Like the gardens of Babylon
Will beckon me to a Sultan's bed.
And so really your empty head
Is no bad thing. When he has a soul
A person gets too self-absorbed.
And, listen, while we're on the subject;
If you want it, you can gladly
Have an anklet of silver bells;—
It works out well for both of us;
I'll take the place of a soul for you,
And all the rest is—status quo.

[ANITRA *snores.*]

What? She's asleep. Has everything
That I've been saying been chucked away?—
No; it only confirms the power
I have, that she should float along
In dreams on the stream of my love-talk.

[*He gets up and puts jewels in her lap.*]

Here are brooches! And more yet!
Sleep, Anitra! Dream of Peer—
Sleep! By sleeping you have put
A crown on to your Emperor's head!
A conquest of personality
Is what Peer Gynt has achieved tonight.

[*A caravan route. The oasis can be seen in the far distance.*
  PEER GYNT, *on his white horse, is galloping through the desert,*
with ANITRA *in front of him on the saddle-bow.*]

ANITRA. Stop it, or I'll bite you!

PEER.   Little rogue!

ANITRA. What do you want?

PEER.   To play doves and eagles!
  To carry you off! To make merry hell!

ANITRA. For shame! An old prophet like you—

PEER.   Nonsense!
  The Prophet isn't old, you goose!
  Does this look like old age to you?

ANITRA. Let me be! I want to go home!

PEER. You flirt! Go home! To father-in-law!
  Charming! We've escaped like wild birds
  Out of the cage; we must never darken
  His doors again. Besides, one should never
  Stay too long in the same place.
  Familiarity breeds contempt;—
  Especially when you come as a prophet
  Or something of that sort. A fleeting
  Appearance, and then away like a song.
  It's high time my visit came to an end.
  They're fickle souls, these sons of the desert;—
  The incense and prayers had petered out.

ANITRA. But are you a prophet?

PEER.   I'm your Emperor!

[*He tries to kiss her.*]

There's a preening little woodpecker!

ANITRA. Give me the ring on your finger.

PEER.   Take it,
  Anitra love, and the rest of the baubles!

ANITRA. Your words are songs! They hang on my ear!

PEER. It's heavenly to be loved so much.
I'll dismount, and lead the horse like your slave!

[*He gives her the riding crop and dismounts.*]

There now, my rose, my lovely flower;
I'll trudge along in the sand beside you
Until I get a well-deserved sunstroke.
I'm young, Anitra; don't forget it!
Don't take what I do too seriously.
Playing the fool is a sign of youth!
If your understanding wasn't so dense
You would know, my elegant oleander,
Your lover is fooling—therefore, he's young!

ANITRA. All right, you are young. Have you any more rings?

PEER. Aren't I? There; catch! I can leap like a stag!
If there had been any vine-leaves here
I'd have made a wreath to put on my head.
By God, I'm young! I'll have a dance!

[*Dancing and singing.*]

I'm a blessed cockerel!
Peck me, my pullet,
While I pirouette it!
I'm a blessed cockerel!

ANITRA. You're sweating, my Prophet; I'm afraid you'll melt;
Let me carry that heavy bag for you.

PEER. What a kind thought! Carry it always;—
When you're in love, who cares about gold?

[*Dancing and singing again.*]

Scalliwag Peer
He doesn't know where
To put his feet
Because life is sweet
For scalliwag Peer!

ANITRA. Such delight, when the prophet dances!

PEER. To hell with the prophet!—Let's swap clothes!
Come on! Get out of them!

ANITRA.   Your kaftan
Would be too long, your belt too big,
Your stockings too tight for me!

PEER.   Eh bien!

[*He kneels.*]

Make me suffer intensely, then;—
When you're in love, pain is welcome!
Listen, when we get back to my castle—

ANITRA. To your paradise;—how far away?

PEER. Oh, a thousand miles—

ANITRA.   Too far!

PEER.   But, listen;—
You'll be getting that soul I promised you—

ANITRA. Thanks; I'll manage without a soul.
But you want to suffer—

PEER [*getting up*].   By thunder, I do!
Intense, but short—say, two or three days!

ANITRA. Anitra obeys the prophet!—Farewell!

[*She raps him hard across the knuckles and dashes at full gallop back through the desert.*]

PEER [*standing for a long time thunderstruck*].
Well, may I be —— !

[*The same place, an hour later.*
    PEER GYNT, *soberly and thoughtfully, is stripping off his Turkish robes, bit by bit. At last he takes his little travelling-cap out of his coat pocket, and stands once again in his European dress.*]

PEER [*throwing his turban far away from him*].
There lies the Turk, and here stand I!—
Acting the heathen doesn't work.
Lucky it was just a matter of costume,
And not heredity, as they say.—
What was I doing in such a set-up?
It serves you best to live like a Christian,

Not peacock about in fancy costume:
To base your actions on law and morality,
Be your true self, and win in the end
A graveside speech, and wreaths on your coffin.

[*He walks a few steps.*]

That bitch;—she came within an ace
Of making me lose my head altogether.
I should be a troll if I could make out
What fuddled and confused me so.
Ah well; it's a good thing it's over!
If the joke had gone on another minute
I should have looked ridiculous.—
I made a mistake. It's some consolation
That the error was due to my false position.
I wasn't the person responsible.
It was really the routine life of a prophet,
So utterly lacking the salt of activity,
That took its revenge in these lapses of taste.
Being a prophet is a horrible business!
Your duty's to wrap yourself in a mist;
You finish your chances as a prophet
The moment you start behaving sensibly.
And so I was merely doing my job
When I made pretty speeches to that goose.
Nevertheless—[*He bursts out laughing.*]
            To think of it!
I tried to make time stand still by dancing!
To reverse the tide by prancing about!
Playing the lute, hugging and sighing,
And I end up plucked like a cockerel.
Religious fervour with a vengeance!
Yes, plucked!—And plucked to the wide!
Well, I've still got something in reserve;
Some in America, a bit in my pocket;
I'm not down on my uppers yet.—
And the middle of the road is the best position.
I'm not cluttered with a horse and a coachman;
No transport or luggage to worry about;
In short, I'm master of the situation.

Which way shall I choose? Of all the many
Possibilities? Choice is how
You can tell an intelligent man from a fool.
My business career is a closed chapter;
My love-life is a cast-off garment.
I won't go backwards like a crab.
'Forward or back, it's the same distance;
'Out or in, it's equally narrow',—
As I once read in some high-flown article.—
So now something new; a great enterprise;
A purpose worth the money and effort.
What if I write my life story,
Keeping nothing back,—a book that will set
A fine example, a guide to living?—
Or, wait! I've all the time in the world;—
Suppose, as a well-travelled scholar,
I studied the whole glut of the ages!
Yes, yes; *that's* the thing for me!
I read enough legends when I was small,
And I've kept it up, more or less, ever since.—
I'll record the progress of the human race!
I'll float like a feather on the stream of history,
Make it live again, as though in a dream,—
See the heroes battling for power and right,
As an onlooker, from a safe distance,—
Watch thinkers perish, and martyrs bleed,
Watch kingdoms rise and kingdoms fall,—
Great epochs growing from small beginnings;
In short, skim off the cream of history.—
I must try to get hold of a copy of Becker,
And go through it chronologically,
As far as I can.—Of course it's true
That I haven't much grounding in the subject,
And history's inner workings are subtle;—
But when the starting-point is weakest
The result is often the most original.—
Marvellous to have such a task in hand
And plunge right through it, like flint or steel!

[*With quiet emotion.*]

To sever the ties that are holding you
On every side to home and friends,—
Blow all your worldly goods sky-high,—
Bid a fond farewell to the pleasures of love,—
All to discover the clue to Truth.—

> [*He wipes a tear from his eye.*]

That's what makes the authentic inquirer!—
I feel immeasurably happy.
I have solved the riddle of my destiny.
I must stick to it now through thick and thin!
It's excusable to hold up my head
And be proud of being the man Peer Gynt,
Alias: the Emperor of Human Experience.—
I shall have the absolute key to the past;
No longer have to cope with the living;
The present isn't worth an old boot;
The conduct of men is perverse and gutless;
No wings to their spirits, no weight to their deeds;—

> [*He shrugs his shoulders.*]

And women,—there's a flimsy collection!

> [*He goes.*]

[*A summer's day. Far in the north. A hut in the deep forest. The door, with a big wooden bar, stands open. Reindeer antlers above the door. A flock of goats by the wall of the hut.*

A middle-aged woman, fair-haired, beautiful, sits spinning in the sun.]

THE WOMAN [*gazing down the pathway as she sings*].

> Winter may go, and spring appear,
> Next summer pass, and all the year.
> And yet a time there *will* be, when
> My love is in my arms again.

[*She calls the goats, and returns to her singing and spinning.*]

> God bless you in your journeying,
> And to his peace your spirit bring.
> Here shall I wait until my end,
> Or meet with you in heaven, friend.

[*In Egypt. Dawn. The statue of Memnon rising out of the sand.*
PEER GYNT *wanders in, and gazes round him.*]

PEER. Here's a good place to begin my wanderings.—
Now I'm Egyptian for a change;
But Egyptian based on the Gyntian ego.
Later, I'll make my way to Assyria.—
If I start with the first day of creation
It's bound to end in total disaster;—
I shall side-step Biblical history;
Its secular traces I'll come across everywhere;
But to go into its details thoroughly
Lies outside my province and my powers.

[*He sits on a stone.*]

I'll sit in patience, and wait for the statue
To sing its usual hymn to sunrise.
And after breakfast I'll climb the pyramid;
If there's time, I can look at the inside later.
Then by land I'll follow the Red Sea;
Perhaps I can find King Potiphar's grave.—
An Asiatic, in Babylon
I'll look about to find the famous
Hanging Gardens and the whores:
The chief traces of culture, in fact.
And then at one bound to the Trojan walls.
From Troy there's a direct sea-route
Across to the glory that was Athens;—
There, stone by stone, on the actual spot,
I'll survey the pass that Leonidas guarded;—
I'll acquaint myself with the better philosophers,
Find where Socrates was martyred;—
No, I forgot,—there's a war going on there!
Yes; well, Hellenism must wait.

[*Looking at his watch.*]

It's ridiculous how long it takes
For the sun to rise. I haven't much time.
Well, from Troy—I had got as far as that—

[*He gets up and listens.*]

Z1

What in the world is that howling noise?

[*The sun rises.*]

STATUE OF MEMNON [*singing*].
>   From the demi-God's ashes are rising
>   The birds delighting.
>   Zeus, All-surmising,
>   Created them fighting.
>   O wise owl, where
>   Sleep my birds of the air?
>   You must die or guess
>   The song's mysteries.

PEER. No joking,—I'm sure a sound was made
By the statue! Music of the Past.
The stony voice was rising and falling.—
I'll write this down, for scholars to mull over.

[*He makes notes in his pocket-book.*]

'The statue sang. I distinctly heard it,
But didn't quite follow the sense of it.
The whole thing clearly hallucination:—
Nothing else of importance observed today.'

[*He goes on his way.*]

[*Near the village of Gizeh. A great Sphinx carved out of the rocks. In the distance Cairo's spires and minarets.*

PEER GYNT *enters. He looks attentively at the Sphinx, now through his eyeglasses, now through his cupped hand.*]

PEER. Now, where in the world have I seen something
I dimly remember, like this monster?
For seen it I have, in the north or south.
A person? And if it was, then who?
It occurred to me afterwards that Memnon
Was like the so-called ancients of Dovre,
The way he sat there, as stiff as a ramrod,
With his bottom planted on stumps of pillars.—
But this fantastic mongrel creature,
This changeling, half lion and half a woman,—

Is he out of some legend, as well?
Or does he belong to some actual memory?
A legend! Now I remember the fellow!
Of course, it's the Boyg whose skull I thumped,—
I mean, dreamed I did—in a high fever.—

[*He moves closer.*]

The self-same eyes, and the same lips;—
Not quite so ponderous; rather more wily;
But, in every other way, identical.—
So that's it, Boyg; you look like a lion
When you're seen from behind, and in the daylight!
Do you still know riddles? Suppose we try.
Let's see if you answer the way you did last time

[*Calling to the Sphinx.*]

Hi, Boyg, who are you?

VOICE [*behind the Sphinx*]. Ach, Sphinx, wer bist du?

PEER. What! Echo answers in German! Astonishing!

VOICE. Wer bist du?

PEER.   Speaks the language fluently!
That's a new observation; my own entirely.

[*He makes a note in his book.*]

'Echo in German. The Berlin dialect.'

[BEGRIFFENFELDT *comes from behind the Sphinx.*]

BEGRIFFENFELDT. A human being!

PEER: Oh, so that's who was talking.

[*Makes another note.*]

'Arrived at a different conclusion later.'

BEGRIFFENFELDT [*gesticulating excitedly*].
Mein Herr, excuse me—! Eine Lebensfrage—!
What brought you here on this day of all days?

PEER. A visit. To greet a boyhood friend.

BEGRIFFENFELDT. Really? The Sphinx—?

PEER [*nodding*].   I used to know him.

BEGRIFFENFELDT. Staggering!—And after such a night!
My forehead is pounding as though it would burst!
You really know him? Tell me! Answer me!
Can you say what he is?

PEER.   What he is? Quite easily.
He is himself.

BEGRIFFENFELDT [*with a leap*]. Ha, the answer to the riddle of life
Flashed across my eyes like lightning!
You're absolutely sure he's himself?

PEER. Well, that's what he says, at any rate.

BEGRIFFENFELDT. Himself. Revolution is at hand!

[*He takes off his hat.*]

May I know your name?

PEER.   I was christened Peer Gynt.

BEGRIFFENFELDT [*in quiet admiration*].
Peer Gynt! An allegory! I might have guessed.—
Peer Gynt? Which means, of course, the Unknown,
The arrival, whose coming was foretold me—

PEER. Is that so? You mean you came here to meet—?

BEGRIFFENFELDT. Peer Gynt! Profound! Mysterious! Penetrating!
Each word is a fathomless pit of knowledge!
What are you?

PEER [*modestly*].   I've always attempted to be
Myself. For the rest, you can see my passport.

BEGRIFFENFELDT. Again, you see, that mysterious word!

[*Grasping his wrists.*]

To Cairo! Revelation's Emperor is found!

PEER. Emperor?

BEGRIFFENFELDT. Come!

PEER.   Am I really known—?

BEGRIFFENFELDT [*dragging* PEER *along with him*].
Revelation's Emperor—enthroned on Self!

[*In Cairo. A large courtyard surrounded by high walls and buildings.
Barred windows; iron cages.*
THREE KEEPERS *in the courtyard.* A FOURTH *enters.*]

NEWCOMER. Schafmann; have you seen the director?

A KEEPER. He drove out long before it was light.

1ST KEEPER. I think he has been upset by something,
Because last night—

ANOTHER.   Sh! Be quiet;
He's here at the door!

[BEGRIFFENFELDT *leads* PEER GYNT *in, locks the gate and puts the key in
his pocket.*]

PEER [*to himself*].   He really is
A wonderfully gifted man; almost
All he says is incomprehensible.

[*He looks round him.*]

So this, then, is the Scholars' Club?

BEGRIFFENFELDT. Yes, you'll find the whole lot of them here;—
The Circle of the Seventy Commentators;
Recently increased by a hundred and sixty—

[*Calling to the* KEEPERS.]

Mickel, Schlingelberg, Schafmann, Fuchs,—
Get into the cages; hurry, now!

KEEPERS. We?

BEGRIFFENFELDT. Who else? Come along, come along!
It's a twizzling world; we must twizzle with it!

[*Forcing them into the cages.*]

He arrived this morning, the mighty Peer;—
You must join the rest;—I needn't say more.

[*He locks the cage and throws the key into a well.*]

PEER. But, my dear Herr Doctor and Director—?

BEGRIFFENFELDT. Neither one nor the other! I used to be.—
Herr Peer, can you keep a secret?
There's something I want to get off my mind—

PEER [*increasingly uneasy*]. What is it?

BEGRIFFENFELDT.   Promise me not to tremble.

PEER. I'll do my best—

BEGRIFFENFELDT [*drawing him into a corner and whispering*].
                    Absolute Reason
Dropped dead last night at eleven o'clock.

PEER. God save us—!

BEGRIFFENFELDT.   Yes, it's most deplorable.
And in my position, as you can imagine,
Doubly unfortunate; because
Up to now this institution
Has been what is called a mad-house.

PEER.   A mad-house!

BEGRIFFENFELDT. Not now, you understand!

PEER [*pale, quietly*].   I realize
At last what this place is! And the man
Is a lunatic;—and no one knows it!

                    [*He tries to move away.*]

BEGRIFFENFELDT [*following him*].
I hope you have followed my meaning so far?
When I say 'dropped dead' I'm talking nonsense.
He's beside himself. Jumped out of his skin,—
Like my compatriot Münchhausen's fox.

PEER. Excuse me a moment—

BEGRIFFENFELDT [*holding on to him*]. I mean like an eel;—
Not like a fox. Impaled through his eye;—
He writhed on the wall—

PEER.   How can I save myself?

BEGRIFFENFELDT. A nick in the neck, and off comes his skin!

PEER. Demented! Utterly off his head!

BEGRIFFENFELDT. Now it's evident, and can't be kept hidden,—
This *Von-Sich-Gehen* must result
In complete revolution on land and sea.
The individuals once called mad
In fact became normal last night at eleven,
To conform with the new conditions of Reason.
And, if you look deeply into the matter,
It's apparent that at the aforesaid time
The so-called intelligent started to rave.

PEER. Talking of time, my time is limited—

BEGRIFFENFELDT. Your time? You've reminded me of something!

[*He opens a door and calls.*]

Come out! The future has been revealed!
Reason is dead. Long live Peer Gynt!

PEER. No, my dear chap—!

[*The* LUNATICS *gather one by one in the courtyard.*]

BEGRIFFENFELDT.   Come and pay your respects;
Greet the rosy dawn of deliverance—
Your Emperor is here!

PEER.   Their Emperor?

BEGRIFFENFELDT. Certainly!

PEER.   This is too great an honour,
Far too much—

BEGRIFFENFELDT. Don't let false modesty
Affect you at a time like this.

PEER. But let me consider! No, I'm not the answer
You've stupefied me!

BEGRIFFENFELDT.   What, a man
Who has solved the mystery of the Sphinx?
Who is Himself?

PEER.   That's just the trouble.
I am myself, in every respect.
But here, if I understand, it's all
A matter of being beside yourself.

BEGRIFFENFELDT. You're making a curious mistake.
Here, a man's himself with a vengeance;
Himself, and nothing else whatsoever;—
The self full sail, full speed ahead.
Each one shut up in the cask of self,
Immersed in a fermentation of self,
Hermetically sealed with the bung of self,
The barrel pickled in a bath of self.
No one has tears for other men's pain;
No one accepts other men's notions.
We're ourselves here, thought, word and deed,
Ourselves right to the edge of the diving-board,—
And so, now we come to elect an Emperor,
You are obviously the perfect man.

PEER. Devil take it—!

BEGRIFFENFELDT.   Now don't be downhearted;
Most things on earth are new to begin with.
'One's self';—come; let me give an example;
I'll pick one out at random for you—

                    [*To a gloomy figure.*]

Good day, Huhu! Well, my lad,
Still walking around looking miserable?

HUHU. What else can I do when generations
Of people die one after another
Without having themselves explained?

                    [*To* PEER GYNT.]

You're new in this place; would you like to hear?

PEER [*bowing*]. By all means!

HUHU.   Lend an ear, then.—
In the East, the Malabaric beaches
Clasp the sea like a golden girdle.
Portuguese and Dutchmen grip
The countryside with their own culture.

Swarms of genuine Malabaris
Live there, too. And so the language
Got itself in a hopeless muddle;—
Now they're in control of the country,
But at one time, long ago,
The ruler was the orangoutang.
He was the master of the forest,
Free to flail around and snarl
Just as the hand of nature made him;
He could bare his teeth and gawp
And scream away to his heart's content,
Top dog in his own kingdom.—
Alas, then the foreign invaders
Ruined the old language of the jungle.
Four hundred years of unbroken night
Brooded over the monkey world;
And, as we know, a night of that length
Leaves its mark on a population.—
The ancient forest voice is silent;
Not so much as a growl is heard there;—
But if we want to express our thoughts
We have to have speech to help us do it.
No one can avoid the problem.
The Dutchmen or the Portuguese,
Mixed races like the Malabari,
They're all of them in the same boat.—
I've been trying to fight a battle
For our authentic forest lingo,
To reinvigorate the corpse,—
Asserting the people's right to shriek,—
Shrieked myself, to urge the need
For shrieking in folk-literature.—
And small thanks I've had for it.—
Perhaps now you can understand
My worry. Thanks for listening;—
If you've any advice I'd welcome it!

PEER [*to himself*]. The saying is: when wolves are about
It's best to howl. [*Aloud.*]
            As I remember

Dear friend, in the Moroccan scrub
There's a tribe of orangoutangs
Who do without any spokesmen or poets;
Their language decidedly Malabarish!—
Charming and unimpeachable,—
Now if you, like other notables,
Went overseas, for the good of your country—

HUHU. Thanks, for paying such close attention;—
I'll do exactly as you say.—

[*With an expansive gesture.*]

The East has dispossessed its poets.
The West still has its orangoutangs! [*He goes.*]

BEGRIFFENFELDT. Now, was he himself? I should say he was.
Full of himself, not another thing,
Himself in every syllable,—
Himself because he's beside himself.
Come here! I'll show you another one,
Who since last night is equally rational.

[*To a* FELLAH *with a mummy on his back.*]

King Apis, how are you doing, Your Highness?

FELLAH [*to* PEER]. *Am* I King Apis?

PEER [*getting behind the doctor*]. I regret to say
I haven't quite grasped the situation;
But, from your manner, I can well believe it—

FELLAH. You are lying, as well.

BEGRIFFENFELDT.   Your Royal Highness
Should tell us just how the matter stands.

FELLAH. I'll tell you, then.
            [*To* PEER GYNT.] Do you observe
Who it is I'm carrying on my back?
He used to be called King Apis; now
He goes under the name of mummy;
What's more, he is altogether dead.

He erected all the pyramids,
And hewed out the Great Sphinx,
And fought, as the doctor would say,
Rechts and *links* against the Turk.
Because of that the whole of Egypt
Has adored him as a god,
And set him up in all the temples
In the likeness of a bull.
     But *I'm* King Apis; that's as clear
As daylight to me. If you can't
Understand me yet, you will.
You see, one day when King Apis
Was out hunting he dismounted
And went off by himself for a while,
On to my great-grandfather's land.
     But the field that King Apis dunged
Yielded the corn I was nourished on;
And, if you want any further proof,
I can tell you I've got invisible horns.
Don't you think it's iniquitous
That nobody recognizes my power?
By birth I am Apis, of the land of Egypt,
But people think I'm only a peasant.—
Tell me what I should do; give me
Your honest advice;—the problem is how
To become more like King Apis the Great.

PEER. Your Highness will have to build pyramids,
     And carve an even greater Sphinx,
     And fight, as the doctor would say,
     Rechts and *links* against the Turk.

FELLAH. Oh, yes, it's all very well to talk!
     A peasant! A poor starving louse!
     I've enough to do keeping my hut
     Clear of rats and mice.—Quick, man,—
     Think of something better than that,
     A way to make me great and secure;—
     And, what's more, identical
     With King Apis here on my back!

PEER. Suppose Your Highness should hang yourself.
And then, in the bosom of the earth
Within the coffin's natural frontiers,
Remain immaculately dead?

FELLAH. So I will! My life for a halter!
Off to the gallows with flesh and blood!—
At first it will seem rather different,
But time will soon take care of that.

[*He goes to prepare to hang himself.*]

BEGRIFFENFELDT. There's a personality for you,—
A man of method—

PEER.   Yes, yes; I see;—
But he really means to hang himself!
God save us! I shall be sick;—
My thoughts are out of control!

BEGRIFFENFELDT.   A question
Of readjustment; it won't last long.

PEER. Readjustment? To what? Excuse me,—
I have to leave here—

BEGRIFFENFELDT [*restraining him*]. Are you mad?

PEER. Not yet.— Mad? Heaven forbid!

[*Uproar.* HUSSEIN, *a political minister, forces his way through the crowd.*]

HUSSEIN. I've been told an Emperor came here today.

[*To* PEER.]

Is it you?

PEER [*desperately*]. Yes, it's all been decided!

HUSSEIN. Good.—You have communications
Needing an answer?

PEER [*tearing his hair*]. Come on! That's right;—
The worse, the better!

HUSSEIN.   Will you do me
The honour of dipping me in the ink?

[*Bowing deeply.*]

I am a pen.

PEER [*bowing still lower*]. And I am simply
A crumpled sheet of imperial parchment.

HUSSEIN. My history, sire, is briefly this:
They think I'm a sand-box; I'm really a pen.

PEER. And mine, Mr. Pen, is very soon told:
I'm a piece of paper no one has written on.

HUSSEIN. Men haven't an inkling of what I am for;
They all want to use me for sprinkling sand!

PEER. When a woman owned me I was a book
With a silver clasp. Mad or sane
It's the same typographical error!

HUSSEIN. Imagine the frustration! To be a pen
And never feel the edge of a penknife.

PEER [*leaping high*]. Imagine: to be a buck, who leaps
From high in the air; comes plunging down,—
And never feels the ground under him!

HUSSEIN. A knife! I'm blunt;—cut me and slit me!
The world will be ruined if I'm not sharpened!

PEER. It's a pity the world, like all home-made things,
Was thought by God to be very good.

BEGRIFFENFELDT. Here's a knife!

HUSSEIN [*grabbing it*].   Ah, how I shall lap the ink!
What an ecstasy to slit oneself!

[*He cuts his throat.*]

BEGRIFFENFELDT [*moves to one side*]. Try not to spatter!

PEER [*in rising panic*].   Get hold of him!

HUSSEIN. Get hold of me! Yes, that's the word!
  Hold! Hold the pen! To a sheet of paper—!

[*He falls.*]

I'm worn out. Don't forget the postscript:
He lived and died a guided pen.

PEER [*fainting*]. What shall I—? What am I? O God—hold on!
  I'm whatever you want,—a Turk, a sinner,—
  A troll—; but help me; something has burst—!

[*He shrieks.*]

I can't for the moment think of your name;—
Help me, you—guardian of all madmen!

[*He sinks down unconscious.*]

BEGRIFFENFELDT [*with a wreath of straw in his hand, leaping astride him*].
  Now he's exalted into the mud;—
  He's beside himself—! His crowning moment!

[*He presses the wreath down on to* PEER GYNT'*s head and shouts:*]

Long life! Long live the Emperor Self!

SCHAFMANN [*in the cage*]. Es lebe hoch der grosse Peer!

ACT FIVE

On board a ship in the North Sea off the Norwegian coast. Sunset. Stormy weather.

PEER GYNT, *a vigorous old man with ice-grey hair and beard, is standing on the poop. He is dressed partly as a seaman, in a pea-jacket and high boots. His clothes are the worse for wear; he himself is weather-beaten and his expression harder. The* CAPTAIN *is standing beside the* HELMSMAN *at the wheel. The* CREW *is for'ard.*

PEER [*leaning on the rail gazing towards the land*].
There's the Hallingskarv in its winter coat,
Parading itself in the evening sunlight.
And his brother Joekel leaning beside him,
Still with his green ice-jacket on.
And the Folgefonn: how superb she is,
Like a virgin asleep under snow-white linen.
Don't try any monkey-tricks, old men!
Stand still; remember you're made of granite.

CAPTAIN [*shouting for'ard*].
Two hands to the wheel—and loft the lantern!

PEER. It's blowing up rough.

CAPTAIN.   We're in for a storm.

PEER. Can you see the peaks of the Ronde from here?

CAPTAIN. Not a chance. They're away behind the snowfields.

PEER. Or the Blaahoy?

CAPTAIN.   No; but you can see
The peaks of Galdhoy from the rigging
On a clear day.

PEER.   Where's Haarteigen?

CAPTAIN [*pointing*]. Somewhere thereabouts.

PEER.   Yes, I thought so.

CAPTAIN. You seem familiar with these parts.

PEER. We sailed this way when I went abroad,
The last you swallow comes back first.

[*He spits and gazes at the coast.*]

Deep in there, in the blue shadows,
Where the valley blackens, like a narrow trench—
And below, beside the open fjords—
Isn't that where the people are tucked away?

[*He looks at the* CAPTAIN.]

The houses are spread out thin in this country.

CAPTAIN. Yes, they're few and far between.

PEER. Shall we make land before daybreak?

CAPTAIN.   Could do,
If the night doesn't bring dirty weather.

PEER. Thick cloud in the west.

CAPTAIN.   So I see.

PEER. When I come to settle up what I owe you,
Don't let me forget—I have a mind,
As the saying is, to contribute something
For the good of the crew.

CAPTAIN.   Thanks!

PEER.   It can't
Be much. I made a mint, but lost it.
Fate and I were at loggerheads.
You know what I've got on board, and that's
The lot; the rest has gone to the devil.

CAPTAIN. It's more than enough to impress your family
When you get back home.

PEER.   I've got no family.
No one's waiting for the rich old rascal.—
But it saves an emotional scene at the quayside!

CAPTAIN. Here comes the storm.

PEER.   Now, do remember,
  If any of the crew are really hard up
  I won't take too close a look at the money.

CAPTAIN. That's kind. Most of them find things difficult;
  They're all got wives and kids at home.
  Their pay alone doesn't go very far;
  But if they came back with something extra
  It would be a reunion they'd never forget.

PEER. What did you say? Wives and kids?
  Are they married?

CAPTAIN.   Married? Yes, all of 'em.
  But the cook is the one most badly off;
  Black hunger is seldom out of his house.

PEER. Married? They've someone waiting at home
  With a warm welcome? Eh?

CAPTAIN.   Why, yes,
  In their simple way.

PEER.   At night, unexpected,
  What then?

CAPTAIN. Somehow the wife would manage
  Some special treat.

PEER.   And light a lamp?

CAPTAIN. Or two, maybe; and schnapps with the supper.

PEER. And sit there snugly? Warm by the fire?
  The children with them? The room full of chatter;
  All talking at once, for the joy of the meeting?

CAPTAIN. Very likely. And all the more so
  Because of the kind suggestion you made
  Of a little extra—

PEER [*thumping the gunnel*]. I'm damned if I do it!
  Do you think I'm mad? Do you really expect me
  To fork out for other people's kids?
  I've slaved enough to earn what I've got!
  Nobody's waiting for old Peer Gynt.

A11

CAPTAIN. Well, please yourself; it's your own money.

PEER. You're right! It's mine, and nobody else's.
As soon as we drop anchor I'll pay
My cabin passage from Panama.
Then a drink for the crew, and that's the lot.
If I give any more you can beat me up!

CAPTAIN. A receipt, not a thrashing, is what I shall owe you.
But excuse me; it's blowing up for a storm.

[*He goes across the deck. It is getting dark; lights are lit in the cabin. The sea gets rougher. Fog and thick clouds.*]

PEER. To have a cartload of kids at home,
Happy to be expecting you;
The thoughts of others for company.
There's no one at all who thinks of me.
A lamp on the table? I'll put that out.
I shall think of a way. I'll make them drunk;
Not one of the bastards will get ashore sober.
They shall greet their wives and children plastered,
Cursing and hammering on the table,
Scaring the family out of their wits!
The wives will run screaming out of the house,
Clutching the brats—all the pleasure shattered!

[*The ship gives a violent lurch.* PEER GYNT *staggers and almost loses his balance.*]

Well, that was a good heel-over. The sea
Couldn't work harder if it was paid to.
Still its old self in these northern waters,
Cross-currents headstrong and raging as ever!

[*He listens.*]

What was that yelling?

LOOK-OUT [*for'ard*].   A wreck to leeward!

CAPTAIN [*amidships, giving orders*].
Helm hard to starboard! Bring her up to the wind!

HELMSMAN. Are there men on the wreck?

LOOK-OUT. I can make out three.

PEER. Lower the boat—

CAPTAIN. One wave would swamp it.

[*He goes for'ard.*]

PEER. Why think about that?
[*To some of the* CREW.] If you're men, to the rescue!
What the hell does it matter if you get a soaking?

BO'SUN. It's impossible in a sea like this.

PEER. They're yelling again! Look, the wind has dropped—
Cook, will you risk it? Quick! I'll pay you—

COOK. Not if you gave me twenty pounds!

PEER. You dogs! Cowards! Don't you realize
They're men with wives and children at home
And waiting—

BO'SUN. Well, patience is a virtue.

CAPTAIN. Keep clear of that sea!

HELMSMAN. The wreck's gone under.

PEER. Suddenly, silence?

BO'SUN. If, as you say,
They were married, the world has got three new widows.

[*The storm increases.* PEER GYNT *goes aft.*]

PEER. There's no faith left among men any more;
No Christianity, as it used to be.
They do little good, and pray even less,
And have no respect for the powers above.—
In weather like this the Almighty's dangerous.
Those brutes should look out, and understand
It's risky playing with elephants.
But they openly snap their fingers at him!
He can't blame *me;* I was standing ready
To make the sacrifice, money in hand.
But what's my reward? The saying is:

'A clear conscience makes an easy pillow.'
Well, that may be true when you're on dry land,
But it's not worth a pinch of snuff at sea
Where a decent man is just one of the mob.
At sea you can't ever be yourself;
You must toe the line with the rest of the ship.
If the hour has struck for the bos'un and cook
I suppose I shall sink with the whole boiling;
One's personal merits count for nothing,
No more than a sausage at pig-sticking time.—
I've made the mistake of being too gentle,
And what thanks have I got for my trouble?
If I were younger I'd change my tactics
And try throwing my weight about a bit.
There's still time! They'll hear in the parish
Peer has come home again in triumph!
I'll get back the farm, by hook or by crook,
Rebuild it into a shining palace.
But I won't let anyone come inside!
They can stand at the gate, twisting their caps,
And beg and pray: there's no charge for that;
But nobody gets a penny of mine.
Since fate has thrashed *me* until I howled
I'll look for someone to thrash in return—

STRANGE PASSENGER [*standing in the dark beside* PEER GYNT *and speaking in
     a friendly way*]. Good evening!

PEER.   Good evening. What—? Who are you?

PASSENGER. Your fellow passenger, at your service.

PEER. Oh? I thought I was the only one.

PASSENGER. A wrong supposition, now rectified.

PEER. It's odd I haven't seen you before.

PASSENGER. I never come up on deck in the daytime.

PEER. You're ill, perhaps? You're as white as a sheet.

PASSENGER. Thank you, no—I'm perfectly fit.

PEER. It's a hell of a storm.

PASSENGER. Yes, what a blessing!

PEER. A blessing?

PASSENGER. The waves are as high as a house.
Doesn't it make your mouth water?
Think of the ships that are going to be wrecked,
And the number of bodies washed ashore!

PEER. Heaven forbid!

PASSENGER. Have you ever seen
A man strangled, or hanged—or drowned?

PEER. That's enough of that!

PASSENGER. The corpses laugh.
But the laughter is forced. The majority of them
Have taken a bite out of their tongues.

PEER. Keep away from me!

PASSENGER. Just one question!
If we, for example, ran on the rocks
And sank in the dark—

PEER. Is the danger likely?

PASSENGER. I don't really know how to answer that.
But suppose I should float, and you go to the bottom—

PEER. Absurd!

PASSENGER. It's just a possibility.
But when a man's on the edge of his grave
He weakens, and starts dealing out presents—

PEER [*putting his hand in his pocket*].
Ah, it's money you want!

PASSENGER. No it isn't;
But would you be so good as to make me
A gift of your esteemed cadaver?

PEER. Now you've gone too far!

PASSENGER. Simply the corpse!
For scientific research—

PEER.   Go away!

PASSENGER. My dear sir, it would be to your own advantage!
  I'll open you up to the light of day.
  I'm mainly looking for the seat of dreams,
  But I'll carefully probe every gusset of you.

PEER. Be off!

PASSENGER.   My dear chap—just a drowned body!

PEER. Blasphemer! You're encouraging the storm!
  It's too bad! We've already got wind and rain
  And a mountainous sea, every indication
  That we're not likely to make old bones,
  And you're doing your best to hurry it on!

PASSENGER. I see you're not in the mood for business,
  But, as you know, time brings its changes.

                    [*With a friendly bow.*]

  We shall meet when you're drowning, if not before.
  I may find you then in a better humour.

                    [*He goes into the cabin.*]

PEER. Sinister fellows, these scientists!
  Such Godless talk.

              [*To the* BO'SUN *as he passes.*]

                    A word with you, friend:
  That passenger? What lunatic is he?

BO'SUN. You're the only passenger that I know of.

PEER. Just me? This is going from bad to worse.

          [*To a* SHIP'S BOY *coming out of the cabin.*]

  Who just went down the companion-ladder?

BOY. The ship's dog, sir! [*He goes.*]

WATCH [*calling*].   Land close ahead!

PEER. My trunk! My cases! All baggage on deck!

BO'SUN. We've other things to attend to.

PEER. Captain!
It was all nonsense, only a joke—
Of course I'm willing to help the cook.

CAPTAIN. The jib has gone.

HELMSMAN. There goes the foresail!

BO'SUN [*shouting from for'ard*]. Breakers under the bow!

CAPTAIN. She's smashing up!

[*The ship strikes. Noise and confusion.*]

[*Close to land among the rocks and breakers. The ship is sinking. A dinghy with two men in it can be dimly seen through the fog. A wave breaks over it and swamps it; it overturns; a scream is heard; then everything silent for a while. Shortly afterwards the boat appears floating bottom upwards.*

PEER GYNT *comes to the surface near the boat.*]

PEER. Help! Send out a boat! Help! I'm drowning!
Save me, good Lord—as the prayer-book has it!

[*He clings on to the keel of the boat.*]

COOK [*coming up on the other side*].
Ah, heavenly Father—for my children's sake,
Have mercy! Let me get back to land!

[*He clings to the keel.*]

PEER. Let go!

COOK. Let go!

PEER. I'll fight!

COOK. So will I!

PEER. I'll push you under with my feet!
Get off! It won't carry both of us!

COOK. I know that. Give up!

PEER. You give up!

COOK. Oh, yes?

[*They fight; the* COOK's *hand is damaged; he clings on with the other one.*]

PEER. Take that hand away!

COOK. Oh, kind sir, spare me!
Remember my little ones at home!

PEER. I need life more than you: I still
Haven't got any children.

COOK. Let go! You've lived
Your time; I'm young!

PEER. Be quick and sink—
You're dragging us down.

COOK. Have mercy on me!
Let go in the name of God! You've no one
Who's going to miss you and grieve for you.

[*He screams and lets go.*]

I'm drowning!

PEER [*grabbing him*]. I'll hold you up by the hair—
Say the Lord's prayer!

COOK. I can't remember—
Everything's going dark—

PEER. Repeat
The important bits!

COOK. 'Give us this day—'

PEER. Skip that, cook; you're going to get
As much as you can swallow.

COOK. 'Give us this day—'

PEER. The same old song! You're a cook all right.

[*The* COOK *slips from his grasp.*]

COOK [*singing*]. 'Give us this day our—'

[*He goes under.*]

PEER.   Amen, my boy!
   You remained yourself to your last gasp.

                [He swings himself up on to the boat.]

   While there's any life there's hope.

PASSENGER *[catching hold of the boat].*
   Good morning!

PEER.   Hell!

PASSENGER.   I heard the shouting.
   It's amusing to come across you again.
   Well? You see, my prediction was true!

PEER. Let go! There's hardly room for one!

PASSENGER. I'm swimming with my left leg—
   Floating, with only my fingertips
   Touching the hull. But about your corpse—

PEER. Shut up!

PASSENGER.   The rest is over and done with.

PEER. Keep quiet, will you?

PASSENGER.   Just as you like. *[Silence.]*

PEER. Well?

PASSENGER. I'm keeping quiet.

PEER.   You demon!
   What do you mean to do, then?

PASSENGER.   Wait.

PEER *[tearing his hair].*
   I shall go mad! What are you?

PASSENGER *[nodding].*   Friendly.

PEER. What else? Tell me!

PASSENGER.   What do you think?
   Who else do you know like me?

PEER.   The devil!

PASSENGER [*quietly*]. Does he usually carry the lantern
  On life's way through the night of fear?

PEER. I'm catching on! When we get down to it
  You mean you're a messenger of light?

PASSENGER. Friend, have you even once in six months
  Felt the reality of dread?

PEER. When a man's in danger, naturally
  He's afraid; but your words have a twist to them—

PASSENGER. Yes. Have you even once in your life
  Known the victory fear can give you?

PEER [*looking at him*]. If you came to open a door for me
  It's a pity you didn't come a bit sooner.
  What's the sense in choosing a time
  When the sea is about to swallow us up?

PASSENGER. The victory would be greater, you think,
  If you sat in comfort beside the fire?

PEER. Maybe not, but your talk was ridiculous.
  What effect did you think it could have?

PASSENGER. Where I come from the comic style
  Is valued as highly as the pathetic.

PEER. There's a time for everything; what floats
  A publican, as the saying goes,
  Would scupper a bishop.

PASSENGER.   The multitude
  Whose dust sleeps in the grave, don't wear
  The tragic mask day in, day out.

PEER. Leave me, you nightmare! Disappear!
  I don't want to die! I must get to land!

PASSENGER. As for that, don't worry; a fellow doesn't
  Die in the middle of the fifth act.

[*He glides away.*]

PEER. So I got it out of him at last.
  What an unpleasant moralizer!

[*A churchyard in a high mountain parish. A funeral.* A PRIEST *and*
PARISHIONERS. *The last verse of a psalm is being sung.* PEER GYNT
passes on the road.]

PEER [*at the gate*]. Here's a man going the way of all flesh.
 Praise be to God it isn't me.

[*He enters the churchyard.*]

PRIEST [*speaking at the graveside*].
 And now, when the soul has gone its way to judgement,
 And the flesh reposes here like an empty pod,
 Now, dear friends, we have a word to say
 About this dead man's journeying on earth.
  He wasn't rich, or of great understanding;
 His voice was small, he had no manly bearing;
 He gave his opinions shyly, uncertainly;
 Was scarcely master in his own house.
 In church, he walked like someone who would ask
 Permission to sit there among the others.
  He came from the Gudbrands valley, as you know.
 When he settled here he was hardly more than a boy;
 And you all remember how, up to the last,
 He always kept his right hand in his pocket.
  This right hand in the pocket was the thing
 That impressed the man's image on one's mind;
 And also the uneasiness, the shy
 Reticence when he walked into the room.
  But though he preferred to go his quiet way,
 And though he seemed a stranger here among us,
 You all know (though he tried hard to conceal it)
 There were only four fingers on the hand he hid.—
  I remember, on a morning many years ago,
 A meeting at Lunde to enrol recruits.
 It was war-time. Everybody was discussing
 The country's ordeal, and what lay ahead.
  I stood watching. Sitting behind the table
 Was the Captain, the parish clerk and some N.C.O.s.
 They took the measure of one boy after another,
 Swore them in and took them for the army.
 The room was full, and outside you could hear
 The crowd of young men laughing in the yard.

Then a name was shouted. Another lad came forward,
Looking as pale as the snow on a glacier.
They called him nearer; he approached the table;
A piece of rag was tied round his right hand.
He gasped, swallowed, groped about for words,
But couldn't speak, in spite of the Captain's order.
However, his cheeks burning, stammering still
And speaking very quickly, he managed at last
To mumble something about an accidental
Slip of a scythe that sheared his finger off.
Silence fell on the room, as soon as he said it.
Men exchanged looks, and their lips tightened.
They all stoned the boy with silent stares.
He felt the hail-storm, but he didn't see it.
The Captain, an elderly, grey-haired man, stood up,
Spat, pointed a finger, and said Get out!
And the boy went. Everyone drew aside
So that he had to run the gauntlet between them.
He got as far as the door, then took to his heels
• Up and off, across the fields and hillside,
Scrambling on over the shale and rocks,
To where his home was, high on the mountainside.
Six months later he came to live down here
With a mother, a newborn child, and his wife-to-be.
He leased a plot of ground way up on the hill
Where the derelict land joins the parish of Lom.
He married as soon as he could; put up a house;
Ploughed the stony ground, and made his way,
As the waving gold of the little fields bore witness.
At church he kept his right hand in his pocket,
But back at home no doubt those nine fingers
Did the work of other people's ten.—
One spring a flood carried it all away.
Only their lives were spared. Everything lost,
He set to work to make another clearing,
And by the autumn smoke rose up again
From a hillside farm, this time better sheltered.
Sheltered? Yes, from flood; but not from glaciers.
Two years later it all lay under the snow.
Yet not even an avalanche could crack his courage.

He dug, and cleared, and carted away the debris,
And before the next winter-snows came drifting
His little house was built for the third time.
   He had three sons, three fine vigorous boys;
They should go to school, but the school was a long way off.
They could only reach the end of the valley road
By going through a narrow, precipitous pass.
What did he do? The eldest looked after himself
As best he could, and where the track dropped steeply
This man roped him round to give him support;
The others he bore in his arms and on his back.
   He toiled like this, year after year, until
The sons were men. Time, you would have thought,
To get some return. Three prosperous gentlemen
In the New World have managed to forget
Their Norwegian father and those journeys to school.
   His horizon was narrow. Apart from the few
Who were nearest to him, nothing else existed.
The ringing words that rouse other men's hearts
Meant nothing to him, more than a tinkle of bells.
Mankind, the fatherland, the highest ambitions
Of men, were only misty figures to him.
   But he had humility, humility, this man;
And after that call-up day he always carried
The shame of the verdict, as surely as his cheeks
Carried the burn of shyness, and his four
Fingers hid in his pocket.—An offender
Against the laws of the land? Yes, indeed!
But there's one thing that shines above the law,
As truly as the bright tent of Glitretind
Has even higher peaks of cloud above it.
He was a poor patriot. To State
And Church, an unproductive tree. But there
On the brow of the hill, within the narrow
Circle of family, where his work was done,
There he was great, because he was himself.
He matched up to the living sound he was born with.
His life was like a music on muted strings.
   So peace be with you, silent warrior,
Who strove and fell in the peasant's little war!

We won't try to probe the ways of his heart.
That's for his Maker, not for us, to do.
But I can hold this hope, with little doubt:
He is not maimed now as he stands before his God.

[*The* CONGREGATION *disperses and goes. Only* PEER GYNT *is left.*]

PEER. Now that's what I call Christianity!
Nothing unpleasant to jar the mind;
And the theme—to be your unshakeable self,
Which was central to his argument—
Was, on the whole, just as uplifting.

[*Looking down into the grave.*]

Was it he who hacked through his knuckle, I wonder,
That day I was chopping trees in the forest?
Who knows? If I wasn't standing here
With my stick by the grave of this kindred spirit,
I could believe it was I who slept
In a living dream, hearing my praises.—
It's a good and generous Christian habit
To throw a benevolent backward glance
Over the life of the departed.
I wouldn't at all mind being judged
By such an excellent parish priest.
Well, I dare say there's enough time left
Before the gravedigger asks me in;
Leave well alone, as the scriptures say;
And 'Cross your bridge when you come to it'—
And 'Don't pay for your funeral till you've had it'.
The Church, after all, is the true consoler.
I didn't appreciate that before;
But now I can see how soothing it is
To be reassured, on the best authority,
That as you sow, so shall you reap.—
You must be yourself: look after yourself
And yours, in small things as well as great.
If luck goes against you, at least there's the comfort
That you lived according to the instructions.—
Now home! Though the road is steep and narrow
And Fate ironical to the last,

Old Peer Gynt will gang his own gait
And be what he is: poor but virtuous.

[*He goes.*]

[*A hillside with a dried river-bed. A mill in ruins beside the river;
the ground torn up; desolation all around. Higher up a large farmhouse. An auction is going on in front of the house. A large crowd,
drinking noisily.*

PEER GYNT *is sitting on a heap of stones by the mill.*]

PEER. Forward or back, it's the same distance;
Out or in, it's equally narrow.
Time consumes, and rivers erode.
Go round and about, said the Boyg.—You have to
Here!

A MAN IN MOURNING. Now only the rubbish is left.

[*He sees* PEER GYNT.]

Strangers, as well? God bless you, friend.

PEER. Well met. This place is lively today
Is it a christening or a wedding?

MAN IN MOURNING. Better to call it a house-warming.
The bride is lying in a bed of worms.

PEER. And the worms are fighting over what's left.

MAN IN MOURNING. It's all finished now. The end of the song.

PEER. All songs wind up in the same way;
And I sang them all when I was a boy.

A TWENTY-YEAR-OLD [*with a casting-ladle*].
Here, look at the fine thing I've bought!
Peer Gynt made silver buttons in this.

ANOTHER. How about this? A ha'penny for the money-bag!

A THIRD. That all? The pedlar's pack was tuppence!

PEER. Peer Gynt? Who was *he*?

MAN IN MOURNING. He was part of the life
Of the dead woman and Aslak the smith.

A MAN IN GREY. You're forgetting me! Are you drunk and stupid?

MAN IN MOURNING. You're forgetting the door of the storehouse at Haegstad!

MAN IN GREY. That's true; but you've never been very particular.

MAN IN MOURNING. As long as she don't make a fool out of Death—

MAN IN GREY. Come on, brother! Let's drink to our fellowship!

MAN IN MOURNING. Fellowship be damned. You're pissed already.

MAN IN GREY. Nonsense. Blood's not so thin we don't
  Know we're all a part of Peer Gynt.

                       [Takes him off with him.]

PEER [*to himself*]. I seem to have come on some old acquaintances.

A BOY [*calling after the* MAN IN MOURNING].
  Your poor old mother will be after you, Aslak,
  If you drink too much!

PEER [*getting up*].   That old country saying
  Doesn't hold good in this neighbourhood:
  'The deeper you dig the better the smell.'

A BOY [*with a bear skin*].
  Look, the Cat of Dovre! Well, only the skin.
  The one that chased the trolls away
  On Christmas Eve.

ANOTHER [*with a reindeer skull*]. Here's the marvellous
  Buck that carried Peer Gynt on its back
  Along the razor-edge of the Gjendin.

A THIRD [*with a hammer, shouting at the* MAN IN MOURNING].
  Hey, Aslak, remember this sledge-hammer?
  Isn't it the one that you were using
  When the Devil flew up and split the ceiling?

FOURTH [*empty-handed*]. Matt Moen, here's the invisible cloak
  Peer Gynt and Ingrid flew through the air in.

PEER. Give me some brandy! I'm feeling old;
  I'll hold an auction of all my junk!

A BOY. What have you got to auction?

PEER.   A palace;
Solidly built, up in the Ronde.

BOY. A button is bid!

PEER.   Why not make it a schnapps?
A terrible shame to bid less than that.

ANOTHER. He's a humorist, this old man!

PEER [*shouts*].   My horse,
Greycoat,—who bids?

ONE IN THE CROWD. Where is he?

PEER.   Away
In the west by the sunset! He can gallop
As fast—as fast as Peer Gynt could lie.

VOICES. What else is there?

PEER.   Gold and scrap metal!
Bought with a shipwreck; I'll sell at a loss.

A BOY. Put it up!

PEER.   First lot: a dream
About a book with a silver clasp.
I'll let it go for a hook and eye.

BOY. To hell with dreams!

PEER.   Second lot: my Empire!
I'll throw it to the crowd; you can scramble for it!

BOY. And the crown with it?

PEER.   Of lovely straw,
It will fit the first man who puts it on.
And here's still more! An addled egg!
A madman's grey hair! A prophet's beard!
All these to whoever shows me a signpost
That says: This is the road to go!

BAILIFF [*who has come up*].
The way you're behaving, my man, your road
Is going to lead you straight to the lock-up.

B11

PEER [*hat in hand*]. Most likely. But, tell me, who was Peer Gynt?

BAILIFF. Come off it—

PEER.   No, really, I want to know.

BAILIFF. An appalling story-teller, they say.

PEER. Story-teller?

BAILIFF.   Yes—he pretended
  He'd done every mighty thing in the book.
  But, excuse me, I've other things to do—

[*He goes.*]

PEER. And where is he now, this remarkable man?

OLDER MAN. He went overseas to a foreign land;
  And came off badly, as you might expect.
  A long time ago now he was hanged.

PEER. Hanged? Well, well! I thought as much;
  Poor Peer Gynt was himself to the last.

[*He bows.*]

Goodbye—and thanks for the pleasant day!

[*He walks a few steps and stops again.*]

Well, boys and girls, by way of return
Would you like to hear a traveller's tale?

SEVERAL. Yes, can you tell one?

PEER.   Nothing can stop me.

[*He comes nearer; a strange look comes over him.*]

I was digging for gold in San Francisco.
The whole town was swarming with mountebanks.
One played the fiddle with his toes;
One danced a fandango on his knees;
Another, I heard, went on reciting
While a hole was being bored through his skull.
This motley lot were joined by the Devil,
To try his luck, like so many others.

His line was this: to be able to grunt
Convincingly like a real pig.
His personality drew the crowd
Even though they didn't know who he was.
The house was full; expectation high.
With a swirl of his cloak he took the stage;
Man muss sich drappieren, as the Germans say.
But under his cloak—nobody knew it—
He had managed to smuggle in a pig.
And now he started on his performance.
The Devil pinched, and the pig sang out.
It was all a kind of extravaganza
On porcine life, enslaved and free:
The finale a squeal, as the creature is butchered;
After which the performer bowed low and withdrew.—
The experts started appraising the act:
The artistic effect was condemned and praised;
Some found the vocal quality thin;
Others considered the death-shriek too studied;
But everybody agreed, *qua* grunt,
The performance was grossly overdone.—
So that's what he got for being a fool
And failing to gauge the taste of his public.

[*He bows and leaves. An uncertain silence falls over the crowd.*]

———————————

[*Whitsun Eve. Deep in the forest. A little way off, in a clearing, a cottage with reindeer horns over the door.*
    PEER GYNT *on his hands and knees looking for wild onions in the undergrowth.*]

PEER. This is one stage of the journey. Where next?
    Try everything, and then choose the best.
    Which is what I've done—starting with Caesar,
    And all down the scale to Nebuchadnezzar.
    So I *couldn't* leave Biblical history out.
    The old boy has had to run back to his mother.
    'From earth art thou come', as they say in the scriptures.
    The main purpose in life is filling the belly.
    Fill it with onions? That isn't much good;

I shall have to be cunning and set some traps.
There's a stream of water, I shan't be thirsty,
And at least I rank first in the animal world.
And when I die—which I shall, most likely—
I'll crawl under a fallen tree,
Heap dead leaves over me, as a bear does,
And scratch on the tree-trunk in big letters:
Here lies Peer Gynt, that decent fellow,
Emperor of all the other animals.
Emperor? [*He laughs inwardly.*]
           You soothsaying jackass!
You're no Emperor; you're an onion.
Now I shall peel you, good old Peer!
It won't help, either, to cry for mercy.

[*He takes the onion and peels off the layers.*]

Off with the outer, tattered layer;
The shipwrecked man hanging on to the boat.
Here's the passenger, shabby and thin,
But the taste has a hint of the real Peer Gynt.
And, inside that, the gold-digging me;
The juice has gone—if it ever had any.
This coarse bit here, with the thick skin,
Is the fur-trapper from Hudson Bay.
The next bit looks like a crown; many thanks!
We'll throw that away without further comment.
Now the ancient-historian, brief but vigorous.
This one's the prophet, fresh and sappy,
Stinking of lies, as they say, enough
To make an honest man's eyes water.
This veil, which rolls so smoothly off,
Is the gentleman living in luxury.
The next seems sick. It's got black streaks:
The black represents either priest or nigger.

[*He pulls several layers off at once.*]

What a tremendous number of layers!
Will the heart of it never come to light?

[*He pulls the whole onion to pieces.*]

My God, no, it won't! Right to the centre
It's all made of layers—but smaller and smaller.
Nature is witty! [*He throws the rest away.*]
             To hell with brooding!
Trudging round your thoughts you can come a cropper.
Well, that's not something that need worry me
Since I'm already down on all fours.

                [*Scratching his neck.*]

A peculiar business, this whole affair!
Life, they say, has a card up its sleeve.
But it disappears when you try to take it,
And you've something else in your hand—or nothing.

   [*He has come near to the hut, suddenly sees it and starts.*]

This hut? On the moor—! Ha! [*Rubs his eyes.*] It's just
As if I had known it before at some time.—
The reindeer horns branching over the door!
A mermaid, fish from the navel downwards!
Lies! There's no mermaid—Nails, planks,
And a lock to keep out hobgoblin thoughts . . . !

SOLVEIG [*singing inside*].
          Now all is ready for Whitsun Eve,
            Distant lover, dearest and best:
              Will you come back soon?
            Is the burden so very great?
              Take time to rest.
             I still shall wait
         Here as I promised, under the moon.

PEER [*getting up, quiet and deathly pale*].
One has remembered—and one has forgotten.
One has squandered, and one has saved,
O truth! And time can't be redeemed!
O terror! Here's where my empire was!

      [*He runs away down the forest path.*]

          ——————

[*Night. A heath; fir-trees. A forest fire has been raging; charred
tree-trunks for miles around. White trails of mist here and there over
the ground.*
   PEER GYNT *runs across the heath.*]

PEER. Scuds of fog, dust in the wind,
   And ashes—here's enough to build with!
   Stench and decay at the centre of it:
   All a whited sepulchre.
   The pyramid is founded on
   Fantasy, dreams, and still-born knowledge;
   And over them the edifice
   Goes up and up in steps of lies.
   Truth scorned, repentance shunned,
   Flaunt like a banner at the summit,
   And sound the trump of doomsday with their
   'Petrus Gyntus Caesar fecit!' [*He listens.*]
   Why are children's voices weeping?
   Weeping, and yet almost singing.—
   And balls of yarn roll at my feet!

[*Kicking.*]

   Get out of the road! You're in my way!

BALLS OF YARN [*on the ground*].
            We are thoughts:
            You should have thought us,
            Taught us
            How to use our legs!

PEER [*going round them*].
   I gave my life to one thought only—
   A botched-up job, with a crooked shinbone!

BALLS OF YARN.   We should have soared aloft
            Like ringing voices—
            Instead we have become
            Grey balls of yarn.

PEER [*stumbling*]. Bundle! You damned underling!
   Trying to trip up your father, are you?

[*He runs from them.*]

WITHERED LEAVES [*flying before the wind*].
            We are the password
            You should have given!
            Look how your lethargy

Stripped us to skeletons.
Worms have devoured us
Down to the veins;
We have never held fruit
In our cupped green hands.

PEER. But still, you haven't been born for nothing.
Lie quiet on the ground, and make good compost.

A SIGHING IN THE AIR.

We are songs;
You should have sung us!
Thousands of times
You have stifled us.
We have been waiting
Under your heart,
But were never sent for.
Death to your voice!

PEER. And death to you, you ludicrous jingle!
What time did I have for versifying?

[*He tries to take a short cut.*]

DEWDROPS [*dripping from the branches*].

We are the tears
You never let fall.
We could have melted
The skewering ice.
But the point has gone
Far into your breast,
And the flesh closed up.
We can do nothing now.

PEER. Thanks; I wept in the Ronde mountain,
And ended up with a tail of woe.

BROKEN STRAWS.   We are the deeds
That you left undone.
Doubt, like a strangler,
Choked and destroyed us.
On Judgement Day
We shall come crowding

And tell all we know—
You'll pay for it then!

PEER. Scoundrels! How dare you indict me
Because of things I *haven't* done?

[*He hurries away from them.*]

AASE'S VOICE [*far away*].
Lord, what a reckless driver!
Hey, you've tipped me over!
There's snow on the ground, my boy.
I'm smothered and rolled in flour.
You brought me the wrong road.
Eh, son? Where's the castle?
The Devil has nousled you
With that stick out of the cupboard!

PEER. The sooner I'm out of here the better.
If a chap has to carry the sins of the Devil
He wouldn't take long to be flat on the ground.
One's own weigh quite enough, without that.

[*He runs off.*]

————————

[*Another part of the heath.*]

PEER [*sings*]. Sexton! Sexton! What are you at?
Sing of what lying under the sod is!
A piece of crêpe round the brim of the hat—
I've a host of dead, and follow their bodies!

[*The* BUTTONMOULDER, *with his box of tools and a large casting-ladle, comes from a side path.*]

BUTTONMOULDER. Well met, good old man!

PEER.   Good evening, friend!

BUTTONMOULDER. The man's in a hurry. Where is he off to?

PEER. To a wake.

BUTTONMOULDER. Indeed? I don't see very well;
Excuse me, your name wouldn't be Peer?

PEER. Peer Gynt, as they say.

BUTTONMOULDER. What a piece of luck!
Peer Gynt is the man I was sent to find.

PEER. Really? What do you want?

BUTTONMOULDER. I'll tell you.
I'm a buttonmoulder. You have to go
Into my ladle.

PEER. Why into your ladle?

BUTTONMOULDER. To be melted down.

PEER. Melted down?

BUTTONMOULDER. Here it is, well scoured and empty.
Your grave is dug, your coffin reserved.
The worms will luxuriate in your carcass,
But my orders are to fetch your soul
On my master's behalf, as soon as I can.

PEER. Impossible! Not like this, without warning!

BUTTONMOULDER. It's an old custom with births and deaths
To choose the festive day in secret
Without informing the guest of honour.

PEER. Yes, of course.—I'm a bit confused.
You are—?

BUTTONMOULDER. I told you: a buttonmoulder.

PEER. I understand! A favourite child
Has a lot of nicknames. Well, then, Peer:
So this is where you're ending up!
But it's grossly unfair treatment, old chap!
I know I deserve more consideration;
I'm not as bad as you seem to think;
I've done a great deal of good in the world.
At the very worst you can say I'm a bungler,
But certainly not an exceptional sinner.

BUTTONMOULDER. No, that's exactly the complication.
Not a sinner at all, in the deeper sense;

Which is why you're excused the pains of torment,
And arrive, like others, in the casting-ladle.

PEER. Call it what you like—ladle or limbo;
Mild or bitter, they're both still beer.
Get behind me, Satan!

BUTTONMOULDER.   Are you being so rude
As to think I trot round on a horse's hoof?

PEER. On a horse's hoof or a fox's claws—
Clear off; and be careful what you get up to!

BUTTONMOULDER. There seems to be some misapprehension.
We're both in a hurry, so, to save time,
I'll try and explain what it's all about.
You're not—as you yourself have said—
A sinner on any heroic scale;
Not really even mediocre—

PEER. Now you're talking sense.

BUTTONMOULDER.   Just wait a minute.
To call you good would be going too far—

PEER. I never laid claim to any such thing.

BUTTONMOULDER. Neither one nor the other, merely so-so.
Sinners of really impressive stature
Aren't to be met with nowadays.
It takes more than paddling in the dirt;
It takes strength and a serious mind to sin.

PEER. Yes, I agree with all you say;
One must go full blast, like the old Berserks.

BUTTONMOULDER. But you, on the contrary, took sin lightly.

PEER. On the surface, friend, like a splash of mud.

BUTTONMOULDER. We begin to agree. Fire and brimstone
Aren't the things for a mud-splashed man.

PEER. And, therefore, I can go as I came?

BUTTONMOULDER. No; therefore, friend, I must melt you down.

PEER. What sort of tricks have you been inventing
  Here at home, while I've been away?

BUTTONMOULDER. A technique as old as the serpent in Eden,
  For keeping up the standard of values.
  You've worked at the craft; you know how often
  A casting turns out to be—if I
  May put it plainly—no better than shit.
  Sometimes the buttons had no eyelets.
  So what did you do?

PEER.   Threw the trash away.

BUTTONMOULDER. That's right; Jon Gynt was famous for squandering
  While there was anything left in his purse.
  But the Master, you see, is a thrifty one,
  Which is why he's become so immensely well-off.
  He doesn't throw anything away
  Which he thinks he can use as raw material.
  You were meant to be a glinting button
  On the world's coat, but the eyelet split;
  So you have to go into the reject-box,
  And merge with the masses, as they say.

PEER. You're not really intending to melt me down
  With Tom, Dick and Harry into something different?

BUTTONMOULDER. Yes, that's precisely what I *am* intending.
  We've done it plenty of times before.
  At Kongsberg they do the same thing with coins
  Which have worn smooth in circulation.

PEER. But this is nothing but sordid cheese-paring!
  My very dear friend, you must let me off!
  A smooth coin, an imperfect button—
  What's that to a man in your Master's position?

BUTTONMOULDER. Ah, but since, and so far as, the spirit is in you,
  There's always the value you have as metal.

PEER. No, I say, no! I'll fight tooth and nail!
  Anything, anything rather than that!

BUTTONMOULDER. But what? Come now, have some commonsense.
    You're not light enough to go up to heaven.

PEER. I'm easily pleased; I don't aim high;
    But I won't give up a grain of my Self.
    Put me on trial, as it's always done!
    Let me serve a term with him of the hoof—
    For a hundred years, if it has to be;
    I dare say that could be endured
    As it's only a matter of moral torment
    And therefore can't be so monumental.
    It's a metamorphosis, as the fox said
    When it was skinned; one waits; the hour
    Of deliverance comes; you fill in time,
    And look forward meanwhile to better days.
    But this other idea—to be absorbed
    Like a molecule into a foreign body—
    This ladle affair, this Gynt destruction,
    Rouses my innermost soul to revolt!

BUTTONMOULDER. But, my dear Peer, you needn't get
    So worked up over such a minor matter.
    Up to now you've never been yourself;
    What difference does it make if you vanish completely?

PEER. I've never been—? I could almost laugh!
    Peer Gynt has been something else, is that it?
    No, buttonmoulder, you judge without seeing.
    If you could scrutinize my vitals
    You would find Peer there, and only Peer,
    And nothing but Peer, neither more nor less.

BUTTONMOULDER. That isn't possible. Here are my orders.
    You can see for yourself: Collect Peer Gynt.
    He defied the purpose of his life.
    Put him in the ladle as damaged goods.

PEER. What nonsense! They must have got the name wrong.
    Does it really say Peer? Not Rasmus or Jon?

BUTTONMOULDER. They were melted down a long while ago.
    Come quietly, and don't waste any more time!

PEER. I'm damned if I will! A pretty thing
If tomorrow you found it meant somebody else.
You ought to be jolly careful, my man!
Remember what you'll be accountable for—

BUTTONMOULDER. I have it in writing—

PEER. At least give me time!

BUTTONMOULDER. What good will it do you?

PEER. I'll prove to you
That I was myself all through my life;
Isn't that what we're arguing over?

BUTTONMOULDER. Prove? What with?

PEER. With witnesses
And testimonials.

BUTTONMOULDER. I'm sorry,
But I think the Master will turn them down.

PEER. Impossible! Well, we won't cross our bridges.
Dear man, let me borrow myself for a bit.
I won't be long. You're born only once,
And you like to hang on to the self you began with.
Well, is it agreed?

BUTTONMOULDER. All right, so be it.
But we'll meet at the next cross-road, remember.

[PEER GYNT *runs off.*]

[*Further on across the heath.* PEER GYNT *enters at full speed.*]

PEER. Time is money, as the saying goes.
I wish I knew where that cross-road is—
It might be near, or a long way yet.
The earth's as hot as a branding iron.
A witness! A witness! Where can I find them?
It's almost unthinkable here in the forest.
The world's a mess! What a state of affairs
When a man has to prove his obvious right!

[*A* CROOKED OLD MAN, *with a stick in his hand and a bag over his shoulder, trudges up to him.*]

OLD MAN [*stopping*]. A copper for a poor beggar, dear sir!

PEER. Sorry; I've no small change at the moment.

OLD MAN. Prince Peer! Surely not? Fancy us meeting!

PEER. Who are *you*?

OLD MAN.   Do you mean you don't remember
The old man in the Ronde?

PEER.   You're not—?

OLD MAN. The Master of Dovre.

PEER.   The Master of Dovre?
Really? The Master of Dovre? You swear it?

DOVRE-MASTER. Alas, I've come down in the world since then.

PEER. Done for?

DOVRE-MASTER. Stripped of all I possessed.
I'm plodding the roads, like a starving wolf.

PEER. Hurrah! A witness as useful as you
Doesn't grow on trees!

DOVRE-MASTER.   Your Highness the Prince
Has gone grey, too, since we last met.

PEER. My dear father-in-law, the years are locusts.
Well, we won't think of our private affairs—
Particularly about family quarrels.
I was a madman in those days—

DOVRE-MASTER.   Yes,
The Prince was young. And what don't we do then?
But the prince was wise to turn down his bride;
It saved him a lot of shame and resentment.
Since then, I'm afraid, she has gone to the dogs.

PEER. Is that so?

DOVRE-MASTER. The world turned its back on her.
And, imagine, she's living now with Trond.

PEER. Which Trond?

DOVRE-MASTER.   The Val-mountain Trond.

PEER.   With him?
The one I stole the goat-girls away from!

DOVRE-MASTER. But my grandson's turned into a strapping fellow,
With bouncing children all over the country.

PEER. Well, save all that for some other time;
Something quite different is troubling me.—
I find myself in a tricky position,
And need someone to give me a character.
Help me in this, father-in-law.
And I'll scrape up the price of a drink for you.

DOVRE-MASTER. Can I really be useful to the Prince?
Will you give me a reference in return?

PEER. Gladly. I'm rather short of cash,
Have to economize all ways up.
But let me explain what's wrong. You remember
The night I asked for your daughter's hand?

DOVRE-MASTER. Of course, my Prince!

PEER.   Stop calling me Prince!
Anyhow, you wanted by sheer brute force
To distort my vision with a slit in the eye,
And change me from Peer Gynt into a troll.
What did I do? I stood out against it,
Swore I would stand on my own two feet;
I sacrificed love and power and glory
For the sake of remaining my own true self.
This is what you must swear to in court.—

DOVRE-MASTER. But I can't!

PEER.   What are you talking about?

DOVRE-MASTER. Is he going to force me to tell a lie?
He surely remembers he put on troll breeches,
And tasted the mead—?

PEER.   You pushed me that far,
But I flatly refused the final test.
And that's how you know what a man is worth.
It's the ultimate verse that makes the point.

DOVRE-MASTER. But the end of it, Peer, was quite the opposite.

PEER. What do you mean?

DOVRE-MASTER.   When you left the Ronde
You wrote on your heart my favourite maxim.

PEER. What maxim?

DOVRE-MASTER.   The potent, thundering Word.

PEER. The Word?

DOVRE-MASTER.   Which separates mankind
From trolls: to yourself be all-sufficient!

PEER [*recoiling a step*]. Sufficient!

DOVRE-MASTER.   And for all you're worth
You've been living up to it ever since.

PEER. I? Peer Gynt?

DOVRE-MASTER [*weeping*]. What ingratitude!
You've lived as a troll without admitting it.
The word I taught you gave you the power
To hoist yourself up to the top of the ladder;
And then you come here and turn up your nose
At me and the word you owe it all to.

PEER. Sufficient! A mountain troll! An egoist!
This must be nonsense, I'm perfectly certain!

DOVRE-MASTER [*pulling out a bundle of old newspapers*].
I suppose you think we haven't got newspapers?
Wait: I can show you in black and red
How the *Bloksberg Post* applauds and reveres you;
As the *Hekle Mountain Times* has done
Ever since the winter you left the country.—
Would you care to read them? You're very welcome.
Here's an article signed 'Stallionhoof'.

And look at this: 'On Troll Nationalism'.
The writer makes a point of the fact
That horns and tails are of small importance
As long as a good skin-grafting is there.
'Our sufficiency', he concludes, 'gives a man
The hall-mark of the troll', and then
He goes on to quote *you* as a fine example.

PEER. A mountain troll? I?

DOVRE-MASTER.   Of course.

PEER. As if I had never gone away?
    Could have sat in the Ronde in peace and comfort?
    Saved all that trouble and effort and shoe-leather?
    Peer Gynt—a troll? It's absurd! Goodbye!
    Here's something to buy yourself some tobacco.

DOVRE-MASTER. No, kind Prince Peer!

PEER.   Let me go! You're mad
    Or in your dotage. Find a hospital!

DOVRE-MASTER. Ah, that's just what I'm on the look-out for.
    But my grandson's offspring, as I said before,
    Have made themselves such a power in the land;
    And they say I only exist in books.
    It's said: One's kin are less than kind.
    Poor me, I've learnt the truth of that.
    It's a terrible life, being a legend!

PEER. Dear man, you're not the only one
    To suffer from that.

DOVRE-MASTER.   And we haven't even
    A pension fund, a savings bank
    Or a poor box. In the Ronde, of course,
    Such things would be unthinkable.

PEER. Their damned 'Sufficient' was all that mattered.

DOVRE-MASTER. The Prince can't complain about that word,
    Or if, in some way or other, he could—

PEER. Look, you've got things completely wrong;
    I'm on my beam ends myself, as they say.

C11

DOVRE-MASTER. Is that possible? The Prince a pauper?

PEER. Totally. My royal ego's in hock.
  And it's all your fault, you bloody trolls!
  That's what comes of keeping bad company.

DOVRE-MASTER. So my hopes have come unstuck again!
  Farewell! It's best I make for the town.—

PEER. What will you do there?

DOVRE-MASTER.   Go on the stage.
  They've been advertising for national types.

PEER. The best of luck; remember me to them.
  If I can get free I'll follow your lead.
  I'll write a farce of crazy profundity
  And call it 'Sic transit gloria mundi'.

[*He runs off down the path; the* DOVRE-MASTER *calls after him.*]

[*At a cross-road.*]

PEER. Now all is at stake as never before!
  The trollish word has sealed my fate.
  The ship's gone down; I must cling to the flotsam.
  Anything, except the rubbish heap.

BUTTONMOULDER [*at the cross-road*].
  Well, have you got your recommendation?

PEER. Have we come to the cross-road? That's quick work!

BUTTONMOULDER. I can see on your face, like a public announcement,
  What the note says, before I've read it.

PEER. I was tired of searching; I might have got lost—

BUTTONMOULDER. Yes; and where in the world does it lead you?

PEER. Where, indeed! In the forest, with night coming on.

BUTTONMOULDER. But here's an old tramp. Shall we ask him over?

PEER. No, let him go. He's drunk, my dear man!

BUTTONMOULDER. But he might be able—

PEER.   Ssh! No—ignore him.

BUTTONMOULDER. Well, shall we begin?

PEER.   There's just one question.
What, exactly, is 'being one's self'?

BUTTONMOULDER. A curious question, especially
From a man who not very long ago—

PEER. Give me a short, straightforward answer.

BUTTONMOULDER. To be one's self is to kill one's self.
I doubt if that answer means anything to you.
So we'll put it this way: to show unmistakably
The Master's intention whatever you're doing.

PEER. But what if a man has never discovered
What the Master intended?

BUTTONMOULDER.   Then he must sense it.

PEER. But such guesses are often wide of the mark,
And one goes *ad undas* in mid-career.

BUTTONMOULDER. Exactly, Peer Gynt; incomprehension
Gives the Devil his best catch.

PEER. It seems incredibly complicated.—
Look here, I'll give up being myself—
I can see it's not going to be easy to prove.
I accept that part of my cause as lost.
But just now, wandering alone on the moor,
I felt the shoes of my conscience pinching;
I said to myself: after all, you're a sinner—

BUTTONMOULDER. Now you're taking us back to where we began.

PEER. Not quite; I mean a tremendous sinner;
Not only in deed, in word and intention.
Abroad I lived one hell of a life—

BUTTONMOULDER. No doubt; may I see the testimonial?

PEER. All right; don't rush me. I'll find a priest,
Make a quick confession, and bring back his verdict.

BUTTONMOULDER. Yes, if you do that you obviously
   Needn't end up in the casting-ladle.
   But my orders, Peer—

PEER.   That paper's old;
   It clearly dates back to ages ago
   When I slopped around like a good-for-nothing,
   Playing the prophet and trusting in Fate.
   Well, may I try?

BUTTONMOULDER. But—!

PEER.   Dear, good friend,
   I'm sure you haven't got much to do.
   It's marvellous air in this part of the world;
   It can lengthen your life by several years.
   Remember what the Jostevale parson wrote:
   'People forget to die in this valley.'

BUTTONMOULDER. As far as the next cross-road; no further.

PEER. A priest, if I have to grab him with tongs!

[He runs off.]

———

[A heathery hillside. A path winds up over the hill.]

PEER. This may be useful in lots of ways,
   Said Espen, picking up a magpie's wings.
   Who'd have thought my catalogue of sins
   Would extricate me on the last evening?
   But the situation is still very awkward;
   It's out of the frying pan into the fire.—
   But there's a well-tried proverb which says:
   While there is any life there's hope.

[A THIN PERSON *in a priest's cassock tucked up high, with a butterfly net over his shoulder, comes running along the hillside.]*

PEER. Who's this? A priest with a butterfly net!
   Hi-de-ho! I'm fortune's favourite!
   Good evening, Herr Pastor! It's a rough road—

THIN MAN. It is; but what wouldn't one do for a soul?

PEER. Aha! Then someone is heading for heaven?

THIN MAN. No; in a different direction, I hope.

PEER. May I go along with you for a bit?

THIN MAN. With pleasure; I'm always glad of company.

PEER. I've a weight on my mind—

THIN MAN.   Heraus! Fire ahead!

PEER. You see before you a decent man.
　　I've strictly obeyed the country's laws;
　　I've never been put in jug for anything;
　　But sometimes you miss your footing and trip—

THIN MAN. Ah, yes; it happens to the best of us.

PEER. These trifles, you see—

THIN MAN.   Only trifles?

PEER.   Yes;
　　I've always steered clear of sins *en gros*.

THIN MAN. In that case, dear man, leave me in peace.
　　I'm not who you seem to think I am.
　　You observe my fingers? What do you think of them?

PEER. A most unusual output of nail.

THIN MAN. What now? You're looking down at my foot?

PEER [*pointing*]. Is that hoof natural?

THIN MAN.   I'm pleased to think so.

PEER [*raising his hat*]. I could have sworn you were a priest;
　　But I have the honour—. Well, best is best;
　　When the front door's open don't choose the back;
　　If the king's to be met with, avoid the footman.

THIN MAN. Shake hands! You seem without prejudice.
　　Well, my dear, what can I do for you?
　　You mustn't ask me for power or wealth.
　　I couldn't supply them, not if you hanged me.
　　You wouldn't believe what a state trade is in.

The turn-over's almost non-existent;
No supply of souls; only once in a while
Some individual.—

PEER.   Have men so improved?

THIN MAN. On the contrary; sunk shamefully low.
They mostly end up in a casting-ladle.

PEER. Ah, yes—I've heard that ladle mentioned.
It's really the reason why I'm here.

THIN MAN. Speak your mind!

PEER.   If it isn't too much to ask,
I'd very much like—

THIN MAN.   A refuge? Is that it?

PEER. You have guessed my request before I made it.
You tell me business isn't flourishing,
So perhaps you won't be over-particular—

THIN MAN. But, my dear—

PEER.   My requirements aren't extravagant.
A salary isn't really necessary;
Just some sociability now and then.

THIN MAN. A heated room?

PEER.   Not too much heat;
And I'd like a permit to leave again
With no trouble—what they call 'no strings'—
If a better position offers itself.

THIN MAN. Dear friend, I'm really extremely sorry,
But you wouldn't believe how many requests
Of a similar nature people send me
When they have to wind up their earthly affairs.

PEER. But when I consider my past behaviour
I know I have every qualification—

THIN MAN. You said it was trifling—

PEER.   Yes, in a sense;
But I've just remembered I traded in slaves—

THIN MAN. There are men who have traded in wills and minds,
　　But so stupidly they failed to get in.

PEER. I've shipped Brahman idols into China.

THIN MAN. Flim-flam! That just makes us laugh.
　　People export much uglier images
　　In sermons and art and literature,
　　And we don't accept them.

PEER.　　　　　　　　　Maybe. But do you
　　Know what?—I pretended to be a prophet!

THIN MAN. Abroad? Humbug! Most transcendentalists
　　End up in the casting-ladle.
　　If that's all you've to back your claim
　　I can't possibly house you, much as I'd like to.

PEER. But listen! In a shipwreck I clung to a boat—
　　A drowning man grasps at a straw, you know;
　　And every man for himself, as they say.
　　I more or less robbed the cook of his life.

THIN MAN. I'd be just as pleased if you'd more or less
　　Robbed a housemaid of something else.
　　What is all this more-or-less palaver,
　　With due respect? Who do you think
　　Is going to waste expensive fuel
　　In times like these on such gutless nonentities?
　　Now, don't get upset; it's your sins I scoffed at;
　　And excuse me for not mincing matters.
　　Listen, my friend, put it out of your mind,
　　And get used to the thought of the casting-ladle.
　　What would you gain if I housed and fed you?
　　Think of it; you're a sensible man.
　　You'd still have your memory, yes, that's true;
　　But the view you would get down memory lane
　　Would be (to your heart, and mind as well)
　　What a Swede would describe as 'good bad fun'.
　　You've got nothing either to sob or smile about;
　　No cause for rejoicing or despair;
　　Nothing to chill or warm your blood;
　　Merely something to irritate you.

PEER. They say: It's not easy to find out where
  Your shoes pinch when they're not on your feet.

THIN MAN. That's true. I have—Who's-it be praised—
  No occasion to use more than one boot.
  But how fortunate we mentioned boots;
  It reminds me I've got to be on my way.
  I've a joint to collect, a fat one, I hope.
  I mustn't stand about gossiping.

PEER. And dare one ask what diet of sin
  Put flesh on this fellow?

THIN MAN.   I rather gather
  He has been himself, all his nights and days,
  And that's what's important in the long run.

PEER. Himself? Do such people come under your aegis?

THIN MAN. It depends; at least the door's left open.
  Don't forget there are two ways of being yourself;
  The right and the wrong side of the garment.
  You know that in Paris they've found the way
  To make portraits with the help of the sun.
  You can either show the straightforward picture
  Or else what is called the negative.
  In the latter light and shade are reversed;
  To the unaccustomed eye it seems ugly;
  But the likeness is in that, too, all the same;
  It only needs to be brought out.
  Now, if a soul has been photographed
  During its life in the negative way,
  The plate's not rejected because of that—
  Quite simply, they hand it on to me.
  And I subject it to further treatment,
  And transform it by the accepted method.
  I dampen, I plunge, I burn, I rinse
  With sulphur and other ingredients,
  Till the image emerges as held in the plate:
  Namely, what's known as the positive.
  But if someone like you half rubs himself out
  Neither sulphur nor potash can help at all.

PEER. So you have to be as black as a crow
To be made as white as a snowy owl?
May I ask what name is on the plate
You're going to develop into a positive?

THIN MAN. It says Peter Gynt.

PEER. Peter Gynt! I see!
And this Mr. Gynt is 'himself'?

THIN MAN. So he says.

PEER. You'll find he's a very reliable man.

THIN MAN. Do you know him, then?

PEER. Well, yes, in a way—
One knows so many.

THIN MAN. I've not much time;
Where did you last come across him?

PEER. Down
At the Cape.

THIN MAN. Di buona speranza?

PEER. Yes,
But he's off again soon, I understand.

THIN MAN. Then I must set off at once hot-foot.
I only hope I'm in time to catch him!
That Cape of Good Hope—I never liked it:
Full of damned missionaries from Stavanger.

[He rushes off southwards.]

PEER. The stupid hound! He's gone bounding off
With his tongue hanging out. He'll find he's been conned!
What a pleasure it was to pull his leg!
Him, playing rich and lording it over me!
What has he got to be cocky about?
He won't get fat in his present business;
He'll come off his perch with the whole bag of tricks.
But I'm not too firm in the saddle myself
Since I got the push, as you might say,
From the self-owning aristocracy.

[A shooting-star is seen; he nods at it.]

Greetings from Peer Gynt, brother meteor!
Sparkle, slip, and go into the dark—

[*He clutches himself as though in terror, and goes deeper into the mist; he pauses, and then shouts:*]

Is there no one, no one on the swarming earth,
No one in hell, no one in heaven—!

[*He reappears further down the road, throws his hat on the ground, and tears his hair. After a moment or two quiet descends on him.*]

So utterly destitute, a soul
Can return to nothing in the grey mist.
Excellent earth, don't be angry
That I trampled your grass to no purpose.
Excellent sun, you have thrown away
Your blessing of light on an empty shell.
No one was there to be warmed and ripened;
The owner, they tell me, was never at home.
Excellent sun, excellent earth,
You were fools to hold and shine on my mother.
The spirit is mean, and nature generous.
Life's a high price to pay for your birth.—
      I'll clamber up to the highest peak;
I would see the sun rise once again,
And stare at the promised land till I'm tired;
Then heap the snow over my head.
They can write above it: Here lies No one;
And afterwards—then—! Things must go as they will.

CHURCHGOERS [*singing on the forest path*].
                Blest morning,
                When God's might
        Spears earth with burning light:
                We, the inheritors,
                Sing out to heaven's towers
        The Kingdom's battle-cry against the night.

PEER [*crouching in fear*].
Don't look that way! It's all a desert.
Alas, I was dead long before I died.

[*He tries to slink away through the bushes, but comes to the cross-road.*]

BUTTONMOULDER. Good-morning, Peer Gynt! Where's your list of
    sins?

PEER. Don't you think I've been whistling and shouting
    For all I'm worth?

BUTTONMOULDER.   And met with no one?

PEER. No one, except a strolling photographer.

BUTTONMOULDER. Well, the time's run out.

PEER.   Like everything else.
    The owl smells its prey. Do you hear it hooting?

BUTTONMOULDER. It's the bell for matins.

PEER.   What's shining there?

BUTTONMOULDER. Just the light from a hut.

PEER.   And the sound I hear?

BUTTONMOULDER. Just a woman singing.

PEER.   That's where I'll find
    The list of my sins—

BUTTONMOULDER [*catching hold of him*]. Set your house in order!

[*They have come out of the thicket and stand outside the hut. Dawn.*]

PEER. Set my house in order? It's there! Leave me!
    If the ladle were as big as a coffin
    It would still be too small for my sins and me!

BUTTONMOULDER. Till the third cross-road, then; but after that—!

[*He turns and goes.*]

PEER [*moving towards the hut*].
    Forward or back, it's the same distance;
    Out or in, it's equally narrow.

[*He stops.*]

No!—it's a wild, endless lament
To go in, go home, be back.

[*He takes a few steps, but stops again.*]

Round and about, said the Boyg! [*Hears a song in the hut.*] No; this
time
Straight to it, however narrow the path is!

> [*He runs towards the hut as* SOLVEIG *appears in the doorway, dressed
> for church, a prayer-book wrapped in her handkerchief, a stick in her
> hand. She stands there upright and gentle.*]

PEER [*throwing himself down on the threshold*].
Now condemn me, however you will!

SOLVEIG. He's here! He's here! God be praised!

> [*She gropes for him.*]

PEER. Rate me with all the wrongs I have done!

SOLVEIG. You've done no wrong, my only boy!

> [*She gropes again, and finds him.*]

BUTTONMOULDER [*behind the house*].
The list, Peer Gynt?

PEER.   Cry out my guilt!

SOLVEIG [*sitting down beside him*].
You made my life a cause for singing.
Bless you, for coming back at last!
And blessed our meeting at Whitsuntide!

PEER. I'm lost, then!

SOLVEIG.   There is one who leads.

PEER [*laughing*]. Lost! Unless you can answer a riddle!

SOLVEIG. Name it.

PEER.   Name it? All right, I will!
Say where Peer Gynt has been all these years!

SOLVEIG. Been?

PEER.   With his destiny clearly marked
As he first sprang from the mind of God!
Can you tell me that? If not, homeward
For me is down to the land of mists.

SOLVEIG [*smiling*]. It's an easy riddle.

PEER.   Then tell me the answer!
Where was I myself, the entire, true man?
Where did I have God's mark on my forehead?

SOLVEIG. In my faith, in my hope, and in my love.

PEER [*recoiling*]. What are you saying? Quiet! You're mocking me!
You have mothered that thought of the man yourself.

SOLVEIG. Indeed, I did; but who is the father?
He who forgives when the mother beseeches.

PEER [*a ray of light goes over him, and he cries out*].
My mother; my wife; purest of women!
Hide me there, hide me in your heart!

[*He clings to her and hides his face in her lap. A long silence. The sun
rises.*]

SOLVEIG [*singing softly*].
                    Sleep, my boy, my precious dear.
                    I will rock you, you my care.

                    The boy has sat on his mother's knee
                    All the day long the two at play.

                    He has slept on his mother's breast
                    All the day long. God give him rest.

                    The boy has lain in my heart's eyrie
                    All the day long. He is weary, weary.

                    Sleep, my boy, my precious dear.
                    I will rock you, you my care.

BUTTONMOULDER [*behind the house*].
We shall meet at the last cross-road, Peer;
And *then* we'll see whether—; I say no more.

SOLVEIG [*singing more loudly in the growing light*].
                    I will rock you, you my care;
                    Sleep, and dream, my home-returner.

APPENDIX I

BRAND: COMMENTARY

1. Dates of composition
2. Manuscripts
3. Some pronouncements of the author
4. Public reception

1. DATES OF COMPOSITION

Three distinct stages in the genesis of *Brand* are clearly identifiable, and manuscripts from each of these stages have survived: the so-called 'epic Brand'; the draft version of the drama of *Brand*; and the final version of the drama. Over and above these stages, there is some circumstantial (though not wholly convincing) evidence to suggest that there was an even earlier dramatic version of *Brand*—if not in draft then at least in conception—which preceded the epic version. Some years later, Ibsen pinpointed the moment of conception for *Brand* as the first days of his own self-imposed exile in the spring of 1864. In his letter to Peter Hansen of 28 October 1870, he explained: 'I wrote a poem "A brother in distress" [14 Dec. 1863]. Naturally it had no effect when it came up against the American-ness of the Norwegians which had defeated me at all points. So I went into exile! Dybbøl fell as I arrived in Copenhagen. In Berlin I saw King Wilhelm hold a triumphal procession with trophies and war booty. In those days *Brand* began to grow within me like a foetus.' When one sets this information alongside the letter he wrote on 17 April 1864 from Copenhagen to Bernard Dunker—'As soon as I get to Rome, I shall start a new five-act drama, which I hope to have ready in the course of the summer'— there is some encouragement for thinking that he was referring to a drama on the theme which eventually grew into *Brand*. The possibility must also be allowed, however, that the reference was to a drama about Julian the Apostate, a theme which is known to have occupied some part of his plans during these and subsequent months; or even, though perhaps less plausibly, to a drama based on the career of Magnus Hejnessøn, about whom Ibsen was actively collecting material. (Some notes on this topic were discovered along with the *Brand* manuscripts.)

The most important testimony among those who believe that work on a dramatic version of *Brand* preceded even the epic drafts is that of Lorentz Dietrichson. In his *Svundne Tider* (Kristiania, 1896, I, pp. 334 ff.), which tells of his association with Ibsen in Genzano and Rome in the latter part of 1864, he reports: 'At that time it was clear to see that he was brewing up something big; and I remember that one day he burst out rather earnestly: "Why can one not write a drama in ten acts. I simply cannot find room in five." And shortly after he told me that he had decided to change the dramatic form of what he was working on into an epic poem.' None of this is very clear-cut evidence, however; and no manuscripts of Ibsen's work of these months appear to have survived.

Work on the 'epic Brand' apparently began some time in the summer of 1864, possibly as early as July. On 16 September 1864 Ibsen wrote in a letter to Bjørnson that he was currently 'preparing a tragedy "Julius Apostata" and working on a longer poem [et større Digt].' This time it is probable, but still not certain, that he was referring to the 'epic Brand'. Clearly, during these months a number of incidents and experiences made their contribution to the development of the Brand theme; one thinks, for example, of the press report of the young Norwegian peasant who cut off his finger to avoid military service (an item that finally lodged in its definitive place in *Peer Gynt*), and of his acquaintanceship with Christopher Bruun, whose career and personality supplied many traits for Brand. Dietrichson (op. cit.) further reports that one day in the spring of 1865 Ibsen read out to him part of a poem satirizing Norwegian Independence Day (17 May) and the way it was traditionally celebrated; this almost certainly was part of the section of the epic draft entitled 'The ways to church', though at the time of writing his book (1895) the existence of the epic was not known to Dietrichson, and he associated the sentiments in the poem rather with *The League of Youth*.

Ibsen apparently worked on the epic for about a year, from July 1864 to July 1865. Ibsen's letter to Bjørnson of 12 September 1865 gives the clearest account of how and when the drama displaced the epic. Acknowledging that there had been moments earlier when his work did not seem to be making headway, he then went on:

'Then one day I went into St. Peter's—I was in Rome on an errand—and there, suddenly, the form for what I had to say came to me, forcefully and clearly. Now I have thrown overboard the thing that has been tormenting me for a whole year without my having got anywhere with it; and in the middle of July I began on something new, which progressed as nothing has ever progressed for me before. It is new in the sense that the writing of it began then; but the content and the drift of it have been hanging over me like a nightmare since those many unhappy events back home made me look within myself and to look at our way of life there, and to think about things that previously went drifting by me and which in any case I never gave serious thought to. It is a dramatic poem, with a contemporary theme, serious-minded in content, five acts in rhyming verse (no *Love's Comedy*!).

Act Four will soon be complete, and I feel I can write the Fifth within eight days. I work morning and evening, something I have never been able to do before. It is blessedly peaceful out here [i.e. in Ariccia], no callers; I read nothing but the Bible—it is powerful and strong.'

The work continued to make the same excellent progress throughout the autumn. During October and November, instalments of the completed play went off in fair copy from Ibsen to his new publisher, Frederik Hegel of Gyldendal, in Copenhagen. The first third of the play went off from Rome on 25 October and arrived in Copenhagen on 6 November, apparently suffering some delay in the posts *en route*. Hegel promised to do all he could to get the book into the Copenhagen and Christiania bookshops before Christmas, and was reasonably optimistic provided Ibsen could hold to his promise of letting him have the completed play by mid-November. Ibsen in fact despatched the final instalment on 15 November. The proofs of the first three Acts were sent to Rome from Copenhagen on 18 November. By the first week in December the entire book was set up and ready to go to press.

In the event, however, and as the result of a series of accidents and mis-understandings, publication was delayed until March 1866. Hegel had not stayed to read the first instalment of the play that reached him in early November, but to save time had sent it straight off to the printer. When a week or two later he found occasion to read what Ibsen had sent him, he was startled. He had been led to expect, from what Bjørnson had told him, that the play was going to be a historical drama, drawing its material from the distant past. This contemporary theme was something very different, and he began to have doubts about the kind of appeal it would have for the public. Moreover, there were rather a lot of Norwegianisms in the language which he felt might not be immediately intelligible to a Danish reading public. He therefore wrote to Ibsen on 23 November 1865 (see L. C. Nielsen, *Frederik V. Hegel, Et Mindeskrift*, Copenhagen, 1909, vol. I, p. 217) suggesting that instead of printing 1,250 copies as had been agreed, he should initially print only half that number, though without any reduction in the agreed fee. To this proposal Ibsen replied by return, on 2 December, giving his approval. Unfortunately this letter apparently went astray and never reached Copenhagen. When still no answer had arrived from Ibsen by 7 December, and since the schedule was a very tight one if the book was to appear for Christmas, Hegel wrote again; he reported that by dint of strenuous efforts by the printers the book was now ready to go to press, but explained that he felt unable to give the word to start until he had Ibsen's answer. Ibsen for his part felt that nothing he could now say could affect the matter of a Christmas publication, and that in any case he *had* given his answer in his reply of 2 December, which he supposed must surely have arrived in the meantime. He therefore left this letter unanswered.

This produced an impasse which caused irritation and impatience to build up on both sides, and which was not resolved until a full three months later. Two letters from Hegel to Bjørnson (see L. C. Nielsen, *Frederik V. Hegel*, ed. cit., vol. I, pp. 218 f.), one from Ibsen to Bjørnson, and another two from Ibsen to Hegel make clear what must have in fact happened (see also Martin B. Ruud, 'The story of the publication of Ibsen's *Brand*', *Scandinavian Studies and Notes*, v, 1819–19, pp. 91–5).

On 18 February 1866, Hegel wrote to Bjørnson:

'I cannot understand Henrik Ibsen. You know how matters are, for I recently wrote to you about it. Because I did not feel that his book would appeal to the wider public, I wanted to test things by publishing half of the edition proposed, but to leave the type set and publish the remainder if required. I wrote, with due tact and politeness, first on 23 November, and again by way of reminder on 7 December, informing him that the book was in proof and corrected. But he has not made any answer. I should regret it if, quite unintentionally, I had offended him. I would much rather stand any loss involved.'

During the first week of March, both parties found themselves complaining to Bjørnson in puzzled terms about the awkwardness of the other. On 4 March, Ibsen wrote to Bjørnson:

'My book is presumably being published sometime about now. You call Hegel a noble man, and Fru Thoresen does the same; but I think his nobility must be of a "Ditmar Meidell" type [a reference to the editor of a contemporary periodical]. He is cautious and fearful of giving offence. I have had a thousand difficulties with him, and given way on everything in order to get my book out by Christmas; then it didn't appear. Among other things he said, long after printing had started, that you had described my work to him as set in ancient times. Is there some misunderstanding here? I distinctly remember once writing to you that the content was taken from contemporary life, but that it was no *Love's Comedy*. As you might well expect, I have during all this neither demanded nor accepted any further advance from him. And how I am now situated, waiting, consumed by suspense and disquiet, anticipating all kinds of conflict and attacks on the book, incapable amidst all this of beginning on anything new, though it lies fully formed within me—about all this I will not proceed to write.'

While on 7 March Hegel also wrote to Bjørnson: 'It is odd that Herr Ibsen has not answered with a word. And now we are into March, and I dare not let things drag on any longer. I feel that I must now issue it next week, and I shall publish it in accordance with the terms agreed earlier.'

Finally, the two men wrote direct to each other—Hegel on 6 March and

Ibsen on 7 March—and inevitably their letters crossed; but it was sufficient at last to clear up the mystery. Ibsen's letter is in the stilted business style he often adopted for correspondence of this nature:

'After informing you on 2nd December last that I accepted your suggestion of printing my book in a reduced edition, together with your proposals regarding author's royalties, I received from you a communication dated 7 December in which you informed me that the book could not be made ready by Christmas. This required no answer from my side, since I had already in my above-mentioned letter given you express authority to proceed on my behalf in this matter as seemed to you best, for I assumed then, as I do now, that you would act in my best interests. But in one of your letters you say that *February* is the most appropriate time for publication, and in another you mention the beginning of *March* because the book ought to appear more or less simultaneously in Norway and here. From the Norwegian newspapers I see that a packet steamer arrived as early as 20 February in Christiania from Copenhagen; but I hear nothing about my book. I sit here in suspense and anticipation which is indescribable and will soon become unbearable. The publication of this book has in truth cost me dear. I will not speak of the reduced royalty payment which naturally I had to accept since the proposal came so late that it left me no choice if I wanted to have my book out by Christmas—which was my main concern and which you, in the same letter in which you made your proposal, still claimed was practicable. But it has cost me even more dearly. Because of this tension, I have not been able to get down in earnest to my new work. Since I am not able to claim the publication of any new literary work, I am debarred from making application to the government for a renewal of my travelling scholarship, the final date for which is in three weeks' time. I beg you not to think that I blame you for this; I have at all times boundless confidence in your integrity and good-will; but I most urgently request you not to delay publication any longer. The blame for what has happened I put on circumstances; but now, from what you say, the moment is favourable.'

Ultimately Hegel's letter of 6 March arrived, in which Hegel—fearing he had given unforgivable offence by suggesting new terms—offered to revert to the original terms of their agreement. But for Ibsen the relief of knowing that publication would be soon was enough:

'Yesterday I received your esteemed and welcome communication of 6 inst., and I hasten to reply with these lines. Your letter of 23 November last was answered by me on the very day of receipt, namely Saturday 2 December. Since I neither write rough drafts nor keep copies but merely note the date of despatch of my letters, I cannot now of course repeat the precise wording of this letter, but the main import of it was that I agreed to your proposals.

... That a letter to this effect was written and posted by me on the above-mentioned date I swear on my honour; and if you have not received it, it must have got lost *en route*. But the possibility of this having happened never occurred to me until now; and this is why I did *not* answer your letter of 14 December (presumably wrongly dated, since the Copenhagen postmark shows that it went off on the 13th); because anything in it requiring an answer had already been answered in the (missing) letter, which at that time I assumed had merely been delayed and delivered to you a few days later.'

Brand was published on 15 March 1866 in an edition of (after all) 1,250 copies. It was an immediate success with the public. A second, a third, and a fourth edition followed that same year, on 24 May, 16 August, and 14 December 1866. By the end of the century it had reached fourteen editions.

2. MANUSCRIPTS

A. THE 'EPIC BRAND'

The 'epic Brand' is a structurally incomplete work, even in its draft form. The text which has formed the basis of the present (prose) translation was arrived at by collating a number of different manuscript items (Royal Library, Copenhagen, Collin Collection, MS. 2869, 4°); as it stands, thus pieced together, it totals 1,640 lines, arranged in 212 stanzas. Apart from stanzas 70–75, 82–86, and 90–93 (all inclusive), the work is in octets, rhyming for the most part a b a b c d c d (though the alternative forms a b b a and/or c d d c are not uncommon) and written in iambic pentameters, with mostly alternating masculine and feminine rhymes. Stanzas 70–75 (the Einar/Agnes song) and stanzas 82–86 (Einar's song) are in rhyming quatrains, a b a b; whilst stanzas 90–93 (Brand's song) are in pentastiches, rhyming a b a a b.

The poem is in five sections of unequal length, with titles to the sections as follows:

'To my fellows in guilt' (stanzas 1–9)
'From the time of ripening' (stanzas 10–48)
'Over the great mountain' (stanzas 49–131)
'The ways to church' (stanzas 132–189)
'By the church' (stanzas 190–212).

For the present translation, stanzas 1–44 were taken from the manuscript item described below in A2(*a*); stanzas 45–48 from A1(*c*); stanzas 49–60 from A1(*a*); stanzas 61–65 from A1(*b*); stanzas 66–189 from A2(*b*), with the exception of stanzas 75 and 162, which are found only in A1(*b*) and A1(*d*) respectively; stanzas 190–206 from A1(*d*); and stanzas 207–212 from A1(*e*).

1. A total of twenty-nine quarto leaves of corrected drafts of 'Brand' in epic form have survived:

(a) Two unnumbered loose leaves (originally the last two leaves of a four-leaf gathering, from which the first two leaves had been cut away) containing a corrected draft of stanzas 49–60, i.e. the first twelve stanzas of 'Over the great mountain'. Stanza 52 was written on a separate piece of paper and stuck on to the reverse side of the first leaf. The first side was originally headed '2', which suggests that the two leaves which originally preceded this and which were cut away, contained the first draft of the nine stanzas of 'To my fellows in guilt', and were originally headed '1'. The original heading '2' was subsequently crossed out, and renumbered '3', doubtless to accommodate a new section '2', i.e. 'From the time of ripening', written later. Finally these figures were deleted altogether and replaced by the heading 'Over the great mountain'.

(b) Three gatherings, each of four leaves, originally numbered 2–4 in the top left-hand corner of the first side of each gathering; these evidently followed directly on A1(a) above in the first instance, but they were later renumbered 4–6, again to accommodate the new section 'From the time of ripening'. They contain a draft version, with a fair number of alterations and deletions, of stanzas 61–136, i.e. the remainder of the section 'Over the great mountain', together with the first five stanzas of 'Two on the way to church', later in the fair copy entitled 'The ways to church'.

(c) One unnumbered folded sheet (two leaves) containing a fairly heavily corrected draft of stanzas 37–48, i.e. the last twelve stanzas of 'From the time of ripening'. This may well be the one surviving fragment of a fuller draft version of the whole of 'From the time of ripening', the remainder of which was destroyed when the fair copy described in A2(a) was made.

(d) Three gatherings, each of four leaves, numbered 7–9, containing stanzas 137–206, i.e. the section (less the opening five stanzas) of 'Two on the way to church', together with the first seventeen stanzas of 'By the church'.

(e) One single leaf, numbered 10, originally presumably the first leaf of a four-leaf gathering as in A1(d), and obviously the continuation of that series of gatherings; it contains stanzas 207–212, i.e. the last six stanzas of what remains of the section 'By the church'.

2. Twenty-eight leaves of fair copy, clearly based on the preliminary drafts A1(a)–(d), have survived:

(a) Two unnumbered gatherings, each of four leaves, containing stanzas 1–44, i.e. the section 'To my fellows in guilt', and the first 35 stanzas of 'From the time of ripening'.

(b) Five unnumbered gatherings, each of four leaves, containing stanzas 66–189, less stanzas 75 and 162; this item includes 'Over the great mountain', less its opening seventeen stanzas, and 'The ways to church'.

3. Three quarto leaves of a revision of the opening stanzas, made up of one loose leaf (the torn half of what was originally a folded sheet) and one folded

sheet of two leaves (the last side of which is blank). These contain stanzas 1–11, rewritten in a much freer rhythm approximating to the style of folk poetry; this covers 'To my fellows in guilt' and the first two stanzas of 'From the time of ripening'.

The overlapping of the various items listed above, and the basis of collation adopted for this present translation of the 'epic Brand', are shown diagrammatically on p. 432.

Four features of these manuscript items allow one tentatively to arrange them in sequence of composition:

(i) At one point the names of the main characters change from Koll, Axel, and Dagmar to Brand, Einar, and Agnes respectively. In A1(*a*), the name Dagmar was originally used once, in stanza 54, and subsequently altered on the manuscript to Agnes. In A1(*b*), the name Koll (uncorrected) appears twice, in stanzas 96 and 99; the name Axel (uncorrected) appears four times, in stanzas 96, 98, 115, and 130; and the name Dagmar (altered on the manuscript to Agnes) appears three times, in stanzas 70, 72, and 82. All these occur in the section 'Over the great mountain'. On the last side of the manuscript, however, in the section 'Two on the way to church', the name Brand is used directly (i.e. not amended from Koll) in stanza 135. In A1(*c*) no proper names occur. In A1(*d*), A1(*e*), A2(*a*) and A2(*b*), the names Brand, Einar, and Agnes are used directly throughout.

(ii) In the course of composition, Ibsen changed the convention he had adopted for capitalizing verse. His original practice was to have capitals at the beginning of each new line of verse; he then changed to having capitals only when sense and prose punctuation required it. Full capitalization is found throughout A1(*a*), except for stanza 52 which was the one inserted later, and also in A1(*b*) until just before Brand's song, i.e. in stanzas 61–89. (Ibsen also used full capitalization for the last verse of Brand's song, stanza 93, but this was probably an oversight.) All the subsequent manuscript items use upper and lower case for the beginning of the lines.

(iii) Ibsen also, during the writing of the 'epic Brand', changed his spelling of the word 'til' to 'till'. He used 'til' throughout A1(*a*), A1(*b*)—including stanzas 132 and 136 of 'Two on the road to church'—and A1(*c*); and he uses the form 'till' throughout A1(*d*), A1(*e*), A2(*a*)—except for one use of 'til' in stanza 15—A2(*b*), and A3.

(iv) There is a change in the colour of the ink used from a relatively pale colour to a pronounced dark colour. Of the corrected draft versions, A1(*a*), (*b*) and (*c*) are written in the paler ink (but have corrections in both pale and dark ink), whilst A1(*d*) and (*e*) are written in the darker ink. In other words, the main break in this respect seems to come after the fifth stanza of 'Two on the way to church'.

There is one other point that seems to bear on the sequence of composition. The first line of stanza 97 of A1(*b*) originally ran: 'They were *a* [editorial italics] pair of schoolboy friends . . . '; this was subsequently changed to 'They were that [lit. 'yon'] pair of schoolboy friends . . . ', which seems to reinforce the suggestion that A1(*c*) was written later than A1(*b*), despite their relative positions in the final work.

Using the above pointers, the following sequence of composition seems to suggest itself: A1(*a*); A1(*b*); A1(*c*); then possibly A2(*a*); A1(*d*) and (*e*); A2(*b*); A3. It is possible, however, that A1(*c*) was written before the last two sides of A1(*b*)—the start of the section 'Two on the way to church'—since this latter was clearly numbered '4' originally, before the figure itself was crossed out and a title substituted; this presupposes that the new section '2' ('From the time of ripening') was either already written or else firmly planned, otherwise these last two sides of A1(*b*) would have originally been numbered '3' to be in line with the original numbering of 'Over the great mountain' as '2'.

The history of how the manuscript of the 'epic Brand', together with that of the draft of *Peer Gynt*, came to light is outlined in Karl Larsen, *Henrik Ibsens episke Brand* (Copenhagen, 1907), pp. 1–10. Andreas Reiersen Pontoppidan was a Danish collector, resident in Rome in the nineties. One day he discovered in a secondhand bookseller's in Rome a packet of manuscript papers, written in Norwegian. Later scrutiny revealed that they were an early draft of *Peer Gynt*, and the manuscript of a work that was believed to be lost: the earlier epic version of *Brand*. Larsen recalls that when Ibsen left Rome in 1868, he lodged with the Scandinavian Association there a trunk of books and papers and other things. Some ten years later, the Norwegian-Swedish Consul in Rome informed Ibsen that moths had got into the trunk, and that they had had to remove the contents:

'When Ibsen now wanted his effects back, ten years after having entrusted them to the Association, there was only the old, worn sealskin trunk itself, and in it a copy of Vilhelm Bergsøe's *Fra Piazza del Popolo* which the author had presented to Ibsen in 1866. That it proved impossible to find the other things will be understood by anyone who knew the prevailing conditions in the Scandinavian Association at that time. Its quarters were in Palazzo Corea, via dei Pontefici. One entered by a large, gloomy anteroom which was used partly as a cloakroom and partly as a coalhouse. In its capacious corners there often stood cases, boxes, and the like which were stored there for members of the Association. Swing doors led from the corridor into a large room, from which further swing doors led to the somewhat smaller library. Beyond that lay a few other dark rooms, containing among other things a huge cabinet with panelled double-doors which was called "The Archive", in which the management put things for safe keeping, including bundles of the Association's accounts over a number of years. Ibsen's trunk

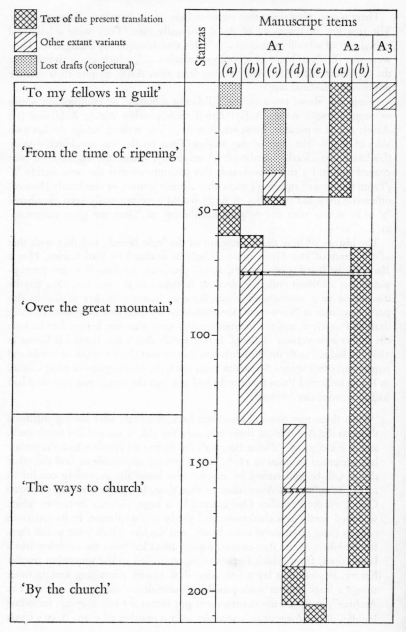

must surely have stood out in the anteroom; and after his trunk had been opened, his manuscripts were probably placed in the not altogether tidily arranged "Archive", where they easily got lost in ten years' growth of papers —all the more easily since the Association's officials changed several times between 1868 and 1878. At all events, Ibsen could not find his possessions in the Association. . . . He later never made reference to what had disappeared. In the spring of 1886, the Scandinavian Association in Rome moved to the Via Condotti.'

According to the secretary of the Association at the time, the 'Archive' and a large part of the library were sold at this time, since they could not be fitted into the new premises; and thus, doubtless, found their way on to the second-hand market.

B. DRAFT VERSION OF THE DRAMA *BRAND*

1. A scrap of notepaper containing four lines of dramatic dialogue, corresponding to the first four lines of stanza 104 of the 'epic Brand':

First: See, she stares carefully at him,
          Spying as though at an enemy camp.
Second: Now she seeks her friend's eye,
          Waiting silently for the victorious answer.

2. Complete draft version of the drama: thirty-five numbered gatherings, each of four leaves, quarto, preceded by one folded sheet of two leaves containing title page and list of characters—the whole making 142 leaves in all. The manuscript of this draft now forms part of the Jonas Collin MS. Collection in the Royal Library, Copenhagen.

One of the preliminary pages originally contained a motto, which was subsequently crossed out: 'And He created Man in His image. *Genesis.*' The handwriting throughout is uneven: some of it carefully formed and obviously copied from an earlier draft; some of it hasty and still uncertain. The first ten gatherings in particular are fairly heavily corrected. Many of the differences between this draft and the final version are minor, and often do not show up particularly well in translation. Some of the more significant deviations are shown below.

(*a*) In the list of CHARACTERS (see p. 75), the SEXTON and the SCHOOLMASTER were added to the list later; 'PRIESTS and OFFICIALS' originally read 'SEVERAL PRIESTS'; and the Norwegian word for 'wilderness' in THE TEMPTER IN THE WILDERNESS was originally 'Ørkenen' (i.e. wilderness/desert) and later changed to 'Ødemarken' (i.e. wilderness/wasteland).

(*b*) BRAND's soliloquy in Act I following the departure of the PEASANT and his SON originally had a somewhat different form (cf. pp. 81–3):

BRAND [*appears again, looking in the direction in which the* PEASANT *went*].
There they plod. One of them falls,
Probably the boy; the peasant curses.
Oh, he hasn't suffered any damage.
It's all right. Those people have hard heads.
Now look! Both of them have fallen,
And the peasant seems to have lost his shoe.

[*Moves on.*]

Yes, life, life! To people like these
How very dear life seems. Every little runt
Lays so much store by life you might think
The salvation of the world, the spiritual welfare
Of all mankind lay on *his* puny shoulders.
They will readily make any reasonable sacrifice . . .
Except . . . life! Life must be saved at all costs!

[*Smiles as though remembering something.*]

Two things have often occurred to me
That made me shake with inward laughter;
They got me many a hiding
When the schoolmaster was feeling nasty.
The first was an owl afraid of the dark,
A fish afraid of water was number two.
I tried to put them from my mind
But still they stuck there like burs [*lit.* like a claw].
They intruded into everything I did,
They visited me in the chimney corner,
They accompanied the train of my inward visions
At home, at school, and at church.
What caused these sudden fits of laughter?
I suppose the dimly apprehended gulf
Between what is and what ought to be,
Between having to bear the burden, and
Finding the burden too heavy to bear.
But from the high peak of this laughter
I take my pondered view of the world,
And clearly see that things are turned upside down,
That the demands of life are far from being its practice.
Every man in this land, whether sick or well,
Is just such an owl, just such a fish.
He was created to infinite toil,
And was meant to have his being in the dark.

Yet these are the things that make him tremble.
He shrinks back from the shores of night,
He dreads his own star-bright chamber,
And longs to enter the fires of noon.
You frightened owl, you sickly fish,
When will someone come to heal you?
He'll come for sure. God infects nobody
Unless he has a remedy for the thing!

[*Halts for a moment, listening.*]

What was that? It sounded like singing!
Yes, it is singing mingled with laughter.
Hark at them! Such a joyful shout!
And another . . . and another . . . and yet another!
How the sunlight streams down there!
The mists are lifting. Now
I see the fields all white with snow.
Look! Up there in the morning sunlight,
On that high ridge, I glimpse
A happy band of friends, their shadows
Cast westward across the desolate snowfields.
They are exchanging a few last words;
They are giving each other their hands.
And now they are parting. They are all
Turning to the east, all but two,
Who are now turning towards the west.
They are shouting their last goodbyes,
Waving caps, veils, hands.

[*He moves to a higher point and looks out.*]

These two approaching . . . light shines about them,
As though the mist gave way before them,
As though the rough heather were spreading
Soft carpets on the rocks at their feet,
And the heavens seem to laugh around them both.
They smile as though an entire world
Of youthful happiness was in all this.
Forgotten are their friends and what they do,
As a passing cloud is forgotten.
They look neither forward nor back;
They must be brother and sister. . . . [etc.]

(*c*) BRAND's scornful description of EINAR's God (see pp. 91–2) was different
in certain details in its earlier formulation:

BRAND.   Of course.
   And grey? With an old man's bald pate,
   And a long beard like threads of silvery ice?
   Kindly looking, but forbidding enough
   To scare the children off to bed with?
   And in so far as your God is old,
   I'm prepared to guess he uses a footstool;
   Moreover it is quite in the nature of things
   That he makes what use he can of the world.
   How far he also has carpet slippers . . .
   Well, we won't go into that.
   But I'm sure he'd really look the part
   If he wore a pair of specs and a skull-cap.

EINAR. What's all this . . . !

BRAND.   See what I mean?
   That's exactly the way he looks,
   This household god of our native land.
   Just as the Catholics have made
   A baby-faced brat of our Saviour here,
   The people of this land make of our Lord
   A doddering old man in his second childhood,
   An amiable grandfather up in heaven
   Who enjoys the bustle here on earth,
   Who is pleased when he hears his grandsons
   Every Sunday lisping their prayers;
   And who, aghast, is ready to scold
   If anybody gets a bit above himself.
   Your art, your poetry gets cut down;
   You do not satisfy any real demands.
   You strive to elevate your souls,
   But not to live the full life.
   For this kind of holy decrepitude
   You need a God who turns a blind eye.
   And therefore his image must turn grey,
   And he must be painted wearing a skull-cap.
   But this God is not my God.
   Mine advances with steps of thunder;
   He is an eternal Hercules,
   Not some greybeard in his dotage.
   The world hearkened to his voice
   When in the blazing bush of thorns
   He stood before Moses on Mount Sinai;

He did stay the sun in the Vale of Gibeon,
And did perform unnumbered miracles,
And would still be working wonders
If the people weren't like her and you.

(d) BRAND's speech in the opening scene of Act II, beginning 'Oh, if all the blood within my heart and body' and ending ' . . . not worthy of salvation' (pp. 102–3) did not belong to the original draft, but was added at a later stage.

(e) The scene between BRAND and THE MAN in Act II (p. 110) originally had an extra passage which was subsequently crossed out:

BRAND. Even if you give everything, but not your life,
 Remember that you have given nothing.

MAN. That may well be as it will;
 We gave because it was required.

BRAND. Farewell!

MAN. Listen, priest! One word more!
 Go through the village, farm by farm,
 And you'll see that you'll find real men,
 Though not folk altogether like myself.
 Follow me down to our churchyard
 Which *we* can scarcely call *ours*;
 And you shall see, and wonder,
 That all the mounds are so small.
 That is because women and children
 Do not need very large resting places. . . .
 Read yourself, and see how often you find
 A man's name painted on the cross above.

BRAND. And where are the village men?

MAN. Ask the rocks,
 Ask the mountain where the avalanche fell,
 Ask the tarn, and ask the landslide slope,
 But first of all ask the sea and fjord.

BRAND. And why do you tell me this?

MAN. I want you to see things properly.
 Every day, every moment, one's hour is at hand,
 Wherever you practise your livelihood here.
 Yet no one regards as anything great
 What each man's father has done before him.
 If that man lying dead . . . [etc.]

(*f*) BRAND's speech after the departure of THE MAN in Act III (p. 135) originally had an extra six lines:

. . . open to bargaining.

[*Lifts his hands to heaven.*]

You God of Truth who are displaced . . .
Slung into the dark, sunk in oblivion,
You are my arm; the way of my will
Shall form a bridge from men to you.
Your flag I shall keep high at the masthead,
Until you are also raised up in Man!

(*g*) One of BRAND's speeches to the MAYOR in Act III (p. 140) originally had an extra six lines:

. . . 'We are only a small nation', hoping to be spared.
Is not each community like a tree
In the great soul forest of the spirit?
One grows openly, one in a corner,
One stands exposed, one is in shelter,
One casts the shadow of a hundred branches,
One grows green over one man alone.

(*h*) One of BRAND's speeches in his scene in Act IV immediately following the MAYOR's departure (p. 178) was originally longer by twenty-six lines:

. . . from the bloodiest wrong.
But who dare come forward with demands
For annulment, when he himself gave,
When he himself has murdered souls
With the poison that struck down his own.
For where is the one who stands alone,
Uncontaminated by the sores of his society . . .
By the pestilence of the past, by the cancer of the age,
Untouched, even by so much as the scent?
See, therein rests the lie, concealed,
Which has hollowed out this society.
They still gnaw on the old text
Which inhibits both flight and growth.
They complain about the rigours of nature
That holds thought confined in a cage.
They blame the force of temptation
That inhabits their powerlessness.
They will twist aside from sacrifice
By claiming to be placed at a disadvantage.

This is where the lie is found. No soul
Went free of the inheritance of the Fall.
In the community, whether great or small,
Every single soul must *will* the goal.
In the world's turmoil, by the silent shore,
The *same* achievement must be attempted.
Doomed is the man who flees the camp
And does not see victory in the Fall itself.

C. FAIR COPY OF THE DRAMA

Fourteen numbered gatherings, each of ten leaves, plus a fifteenth consisting of one folded sheet of two leaves, making 142 leaves in all, all in a careful hand.

3. SOME PRONOUNCEMENTS OF THE AUTHOR

1. At Christmas there will be published a dramatic poem of mine which I earnestly beg you to treat as kindly as ever your conscience can permit you. The sense of hopelessness and mean-mindedness back home has compelled me to examine both my own inner self and the state of affairs generally; this is what has given rise to the mood and content of the work. You once wrote to me that verse form with symbolic undertones was my natural bent. I have often thought about this; I believe the same myself; and it is in accord with this view that the work has taken shape. But I have not been able to avoid making some sharp attacks. I beg you, if you can, not to set this aspect of things under the magnifying glass. Your criticism will decide what reception my countrymen give to the work and to those truths which I have not been able to withhold; but naturally I want as far as possible to avoid any kind of martyrdom. Those who write newspaper criticism in Norway will not understand it. I therefore urgently beg you quickly and firmly to support me at all points where you feel that I and the matter in question deserve it. If you have anything to say to me which does not find a place in your public review (which I look forward to with confidence and with pleasure), I would be most sincerely grateful if you could drop me a line or two. I have an unbearably oppressive feeling of standing alone. (*Letter of 4 Dec. 1865 to Clemens Petersen, a leading Danish critic.*)

2. If my book [*Brand*] has not already appeared, it will do so very shortly. Already last autumn I gave instructions to my publisher to send you a copy; and if, after having read it, you felt like giving me your full and frank opinion of it, I would be more than delighted . . . whatever the direction your judgement took. I have experienced much on this trip, perhaps more inwardly than outwardly; and perhaps it is mainly the conditions back home, compared with what I have seen is possible out

here, that has had an effect on me. The book has emerged as a result of this; but despite my unshakeable certainty that I am right, I don't know if many will join me. I often wonder anxiously how you in particular will take it; for you have been one of the few spectators I have always in my imagination seen sitting in the first row as the work progressed. (*Letter of 4 March 1866 to Bernhard Dunker.*)

3. I have written to Clemens Petersen and begged him to be as kind to my book as his conscience will allow him. I expect nothing by way of clarification from the critics in Norway; naturally I expect attacks. Well, so be it; I have right on my side, and they won't get me to bend. (*Letter of 4 March 1866 to Bjørnstjerne Bjørnson.*)

4. To His Majesty the King!

Henrik Ibsen, the undersigned, herewith makes humble application that it may graciously please Your Majesty, through the Royal Norwegian Government, to petition the assembled Storting to grant me an annual subvention of 400 Speciedaler to enable me to devote myself exclusively to my calling as poet.

After receiving in two successive years, 1862 and 1863, by royal resolution scholarships of 100 Speciedaler on each occasion to enable me to undertake journeys within Norway during the summer months, in 1863 I was awarded a grant of 400 Speciedaler by the Fund for Artists' and Scholars' Visits Abroad, by virtue of which I set out abroad at the beginning of 1864 and have since that time been resident mainly in Italy.

The first fruits of my trip have now reached the public: a dramatic poem, entitled *Brand*, recently published in Copenhagen and which already, a few weeks after publication, has attracted attention also outside the frontiers of my native land. But I cannot live from these expressions of gratitude; nor in the circumstances are the relatively generous royalties sufficient to enable me to continue my stay abroad, or even to guarantee my immediate future. . . .

I am not seeking to claim any kind of carefree existence; I am battling for the mission which I implicitly believe in and know that God has placed upon me—the mission which is for me the most important and most necessary in Norway: to rouse the people and make them think big. . . . (*Petition, 15 April 1866.*)

5. Here it is wonderful, splendid, like a fairy tale. I have a capacity for work, a strength so great I could rend a bear in pieces. I wrestled with my poem in my thoughts for a year before it took a clear form; but once I had that, I wrote from morning till night and completed it in less than three months. About Rome it is impossible to write, especially if one knows it inside out, as I do. I have at various times wandered through most of the Vatican State on foot, with my knapsack on my back. . . . You say that scholars

are baffled by 'quantum satis'. It was good enough Latin in my day—though admittedly *doctor's latin*. Any medical man will be able to tell you that it is a standard formula for prescriptions where no particular amount of a substance by weight is prescribed, but only as much as is necessary, an adequate amount. That is incidentally why it is the *Doctor* who first uses the expression in my work, and it is the memory of this that brings Brand to repeat it. How far 'caritas' is a classical expression, I don't know; but in modern Catholic Latin it is used (in contrast to 'amor' = earthly love) to signify the heavenly kind; thus also in Italian 'carità'. (*Letter of 4 May 1866 to Michael Birkeland.*)

6. Many thanks for the reviews which you sent me! I have read Helveg's book [F. Helveg, *Bjørnson and Ibsen in their two latest works*, Copenhagen, 1866] with much interest; it corrects many things which most critics got wrong. . . . About Helveg's book, I must in truth say that what is suggested there is in fact not the case: that it is supposed to be S. Kierkegaard who served in the first instance as my material, or something like that; the fact is that any depiction of a life that aims at achieving some ideal will always at certain points coincide with S. Kierkegaard's. (*Letter of 9 July 1866 to Frederik Hegel.*)

7. I don't know if you read the Norwegian newspapers; if you do, you will have noticed that in some of them—particularly *Morgenbladet*, *Nyhedsbladet* and *Aftenbladet*—a whole literature has developed over *Brand*. The best thing which has been written about the work from the Norwegian side is in my view the articles in *Morgenbladet* for 1 and 4 December; I am ignorant of the author. (*Letter of 5 Jan. 1867 to Frederik Hegel.*)

8. *Brand* has been misinterpreted, at least as far as my intentions were concerned—to which you may rightly reply that the intention is no concern of the critic. The misinterpretation clearly has its roots in the fact that Brand is a priest and that the problem is set in religious terms. But both these circumstances are quite without significance. I would have been quite capable of making the same syllogism just as well about a sculptor or a politician as about a priest. I could have achieved the same release of that mood that drove me to write what I did if, instead of Brand, I had for instance treated Galileo—with the modification, of course, that he would have had to stay stubborn and not admit that the world stood still. Yes, who knows—had I been born a hundred years later, I might just as well have treated you and your fight against Rasmus Nielsen's philosophy of compromise. There is in general more masked objectivity in *Brand* than has generally been spotted up till now. . . . (*Letter of 26 June 1869 to Georg Brandes.*)

9. What I said about *Brand* I must hold to. That the work might have given pietism something to lean on is nothing they can blame me for. They

might just as well reproach Luther for introducing philistinism into the world; that was not part of his intention, and he need therefore have no regrets. (*Letter of 15 July 1869 to Georg Brandes.*)

10. As a curiosity, let me tell you that a young lady in Norway has published a novel this winter which is supposed to be a continuation of *Brand* and is called *Brand's Daughters.* It is said to have attracted some attention; I am, however, not familiar with it. (*Letter of 28 Feb. 1870 to P. F. Siebold.*)

11. For your courtesy in dedicating your book to me I ask you to accept my sincerest thanks. Were I, however, to have to express any opinion about the work, I should find myself in something of an embarrassment. You would of course wish to have the book regarded as a work of edification, and I do not know how to judge literature of that kind. What attracted and interested me on reading it was the character drawing and particularly your unmistakable talent for the purely poetic. But how far this is praise in your eyes, I simply do not know.

It almost seems as though you would be terrified at the thought that you had written 'a novel'. If that were so, then we two do not understand each other: *Brand* is an aesthetic work wholly and completely, and nothing else. What it might have depraved or edified has absolutely nothing to do with me. It developed in its day as the result of something lived through —not merely observed. It was imperative for me to free myself in the form of literature of something which, inwardly, I was finished with; and when by this means I had rid myself of it, my book no longer had any interest for me. . . .

Are you thinking of continuing on the path of authorship? That needs something other, something more than mere natural talent. One must have something to write about, a content to life. If one lacks that, one does not write literature, one merely writes books. Now I know very well that a life in solitude is not a life lacking in content. But in cultural matters man is a long-sighted creature; we see clearest at a great distance; details confuse; one must stand outside to judge; one describes summer best on a winter's day. (*Letter of 11 June 1870 to Laura Kieler, authoress of the novel,* Brand's Daughters.)

12. So I went into exile! As I arrived in Copenhagen, Dybbøl fell. In Berlin I witnessed Kaiser Wilhelm's triumphal procession with trophies and booty. Those were the days when *Brand* began to grow within me like an embryo. When I arrived in Italy, unification was complete as a result of a boundless spirit of self-sacrifice, whilst at home in Norway . . . ! Add to this Rome with its ideal air of peace, and my association with the carefree artistic world, an existence which can only be compared with the mood of Shakespeare's *As You Like It*—there you have the pre-conditions for *Brand.* It is a complete misunderstanding to imagine that I have

described the life and career of Søren Kierkegaard. (I have in any case read very little of S.K. and understood even less.) That Brand is a priest is really immaterial; the demand of All or Nothing is valid for all aspects of life, in love, in art, etc. Brand is myself in my best moments—just as I have also by self-dissection brought out many features in both Peer Gynt and Steensgaard.

While I was writing Brand I had standing on my desk an empty beer glass with a scorpion in it. From time to time the creature became sickly; then I used to throw a piece of soft fruit to it, which it would then furiously attack and empty its poison into; then it grew well again. Is there not something similar to that about us poets? The laws of nature are also valid in the world of the spirit.

After *Brand, Peer Gynt* followed as it were of its own accord. (*Letter of 28 Oct. 1870 to Peter Hansen.*)

13. I always read your letters with strangely mixed feelings. The things you write are more poems than letters; they come to me like a cry for help from one who is the sole survivor in a great devastated land. So I can only feel delight and gratitude that you should direct your cry for help to me. On the other hand it fills me with concern as I ask myself: where will such a state of mind lead to? And I have nothing to comfort myself with but the hope that it is only transitory. To me it seems as though you are now facing the same crisis as I did in the days when I turned to the writing of *Brand;* and I am sure you will also find the remedy that will drive the sickness from the body. Energetic production is a splendid cure. What I wish you first and foremost is some really full-blooded egoism which will drive you to value your own self as the one thing of worth and significance, and all other things as non-existent. Do not regard this as a sign of something brutal in my nature! You cannot benefit society in any better way than to mint the metal you have within yourself. I have never had any strong feelings for the notion of solidarity; I have generally taken it only as a conventional expression of faith—and if one had the courage to disregard it wholly and completely, one might perhaps be rid of the ballast that weighs most heavily on the personality. On the whole there are times when the entire history of the world strikes me as being one enormous shipwreck; what matters is saving oneself. I don't expect anything from particular reforms. The whole human race is on the wrong track—that is the fact of the matter. Or is there really anything to hold to in the present situation? All this about unattainable ideals and things like that? Whole successions of generations seem to me like a young man who has left his last and gone to the theatre. We have made a fiasco of things both as lovers and as heroes. The one thing we have shown a bit of talent for is naïve comedy; but with our more developed self-consciousness even that does not operate any longer. I do not believe

that things are much better in other countries than at home; the masses stand outside any comprehension of higher things both at home and abroad. (*Letter of 24 Sept. 1871 to Georg Brandes.*)

14. Last week I wrote to my publisher in Copenhagen and requested him to send you *Love's Comedy*, a play in three acts, together with the two other books you require. *Love's Comedy* is actually to be regarded as a forerunner to *Brand*, in so far as I have described there the conflict that prevails in our social conditions between reality and the demands of the ideal in everything that concerns love and marriage. When it appeared, the book raised a wild storm of indignation in Norway, the reasons for this you will gather from my preface to the second edition which is being sent to you. *Peer Gynt* is Brand's opposite. . . . (*Letter of 30 April 1872 to Edmund Gosse.*)

15. In the—to me—wholly flattering preface I find everything said about *Brand* that is in any way necessary for a correct understanding of the work, and moreover expressed in a most brilliant and profound fashion. The purpose of the work I have never before seen presented so clearly. (*Letter of Dec. 1876 to Alfred von Wolzogen, author of the third translation of* Brand *into German.*)

16. The same goes for the projected [German] translation of *Brand*. This work is not meant for the theatre either; and if, despite the existence of three other German translations already, you venture to make a fourth, I can only regard this as evidence on your part of a highly flattering interest in my work. (*Letter of 17 Aug. 1881 to Ludwig Passarge.*)

17. I spoke to him about Kierkegaard, and he declares it is all nonsense that Brand has anything to do with Kierkegaard. He says he always draws from models to some degree, and that a man who formed a sort of model for Brand was a certain Pastor Lammers. This man went out of the State Church, taking any number of people with him; then he saw he was on the wrong track, but neither could nor would take his followers back into the fold, and so left them in the wilderness and came abroad. Ibsen knew him in Dresden. However, he can't have been by any means an exact prototype of Brand, for Ibsen says he was full of the joy of life, went to the theatre, and was something of a painter and musician. Brand played the organ, but that was his only accomplishment that I ever heard of. (*William Archer in conversation with Ibsen in Rome in early 1882, reported in* The Monthly Review, *June 1906, pp. 8–9.*)

18. He spoke of the mission which the Government had assigned him in his youth, to travel through the country and collect folk-songs. As a matter of fact, he picked up no folk-songs at all, but brought back a store of folk-tales—all told him by one man, however. On the other hand, he

gathered many impressions which he afterwards used in *Brand.* He came to one valley where the parsonage had just been destroyed by an avalanche. The pastor and his wife were living in one room of a peasant's house. The wife, who had just given birth to a child, occupied a screened-off corner, while the husband transacted all the business of the parish in the remainder of the room. The scenery of *Brand* was mainly suggested to him by a side valley of the Geiranger Fjord—the Sunnelvsfjord I think he said. He also spoke of coming down from the Jotunfjeld at a place where he looked straight down upon a steeple in the valley hundreds of feet below, and could see no possible way of descent. It appeared, however, that there was a path cut in the face of the precipice, and by this he made his way down, in company with a Catholic priest and a sick woman tied on to a horse.

He wrote *Brand* and *Peer Gynt* (which appeared with only a year's interval between them) at very high pressure, amounting to nervous overstrain. He would go on writing verses all the time, even when asleep or half awake. He thought them capital for the moment; but they were the veriest nonsense. Once or twice he was so impressed with their merit that he rose in his night-shirt to write them down; but they were never of the slightest use. At Ariccia he used to get up at four or five in the morning and go for a long walk; then, when he came back, he was in good trim for writing. (*William Archer in conversation with Ibsen in the late summer of 1898, reported in* The Monthly Review, *June 1906, pp. 17–18.*)

19. I can, however, say that he very definitely denied to me that Lammers was the model for Brand. I never knew Lammers, he said. And he did not conceal that the man he thought of when he wrote *Brand* was Christopher Bruun, parish priest of St. John's church; he told me this once when we met Bruun and stopped to say hello to him. And Ibsen added that Bruun's sister, whom he met in Rome, was the model for Agnes. (*Arnt Dehli, Ibsen's masseur and companion 1901–6, reported in* Aftenposten, *14 March 1928, p. 8.*)

4. PUBLIC RECEPTION

The impact made by the book on the Scandinavian public was immediate and immense; and the fact that it ran through four editions in less than a year, but had to wait nearly twenty years for its first production in a theatre anywhere in Scandinavia (and many more before it was finally performed in Norway in full), underlines the recognition that it was through the medium of the printed page that it exerted its prime influence, and not by way of the theatre.

It was much reviewed in the Norwegian press; and, particularly, a long critique of the work by M. J. Monrad (in four instalments in *Morgenbladet,* nos. 242, 249, 256 and 263), in which he claimed that Brand's extremism derived from a complete misconception of the true nature of idealism, pro-voked a great deal of correspondence and discussion in both *Morgenbladet* and *Aftenbladet*. A. O. Vinje contributed to the general debate with pieces in his periodical *Dølen* (see his *Skrifter i Utval*, IV, pp. 86–102 and 141–54), in which he asserted that *Brand* was 'too mad to be taken seriously'. Bjørnson, on his first reading of the play, greatly disliked it; he gave it as his view that within two months the book would be dead. The most distasteful thing about it for him was that it seemed to strike at the roots of true religion; and although he recognized the power that resided in the work, he felt that it was too deficient in feeling to stand as true poetry. (It is fair to add that over the years Bjørnson's opinion of the play changed somewhat; and in 1878, in a letter to Georg Brandes, he admitted that he had not fully grasped the play at first, but that now he understood it better—see his *Brev*, Grotid II, pp. 189–93 and Brytningsår II, p. 259.)

The play was also widely reviewed in Denmark on its publication, including the inevitable piece by Clemens Petersen, in *Fædrelandet*, no. 80, 1866. There was also published in Denmark, before the year was out, a short monograph by F. Helveg dealing with Ibsen's and Bjørnson's most recent works— *Bjørnson og Ibsen i deres to seneste Værker*—with a section (pp. 26–67) devoted to *Brand;* it was here that the suggestion was first made that Brand might be regarded as a portrait of Kierkegaard. Shortly after this, and stimulated no doubt by the attention which *Brand* had aroused, there appeared a biographical account of Ibsen in the Danish *Illustreret Tidende* for 27 Jan. and 3 Feb. 1867. It was, however, Georg Brandes's account and criticism of *Brand*, in *Dansk Maanedsskrift*, II, 1867, pp. 228 ff., that did most to establish Ibsen's wider reputation in Scandinavia. He drew attention to the passionate intensity which was the most conspicuous characteristic of the work, to Ibsen's hatred of falsehood and deceit, and to the strength of his moral indignation. At the same time he found disapproval for certain other aspects of the work: compared with the rich poetry of *The Pretenders*, *Brand* marked (he believed) a false step. Ibsen would have to abandon the direction he had taken with *Love's Comedy* and with *Brand* and return to the path of true poetry. Largely through Brandes's encouragement, *Brand* became required reading for the younger and more radical spirits in Scandinavian literature—the 'men of the modern break-through', as they came to be called. A Swede among them, Gustaf af Geijerstam, spoke later of the unbounded enthusiasm with which the generation of writers to which he belonged discussed Ibsen's work, and particularly *Brand*; and, on a somewhat different plane, Fritjof Nansen is reported to have said that for himself and for a great many of his contemporaries no book had had greater formative influence.

The first translations of *Brand* to appear—apart from a Swedish version that came out in 1870—were German. By 1882 no fewer than four different and independent translations had been published in Germany: by P. F. Siebold in 1872; by Julie Ruhkopf in 1874, which included the text, in the original language and in German translation, of a letter of June 1873 from Ibsen acknowledging the work as one 'wholly characterized by the spirit of the work as manifested in the original, together with complete understanding of all details, which in all seem to have been rendered with the greatest possible fidelity'; by Alfred Freiherr von Wolzogen in 1876 (see also Ibsen's letter to Wolzogen, Dec. 1876, p. 444 above); and by Ludwig Passarge, in Reclams Universal-Bibliothek, in 1882 (see Ibsen's letter of 17 Aug. 1881 to Passarge, p. 444 above). The version that eventually established itself in Germany, however, was that made by Christian Morgenstern, published in 1898 as part of the collected German edition of Ibsen's works, edited by Georg Brandes, Julius Elias, and Paul Schlenther.

The first introduction which the English reading public was given to *Brand* was in Edmund Gosse's article 'Ibsen, the Norwegian Satirist' in *Fortnightly Review*, xiii, no. 73, 1 Jan. 1873, pp. 74–88, also in *Every Saturday* (Boston), 14, 1873, pp. 133 ff., and eventually included in Gosse's *Studies in the Literature of Northern Europe*, London, 1879: 'It is not that *Brand* is more harmonious in conception than the earlier works—for let it be distinctly stated, Ibsen never attains to repose or perfect harmony—but the scope was larger, the aim more Titanic, the moral and mental horizon wider than ever before. Brand, the hero of the book, is a priest in the Norwegian Church; the temper of his mind is earnest to the point of fanaticism, consistent beyond the limits of tenderness and humanity. He will have all or nothing, no Sapphira-dividings or Ananias-equivocations—the whole heart must be given or all is void.'

In America, there was a review of *Brand* by Rasmus B. Anderson in *Literary World*, xiii, 1882, pp. 325–6; and articles in 1890 by A. H. Palmer, 'Henrik Ibsen's *Brand*', in *The New Englander and Yale Review*, liii, pp. 340–73, and in 1891 by Wilbur L. Cross, 'Ibsen's *Brand*', in *The Arena* (Boston), iii, pp. 81–90.

Meanwhile, in England, George Bernard Shaw had delivered his Fabian lecture on Ibsen at the St. James's Restaurant on 18 July 1890, which grew into his book *The Quintessence of Ibsenism*, first published in 1891: 'Brand the priest is an idealist of heroic earnestness, strength and courage. Conventional, comfortable, sentimental churchgoing withers into selfish snobbery and cowardly weakness before his terrible word. . . . Brand . . . declares himself the champion, not of things as they are, nor of things as they can be made, but of things as they ought to be . . . Brand spares neither himself nor anyone else. Life is nothing: self is nothing: the perfect Adam is everything' (pp. 45–6). And Philip H. Wicksteed, whose lectures delivered in Chelsea Town Hall were subsequently collected and published under the title *Four Lectures on Henrik Ibsen* (London, 1892), remarked how 'in *Brand* the poet turns fiercely upon his native land, but amid all his passion and contempt learns and tells the truth that there is no redeeming power save in love'.

During these years in the early nineties, three different English translations of *Brand* were published: (i) William Wilson (pseudonym for More Adey) published a prose translation: *Brand: a dramatic poem*, by Henrik Ibsen (London,

1891); (ii) C. H. Herford, who in 1891 had published the translation of 'A Scene from Ibsen's *Brand*' in *Contemporary Review*, lix, March 1891, pp. 407–22, brought out his verse translation: *Brand* (London, 1894); (iii) F. E. Garrett also published a verse translation: *Brand: a dramatic poem*, by Henrik Ibsen (London, 1894). Among the commentaries on these occasions may be noted: an anonymous review of Wilson's translation in *Saturday Review*, lxxii, 19 Dec. 1891, p. 705; an article by C. H. Herford, 'Two books on Ibsen', in *Academy*, xli, 1036, 12 March 1892, pp. 247–9, being a review of Wicksteed's *Four Lectures on Ibsen* and of Wilson's translation; R. Brimley Johnson's 'Two Translations of *Brand*' [i.e. Herford's and Garrett's] in *Academy*, xlv, 1155, 23 June 1894, pp. 510–11; and a review by W. M. Payne of Herford's translation in *The Dial*, xvi, 1894, pp. 236–40.

Two other publications of the nineties are also noteworthy in this connection, though for different reasons: W. B. Yeats's views on *Brand* and *Peer Gynt* in *The Bookman*, 8, 1897, pp. 20 ff.; and M. A. Stobart's quite remarkable article, 'New Light on Ibsen's *Brand*', in *Fortnightly Review*, lxvi (New Series), 1899, pp. 227–39. This latter piece is discussed in some detail by Brian W. Downs, *A Study of Six Plays by Ibsen* (Cambridge, 1950), pp. 58 ff., who calls it 'one of the completest alignments of *Brand* to Kierkegaard's philosophy'.

By the end of the century, translations had been published in Dutch (1893), in French (prose) by Count Prozor (1895), in Finnish (1896), and in Russian (1897). For a fuller list of English translations, see the Bibliography.

The play proper was not performed on the stage until nearly twenty years after it had first been published, although Act IV had on occasion served separately to mark various jubilee or benefit occasions: with Laura Gundersen as Agnes in the Students' Union in Christiania in 1866; in June 1867 in the Christiania Theatre as a benefit performance; and in the early seventies by a travelling company in a number of Norwegian provincial towns. (See also Ibsen's letter of 12 May 1888 to Laura Gundersen gladly acceding to her request to put on Act IV as part of her husband's jubilee celebrations.) It is of interest to note that this Act was also performed on occasion in England as an independent item: it was played in June 1893 as a curtain-raiser to *The Master Builder* at the Opera Comique; and again in November 1911 by the Ibsen Club at the Rehearsal Theatre.

When, eventually, the play proper was performed in the theatre, neither Christiania nor Copenhagen provided the venue, but Stockholm. It was played, in Swedish translation, at the New Theatre on 24 March 1885, in a version that is reported to have lasted from half past six in the evening until a quarter past one in the morning. Writing the previous month from Rome, Ibsen had informed his publisher that *Brand* was soon to be performed in Stockholm:

'*Brand* was long ago accepted for performance at Nya Theatern in Stockholm. It should have been performed there already last season; but circumstances arose which made it preferable to wait. Now nothing stands in the way; the necessary cast are there and ready, and one can expect the first performance in the very near future. I am waiting excitedly to hear how Director Josephson will cope with this difficult assignment which he is obviously so keenly interested in. It was he who so effectively staged *Peer Gynt* in Christiania some time ago.'

News of the production and its reception reached Ibsen in Rome at the beginning of April; and on 9 April he wrote in the following terms to Josephson:

'These last few days I have received a number of reports and accounts from Stockholm which express themselves with unusual unanimity about the performance of *Brand* at Nya Theatern.

'The performance of the play took me by surprise and unawares; I did not know that it was so imminent. I was already beginning to fear that it had been put off to next year.

'How much greater was thus my delight to receive your and my son's telegrams, and to learn from them that your courageous—I might almost say reckless—undertaking had been crowned with such a decisive triumph.

'It is now over ten years ago that you first sketched out to me the plan which you have now so happily accomplished. In the meantime I had almost lost sight of the matter; but I now see that you held on loyally until the plan could be carried out. And for a number of reasons I believe that a more fortunate point in time than the present one could not have been chosen.

'Allow me therefore to send you my sincerest and most affectionate thanks for the fact that once again you have applied your supreme talents and ability as a director to an enterprise which once again links our names in the history of our dramatic art. . . . '

A further ten years elapsed before the European theatre again found courage of this order: on 21 January 1895 Lugné-Poë played the title role in a production in Paris by the Théâtre de l'Œuvre. In the autumn of that same year, August Lindberg took his (Swedish) travelling company with a shortened version of the play to Christiania (21 Oct. 1895), Bergen, and Trondheim, rounding off his Scandinavian tour with performances in May 1896. In March 1898, it was performed in German at the Schiller Theatre in Berlin in honour of Ibsen's 70th birthday. Halvdan Koht, Ibsen's biographer, happened to be in Berlin at the time, and was not impressed: 'To me it seemed utter parody, and the German spectators must have looked upon the drama as something foreign and strange, rather than as a revelation of the human soul' (*The Life of Ibsen*, 1931, vol. I, pp. 295-6). On 3 April 1898, also as part of Ibsen's 70th birthday celebrations, *Brand* was performed at the Dagmar Theatre in Copenhagen, with a prologue written by Holger Drachmann, and in the presence of the author. It was the first time in his life that Ibsen had seen *Brand* performed;

P. A. Rosenberg, who directed the play, afterwards reported that Ibsen 'seemed moved and several times wiped away a tear during the scenes in Act Four'. Rosenberg then reports a subsequent conversation with Ibsen:

' "You didn't have to cut much in *Brand*", he said. I started. In fact I had had to cut about a third of the play.

' "May I see the prompt book?" I brought it to him with a beating heart. Page after page was crossed out.

' "Devil take it," he murmured, as he thumbed through the book. "I've obviously forgotten most of it." ' (*Nationaltidende,* 28 July 1926.)

Koht also saw this production, and he commented that 'if Martinius Nielsen [in the title role] was somewhat monotonous and colourless in his declamation, he had still some of the enthusiasm and intense strength that lived in Brand, and he was able to wrest, as it were, the victory from untoward circumstances' (op. cit. p. 296).

It was first played in full in Norway at the National Theatre in Christiania on 14 Sept. 1904, and has appeared repeatedly in the repertory of that theatre ever since.

The play made a great impression in Russia when it was first introduced in Jan. 1907 into the repertory of the Moscow Art Theatre, and then later taken on tour.

In England, the first performance of the full play was on 11 Nov. 1912 at the Court Theatre in London, with H. A. Saintsbury as Brand, Phyllis Relph as Agnes, and Mignon Clifford as Gerd, produced by W. G. Fay. There was a production of the play at Manchester University on 23 April 1914; the Gate Theatre, Dublin, produced it on 11 Dec. 1936, with Micheál Mac Liammóir as Brand; and the Cambridge Amateur Dramatic Society produced it in the academic year 1945–6. It was not, however, until 8 April 1959 that the play finally established itself in Britain, with a memorable production at the Lyric, Hammersmith, in Michael Meyer's translation, with Patrick McGoohan as Brand, Dilys Hamlett as Agnes, Harold Lang as Einar, Patrick Wymark as the Mayor, Peter Sallis as the Provost, and Olive McFarland as Gerd, in Michael Elliott's production.

Radio productions of *Brand* include: 11 Dec. 1949 (recorded repeat 16 Dec.) with Ralph Richardson as Brand, Sybil Thorndike as Brand's Mother, Margaret Leighton as Agnes, and Hamilton Dyce as the Sheriff; 30 Dec. 1956 (recorded repeat 4 Jan. 1957) with Stephen Murray as Brand, Fay Compton as Brand's Mother, Ursula Howells as Agnes, June Tobin as Gerd, and Arthur Young as the Sheriff; 29 April 1963 with Stephen Murray as Brand, Mary O'Farrell as Brand's Mother, Ursula Howells as Agnes, June Tobin as Gerd, and Malcolm Hayes as the Sheriff. *Brand* was produced on BBC Television on 11 Aug. 1959 with Patrick McGoohan as Brand, Enid Lorimer as Brand's Mother, Dilys Hamlett as Agnes, James Maxwell as Einar, Olive McFarland as Gerd, and Patrick Wymark as the Mayor.

APPENDIX II

PEER GYNT: COMMENTARY

1. The genesis of the play
2. Scenario and draft manuscripts
3. The folk-tale Per Gynt and the Boyg
4. Some comments by the author
5. Public reception
6. Collaboration with Grieg

1. THE GENESIS OF THE PLAY

After *Brand*, Ibsen was for a long time uncertain about what subject to turn to next. As early as 7 March 1866, he confided to his publisher, Frederik Hegel, that his new work was to be a historical play set in the time of Christian IV's youth, and 'intended for stage production'. Two and a half months later his interest seems to have reverted to the subject of Julian the Apostate, a theme which had already exerted some attraction for him earlier (see *Oxford Ibsen*, vol. iv, pp. 557–8); on 21 May he wrote to his publisher: 'In the near future I shall be able to tell you which work I shall set about first. I feel more and more inclined to start in earnest on "Emperor Julian", which I have been thinking about for two years.' On 2 November 1866 he again wrote from Rome, still clearly in some doubt as to which subject to settle for:

> 'I see from your letter that there is some slight misapprehension concerning one of my projected works. It is not intended to be *about* Christian IV's youth; but the material is taken from that period. Whether this work will be the *first* one I shall complete, I do not know for certain. I still have a few other subjects in mind; but it is precisely this dispersal in my interests that shows that none of them has yet reached sufficient maturity; yet I feel certain that this will soon take place, and I hope to be able to submit the completed manuscript to you by next spring.'

By the early days of the new year these uncertainties had wholly disappeared; he had then committed himself to the theme of Peer Gynt, the general plan of which had been quite fully worked out and a start made on the first Act. On 5 January 1867 he wrote to Hegel:

> 'Finally I must tell you that my new work is fully into its stride and will, if nothing upsets things, be complete in the early summer. It will be a large-

scale dramatic work, the main character of which is one of those half mythological and fairy-tale figures from *recent* times, and widely known to the Norwegian public. It will show no resemblance to *Brand*, and is without direct polemics, etc.—I have had the subject matter in mind for a long time; now the entire plan has been worked out and set down on paper, and a start has been made on the first Act. As I work on it, it grows; and I am sure you will be satisfied with it. May I ask, however, that this be kept confidential for the present.'

Nevertheless, there was still a fair amount that was tentative at this stage. He later admitted to Vilhelm Bergsøe (*Henrik Ibsen paa Ischia*, Copenhagen, 1907) that at this time he had no idea, for instance, that he was going to send Peer to North Africa and Egypt. Whether the fragment of a scenario (see below) which has survived dates from these early days, and whether it is in fact the 'entire plan' referred to in the letter of 5 January, is uncertain; the general weight of the evidence suggests a somewhat later date for it.

On the manuscript of the surviving draft, the beginning of Act I is dated 14 January 1867. The slight discrepancy between this date and the chronology suggested by the letter of 5 January quoted above is, however, not enough for one to assume with any certainty the existence of any earlier draft of a comprehensive kind. Ibsen probably worked from a provisional scenario and from scattered notes and fragments relating to that scenario. There is also a strong likelihood that—in the case of some passages, at least—he worked up the final verse formulation from a prose draft of the dialogue.

Two sets of dates allow one to place the composition of *Peer Gynt* in time with some accuracy: those dates that appear at certain key points in the draft manuscript; and the reports of his progress which he sent to his publisher. On the manuscript, the end of Act I is dated 25 February 1867, and the beginning of Act II 3 March; and by 8 March he could confidently announce to Hegel not only the number of Acts the play would have but also the number of printed pages it would fill—a prediction which turned out to be very close to reality: 'In my new dramatic poem I have now progressed as far as the middle of the second Act (there will be five in all), and as far as I can calculate in advance it will be about 250 pages long. If you wish, I will be able to send you the manuscript in July.' The tone of this letter suggests that by this date he not only had a clear view of how the play was to develop, but possibly also had a fair amount of the later Acts of the play in the form of loose notes and jottings; indeed the possibility that some kind of antecedent draft version of these Acts was in existence at this stage cannot be wholly ruled out.

This notion is given some reinforcement by the fact that the work of making a fair copy of the earlier Acts ran concurrently with the drafting of the later ones. On 27 March 1867 he wrote to Hegel: 'Towards the end of May I hope to be able to send you the first three Acts of my new work and the remainder in the course of the summer. The first two Acts are ready, and Act I is in fair copy. I shall complete all three in Rome, and then will leave for Sorrento or some other place on the coast.' In the May he moved to Ischia.

In the event, Ibsen did send off the first three Acts in fair copy to the printer before even beginning work on the drafts (as we now have them) of Acts IV and V, which indicates that he must have been pretty confident of both the scope and the direction of the two final Acts, and also reasonably certain that they would not impose any subsequent revision upon the earlier portion of the work. Act III—the first and last pages of which in the Draft are dated 15 June and 2 July respectively—was sent off together with Acts I and II on 8 August in fair copy; and a covering letter went separately from Cacamicciola, Ischia:

'I have to report to you that today I sent off to you—via Danchertsen, the Consul General in Naples—the manuscript of the first three Acts of my new work, entitled: Peer Gynt, a dramatic poem. I hope you will receive the package about the same time as you get these lines. What I have sent off will fill about 120 pages of print, and the remainder will be about the same. I hope to be able to send you the fourth Act towards the end of the month, and the rest not long after that. . . . Assuming that you are satisfied with the work, there remains the question of whether you wish to get the book out by Christmas. Naturally I would prefer that, but I leave the matter to you. . . . I am leaving [soon] for Sorrento, and will turn my hand to the final part of my work. We have been living here in Ischia since the middle of May. At times the heat has reached 30 degrees Réaumur; and then you have to be strong—as praise God I am—to be able to work with good humour.'

The draft of Act IV was complete by 15 September, and sent off on 18 September with a covering letter:

'I enclose the manuscript for Act IV of my work; the remainder will follow as soon as possible. . . . If the first Act is not yet printed, I would like the following alterations made to the list of characters: instead of Two Thieves put *A Thief and a Receiver;* and if the name Trumpeterstraale was written in the Swedish form (with an "å"), please change it to the Danish form. If the list is too long to go on one page, it could well begin on the previous one, where the title could be rearranged. If the setting-up of the list of characters could in general be postponed until I have sent you the remainder, it would be a good thing, because I might well want to introduce one or two extra subsidiary characters; but this is not imperative.'

In other words, although the shape of the last Act was not fully fixed, Ibsen had not left himself a great deal of room to manœuvre; and even though the Draft of Act V is dated 19 September at the beginning and 14 October at the end, there must surely have been in existence before then some kind of draft or detailed plan to enable Ibsen to speak so confidently of its nature. On 18 October he sent off the final consignment from Sorrento.

He was presumably encouraged to take the risk of sending the manuscript

off piecemeal like this in the hope of getting things to the publisher in time for
the Christmas book market—which his letter of 8 August (above) hinted at.
It is likely that the publisher, too, felt the risk was worth taking, and he probably
fed the copy in instalments to the printer before it was all in. The book was
published on 14 November 1867 in an edition of 1,250 copies. Such had been
the impact of *Brand* the previous year, however, that practically the whole of
this first edition was sold out before publication day. A second printing of a
further 2,000 copies came out within fourteen days of the first. By the end of the
century, it had reached its eleventh edition.

2. SCENARIO AND DRAFT MANUSCRIPTS

Those manuscripts of *Peer Gynt* which have survived comprise four main
items: a fragment of a scenario; a draft version, largely complete, of the play;
a number of revisions and additions on separate leaves or folded sheets which
were later inserted into the Draft; and a Fair Copy.

A. FRAGMENT OF A SCENARIO

Two folded sheets of lined notepaper (i.e. four leaves in all), numbered '2'
and '3' and containing part of a scenario for the play. The original folded sheet,
no. '1', which does not appear to have survived, clearly contained the scenario
for Act I and for the beginning of Act II. The extant fragment takes up the
action some way through Act II and continues it into Act IV. All four sides of
folio '2' are written on; sides 1 and 2 contain the plan for Act II (less the two
opening scenes); sides 3 and 4 contain the outline of Act III. Of folio '3', only
the first side and part of the second side are written on.

The fragment begins in the middle of a sentence:

[. . .] remains behind. Solveig asks Aase to tell more about Peer Gynt.
Oh, says Aase, there's no end to telling about him.

On the other side of the lake. Peer Gynt lies on the bank weeping. Solveig
and Helga come to rest a little, whilst the others go searching round the lake.
They stumble across Peer Gynt. If you had danced with me, this wouldn't
have happened, he says. Now she would do so gladly, she answers. He:
Now it will have to be more. Let him speak out; she will do whatever is
in her power. Stay with me, live with me—But in Jesus' name!—Give me
a kiss—But in Jesus' name! Solveig leaves. Peer Gynt weeps. Now let come
what may. He leaves.

In among barren hills. Peer Gynt enters. Three sæter girls are running about
the hills, shrieking and singing. He bumps into them. They are seized by
both laughter and despair. Wild scenes: they continue on further with Peer
Gynt.

In the Rondane Mountains. Evening. Peer Gynt enters, half crazed; he sees
visions. The woman in green meets him. The mountain opens. Dancing,

cheering and wild gaiety. The visions change. He stands in the pitch dark night outside Aase's sæter hut and encounters the great Boyg. Fight with this great invisible thing. Gains entry. It is empty. Fights his way out again. The Boyg is everywhere. Despair seizes him. Alone, alone! All have forsaken him. Bells are rung for him far away; he hears his mother's voice. The Boyg fades away, the visions vanish, it grows light. Peer Gynt collapses.

On the heights at sunrise. Peer Gynt wakes. Lethargy and nausea have taken possession of him. Little Helga brings food and a message from her sister who waits on the slopes below. He sends a message back. Wants to go far away.

3rd Act

Deep within the great mountain forests. Peer Gynt stands, strong and bold, cutting timber. Day-dreams come; he is slaying giants; he dispels them. He takes a log on his back; then he listens. A youth is moving down on the slopes; he looks cautiously round, and cuts a finger off his hand with his axe. Peer Gynt has turned pale; to think of doing that, to will it, this he can understand; but to do it, this he cannot understand.

In Aase's hut. Aase lies sick. All her thoughts turn to her son. The cottager's wife looks after her. She sees to his clothes and other things. She sings.

Outside Peer Gynt's newly built cabin. Peer Gynt is busy with his joinery. It is nearly evening. Solveig enters with a little bundle. Now he may take her in God's name, she says. It was no life down below. She could not do anything else. She has left father, mother and sister. The worst was saying farewell to them all. Peer Gynt dare scarcely believe it. He lifts her high in the air; he thinks she is too delicate, so to speak; he scarcely dare touch her. She goes in. He will fetch some wood. A lame woman in an old green gown, leading an ugly child by the hand, meets him, He must see his son, she says. He has grown fast. They can all live together. Let Solveig go, and she will become beautiful again. She will pursue; if he embraces Solveig, she will be sitting close by. She leaves. Peer Gynt is alone; all his wild moments pass by in his mind's eye. Ingrid and the sæter girls might also come, he thinks. It will become overcrowded. This is not for Solveig, all this; how fair she was. This evening he cannot tell her anything. There is ugliness in this; he must get away from it. Solveig appears at the doorway and calls to him. Peer Gynt tells her to wait. He goes. Solveig stands at the door and waits.

In Aase's hut. Aase lies on a bed of sickness. Peer Gynt enters. She asks about Solveig. He evades the question. She is dying, she says. But not so soon, says Peer Gynt. She is thinking of sending for the priest. But not this evening, he says; not all that unpleasantness this evening. He sits down on the end of the bed. The cat is a horse, he sings, he drives her to glory and happiness. Aase is dead. The cottager's wife enters. She is to have his mother honourably buried, he says; he himself must go far away. Where, she asks. To the sea, he says; he leaves.

4th Act

On the coast of Africa. Palm trees. Out in the bay lies a yacht flying the Norwegian and American flags. Gay company at a splendid lunch. Mattings and awnings. Peer Gynt, a handsome middle-aged gentleman in an elegant suit with gold-rimmed spectacles and gold lorgnette presides as host at the head of the table. Mr. Cotton, Herr Trumpeterstråle and Herr Eberkopf sit at table; M. Ballon a little apart. The conversation turns to great plans, to the lethargy of the age. Peer Gynt hints at his past. M. Ballon, who has been reading the newspapers, jumps up: the Greeks are in revolt. Here is something to seize on.

Now they can all make their fortune. Mr. Cotton will sink mines in Olympus and calculate the horsepower of the Castalia. M. Ballon wants to come along because he is enraptured. Herr Eberkopf wants to civilize the Greeks and bring the culture of the Fatherland to them; moreover he is destitute. Herr Trumpeterstråle will reveal to the world the great pair of spur strap-buckles which are said to be in Bender. But Peer Gynt, who sits high and dry, does not want to go with them. One may embrace such follies when one owns nothing; but one should not squander God's gifts. He is unwilling to go. The rest wish to leave for Greece, but see no solution until Herr Eberkopf suggests annexing the yacht; to this Mr. Cotton acquiesces with the reservation that he will offer compensation in the form of shares in Olympus and Castalia, Eberkopf will dedicate to P.G. his new work on the War of Civilization, Ballon will send him a laurel wreath, and Trumpeterstråle will give him permission to wear three times the great spur strap-buckles which are said to be in Bender. They approve the annexation; they leave.

Near an oasis in the desert. Peer Gynt alone and forlorn. Men are of no use; he renounces them all, and all friendship. A slave with the Emir's stolen horse and clothes. Peer Gynt buys both from him and rides off across the desert. The thief's reflections. His father and grandfather were thieves. He too; it is a duty to Allah to be oneself. Allah is great!—

B. THE DRAFT

In its extant (defective) form, the basic Draft, i.e. excluding the later interleaved insertions, consists of 113 leaves quarto, the greater part of which are in gatherings of four leaves (i.e. double folded sheets), others of which are single folded sheets of two leaves, and in one instance there is one single leaf. The individual sections of the draft manuscript are numbered 1–32 and are made up as follows:

no. 1   One folded sheet of two leaves; on the first side is a title page 'Peer Gynt/A dramatic poem/by/Henrik Ibsen/1867; the second side is blank; the third side is a further title page with '*Peer Gynt*' only; and the fourth side has a list of characters (see E1 below).

nos. 2–14 Thirteen four-leaf gatherings; the last side of gathering no. 3 contains an early prose version of part of the first encounter between Peer and the Smith, heavily scored out; Act I ends one quarter of the way down no. 6, side 5, and Act II begins at the top of side 6; the writing of no. 9 originally ceased abruptly about one quarter of the way down the last side in the middle of an early draft of the scene with the Dovre-Master—see also E13 below—and Act III begins at the top of no. 10; the last side of no. 12 was half-written, then the passage (which comes in the middle of Aase's death scene) was so heavily scored out as to be illegible; Act III ends one quarter of the way down no. 13, side 4, and Act IV begins at the top of side 5.

[no. 15] One four-leaf gathering missing, containing a large part of the opening scene of Act IV from the toast drunk to 'Swedish steel' (p. 332) to within six short speeches of the end of the scene.

nos. 16–24 Nine four-leaf gatherings; Act IV ends on no. 22, side 3, and Act V begins at the top of the following side.

no. 25 One folded sheet of two leaves, containing the last two-thirds of the graveside scene, from 'He got as far as the door . . .' (p. 388) to the end.

no. 26 One four-leaf gathering, half of the last leaf of which has been cut away, immediately following the end of the auction scene; see also E26 below.

no. 27 One four-leaf gathering, which takes up where the truncated no. 26 leaves off, i.e. the 'onion' speech.

no. 28 Originally a four-leaf gathering, now lacking its first and last leaves, i.e. sides 1 and 2, 7 and 8; the missing passages are (i) from the first Buttonmoulder scene, from 'PEER. Impossible! Not like this! Without warning' (p. 401) to 'BUTTONMOULDER. But you, on the contrary, took sin lightly'; and (ii) the last two full lines of speech of that same scene, from ' . . . Well, is it agreed?' and the first sixteen exchanges of the next scene with the Dovre-Master down to and including ' . . . she has gone to the dogs'.

no. 29 One folded sheet of two leaves.

nos. 30–31 Two four-leaf gatherings.

no. 32 One single leaf.

Gatherings nos. 2–9 were stitched together; the later gatherings are merely folded one sheet inside the other. The handwriting as far as the middle of no. 16 is for the most part careful and well-formed; thereafter it is clearly hastier. Throughout the entire draft there are extensive corrections and deletions.

At a number of key points this Draft is dated: 14 Jan. and 25 Feb. 1867 at the beginning and end of Act I respectively; 3 March 1867 at the beginning of Act II; 15 June and 2 July 1867 at the beginning and end of Act III; 15 Sept. 1867 at the end of Act IV; and 19 Sept. and 14 Oct. 1867 at the beginning and end of Act V. A note at the end of Act III runs: 'Despatched in fair copy from Ischia 8 Aug. 1867; and at the end of Act IV: 'Despatched in fair copy from Sorrento 18 Sept. 1867'.

C. THE DRAFT: SUPPLEMENTARY ITEMS

Inserted at various points into the original main draft are a number of supplementary items on separate pieces of paper, both quarto and octavo, single and folded.

1. Between gatherings nos. 8 and 9 was inserted one folded sheet (i.e. two leaves), octavo, written on three sides and containing the revision of a passage that originally began on the last side of no. 8 and continued on no. 9: the monologue in Act II 'in Rondane' (p. 290); see also E11 below.

2. Between gatherings nos. 9 and 10 were inserted five folded sheets (i.e. ten leaves in all), octavo, lettered *a*, *b*, *c*, *d* and *e*, containing a re-cast version of the last three scenes of Act II, together with a fragment of prose dialogue (on *b*, last side) relating to the scene with the Trolls; see E13 and 14 below.

3. Within gathering no. 16 were inserted two separate unnumbered leaves, quarto, containing revisions and extra material for parts of Act IV (Peer's 'nightmare' soliloquy); see E16 below.

D. FAIR COPY

The fair copy consists of 29 unnumbered gatherings, quarto, each gathering consisting of a double folded sheet (i.e. four leaves), with the exception of gatherings nos. 21 and 29 which each consist of six leaves; two further unnumbered leaves containing the title page and the list of characters were added later, making in all a total of 122 leaves. The handwriting is carefully formed throughout; there are, however, a number of alterations on the manuscript of a not very far-reaching kind.

E. DRAFT AND FAIR COPY COMPARED

Very many of the minor drafting changes are such that they are difficult or impossible to convey in translation. The following are some of the more substantial changes.

E 1. The list of characters shows both differences in nomenclature and also significant omissions:

The characters

Aase, a farmer's widow
Peer Gynt, her son
Two old women with corn sacks
The Smith
Wedding guests
The Man at Hæggstad
The Bride, his daughter
Matt Moen, the bridegroom
Sølve⎫
Birgit⎭ new arrivals in the district
Solveig⎫
Helga, a child⎭ their daughters
Several wedding guests
The Steward, the Fiddler, etc.
A woman in green
Three sæter girls
An ugly child
Elfin-folk and trolls
Foreign seamen
Anitra, the Bedouin's daughter
The Statue of Memnon (singing)
The Sphinx of Gizeh (non-speaking part)
Frasenfeldt, a philosopher
Tuhu, a language reformer from the Malabar coast
Hussein junior, an Oriental minister
A living man with a corpse
Sanatorium visitors from various countries
A Norwegian skipper
Mate, cook, sailors
A Priest
A funeral procession

The action which begins in the ⟨previous century and ends in this one *crossed out and replaced by*⟩ early part of this century and ends close to the present day takes place in Gudbrandsdal, in the mountains, on the coast of Africa, in the Sahara Desert, in the lunatic asylum in Cairo, on the sea, etc., etc.

E 2. At a number of points there are changes of versification between the Draft and the final version; Ibsen re-cast some of the stricter metres into freer rhythms more reminiscent of folk song.

E 3. In the Draft, Peer's antecedents were different (cf. pp. 259-60):

> Your father was a gentleman;
> It was as well Our Lord took him
> Suddenly away, before you struck him
> To the heart, you brand of hell!
>
> [*Weeping.*]
>
> Why did you not become a
> Lad like Niels, your eldest brother?
> Ah, he joined the service of the King,
> And met his death away at the wars.
> You, my Peter, became my only one,
> Grew up, became big and strong,
> Were to stand as a staff and a prop
> For your poor old mother,
> Were to see to running the farm,
> To stand in my husband's place,
> And in that of the eldest son—
> Oh, God help me for all the help
> I've had from you, you wastrel.

E 4. The scene as Peer Gynt approaches Hægstad apparently lacked the 'cloud' reverie in its earliest form; sides 5 and 6 of gathering no. 3 originally ran as follows (cf. p. 268):

> [*A small hill covered with scrub and heather. The road goes round the foot of the hillside.* PEER GYNT *appears from above; he stops where the view opens up.*]
>
> PEER GYNT. ⟨There's Hægstad. I shall soon be there.
> I shall tread a dance they'll not easily forget.
>
> [*Pauses a moment.*]
>
> The entire green is swarming with people.
> Should I go? Or should I wait?
> If only they didn't all secretly laugh.
> They all have that habit, both men and girls.
>
> [*Clenches his fists.*]
>
> That hellish laughter! The whole village laughs. . . .
> Not in front of you; not so you see it yourself. . . .
> Puh! You could hit the devils in the face.
> No, they walk past, softly, like cats.
> 'Nice to meet you', they say, and raise their hats.
> But behind you, behind you they turn around,

Pull a sour face, narrow their eyes,
Say nothing, walk on, as quietly as they came.
But they think—behind you. Think so you feel it
Burning and searing its way right through you. . . .
They say nothing; never abuse you.
Just thoughts, wordless thoughts and smiles.
You could scream, like a sawblade being filed.
And behind your back! That's what's nasty!⟩

[*Short pause.*]

If I had a drink to start me off,
Or if I could walk about invisible,
Or if nobody knew me. A good strong drink's
The way to stop the laughter stinging.

[*Suddenly listens, and hides among the bushes. Some* WEDDING GUESTS *go past.*]

A WOMAN [*conversing*].
Well, one wonders where it will all end?

A MAN. In jail, I imagine.

WOMAN. It surely will.

[*They go on.* PEER GYNT *comes forward, hot with shame, and stares after them.*]

PEER GYNT [*softly*].
Was it me they were talking about?

[*With a forced shrug.*]

Well, let them!
I don't suppose slander's likely to kill me.

[*He throws himself down in the heather.*]

⟨For all I care, the Hægstad girl can marry
Anybody she likes. No skin off my nose.

[*Longish pause.*]

My breeches are torn. I'm a grim sight.
If only I'd got something new to put on.⟩

The passages between the angled brackets were later struck out; the opening six lines of his soliloquy in the final version (but without the stage directions) were entered in the margin; and a new start was made at the top of the next side (side 7 of gathering no. 3) with the 'cloud' soliloquy (see p. 269).

E 5. On the last side of the same gathering as above (no. 3), there is a prose version of part of the encounter between Peer and the Smith, heavily struck out:

> There he lies, the swine, sleeping off his drunken stupor.
>
> PEER GYNT [*starts up*]. What the . . . ! Ah, Smith, so it's you!
>
> SMITH. Is it a six-weeks' binge you are lying sleeping off here?
>
> PEER GYNT. Lies!
>
> SMITH. Can you deny that you left the village six weeks ago—after the affair at Lunde?
>
> PEER GYNT. But I haven't been drinking!
>
> SMITH. People say you've been causing trouble in the western mountains . . .
>
> PEER GYNT. I've been doing great things there!
>
> SEVERAL [*under general laughter*]. Oh, tell us, Peer!
>
> PEER GYNT. Not a word. Let me be.
>
> SMITH. Are you going to Hægstad?
>
> PEER GYNT. No!
>
> SMITH. You do right. I'm going there.

Immediately following this deleted passage there follows (beginning on the first side of gathering no. 4) the version in verse of this encounter, more or less as it is in the printed text.

E 6. In the scene in Act I where the Wedding Guests are taunting Peer, there were some additional lines in the draft which were later struck out and not included in the final version (see p. 277):

> PEER GYNT [*throwing up his head*]. I'm able to ride
> Clean through the air on marvellous horses!
> And that's not all I can do, let me say!
> I have a pair of trousers, with their pockets full
> Of silver coins!
>
> [*General laughter.*]
>
> SEVERAL [*laughing*]. Silver! Surely you mean gold!
>
> PEER GYNT [*his passions rising*].
> I could make you as rich as Counts!
>
> SEVERAL. Oh, do that!
>
> PEER GYNT.   Never as long as I live!

ONE OF THE CROWD.
    Take a ride in the air, then!

E 7. When Peer tries to persuade Solveig into dancing with him, he uses
    different arguments from those in the final version (see pp. 279–80):

PEER GYNT. Oh, yes! And then perhaps I'm slightly drunk.
    I did that because the others offended me.
    Will you . . . ?

SOLVEIG.   I dare not, even though I want to.

PEER GYNT. What are you afraid of?

SOLVEIG.   My father, mostly.

PEER GYNT. Your father? I get it. He's a devout one.
    Hangs his head, eh? Well! Answer me!

SOLVEIG. Answer what?

PEER GYNT.   Isn't your father
    Pious, and your mother is probably the same?
    Well, will you answer!

SOLVEIG.   Let me be in peace!

PEER GYNT. Oh, how high you carry your noses!
    Oh, I understood what you were as soon as you came.
    Your mother smirked; he raised his hat.
    He padded by, softly, like some cat.
    You speak nicely and sweetly—by God, yes!
    But your thoughts are of a different brew.

    [*Changing his tone and speaking as in fear.*]

    Solveig, do dance with me!

E 8. Just before Aase makes her appearance at the end of Act I, Solveig is
    allowed in the Draft a two-line comment on Peer (p. 281):

    They are all on to him, like the birds of the day
    Cackling around a poor sun-shy owl.

The last two lines of Act I show the anger of the groom's father rather
than the bride's, and a somewhat different attitude on Aase's part from
her stance in the final version:

GROOM'S FATHER. This deed will cost him his life and health!

AASE. Take farm and land if it can save my son!

E 9. Aase's speech beginning 'The world's fury . . .' (pp. 285–6) and ending ' . . . On the brow of the hill there!' is missing from the Draft.

E 10. Following immediately on the scene between Solveig, Aase and the Man, there was an entire scene with Peer Gynt, Solveig, Aase and Solveig's parents which was later struck out in the Draft; it was followed by the scene with the Three Sæter Girls. The scene originally ran as follows (cf. p. 288):

> [*The other side of the lake.* PEER GYNT *is lying among the blueberry clumps. Now and then he tugs at the heather; he weeps intermittently.*]

PEER GYNT. What will it come to? [*Twists.*] Ah, dear God,
That I did not bethink myself in time!

> [*He looks across at the lake.*]

Perhaps it were best to leap out and into . . .

> [*He again twists and turns.*]

But then one would lie and struggle so long.
And then the others would live.

> [*He is silent for a moment.*]

                        To lie cold and pale.
To be parted from it all, both friends and games . . .
And the sun is shining. . . . If only one could
Douse the sun and drag it down with you.

SOLVEIG [*enters with* HELGA].
Here you can rest until the others get here.

PEER GYNT [*half starts up*]. Ah!

SOLVEIG. Oh, no . . . !

> [*She turns to shout behind her.*]

PEER GYNT [*jumps up*]. Hush! Are there many of you?

SOLVEIG [*pointing*]. Only the old folk.

PEER GYNT.   Ah, only them.
Because I won't be taken captive alive!

SOLVEIG. But Ingrid . . . ?

PEER GYNT.   What of her?

SOLVEIG.   Where is she?

PEER GYNT [*shortly*]. Gone home.

SOLVEIG. Home!

PEER GYNT [*puffing*]. Do you think I care anything for her?

SOLVEIG. But how could you . . . ?

PEER GYNT [*cutting her short*]. Well, now. . . . Let's have done with that!

[SOLVEIG *is silent; he looks quietly at her for a moment, then he says:*]
You should have gone and danced with me.

SOLVEIG. How can you talk of these trifles now?

PEER GYNT. Great or small . . . You see how it goes.

SOLVEIG [*bursts into tears*]. Oh, for shame that you blame it on me.

PEER GYNT. It is no shame. You drove me to violence and anger!

[*He flings on his clothes.*]
It took me to hell.

SOLVEIG. Then God have pity . . . !

PEER GYNT. Will you make amends?

SOLVEIG. Yes, as truly and surely
As God and Jesus Christ shall help me!

PEER GYNT [*looks at her*]. Dance?

SOLVEIG. Dance? Yes, as long as you wish!

PEER GYNT. Thanks, but more is required than that now.

SOLVEIG. Well, then I'll do more.

PEER GYNT. Then stay up here.
We'll tend the deer among the peaks. . . .
We'll build a house that no one shall find. . . .
A royal estate deep within the forest. . . .
Will you?

SOLVEIG. But in Jesus' name!

PEER GYNT. That's just like you!
Yes or no!

SOLVEIG. Can you think such a thing!

PEER GYNT. Can I kiss you then? Then you can go.

SOLVEIG. But in Jesus' name!

PEER GYNT.   Answer! Will you let me? Well!

SOLVEIG. Can you think such a thing!

PEER GYNT [*after a while*].   How stupid of me to ask.
   Go, as you came. It makes no difference to me!

   [*He is about to go; at that moment* AASE *enters, accompanied by*
   SOLVEIG'S PARENTS.]

AASE. Well, we've found you, then: you thief, you robber!
   You'll cleave my heart before you are finished!
   Where's Ingrid, you wretch? Quick, bring her out!

SOLVEIG. No, do not scold him. He's sent her home!

THE MAN. Sent her home?

AASE.   Then the good Lord help us.
   The first was bad, but the last is worse!

SOLVEIG. Worse?

AASE. Home! Dear God, what have you done?

PEER GYNT. Don't preach! I'll see that I make my escape!

THE MAN. Can you run away from sin?

AASE.   My poor boy!

PEER GYNT. Be quiet. You'll end by driving me mad!

AASE. Yes, I'll be quiet. But take to your heels.
   Just tell me where!

PEER GYNT.   It's all the same.

               [*Turns suddenly to the man.*]

   Man, give me your daughter. Let us go together.
   She will bring me both joy and gain.

⟨THE MOTHER. To you! *altered to*⟩

AASE. Oh, yes!

THE MAN.   I'll make a coffin for her first.

PEER GYNT. She shall have a good life.

AASE.   I'll see to some food!

PEER GYNT. You think they'll tear us up by the roots;
With the farm and all wiped out in fines?
Instead I'll build one ten times as big;
Just wait till a year . . . or five or six have passed.

THE MAN. Very well. You shall have her.

PEER GYNT.   You mean it!

THE MAN.   Yes.
On one condition.

PEER GYNT.   Very well. Speak out!

THE MAN. Go down and surrender to the forces of law.
Demand the penalty as the fruit of the crime.
Bear the scorn and contempt of men,
Be strong in the power of a humble mind.
Seven years in prison is what the law says.
Bear all seven as a punishment from above;
And when you have borne them, return to the village;
And if you think as now, you shall have my daughter.

THE WOMAN. Man!

AASE.   Never heard such nonsense!

PEER GYNT. In prison!

THE MAN.   Go through. Will you?

PEER GYNT.   No thanks!

THE MAN. Hear me, hear me, you soul forlorn!
The devil plays for you, do you not see?
Already he's won the best part of you!
Now the rest stands balanced on a single throw.
Never were you bidden to choose as now.
Damned or saved; hosannahs or terror!
Let life's dread smite you wholly asunder,
Smelt you, transform you from raven to dove,
Burn so you rise purified by the flame!
Choose, choose, choose in the name of the Lord!

PEER GYNT. Can you think that way!

THE MAN.   The demand is unjust?

PEER GYNT. How do I know! But first I must live,
First I must try my wings in the world.
I cannot now go and shut myself in,

Perhaps to hard labour, suffering hunger and thirst—
Man, you need to find better conditions.

THE MAN. Raise the tabernacle of the Lord in your heart.
Serve seven years, as did Jacob for Rachel.

AASE. Seven years is long.

THE MAN.   Eternity longer.

⟨*A break seems required here, but is not indicated in the manuscript.
The sense seems to suggest that Ibsen struck out the above scene and
started again, and then once more gave up after a few lines.*⟩

[*The other side of the lake.* PEER GYNT *is poised to jump.* SOLVEIG *has
just encountered him.*]

PEER GYNT. Solveig!

SOLVEIG.   Peer!

PEER GYNT.   So you've come then!

SOLVEIG. But Ingrid . . .

PEER GYNT.   She is far away . . .

E 11. The soliloquy 'in Rondane' in Act II (see pp. 290–2) originally had a
different form:

[PEER GYNT *enters, wild and in despair.*]

PEER GYNT. Stop! Now it disappears again!
Wall and gable and tower and peaks . . .
All things run away to nothing . . .
Ha! look there! Those shining men!
What a throng in every crevice!
See how they make themselves so tall,
See how they grow, and how they lift
Their heron's feet. Well, come along!
You think that you can catch Peer Gynt . . .
That's a thing to wrangle about.
Ah! What's happened to them all?
Now all the heights are empty.
Away they flowed like rainbow rings . . .
What is this that wounds my vision?
And this that sounds from distant parts?
Ah! this tightness round my forehead,
Aching, aching. Who the devil
Screwed this ring about my brow.
I've been hunting all day long,

And moreover—what is worse—
Did I not go chasing off,
Carrying that damned buck on my back!
Dance in the meadows; games and mead . . .
More than that. H'm. Thanks as may be.
Girl, you're blushing, turning pale . . .
Trembling between joy and distress . . .
Say then, was Peer Gynt a braggart.

[*The snowy peaks shine more and more strongly in the evening sun.*]

Look, look there! Grandfather's house!
Lights shine out from every pane!
They have gone, those ancient rags.
The family rises again from the dust.
What a din! Ha! There's a feast!
Dean and captain fling their glasses
And their bottles through the windows!
That's all right! Let them squander!

[*Cries out.*]

The goblin lives in the attic still!
You came from greatness, and great you shall be!

[*Leaps forward, but runs his forehead against the rockface, falls and remains lying there.*]

E 12. In the Draft, the setting of the scene with the Woman in Green was a high-vaulted room, not the hillside (cf. p. 292):

[*A great vaulted hall; lights blink and shine from the roof and from the walls.* PEER GYNT *is lying on a broad bench. A* WOMAN IN GREEN *is sitting bent over him.*]

WOMAN IN GREEN. Is it true?

PEER GYNT.   As true as it is festive here.
As true as you are a beautiful woman.
I shall arrange things nice and fine,
And you shall neither spin nor weave.

WOMAN IN GREEN. And you will not beat me?

E 13. The original scene with the Dovre-Master is incomplete in the Draft, and it is much more satirical, with more contemporary allusions, than is the final version (pp. 294 ff.); this scene in the Draft stops abruptly:

[*The hall of the* DOVRE-MASTER. *Great Troll banquet. The company is sitting at table.* DOVRE-MASTER *on the throne, and by his side* PEER GYNT *and the* WOMAN IN GREEN, *both dressed for a wedding.* TROLLS *of both sexes line the table.*]

CHORUS [*in unison*].
    Then one day we'll surely wake
    And burst our fetters, bonds and straints!
    Let us drain our glasses now
    To Dovre, birthplace of all trolls!

DOVRE-MASTER [*speaking from his throne*].
    The first five songs praised our native land,
    The last eight had no different theme.
    That's fine! It shows a common mind,
    That never looks outwards, always in.
    Now we might in a different way
    Proclaim our Dovre's praise again;
    In place of songs we'll have a speech.
    My son-in-law from the distant vales
    Ought to know the folk he's to live among.
    We'll speak of ourselves, unadorned and plain,
    So we tickle *our* ear and *he* grows wise.

THE COURT TROLL.
    The King will always seize the chance
    To profit and please the mind at once.

THE PROFESSOR TROLL ⟨*altered to:* THE WISDOM TROLL⟩ [*rises*].
    It is doubtless I, though undeserved,
    The King intends should make a speech.
    I'm not prepared; I'm lacking words.
    I'll make the speech I made last year,
    Which I also made two years ago.
    But lots of things are forgotten with time;
    And possibly here and there it held
    The seed of a somewhat golden truth,
    Deserving life; which should not die
    By being forgotten by honourable trolls.
    Well then, as I've said myself before—
    Our strength resides in petrifaction. . . .

DOVRE-MASTER. Stop! It is better that speeches come
    From the mouths of all who know these things.
    All know something, but no one knows all.

THE COURT TROLL. These are wisdom's words!

DOVRE-MASTER.   So if you can,
Tell us what marks a troll from a man?

THE PROFESSOR TROLL.
Out there, under the glimmering sky,
Men say: 'To thine own self be true.'
In the shadowy world of trolls, we say
'To thine own self be—*all-sufficient!*'

THE BISHOP TROLL.
This word 'sufficient' you must mark, my son.
'Sufficient', my son, that potent, thundering
Word you must bear on your coat of arms.

PEER GYNT. Yes, but . . .

DOVRE-MASTER.   You must if you're to be master here.

PEER GYNT. Ah, well, here goes. It might have been worse.

DOVRE-MASTER. Name our domestic way of life,
Praise us all and our Dovre-home.

THE FOLK TROLL.   From the cow we get cake,
                         From the bullock mead;
                         Don't ask if the taste
                         Is sour or sweet.
The main thing is, and don't you forget it,
It's all home-made.

PEER GYNT.   Home-made the devil!
I'll never get used to this country's habits.

DOVRE-MASTER. The bowl goes with it, it's made of gold;
Worth to be drained to the very last drop.

PEER GYNT. Well, it's said 'You must master your instincts';
I suppose in time it won't seem so sour.
Here goes!

DOVRE-MASTER. With that you spoke good sense.
You'll find in time it's not bad here.

[*To the* POET TROLL.]

What is it that gladdens our eyes and ears,
And what is a decent troll to wear?

THE POET TROLL. Our song-girl strums her cat-gut tune in russet;
Our dancing girl goes tripping in short hose;

All's mountain-style, with nothing from the valley
Except the silken bow tied to our tail.

PEER GYNT. But I have no . . .

DOVRE-MASTER.   What you have not can yet be yours.
We shall bind it upon you nice and neat.
You shall have a golden bow to wear,
Which counts as the highest honour among us. . . .

PEER GYNT. Does it not state that man is but dust . . . ?
One has to make some concession to fashion . . .
Here goes!

DOVRE-MASTER. You're a sensible chap.

PEER GYNT [*to himself*].
A tail doesn't make an animal of man.

DOVRE-MASTER.

⟨*The Draft breaks off here abruptly about one third of the way down the last side of gathering no. 9; the whole of the above passage was then subsequently struck out. It is immediately followed by stage directions, which were not struck out, as follows:*⟩

[*The hall of the* DOVRE-MASTER. *Large gathering of* TROLLS. *The* DOVRE-MASTER *is on the throne with crown and sceptre.* PEER GYNT *stands before him. Great alarm among the* ELVES, GOBLINS *and* COURT TROLLS.]

⟨*There then follows a succession of wavy lines in ink, simulating writing and filling up the remainder of the side, which is the last side of gathering no. 9. At the foot of the page there is a note:*⟩

(NB. Here add supplementary sheets *a*, *b*, *c*, *d*, and *e*.)

⟨*These sheets—see* C2 *above—contain the last three scenes of Act II (with the Trolls; with the Boyg; and with Solveig and Helga) very largely as in the printed version.*⟩

E 14. The last side of insert '*b*' (see C2 above) carries, 'upside down', a fragment of prose dialogue, which was subsequently crossed out:

[*The hall of the* DOVRE-MASTER. *Large gathering of* TROLL FOLK, ELVES *and* GOBLINS. *The* DOVRE-MASTER *himself sits on the throne with a crown on his head and a sceptre in his hand.* PEER GYNT *stands in front of him.*]

TROLLS. Eat him! Eat him! The son of a Christian man pays court to the Dovre-Master's daughter!

YOUNG TROLLS. May I pinch a bit of his loins?

OTHERS. May I bite a finger off?

TROLL WITCH [*with a ladle*]. Does he go on the spit or into the pot?

TROLLS. Slaughter him! Flay him! Incredibly crazy fool, paying court to the Dovre-Master's daughter!

DOVRE-MASTER. Ice-water in the blood. That wouldn't have been tolerated in the old days; but we have gone astern, that cannot be denied; and time that wears away the rock face also wears away the rough edges between neighbour and neighbour. There is not nearly so great a distinction now between a Christian man and a troll as there was before.

E 15. A passage of some 27 lines in the opening scene of Act IV in the Draft was not taken up into the final version (see p. 331); the passage originally ran:

PEER GYNT. A small one, but full of wiles
To make a man commit himself.
Stake your money liberally,
And lose it, if it must be so. . . .
You may bear it with equanimity
For next time it's your turn to win;
If not, your losses are in no way such
As to constitute any real difference.
Stake your honour for a while;
You can always have it rinsed
From black to grey, from grey to white;
And if you can't—with honour spotted,
So long as you're wrapped in a golden cloak,
In the eyes of the world it's just as though
You walked about immaculate.
Neither are these losses such
As to constitute any real difference.
Stake your conscience there as well,
Along with what's called inner peace . . .
But unintentionally—please to note.
Even Paul resisted the light,
And stubbornly kicked against the pricks;
Yet who would dare to call him rotten?
Why? Because it was nothing such
As to constitute any real difference.
The whole art contained in this,

The great art of showing courage,
Is this: to keep your freedom of choice
Wherever you find yourself in life. . . . ⟨*etc.*⟩

E 16. One of Peer's monologues—the 'nightmare'—in Act IV shows some differences in the Draft from the version eventually incorporated into the final version (cf. pp. 338–9):

PEER GYNT. A dream! Mere dreams! I'll wake up soon.
She's moving offshore! At a rate of knots!
⟨A dream! I insist upon its being a dream! *altered to*⟩
Sheer illusion! I fell asleep drunk or delirious!
Horrible! Huh! But nevertheless true.
My villainous friends! Hear me, God!
You're an all-wise and righteous judge!
Bid them turn back this very minute!
I cannot possibly end my days here.
It's *me* that matters! Protect me, God!
Take care of me, Father, or I shall perish . . .
Listen! Don't fret about other people;
The world can look after itself for a while!
⟨They're sailing! He's deaf to all entreaty *altered to*⟩
They're sailing! Him! He's deaf as usual!
How nice! A God who's run out of advice.
Quick! Retire, off to your Fathers
If you can't deal with things any better than that.
In the desert. Abandoned. And evening approaching . . .
What shall I do . . . ! Oh, God help and keep me.
It's me, ⟨Peer *altered to*⟩ Peter Gynt, who's calling! Listen!
You cannot intend that I should die!
Haven't I repaid you for looking after me,
And for letting me keep the life you gave me!
Listen! I've got rid of the nigger plantation,
And sent the missionaries across to Asia. . . .
One good turn surely deserves another?
Get me on that boat! . . .

E 17. One passage contained on one of the supplementary leaves inserted in gathering no. 16 of the Draft was not taken up into the final version (cf. pp. 340–1):

PEER GYNT. What's *that*? People here? Somebody snorted . . .
There's a noise in the branches! Ugh—what a screech!
Oh, save . . . ! Pah! It's only a monkey . . . !
And more than just one—this is bloody hell!

Throwing fruit at me. No, something else.
Calamity! Now for a restless night.
Well, watch and ward, as the saying goes.

[*Tries to sleep but is disturbed again.*]

I must put a stop to this persecution!
I must try and catch one of the brutes,
Hang him and skin him, and disguise
Myself, somehow, in his hairy coat.
And perhaps the others will think I'm real.
The main thing is to distort one's speech
And learn the art of wagging one's tail.
⟨They said in Norway—which is very true—
Howl with the wolves that you move amongst *crossed out*⟩
One has to make some concession to fashion.
Ah, what is a man? Only dust.

[*Uneasily.*]

No, not quite. If I keep my health
I'm sure Our Lord will see to salvation.
Just build upon Him. He knows what portion
Of the chalice of need I am able to drink.
He looks on my person with the eye of a father . . .

[*Strikes out wildly.*]

It's that creature again! Ah, I missed him!

[*Continues to fight with the monkey.*]

E 18. The Draft contains (gathering no. 16) a prose version of the dialogue
between 'Horse thief' and 'Clothes thief' (cf. p. 342):

[*Rocky place in the desert. Two* THIEVES *in a ravine with the Emperor's horse and clothes.*]

HORSE THIEF. Tongues of lances here and there on all sides!

CLOTHES THIEF. Tongues of lances flickering like a snake's forked sting.

HORSE THIEF. Licking after our throats; twisting, stretching . . . alas, alas!

CLOTHES THIEF. Allah is great, but why did you bid me listen to evil advice when I have tasted the forbidden drink . . .

HORSE THIEF. He is great, but my father was a thief, and his father and his father's father, and it stays in the blood . . .

All the above passage, with the exception of the stage directions, is crossed out on the Draft; and a revised version in verse follows immediately on the same page. This revised version is very similar to the final version, except that the characters are still designated HORSE THIEF and CLOTHES THIEF, and the double lines of verse are (in all but one instance) written as one line.

E 19. In Peer's monologue following the scene between the two thieves, the Draft contains a passage, some of which was eventually adapted and used for the monologue *preceding* the scene with the two thieves (see pp. 340–1):

> The bed in the palm tree was somewhat narrow,
> Yet despite it all it wasn't too bad.
> But it was a nuisance about that monkey
> Who kept bombarding my neck and back
> With date-palm nuts for half the night.
> If he starts any more again tonight,
> I must put a stop to this persecution;
> I must try and catch one of the brutes,
> Hang him and skin him, and envelop
> Myself, somehow, in his hairy skin.
> And perhaps the others will think I'm real.
> ⟨Perhaps I can manage with simply the tail;
> Wear that, and in the dark one resembles an ell
> Of the same material of which monkeys are made *crossed out*⟩
> They said in Norway—which is very true—
> Howl with the wolves you move amongst.
> You must join forces with those who surround you;
> That's a theory which is borne out in time.
> If the many will not climb up to the one,
> Then the one must descend to the many.

E 20. A passage of four lines, originally in the draft version of Peer's monologue (p. 344), was crossed out and not taken up into the final version:

> [. . .]   Nature is prodigal.
> ⟨A graveland, as big as the face of the moon,
> Death's Holland, low lying, below the sea,
> Created never to be woken to life,
> Born to be buried within the hour *crossed out*⟩

E 21. The passage in the same monologue describing Peer's plans for establishing Gyntiana was originally different at a number of points from the final version (cf. pp. 344–5):

[. . .] to the Upper Nile.
⟨What a priceless gain for humanity,
An undying garland for my brow! *crossed out*⟩
Emperor Peer Gynt! Here I have my land!
I am its creator in the fullest sense.
On a plump oasis in the ocean
I would propagate the Norwegian race,
⟨Ennoble its blood by crossing it with English *crossed out*⟩
A dalesman's blood is almost royal,
And, crossed with English, would do the trick.
⟨Emperor Peer Gynt! That's how it shall be!
Finally, finally, honour would be mine!
Finally I'd have managed to raise the clan
Higher than it had ever risen before *crossed out*⟩
The world is old! Now it's the turn
Of Gyntiana, the land of the future;
Around the bay, on rising ground,
I shall build the main city, Peeropolis—
Given the capital, it's as good as done.
A golden key to the gate of the ocean!
Glad cries of freedom in every land.
Across the world I'll send a call,
Baptize the lands now under a yoke
In the name of freedom and the times to come.
A crusade against Death. The rich skinflint
Can open the sack he sits brooding over.
On now! I must on in east and west!
My kingdom—half my kingdom for a horse!

E 22. The line from Goethe's *Faust* (see p. 349)—'Das Ewig-Weibliche zieht
uns hinan'—was originally set down in the Draft as 'Das evig weibliche
ziet ⟨?⟩ uns herann ⟨?⟩', and subsequently amended on the Draft to
'Das evig weibliche ziehet uns an'. Neither the *Efterladte Skrifter* nor
the *Hundreårsutgave* accurately notes this point.

E 23. One passage in Peer's monologue that follows the Anitra scenes was
quite heavily amended and in the end discarded (see p. 358):

[. . .] pretty speeches to that goose.
But basically that was a matter of chance.
One's bitten, the other escapes with a bark.
Yes, the position is and remains unhappy.
It is written in classical poetry
That truth is found in fuddled madness;
And the saying is right in theory.

But the fuddle one gets from pure nature
Has often a taste of madness mixture.
This happened to me! H'm! Imagine:
To try to make time stand still by dancing!

E 24. Six lines of Peer Gynt's speech immediately before he meets the Strange
Passenger were crossed out in the Draft and omitted from the final
version (cf. p. 380):

[. . .] sink with the whole boiling.
There's something uncanny, quite inexplicable,
In what is called shared responsibility.
There is no guilt, and yet there is punishment
As though the bullet struck by sheer chance.
As though the helmsman ⟨lacked *altered to*⟩ shut one eye
Or at least didn't take too much care—
One's personal merits [. . .]

E 25. The concluding lines of Peer's speech at the end of the graveyard scene
with the Priest originally ran as follows (cf. p. 390):

[. . .] according to the instructions.
There is one saying that cannot fail:
That the Bible's words are valid for all.
Now, safe and content, to follow the road;
Perhaps my reward will be to win my case.
Old Peer Gynt, was he not born and bred
As the rightful heir to that estate.
And if the Lord grants shelter and meat
I'll remember that priest with a Christmas box.

E 26. In the auction scene in Act V, the stage directions were more explicit
than in the final version; in place of '*A mill in ruins beside the river; the
ground torn up; desolation all around. Higher up a large farmhouse*', the Draft
has '*The mill house has long ago collapsed; the river has burst its banks and
torn up the ground; desolation all around. Up at the farmhouse an auction is
being held.*' The MAN IN MOURNING was first designated in the Draft as
the SCHOOLMASTER; the TWENTY-YEAR-OLD was simply A LAD; the MAN
IN GREY at first simply ANOTHER MAN; finally the identities are revealed
in the exchanges:

ANOTHER MAN. You're forgetting me. Are you drunk and stupid?

THE MAN. No, Matt—⟨*altered from* You're forgetting⟩ the door of
the storehouse at Hægstad.

THE FIRST. That's true. But you've never been very particular.

THE MAN. As long as she don't make a fool out of Death—

⟨FIRST *crossed out*⟩ MATT. Come on, brother! Let's drink to our fellowship!

ASLAK. Fellowship be damned. You're pissed already.

MATT. Nonsense. Blood's not so thin we don't
Know we're all a part of Peer Gynt.

E 27. The last side of the truncated gathering no. 26 contains an earlier passage of Peer's 'onion' speech which was struck out (see p. 396):

> How nice it is that man is an onion.
> It's not just clothes but the body itself
> One peels off oneself to the centre bud.
> But what is so fine is that deep down within
> The ⟨innermost *altered to*⟩ juiciest self of the lie is found.
> Now I shall peel you [. . .]

E 28. The Draft contains an earlier version of Solveig's final song (cf. p. 421):

> Sleep, my boy, my dearest one,
> I will rock you, you my care.
> Sleep and dream your way to heaven,
> I shall guard against sun and wind.
> Protect you from the mountain's harm,
> Brush the terror from your brow.
> Sleep, my boy, my precious dear,
> I will rock you, you my care.

F. THE SEQUENCE OF PARTS

Like geological strata in a weathered landscape, a number of different stages stand revealed in these preliminary manuscripts. Handwriting styles offer a useful guide. Gatherings 2–14, mostly written in a fair hand, could well have derived from an earlier and more hastily written draft comparable to the extant gatherings 17–32. Further sub-divisions also suggest themselves. No. 28 is much more carefully formed than no. 27, for instance, and may have been specially rewritten from a version too heavily amended to be carried forward. Conversely, certain passages remained virtually untouched—Act III, for example—whereas some of the other scenes might have needed rewriting several times before they were adjudged suitable or (as in one case) wholly unsuitable.

Occasionally, too, fragments of what must have been very early stages in the play's composition—draft prose passages upon which the final verse

passages were constructed—have survived because Ibsen, cannily or inad-
vertently, used up the other unwritten pages of the folded sheet containing the
prose passages. (The last side of E4 above is possibly a case in point.)

The Scenario fragment presents a special problem. There have been sug-
gestions—the most authoritative of which have been made by the editors of
the Norwegian Centenary Edition—that this scenario might belong to the very
earliest stages of the play's composition, and could well be part of 'the entire
plan . . . set down on paper' to which Ibsen referred in his letter to Hegel of
5 January 1867 (see pp. 451–2). On the other hand, although it is natural to think
of the sequence Scenario/Draft/Fair Copy as being the normal one, there are
aspects of *this* Scenario that seem to put it later in time than some parts of the
Draft. And there is no inherent reason why Ibsen should not at some stage have
revised an earlier draft scenario to bring it into line with his more mature plans.
(We know from other plays, e.g. *Pillars of Society*, that this was often his
practice.) In such a case, the Scenario would serve partly as a summary of
what had so far been done and partly as a design to be followed. The revisions
which Ibsen seems to have made to Act II illustrate the problem very clearly:

1. At one time, the play contained a scene—the third in Act II, though Ibsen
   did not number his scenes—between Peer Gynt and Solveig. In the Scenario,
   the scene is between Peer and Solveig only, with Helga in attendance; in
   the Draft, the scene additionally brings in Aase and Solveig's parents. This
   scene was heavily struck out on the manuscript and a new start on the scene
   made (on the same page), which only progressed a few lines before it was
   also struck out; this scene apparently did not include Helga. Finally, in the
   Fair Copy, the entire scene was omitted. It is difficult to know here whether
   Draft followed Scenario or Scenario Draft: whether the addition of the
   Aase/Solveig's Parents incident was a later *elaboration* on the earlier simpler
   plan, or whether the Scenario was a later simplification of an earlier over-
   elaborate Draft.
2. In the case of the encounter between Peer Gynt and the Woman in Green:
   the Scenario allows for Peer to meet the Woman 'in the Rondane
   Mountains', whereupon the mountain opens; in the Draft, the scene is set
   in 'a great vaulted hall' with Peer lying on a bench and the Woman in
   Green bent over him; in the Fair Copy, the setting is once again in the open
   on a hillside. There is some encouragement here to think that the sequence
   of things was Draft/Scenario/Fair Copy; if not, then Ibsen must have
   changed his mind once in moving from Scenario to Draft, and changed
   it back again when moving on to Fair Copy.
3. In the case of the Boyg, there are strong grounds for believing that it was
   lacking in the basic Draft (i.e. excluding the additional items on separate
   sheets); indeed, the allocation of space in gathering no. 9 for the scenes at
   the end of Act II, and before Act III began in gathering no. 10, allows very
   little room for the quite extensive scenes, including that with the Boyg,

which eventually rounded off this Act. Thus, the Scenario introduces scenes which the Draft originally seems to have lacked; finally, the *additional* draft items incorporate these new ideas, though again with modifications in certain details as compared with the Scenario: in the latter, for example, Peer meets the Boyg outside Aase's house instead of in indeterminate blackness as in the later version, and he fights his way into the house and out again, hears his mother's voice, and so on.

All three points are consistent with a chronology that places the Scenario in time between the original Draft and the interleaved revisions.

Possibly the oldest element in the surviving manuscripts altogether is gathering no. 1, and particularly the List of Characters. Not only does it differ quite significantly from the printed List of Characters, but it also seems to embody a much earlier conception of the play than that represented by the body of the Draft. There are differences in the degree of individuality awarded to the different characters: the Smith and the Bride are left impersonally designated in the Draft List of Characters, though identified by name in the printed version; conversely Matt Moen, Sølve and Birgit were given names in the Draft List and left anonymous in the printed version as the Bridegroom and the 'Newly Arrived Couple', i.e. Solveig's parents, respectively. This could conceivably indicate a more active role for Solveig's parents, for example, in Ibsen's first plans for the play than the part they finally played. The Draft List includes only 'Elfin-folk and Trolls', whereas the Draft and its interleaved insertions specify the Dovre-Master, the Court Troll, the Professor Troll and many more; and the printed List is also much more specific than the Draft List.

Then, too, the order in which the characters appear in the Draft List is different from the final version, which may have something to say about the planned appearance of the characters in the play itself. Solveig and her parents came before the Hægstad farmer and Matt Moen, the Bridegroom—who incidentally is not shown with his parents in the Draft List, though the parents appear in the body of the Draft itself, and of course also in the printed List of Characters and the final version of the play. The Steward and the Fiddler also appear later in the Draft List than in the printed version. Of the characters who make their appearance in Act II, the Draft List follows the sequence Woman in Green/Sæter Girls/Ugly Child/Trolls, whilst the order in the body of the Draft and in the printed List is Sæter Girls/Woman in Green/Trolls/Ugly Child. More important, possibly, than this is that the Draft List lacks mention of either the Boyg or the Cries of Birds, both of which appear in the augmented Draft and in the printed List of Characters.

For Act III, the only difference is the slight one that there is no mention either of 'Kari' or 'Cottager's Wife' in the Draft List.

For the characters making their appearance in Acts IV and V, some of the disparities are highly significant. Where the Draft proper and the final printed List of Characters identifies by names an international troupe of tourists and profiteers—Mr. Cotton, M. Ballon, Herr von Eberkopf, and Herr Trumpeter-straale—the Draft List has only 'Foreign Seamen'. In the Draft List there is no mention of 'A Thief and a Receiver', though in the Draft proper there is a scene involving 'Two Thieves' (see also Ibsen's letter to his publisher, 18 Sept. 1867, p. 453). The differences Frasenfeldt/Begriffenfeldt, Tuhu/Huhu, etc., are minor. Of a completely different order of significance, however, is the fact that the Draft List omits all mention of the Strange Passenger, the Bailiff, the Buttonmoulder or the Thin Man. When taken in conjunction with Ibsen's letter to his publisher of 18 Sept. 1867 (p. 453), in which he intimates that he 'might well want to introduce one or two extra subsidiary characters', the conclusion is clear: that the semi-mythological characters were introduced at a late stage in the play's composition, and at a time, moreover, when all preceding four Acts were actually in the hands of the printer, and therefore not easily changed.

3. THE FOLK TALE PER GYNT AND THE BOYG

The collection of Norwegian fairy tales and folk tales collected and arranged by P. Chr. Asbjørnsen, *Norske Huldre-Eventyr og Folkesagn* (3rd ed., Christiania, 1870), contains two sections that show a direct relevance to Ibsen's drama: the first (pp. 175–6) is a tale told by Thor Ulvsvolden about the exploits of a hunter called Gudbrand Glesne; and the second (pp. 190–6) is an account told by Per Fugleskjelle about an encounter between a hunter called Per Gynt and the Boyg of Etnedal.

1. ' . . . There was a hunter in the Western Mountains. He was called Gud-brand Glesne, and he was married to the grandmother of the lad you saw at the sæter last night, and he is said to have been a fine hunter. One autumn he came across an enormous buck. He fired at it, and from the way it fell it never occurred to him that it wasn't dead. So he went up to it and, as one often does, he sat astride his back and was just about to draw his knife to sever the neck-bone from the skull. But no sooner had he sat on it than up it jumped, cast its horns back pinning him down so he was as though sitting in an armchair; and then it sped off, because the bullet had only grazed the animal's skull and it had lost consciousness. No man surely ever had the kind of ride that Gudbrand had. Right into the wind and weather, across the most awful glaciers and moraines. Then it continued over Gjende Edge; and then he prayed to Our Lord, believing he would never see sun or moon again. But finally the reindeer took to the water and swam right across with the hunter on his back. Meanwhile he had managed to free his knife, and the moment the buck set foot on land, he plunged it into its neck, and it was dead, and surely Gudbrand Glesne would never have done that ride again, not for all the wealth that ever was.'

'I've heard a similar story in England about a deer-stalker that became a deer-rider', said Sir John [Tottenbroom] . . .

'Blicher tells a similar one about Jutland', I said.

'But what sort of edge was the one you mentioned, Thor—Gjender Edge?' he interrupted.

'You mean Gjende Edge?' Thor asked. 'That's the ridge of a mountain running between the Gjende Lakes, and it's so fearfully narrow and steep that if you stand there and throw a stone with each hand, they'll roll down into their separate lakes. Reindeer hunters cross it in good weather, but otherwise it's impassable; but there was a wild man up in Skeager—called Ole Storebraaten—he went over it carrying a grown reindeer on his shoulders.'

'How high is that mountain above the lakes?' asked Sir John.

'Oh, it is not nearly as high as the Ronde mountains', said Thor. 'But it is over seven hundred ells high. . . . '

2. In the old days there was a hunter living in Kvam who was called Per Gynt. He was for ever up in the mountains shooting bears and elk, for in those days there was rather more forest covering the mountains, and wild animals of that sort lived there. Late one autumn, long after the cattle had been brought down from the hills, Per set off into the mountains. Everybody else had returned home from the hills except for three sæter girls. When he had got almost to Høvring where he was meaning to spend the night in a sæter, it was so dark he could not see a hand's turn in front of him; his dogs began to howl and it was all very ghostly. All of a sudden he ran into something; and when he reached out, it felt cold and slippery and big. Yet he didn't seem to have left the path, so he couldn't think what it might be. But it was uncanny.

'Who is that?' said Per, for he felt it moving.

'Ah, it's the Boyg', came the answer. This left Per Gynt none the wiser. But he skirted round the thing a little way, thinking he must be able to get by somewhere. Again he suddenly ran into something; and when he reached out, it too was big and cold and slippery.

'Who is that?' said Per Gynt.

'Ah, it's the Boyg', came the answer again.

'Well, whether you be straight or crooked, you must let me get past', said Per, for he realized he was going round in a circle, and that the Boyg had curled itself round the sæter. At this it wriggled a little and Per got past to the sæter. When he got in, it was no lighter there than it had been outside; and he went fumbling round the walls, wishing to put down his gun and take off his knapsack; but suddenly as he was groping forward, he again felt that cold and big and slippery thing.

'Who is that?' shouted Per.

'Ah, it's the great Boyg', came the answer; and wherever he turned to go, he felt the encircling Boyg. It isn't very good being here, thought Per, since this Boyg is all over the place; but I'll soon settle the hash of this nuisance. So he took his gun and went out again and groped until he found its head.

'What sort of thing are you?' said Per.

'Ah, I am the great Boyg of Etnedal', said the Great Troll. Then Per Gynt let fly and fired three shots right into its head.

'Fire one more!' said the Boyg. But Per knew better than to do that; for if he had fired one more shot, it would have back-fired on him. When this was done, Per and the dogs seized the Great Troll and dragged it out so that they could get into the sæter. And all the while there was laughing and jeering in all the surrounding hills.

'Per Gynt tugged hard, but the dogs tugged harder', it was said.

The next morning he planned to go out stalking. When he reached the high ground, he caught sight of a girl who was calling some sheep across the hillside. But when he got there, the girl was gone, and the sheep too; and all he saw was a large flock of bears.

'Well, I've never seen bears in a flock before', Per thought to himself; but when he got closer, they were all gone, except one. Then there was a voice in a near-by hill:

> 'Watch out for your pig;
> Per Gynt is out
> Together with his tail.'

'Oh, it'll go badly for Per, but not for my pig, because he hasn't washed today', said a voice in the hill. Per washed his hands with what water he had, and shot the bear. There was laughter and jeering in the hill.

'You might have looked after your pig', came a shout.

'I forgot he had a water jug between his legs', the other replied.

Per skinned the bear and buried the carcass among the rocks, but he took with him the skull and the hide. On the way home he met a fox.

'Look at my lamb, how fat it is', said the voice from a hill.

'Look at that tail of Per's, how high it is', said a voice from another hill, as Per aimed his rifle and shot it. He skinned it and took the hide with him, and when he got to the sæter he placed the heads outside with gaping jaws. Then he kindled a fire and put a soup pot on it, but it smoked so terribly that he could hardly keep his eyes open, so he had to open a little window that was there. Just then a troll came and poked a nose through the window so long that it stretched right to the chimney.

'Now you shall see a real snout', came the remark.

'Now you shall feel some real soup', said Per Gynt, and poured the potful over the nose. The troll made off in a bad temper; but there was laughing and jeering in the surrounding hills, and voices shouting: 'Gyri Soup-snout, Gyri Soup-snout!'

Then it was quiet for a while; but it wasn't long before there was more noise and to-do outside again. Per looked out and saw a cart drawn by bears; they collected the Great Troll and went off with him into the mountains. Just then a bucket of water came down the chimney and put out the fire, and Per was left sitting in the dark. Then there began a laughing and a jeering in all the corners, and something said:

'Now it will go no better with Per than with the Vala sæter-girls.'

Per re-lit the fire, took the dogs, shut up the cottage and made off north to the Vala sæter where the three girls were staying. When he had gone some way to the north, there was such a glare it seemed Vala sæter was on fire. Just then he encountered a flock of wolves, some of which he shot, and some of which he beat to death. When he got to Vala sæter it was pitch dark and there was no fire; but there were four strange men in the cottage keeping the sæter-girls company; and they were four hill-trolls and they were called Gust of Værë, Tron Valfjeld, Tjøstøl Aabakken and Rolf Eldførpungen. Gust of Værë was standing outside the door keeping watch, whilst the others were inside courting the girls. Per shot at him but missed, and Gust made off. When Per walked in, they were hard at it with the girls; and two of the girls grew quite terrified and called to heaven, but the third who was called Mad Kari wasn't frightened; she said they could come if they liked and that she would like to see whether such men had anything about them. But when the trolls realized that Per was in the room they began to howl and told Eldførpungen to build up the fire. Thereupon the dogs set upon Tjøstøl and dragged him backwards into the fire so that sparks and embers scattered around him.

'Did you see my snakes, Per?' asked Tron Valfjeld—this was what he called his wolves.

'Now you'll go the same way as your snakes', said Per, and shot him; then be battered Aabakken to death with his rifle butt; but Eldførpungen had escaped up the chimney. When he had done this, he took the girls back to the village, for they didn't dare stay there any longer.

When Christmas was approaching, Per Gynt set out again. He had heard of a farm up in Dovre that became so full of trolls every Christmas Eve that the people had to get out and go to other farms. He wanted to go there because he was very keen on trolls. He put on some tattered clothes, and took with him a fine white bear which he had, and an awl, some pitch and some twine. When he got there, he went in and asked for shelter.

'God help us', said the man. 'We haven't any room for you; we have to leave the farm ourselves, because every single Christmas Eve the place gets filled with trolls.'

But Per Gynt said he might be able to clear the place of trolls, so they let him stay, and furthermore gave him a pig's skin. Then the bear lay down behind the chimney-place, and Per took out the awl and pitch and twine, and started making a big shoe from the entire pig's skin. As laces he put in a thick rope so that he could draw the whole shoe together; and he also had some hand-spikes ready. Just then they all came, with a fiddler playing his fiddle; and some danced, some ate the Christmas fare that stood on the table; some roasted pork, and some roasted frogs and toads and other disgusting things—these Christmas goodies they brought themselves. Meanwhile some of them had caught sight of the shoe Per had made. They all agreed it was for a very big foot. Then they wanted to try it on; and when each one of them had put a foot in it, Per tightened the rope, pushed a hand-spike in and twisted it till they were all caught fast in the shoe. Then the bear put his nose out and smelt the roast meat.

'Would you like some sausage, white pussy?' said one of the trolls and threw a red-hot roast frog straight into its jaws.

'Claw them and strike them, little bear!' said Per Gynt. Then the bear grew so very cross and angry that it leapt up and struck them and clawed them all, and Per Gynt rushed among them with the other hand-spike as if he wanted to beat all their brains in. So then the trolls had to run away, and Per stayed there for the whole Christmas living on the Christmas fare; and they heard nothing more of the trolls for many years. But the man had a light-coloured mare, and Per advised him to breed from it, the foals of which then went among the hills and had other foals.

Then some years later at Christmas time—the man was out in the forest cutting wood for the festival time—a troll came up to him and shouted: 'Have you still got your big white pussy?'

'Yes, lying behind the stove at home,' said the man, 'and now she's had seven kittens, much bigger and fiercer than she is herself.'

'Then we'll never come again to you any more', shouted the troll.

'That Per Gynt wasn't like anybody else', said Anders. 'He was a real story-teller and yarn spinner; you would have enjoyed listening to him. He always pretended he'd taken part himself in all the stories that people said had happened in olden days.'

'What you say may well be true', said Per Fugleskjelle. 'My grandmother knew him; she told me about him more than once.'

4. SOME COMMENTS BY THE AUTHOR

1. I have completed a new dramatic work which will be published at Christmas; it will interest me greatly to know what you think about it. The work is called 'Peer Gynt' after the main character, about whom one reads in Asbjørnsen's folk-tales. I had not very much to build on; but then I could be all the freer to play with the material as I wanted. I hear from Hegel that your new book will not be out until spring, and that it will be a big book. Nothing more is known; but I look forward with great anticipation to getting it. One advantage one does have in living abroad, and that is that one gets the national life from home purified and in extract; one is

spared all the things that go on in the highways and byways, and that is a gain. We have not seen any Norwegian papers more recent than the beginning of May. (*Letter of 15 Oct. 1857 to Magdalene Thoresen, his stepmother.*)

2. I enclose the last of the manuscript to 'Peer Gynt', and let's hope it has good luck. I have no more alterations to make to the list of characters or other things; so it can all go to the printers now at any time. I am impatient to know how the book will be received; but I am not anxious, for the book is written with mature consideration. I am delighted to hear that Brandes wants to write about my works. May I ask you to greet him, thank him and tell him I am most desirous of having his critical opinion in particular; but tell him I would also be glad if he could also include 'Peer Gynt', because this may cause him to modify certain of his views; he will himself say which. (*Letter of 18 Oct. 1867 to Frederik Hegel, his publisher.*)

3. I received your letter the day before we left for Rome. Since then we have divided our time mainly between Ischia and Sorrento. My new work, a dramatic poem which will probably appear next month, I wrote here. I have, as I promised, put the manuscript aside for your father's collection, and I shall send you the packet at the first opportunity. (*Letter of 21 Oct. 1867 to Jonas Collin.*)

4.   9 December 1867
What infernal thing is this that seems to come between us at every step? It is as if the very devil in person came to cast his shadow. I had received your letter. When one writes as you wrote, there is no deception. There are some things one cannot simulate. I had also written a reply straight from a grateful heart; it is not praise that one is grateful for, but to be understood makes one inexpressibly grateful. And now I have no use for my reply. An hour ago I read Mr. Clemens Petersen's review in *Fædrelandet.* If I am *now* to answer your letter I must begin in a different fashion; I must acknowledge receipt of your esteemed communication of such and such a date with the enclosed review in the afore-mentioned periodical.— If *I* were in Copenhagen, with anybody as close to me as Clemens Petersen stands to you, I would have beaten him senseless before I would have allowed him to commit such a tendentious crime against truth and justice. There is a lie running right through Clemens Petersen's article; not in what he says but in what he suppresses. And there is much *deliberately* suppressed. You can tell him what is in this letter, if you wish. As surely as I know that he takes a serious and responsible attitude to those things for which it is worth the discomfort of living in this world, so surely I know that this article will one day come to scorch and brand his soul. For suppression is a lie just as much as is a positive utterance, and Clemens Petersen bears a heavy responsibility. For the Lord has placed upon him a great task. Don't think that I am some blind conceited fool! Believe me

when I say that in my quiet moments I sit and rummage and probe and dissect my own entrails very nicely—and at those points where the pain is worst.—My work *is* poetry; and if it isn't, it shall become it. The concept of poetry in our country, in Norway, will come to conform to the work. There is nothing stable in the world of concepts; the Scandinavians of our century are not the Greeks. He says that the Strange Passenger is the concept of Dread! If I stood at the execution block and could save my life with that explanation, it would never have occurred to me; I have never thought of that; I slipped the scene in as a caprice. And is not Peer Gynt a personality, complete, individual? *I* know that he is. And is not the Mother too?—One can learn much from Clemens Petersen, and I have learned much from him. But there is something *he* would do well to learn, and which I—though I cannot teach him it—nevertheless have to my advantage over him, and that is what you in your letter call 'loyalty'. Yes, that is precisely the word! Not loyalty to a friend or an objective or something like that, but something infinitely higher.

Nevertheless I am glad of the injustice which has been done to me; in it there is God's help and dispensation; for I feel my strength growing with my anger. If there is to be war, then so be it! If I am not a poet, then I have nothing to lose. I shall try as a photographer. I shall take on my contemporaries up there, individually, one by one, as I have done with the language reformers. I shall not spare the child in the mother's womb, nor the thought or feeling behind the words of any living soul who deserves the honour of my attention.

Dear Bjørnson, you are a warm and generous soul, and you have given me more great and splendid things than I can ever repay; but there is something in your nature which could easily cause your good fortune—and precisely that—to be your curse. I have a right to say this to you; for I know that below a crust of fatuousness and swinishness I have lived my life seriously. Do you know that the whole of my life I have withdrawn from my own parents, from all my family, because I could not remain in a state of semi-understanding?—All this that I am writing is pretty incoherent; but the *summa summarum* is: I don't *wish* to be an antiquary or a geographer, I don't *wish* further to develop my talents in the service of Monrad's philosophy; in short, I simply do not wish to follow good advice. But *one* thing I do wish, even though powers within and without drive me to tear the roof down about my own head—I wish always, *so help me God*, to be and remain

Your loyal and sincerely devoted
Henrik Ibsen

10 December.

I have slept on the lines written above, and read them through again in cold blood. They express my feelings of yesterday; but I shall send them just the same.

Now I shall tell you, slowly and composedly, what flows from Herr Cl. Petersen's article.

I will not willingly yield, and Herr Cl. Petersen cannot drive me away; it is too late. Perhaps he can get me to withdraw from Denmark; but in that case I mean to change more than my publisher. I don't undervalue my friends and my following in Norway.—The party whose paper has opened its pages to injustice towards me shall be made to feel that I do not stand alone. Beyond certain limits I recognize no scruples; and if I examine what I can also do by a cold-blooded choice of weapons to match their uncontrolled passion, then my enemies will realize that, if I cannot build up, I am at least man enough to tear down the things around me.

So much for the future. But now I want to say something to you about the present moment. I have had no correspondence with home. Nevertheless I can easily tell you something of what goes on there. Do you know what is being said in Norway these days wherever Carl Ploug's newspaper is read? They are saying: You can tell from Cl. Petersen's review that Bjørnson is in Copenhagen.

If you have reviewed *Peer Gynt* in *Norsk Folkeblad*, then they say: 'Diplomatic move; but not deft enough.'

Some will speak thus from conviction; others vengefully or maliciously. The criticism will come to form parties for and against. You will see.

They will call Clemens Petersen's review a tit-for-tat. Some man unknown to me wrote a number of articles a little time ago in *Morgenbladet* very contemptuous of Herr Petersen's literary activities; and I was favourably mentioned. People will refresh their memory of such combinations. I know the way those people think.

Dear Bjørnson, let us nevertheless try to hold together. Often enough have our friends soured our lives and made the struggle heavier than necessary.

That I do not mistrust you in this matter you can see from the fact that I have written all this to you. I do not take nor shall ever take my followers' side against you. *Vis à vis* your friends—that is a different matter.

Herr Petersen's article—I keep returning to it—will not succeed in harming me. He who is absent always has the advantage that comes from actually *being* absent. But to write the article in the form that it took was not clever. In his article on *Brand* he treated me with respect; and the public will not find anything in the intervening years that exposes me to disrespect. The public will not acknowledge Herr Petersen's right to sweep me on one side the way he is trying to do. He should leave those things to those colleagues of his who live *off* their critical activities; I always thought until now that Herr Petersen lived *for* his.

You I reproach only for your inactivity. It was not nice of you to allow, from neglect, such an attempt to put my literary standing under the auctioneer's hammer in my absence.

Well then! I have written myself into a quiet mood again. Tick me off good and proper, preferably in a long letter, if you feel the need! And accept with a good heart greetings from all of us to you and yours. Don't show your wife this letter; but give her our best wishes for Christmas and New Year and *particularly* for the third and imminent happy event. (*Letter of 9/10 Dec. 1867 to Bjørnstjerne Bjørnson.*

5. A greeting more blessed than which reached me via your letter on Christmas morning I could not have had.

The load of nonsense I shipped to you in my last epistle left me in the interval without a moment of peace or satisfaction. The worst thing a man can do to himself is to do wrong to others. Thank you for being so big-minded as to take the thing the way you did! I could see nothing but enmity and bitterness for a long time ahead; but now, looking back, I see it as quite natural that you took it as you did and in no other way. Every day I read your letter over and over again, to free myself from the tormenting thought that I might have hurt you.

Do not misunderstand what I said in my earlier letter about my seeming to place the essence of poetry elsewhere than where Clemens Petersen would want to put it. On the contrary, I understand him and agree with him. But I believe I *have* satisfied the requirements; he says no. He speaks about our reflective age that allows Macbeth's witches to signify something that takes place within Macbeth himself; but in the selfsame article he lets some distracted ship's passenger signify 'Dread'! Well, at that rate I could offer to turn not only your but all other writers' works into allegory from first to last. Take Götz von Berlichingen! Propose that Götz himself signifies the people's fermenting urge for freedom, the Emperor signifies the concept of the State, etc. And what do you get from that! That it's not poetry!—

However, you mustn't get concerned about my 'paroxysms'; they are not sick, neither in the one sense nor the other. Your advice that I should write a comedy for stage performance is something I think I shall follow. It is possible I shall make for Northern Italy this summer; and where we shall spend next winter I don't know. All I know is it won't be Norway. If I were to return home now, one of two things would happen: either I should within a month have made all men my enemies, or else I should have slipped into all kind of disguises and become a lie both to myself and to others. (*Letter of 28 Dec. 1867 to Bjørnstjerne Bjørnson.*)

6. How is it going with *Peer Gynt*? As far as I can tell from the newspaper reports, it has been well received in Sweden; but are the sales commensurate?

I hear that the work had caused a lot of upset in Norway; this worries me not in the slightest; but both there and in Denmark people have found much more satire in it than I intended. Why can't they read the book like any ordinary poem? For that was how I wrote it. The satirical bits are fairly isolated. But if, as seems to be the case, the present-day Norwegians recognize themselves in the person of Peer Gynt, that is those good people's own business.

I am sincerely obliged to you for the many reviews you have been kind enough to send me. *Morgenbladet* is the only newspaper we get here. If it were possible some time for you to get me Bjørnson's articles in *Norsk Folkebladet,* you would give me great pleasure. (*Letter of 24 Feb. 1868 to Frederik Hegel.*)

7. Concerning those particular parts of *Peer Gynt,* I cannot agree with you. Naturally I bow to the laws of beauty; but I don't worry about its rules. You mention Michelangelo; in my opinion, nobody has sinned more against the rules of beauty than he; but everything he has created is nevertheless beautiful; for it is characterful. Raphael's art has actually never fired me; his figures have their home before the Fall; and in any case, Mediterranean man has different aesthetic values from us. He wants formal beauty; for us, even the formally un-beautiful can be beautiful by virtue of its inherent truth. (*Letter of 15 July 1869 to Georg Brandes.*)

8. After *Brand, Peer Gynt* followed as it were of its own accord. It was written in Southern Italy, in Ischia and in Sorrento. When one is so far away from the intended readers, one becomes reckless. This work contains much that was occasioned by my own youth; my mother served, with necessary exaggerations, as the model for Aase. (Similarly for Inga in *The Pretenders.*)

The locality has a great influence on the forms within which the imagination creates. Can I not, rather like Christoff in [Holberg's play] *Jakob von Tyboe,* point to *Brand* and *Peer Gynt* and say: 'Look, that was when intoxicated with wine'? (*Letter of 28 Oct. 1870 to Peter Hansen.*)

9. *Peer Gynt* is *Brand's* opposite; it is regarded by many as my best work. How far you will find pleasure in it, I don't know. It is wild and formless, recklessly written in a way that I could only dare to write while far from home. It was actually produced during my stay in the summer of 1867 in Ischia and Sorrento. (*Letter of 30 April 1872 to Edmund Gosse.*)

10. Already in Berchtesgaden I had the pleasure of receiving your kind letter of 1 August, along with the enclosed review of *Peer Gynt* in *The Spectator.* A better, clearer or more sympathetic interpretation of my work I could not wish for. I could only wish that the praise you give to my work was sufficiently deserved; the objections which you raise are doubtless well-founded. I can myself in part see the faults now, since during the intervening time I have moved sufficiently away from the book to be able to look back on it as though at the work of a stranger. (*Letter of 14 Oct. 1872 to Edmund Gosse.*)

11. How shall I be able to thank you enough for your last big and exhaustive essay. I won't even attempt to *thank* you; I will only say that you have given me great pleasure. The translated sections of *Love's Comedy* and *Peer Gynt* are masterly, and there is nothing in them I would want to see changed. (*Letter of 20 Feb. 1873 to Edmund Gosse.*)

12. First of all let me thank you most sincerely for the kind interest which you show in my literary activities. Your conception of *Peer Gynt* coincides completely with what I was aiming at when I wrote that book; and I am naturally only delighted that it has found a translator who has with full clarity found his way into the inmost purpose of the work.

But this does not diminish my surprise to learn that you regard this work as suitable for translating into German and publishing. I must confess that I have grave doubts in this respect. Of all my books I regard *Peer Gynt* as the one least constituted to be understood outside the Scandinavian countries. I ask you to remember that by far the greater part of your German readers do not possess your own ability to understand the book. You yourself doubtless possess a very detailed knowledge of the Norwegian landscape and the pattern of Norwegian life; you are familiar with our literature and with our habits of thought; you know people there, and characters. But is not all this necessary in order to find merit in the work? It is on this point that I have considerable doubts, and I did not want to conceal these even though I naturally assumed—what I have indicated here —that you have fully considered all this before deciding to undertake so difficult and wide-ranging a task. (*Letter of 19 May 1880 to Ludwig Passarge.*)

13. I was delighted to learn that you had found a reputable publisher for your translation of *Peer Gynt*. But with the best will in the world, I cannot see myself able to give explanations of the many references in the work that might be incomprehensible to German readers. This is something which for me as a foreigner would be impossible—to judge what needed an explanation and what did not. For the same reasons I regard it as useless to approach Dietrichson or indeed any other Norwegian. I think there is nobody better than yourself to decide this matter; and if you should be uncertain about this or that point, it would not be difficult for you during your planned visit to Norway to find the necessary explanations. Apart from that, I have the impression that you know Norwegian conditions quite as well as any native.

Nor am I in a position to give any further details of the circumstances that led to *Peer Gynt* being written. If any account of that were to be intelligible, I would have to write a whole book about it; and the time for that has not come yet. Everything I have written has a close connection with what I have experienced—not to say observed; every new work has for me had the purpose of serving as a process of spiritual liberation and purification; for one never stands quite without complicity and responsibility within the society one belongs to. That is why I once wrote in a copy of one of my books by way of dedication the following lines:

> 'To *live* is to war with trolls
> In the vaults of the heart and brain;
> To write—that is to pass
> Judgement upon one's self.'

You don't know the word 'pusselanker', and that is not unexpected; for it is not used in the written language. It means: the patter of little baby legs or baby feet, and the expression is only used by mothers and nannies when they talk baby-talk to small children.

The meaning of the lines you ask about is as follows: Peer Gynt pleads, when trying to get admittance to hell, that he has been a slave-trader. To this the 'Thin Man' replies that many people have done worse things, e.g. suppressed the spiritual, the will and the mind in their surroundings; but if this is done 'våset' [stupidly], i.e. without demonic intent, then this is no qualification for getting into hell but only into the 'casting-ladle'. (*Letter of 16 June 1880 to Ludwig Passarge.*)

14. Of course, *Peer Gynt* is in no way designed to be performed, and you will remember that I myself had grave doubts about publishing this work in Germany. (*Letter of 17 Aug. 1881 to Ludwig Passarge.*)

15. One factual inaccuracy in your account you must allow me to correct. My parents on both my father's and my mother's side belonged to the most respected families in Skien at that time. The member of parliament for the district, Mr. Paus, and his brother the judge were my father's half-brothers and were cousins of my mother. And my parents were equally closely related with the families of Plesner, von der Lippe, Cappelen, and Blom, in other words with practically all the patrician families which at that time dominated the place and the surrounding district. My father was a merchant with an extensive business, and the hospitality he offered in his house was quite reckless. In 1836 he was unable to meet his commitments, and there remained nothing for us but a country place near the town. We moved out there and thus lost touch with the circles we had previously belonged to.

In *Peer Gynt* I used the conditions of my own childhood and my memories as a kind of model for describing the life in 'the house of rich Jon Gynt'. (*Letter of 21 Sept. 1882 to Georg Brandes.*)

16. He began *Peer Gynt* at Ischia and finished it at Sorrento. He set to work upon it with no definite plan, foreseeing the end, indeed, but not the intermediate details. For instance, he did not know that Peer was to go to Africa. 'It is much easier', he said, 'to write a piece like *Brand* or *Peer Gynt*, in which you can bring in a little of everything, than to carry through a severely logical (*konsekvent*) scheme, like that of John Gabriel Borkman,

for example.' (*William Archer in conversation with Ibsen, late summer 1898, reported in* The Monthly Review, *June 1906, pp. 17–18.*)

5. PUBLIC RECEPTION

Among the first to review *Peer Gynt* on its publication in Copenhagen was Bjørnstjerne Bjørnson, who chanced to be in Denmark at the time. His account of it is dated 'Copenhagen, 15 November [1867]'—publication day had been 14 November—and it appeared in Christiania's *Norske Folkeblad*, no. 47, 23 Nov. 1867. In his review, Bjørnson welcomed *Peer Gynt* as a work 'quite as great as *Brand*, but not so unpleasant, so unclear, so strained'. One important reason for this in his view was that the closer Ibsen approached satirical comedy, the nearer he approached his natural mode. *Peer Gynt* was a satire on Norwegian self-love, narrow-chestedness [!], self-righteousness, written in a fashion that moved him (Bjørnson) to great belly-laughs, but also prompted him to give thanks for the man who wrote it. The review went on to make the point that *Peer Gynt* was no finished work of literature, but rather a bold contribution to the current debate about Norway's role in Scandinavian and world affairs; the language of it was unpolished, racy, occasionally violent, and marred by unnecessary obscenities; some of the ideas in it were uninhibited and rather wild, and some might even give offence. Bjørnson concluded that one could not be certain whether everybody should be allowed to read this book.

The review that Ibsen was waiting for with more than usual anxiety, however, was that of Clemens Petersen, the doyen of the Danish critics of the day. At the time of the publication of *Brand*, Ibsen had written specifically to Petersen (see p. 439) to express the hope of receiving as sympathetic a review as his (Petersen's) conscience would permit him to write; and while at work on *Peer Gynt*, he had written again to thank Petersen for what he had written, and to hope that the new work he was writing would be thought of as marking a new and important step forward. Two weeks after the appearance of *Peer Gynt*, Petersen published a long review in *Fædrelandet*, no. 279, 13 Nov. 1867, which both infuriated and bitterly disappointed Ibsen. Petersen began his piece ominously by asking: Was this poetry?

'Psychologically and ethically, *Peer Gynt* forms a contrast to *Brand*, and this contrast is so marked even in matters of detail that it was doubtless a quite deliberate thing on the part of the author. In style and in form, on the other hand, the two works are as like as two drops of water; it is therefore natural that a review of *Peer Gynt* should begin where reviews of *Brand* left off— with the question, namely: "Is this then poetry?"

'All poetry is the transmutation of reality into art. Even the most fleeting impressions of beauty in everyday life are precisely this. The view over the harbour when the rain eases and all the ships hoist their sails in the sunlight; the sight of a group of animals, who have stopped motionless in the forest as though Pan were playing for them and who then suddenly, released from their enchantment, go chasing off across the plain; the sight of a man straining with every fibre of his being in quiet self-sacrifice but who nevertheless finds inexpressible joy in it because he is sacrificing himself for something he loves; whenever one encounters something of this kind in real life which leaves on one an impression of beauty and which rouses feelings of poetry, this is due solely to the fact that reality, at such a moment, presents itself to one as art. . . . But if this transmutation of reality into art is to be successful, so that the raw material of reality is absorbed by art's form and thereby wholly becomes poetry, then art makes its distinct demands, just as reality makes its, and if both demands are not completely met, then the transmutation fails and poetry remains absent, even though there may otherwise be sufficient both of art and reality in the work. But this is precisely how things are in Herr Ibsen's last two works: they might rather be said to have come to terms with these demands than fully satisfying them. Neither *Brand* nor *Peer Gynt* are properly poetry, however great or interesting their immediate effect may be.'

Petersen went on to say that there was more wit, more genuine freedom of spirit, less violence, less of a forced quality in this work than in *Brand*; it was a more natural product of the writer's talents, and it left a healthier, more even and thereby more poetic impression than the earlier work. The essential element in all poetry, however, in Petersen's view, was the ideal; and it was precisely this that *Peer Gynt* lacked.

As is well known, Ibsen reacted vehemently against this review (see pp. 487–90); and in his consequent decision to write a 'photographic' prose satire (*The League of Youth*), directed against those back in Scandinavia who lacked any real understanding of life and art, many have seen the essential starting-point of his more obviously 'Ibsenist' career.

Ibsen had almost as little satisfaction from the review by Georg Brandes (in the Danish *Dagbladet*, no. 292, 16 Dec. 1867). Brandes saw in *Peer Gynt* 'one of those literary products, appearing more and more frequently in this country, the purpose of which is to present mankind from its reverse side, morally speaking, and upon whose scapegoat of a hero is heaped all human contemptibility.' Like Petersen, Brandes regretted the lack of 'beauty' in the piece:

'If the fine, old rule of the French Romantics—"The ugly is the beautiful"—is really valid, then *Peer Gynt* would be a work of beauty; but if there is any hint of doubt about this rule, then Ibsen's new work has failed totally. That it has failed *totally* does not of course mean that it is unsuccessful in all or indeed in most details. It is in no wise denied that *Peer Gynt* in part contains great beauties, and in parts informs us—Norwegians and everybody —of a number of great truths; but beauties and truths are worth a good deal less than beauty and truth in the singular; and Ibsen's work is neither beautiful nor true. Contempt for one's fellows and self-hate—the things upon which it is constructed—is a poor foundation upon which to build works of literature. How unbeautiful, how distorted Ibsen's view of life is! What bitter pleasure he finds in besmirching human nature! These efforts must surely now have reached the end of the line! Surely this is enough and must now cease! . . . A poet's destiny is to be more than one who abuses human nature. Yet is Ibsen anything other than this in the whole of Act Four of this work; and can anything be more repulsive than the scene between Peer Gynt and Anitra, the Arab girl?'

Brandes clearly was upset by this fourth Act; he dismissed it as having no relevance to what went before or what came after; he found it unwitty in its satire, crude in its irony, and completely unintelligible in its final stages. Fortunately, he went on, there were admirable things elsewhere in the work:

'In all the other Acts there is, to make up for this, a wealth of poetry and a profundity of thought that is perhaps not exceeded in any of Ibsen's earlier works. The first Act is a fine, vibrant and fascinating exposition, completely free of the quasi-symbolical nonsense the book suffers from later. In this Act there is a strength of imagination and a genuineness of humour that carries one along and builds up tension for what is to come. The second Act is weaker, but it nevertheless contains many fine things in the first conversation between Peer and Ingrid. . . . The third Act is beautiful in almost all ways: there is powerful imagination, deep feeling and a mood of romantic melancholy in the account of Solveig's arrival at the newly-built cabin and in the splendid and moving description of the mother's death. The fifth Act has another poetic pearl of the highest order, in the priest's funeral oration. . . . Moreover this Act has dotted about here and there excellent bits, both profound and beautiful, like the scene where Peer Gynt peels the onion; or the one where the voices around him remind him of what he should have done but in his wretchedness has neglected to do; or the notion of the negative photograph; or of the Button Moulder, etc.; yet here again the allegory has so drained strength from the poetry that even these excellences find it difficult to assert themselves in the midst of all these unclarities and these obscurities.'

Nearly ten years later, in anticipation of the première of *Peer Gynt* at the Christiania Theatre on 24 February 1876, Arne Garborg wrote a long and thoughtful article about the work, including many cross-references to *Brand*, which was printed as instalments in *Aftenbladet*, nos. 20–26, 25–31 Jan. 1876. (This article, along with the Bjørnson, Petersen, and Brandes pieces referred to above, are to be found conveniently collected in the anthology *Omkring 'Peer Gynt'*, ed. Otto Hageberg, Oslo, 1967.) Despite his admiration for the work itself, Garborg was, however, deeply sceptical of the wisdom of performing *Peer Gynt* in the theatre. He suspected that the producer would put an emphasis on the work as a spectacle; and he feared that the public would be drawn more by curiosity than by any deeper interest in the play's worth.

Ibsen was wholly reconciled to the need for cutting the play. On 16 August 1875, just about the time when Grieg announced that he had completed the score of *Peer Gynt*, Ibsen wrote to Hartvig Lassen on this very point:

'It is self-evident that *Peer Gynt* can only be produced in the theatre in a cut version. When I first wrote to Grieg concerning the music, I sketched out for him how I had imagined the fourth Act might be replaced by a tone-poem which would indicate the content and would be accompanied by a few living pictures or tableaux presenting the most appropriate situations in the Act which had been omitted, e.g. Peer Gynt and the Arab girls, Solveig waiting at home in the cottage, etc. I communicated this plan to Herr Josephson, but he did not agree with me; instead he proposed certain cuts in the dialogue—cuts which seemed to me to have been made very conscientiously, and to which I gave my approval.

'Which of the two procedures is to be preferred, I do not dare to decide at this distance. I would rather that you and Herr Josephson should discuss and determine the matter. He has assured me that if his ideas are followed, the play will be a popular and a box-office success. Meanwhile, I would rather stand aside from it all, and I shall be satisfied if only the performance is brought down to a suitable length; if not, it is ruined.'

In the event, the production was a genuine success. It ran for 37 performances, a run that was only terminated by a fire in the theatre that destroyed many of the sets and costumes. On 5 March 1876 Ibsen wrote to Ludvig Josephson, who had produced the play: 'Thanks for Peer Gynt! Your kind telegram was the forerunner of a whole series of happy tidings which I received last week from home. This success of the theatre's audacious undertaking has surpassed all my expectations, even though I entertained no doubts on this score. I knew that the matter was in your hands, and that no other man in our country could carry the thing through as you could. I am also delighted to learn that this is the general and unanimous view back home.'

It had to wait a further ten years before it was given its first Copenhagen production, on 15 January 1886 at the Dagmar Theatre. Grieg himself participated in the rehearsals. On 22 December 1885 he wrote to his friend Frantz Beyer:

'. . . This afternoon I had the first rehearsal with the singers for *Peer Gynt*. As I came up the steps of the Dagmar Theatre, I heard the sæter-girls crowing at the tops of their voices, naturally in hopelessly wrong tempo, too slow; so I'm very glad I was on the spot. But the voices are good, and the girls seem lively, so I am not giving up on this scene which is now better orchestrated than it was before. Then I rehearsed Solveig's songs with Mrs. N. N.; but as Solveig is apparently in the family way, the illusion suffers considerably. Nevertheless she has a good grip on things, and shows genuine musical temperament. Then came the Thief and the Receiver who made such nonsense of their songs that I had to ask them to stop and listen to me. . . .'

A month later, on 21 January 1886, he wrote again:

' . . . Let me rather tell you something of the *Peer Gynt* performance. It was with a strange feeling that I took my seat in the stalls that evening. Klausen was as he was ten years ago in Christiania, perhaps a little less agile, but it seemed to me he managed the last two Acts a little better. The Finn, Miss A., was a complete failure as Aase in the first two Acts, but in her own way excellent in the death scene. The supporting parts were altogether better than in Christiania: Celti was a perfect Dovre-Master; Mrs. Krum an equally perfect Anitra; and in Oda Nielsen's hands, Solveig was a pretty and poetic figure, even though not the Solveig we might have imagined. And she sang beautifully and naturally.

'You would have been amused at me during rehearsals. I was so happy at being able to express my intentions that I put my oar in everywhere. Particularly in the scene with the sæter-girls I wanted to have my way. And this really became something! I stood in the wings with the book open to be able to follow, and stopped them every so often with shouts like: "It says here you have to kiss him—go on then, don't be shy!" And once they had crossed the rubicon, they went really wild and crazy and all as they should be. At the dress rehearsal there were great cheers after this scene; but on the first night, nobody moved. Obviously, they were astounded by it. But, as a whole, I think I may say the music was a success, and the performance quite good.'

This production was followed on 2 February 1892 by its first Swedish production in Gothenburg, under the direction of August Lindberg, who then later, in 1895, went on tour in a number of Norwegian provincial towns. Beginning in March 1892 there was also a run, at the Christiania Theatre, of a version that consisted of the first three Acts only, in which the title role was played by Bjørn Bjørnson, the poet's son.

On 9 June 1893 Edvard Grieg in some irritation wrote a letter to the newspaper *Verdens Gang:*

'I see from the newspaper that yesterday the theatre gave a benefit performance of *Peer Gynt* for Miss Porelius. I have previously informed the producer why I have neither seen nor wish to see the play in this new production; there are good reasons why it is now appropriate to explain this 'Why not' to the public. The matter is very simple: my music is being deliberately ruined. Two instruments (two horns) have been cut from my orchestration; without these the music not only loses all its colour and brilliance, but certain details become musically unlovely, and indeed meaningless. (For those who are not musical: one might just as well cut two parts in a play. The one is as inexcusable as the other.) And this is done —it is said—because these two poor little horn players are not to be found anywhere in the capital city of Norway. These excuses are sheer nonsense; and the ugly fact remains that nobody cares to find the money for these two extra instrumentalists. When *Peer Gynt* was first performed in 1876, and when the state of our music was considerably more primitive than it is now, there was never any thought of this kind of artistic offensiveness. The instrumentalists which the theatre lacked had of course to be found—and were. Now—seventeen years later—they cannot be found. . . . '

From February 1902 onwards, the play figured regularly in the repertoire of the Christiania Theatre in a severely cut form, the nature of which has been reported by Emil Reich (*Henrik Ibsens Dramen*, 14th ed., Berlin, 1925, pp. 140–1):

'Ibsen in 1902 permitted the Norwegian National Theatre very considerable cuts in the very first scene (Peer and Aase), lesser ones in the scene in Act II with the Dovre-Master; whereupon, as the opening scene of Act III, there follows the scene in which Solveig comes to Peer, with the consequence that Peer's scenes with the Boyg, with Helge, alone in the wood, and that with Aase following the distraint are wholly omitted. In the Fourth Act, the greater part of Peer's scene with the four opportunists is cut, the entire scenes with the apes, the theft of the horse, the thief and the receiver, and then the greater part of Peer's monologue before he finds the horse, and a number of lines belonging to Peer the prophet; the moonlight scene is completely cut, the greater part of the scene with Peer and Anitra in the desert and the following scholarly monologue, and the encounter with the Memnon column, and the comparison of Dovre-Master and Memnon. The scenes in the lunatic asylum remain almost whole. In the Fifth Act, Peer's two monologues on the ship disappear, also the fight with the cook and the second encounter with the Strange Passenger; then—particularly noteworthy—the entire churchyard scene in which many commentators claim to find the main sense of the work, as well as the peeling of the onion, the scene on the heath with the puffballs, the leaves, the drops of dew and Aase's voice, much of the exchanges with the Buttonmoulder and of the encounters with the Dovre-Master and the Thin Man, the Devil in priest's robes; all the Solveig scenes are unabridged.'

The first translation into a non-Scandinavian language was that of Ludwig Passarge into German, published in 1881 (see also Ibsen's correspondence with Passarge, pp. 492–3 above). An English translation by Charles and William Archer appeared in 1892; a French version, by Count Prozor, was published in *La Nouvelle Revue*, 1896; and a Russian translation was published in 1897. The earliest account of *Peer Gynt* in English was an unsigned review by

Edmund Gosse in *The Spectator* in July 1872 (no. 2299, pp. 922–3, and re-printed in revised form in *Studies in the Literature of Northern Europe*, 1879, and again in *Northern Studies*, 1890). The greater part of the notice is taken up with a summary of the plot, and such comment as there is is not particularly profound: '. . . These events, and many more, take up the first three Acts, which almost form a complete poem in themselves; these Acts contain little satire, but a humorous and vivid picture of Norse manners and character. To a foreigner who knows a little of Norway and would fain know more, these Acts of *Peer Gynt* are a delicious feast. Through them he is brought face to face with the honest merry peasants, and behind all is a magnificent landscape of mountain, forest, and waterfall.'

The first substantial criticism in English of the drama was Philip H. Wicksteed's article 'Ibsen's *Peer Gynt:* a study' in the *Contemporary Review* for August 1889 (lvi, pp. 274–87), which also formed the basis of his lecture on *Peer Gynt* in the series of four delivered in the Chelsea Town Hall, and subsequently reprinted in his *Four Lectures on Henrik Ibsen* (London, 1892). Like so many subsequent critics, he emphasized the complementarity of *Brand* and *Peer Gynt:*

'In *Brand* the hero is an embodied protest against the poverty of spirit and half-heartedness that Ibsen rebelled against in his countrymen. In *Peer Gynt* the hero is himself the embodiment of that spirit. In *Brand* the fundamental antithesis, upon which, as its central theme, the drama is constructed, is the contrast between the spirit of compromise on the one hand, and the motto "everything or nothing" on the other. And *Peer Gynt* is the very incarnation of a compromising dread of decisive committal to any one course. In *Brand* the problem of self-realization and the relation of the individual to his surroundings is obscurely struggling for recognition, and in *Peer Gynt* it becomes the formal theme upon which all the fantastic variations of the drama are built up. In both plays alike the problems of heredity and the influence of early surroundings are more than touched upon; and both alike culminate in the doctrine that the only redeeming power on earth or in heaven is the power of love.' (pp. 52–3.)

On 18 July 1890 George Bernard Shaw read his paper on Ibsen at the St. James's Restaurant to the Fabian Society—a lecture out of which grew his book *The Quintessence of Ibsenism*, published in 1891. Shaw extended the more obvious comparison with *Brand* to include also Don Quixote:

'There is nothing novel in Ibsen's dramatic method of reducing these ideals [of unconditional self-realization] to absurdity. Exactly as Cervantes took the old ideals of chivalry, and shewed what came of a man attempting to act as if it were real, so Ibsen takes the ideal of Brand and Peer Gynt, and subjects them to the same test . . . Don Quixote, Brand and Peer Gynt are, all three, men of action seeking to realize their ideals in deeds.'

In 1892, there was published the first English translation of *Peer Gynt*, by Charles and William Archer. This produced a crop of reviews and other pieces, among them: two articles by A. T. Quiller-Couch on 'Ibsen's *Peer Gynt*' in *The Speaker*, 8 and 22 Oct. 1892, and later reprinted in *Adventures in Criticism* (London, 1896, pp. 295–309); a piece by C. H. Herford in *The Bookman*, 3, 1892, pp. 85 ff.; a short notice by Justin Huntly McCarthy in *Gentleman's Magazine*, cclxxiii, 1892, p. 533; and an unsigned review in *Saturday Review*, lxxiv, 8 Oct. 1892, pp. 417–18.

The *Saturday Review* for 21 Nov. 1896 (lxxxii, pp. 542–4) printed a full account by George Bernard Shaw of the production by the Théâtre de l'Œuvre in Paris on 12 November—a report in which he also incorporated some discussion of the merits of the Archers' English and the French translation of the drama.

In 1912, R. Ellis Roberts published his new English version of *Peer Gynt*, with an introduction by himself. The keynote of his interpretation is: 'If *Peer Gynt* stands for anything, it stands for this truth, that personality is more important and splendid than any other factor in life or art.' Among the reviews that greeted it one might mention Robert Lynd, 'Ibsen's Masterpiece', *The Bookman*, xliv, April 1913, p. 30. For subsequent translations into English, see Bibliography.

Peer Gynt was first performed in English translation at the Garrick Theatre, New York, on 29 October 1906, with a memorable performance by Richard Mansfield in the title role. An account of his performance was given by Montrose J. Moses in 'Richard Mansfield and Peer Gynt' in *The Times Magazine* (N.Y.), i, Feb. 1907, pp. 313–30; see also his *Henrik Ibsen: the man and his plays* (New York, 1908). A critical account of the play, '*Peer Gynt*: an interpretation', was contributed by Jane D. Stone to *Poet Lore*, xviii, Sept. 1907, pp. 383–92.

In Britain, the first performance appears to have been at the Queen's Hall, Edinburgh, on 14 Feb. 1908. There were performances (excluding Act IV) by the Ibsen Club in the Rehearsal Theatre in London, on 26 Feb. and 30 April 1911, and again on 27 April 1913. However, London had to wait until 6 March 1922 for its first substantial production: at the Old Vic, with Russell Thorndike as Peer, Florence Buckton as Aase, Stella Friston as Solveig, and Rupert Harvey as the Buttonmoulder.

Other London productions since then include: 18 Oct. 1932 at the Gate Theatre, with Peter Godfrey as Peer; 23 Sept. 1935 at the Old Vic, with William Devlin as Peer, Alec Clunes as Aslak, Cecil Trouncer as Mr. Cotton, and Leo Genn as the Boyg; 5 May 1936 at Sadler's Wells, with William Devlin as Peer, Susan Richards as Aase, Alec Clunes as Aslak, Vivienne Bennett as Solveig, Ion Swinley as the Buttonmoulder; 31 Aug. 1944 at the New Theatre, with Ralph Richardson as Peer, Sybil Thorndike as Aase, Joyce Redman as Solveig, and Laurence Olivier as the Buttonmoulder; 26 Sept. 1962 at the Old Vic, with Leo McKern as Peer, Catherine Lacey as Aase, Dilys Hamlett as Solveig, Adrienne Corri as Ingrid and Anitra, James Maxwell as Begriffen-feldt, David William as the Thin Man, and Wilfred Lawson as the Button-moulder. The present translation was first played at the Chichester Theatre on 13 May 1970, with Roy Dotrice as Peer and Beatrix Lehmann as Aase.

Radio productions of *Peer Gynt* include: 9 March 1927, presented by Edward P. Genn and the Liverpool Radio Players, with William Armstrong as Peer, Irene Rooke as Aase, Catherine Scales as Solveig, and Walter Shore as the Buttonmoulder; 10 Aug. 1943, with Ralph Richardson as Peer, Ivy St. Helier as Aase, Marjorie Westbury as Solveig, Powell Lloyd as the Dovre King, and Alexander Sarner as the Buttonmoulder; 2 June, 1944 with Ralph Richardson as Peer, Sybil Thorndike as Aase, Joyce Redman as Solveig, Grizelda Hervey as Ingrid, Russell Thorndike as the Dovre King, and Valentine Dyall as the Buttonmoulder; 30 Dec. 1959 (recorded repeat 17 Jan. 1960) with Michael Redgrave as Peer, Fay Compton as Aase, Frances Cuka as Solveig, Barbara Ashcroft as Ingrid, Peter Claughton as the Dovre King, and Haydn Jones as the Buttonmoulder.

Peer Gynt was produced on BBC Television in two parts, transmitted separately on 31 Oct. and 4 Nov. 1954, with Peter Ustinov as Peer, Mary O'Farrell as Aase, Josephine Crombie as Solveig, Rosalie Crutchley as the Green Clad Woman, Erik Chitty as the Troll King, and Clifford Evans as the Button-moulder. A London Festival Ballet production, with Grieg's music, adapted and produced by Charles R. Rogers, was televised on 28 May 1964, and repeated 16 Oct. 1964.

6. COLLABORATION WITH GRIEG

As *Peer Gynt* approached its third edition, Ibsen conceived the notion of adapt-ing it for stage production, and of reducing it in length by substituting musical passages for some of the scenes. On 23 January 1874 he wrote from Dresden about his plans to Edvard Grieg, at that time a man of thirty-one with a steadily rising reputation:

'Dear Mr. Grieg,

'I address these lines to you to inquire whether you might wish to participate in an enterprise which I have in mind.

'The matter is this. I mean to adapt *Peer Gynt*—the third edition of which will soon appear—for the stage. Will you compose the necessary music for it? Let me give you a brief indication of how I am thinking of arranging the play.

'The first Act is to be retained in full, with only one or two cuts in the dialogue. Peer Gynt's monologue on pages 23, 24 and 25 I wish to treat either as melodrama or partly as recitative. The wedding scene, page 28, must be made more of than there is in the book, by means of a ballet. For this a special dance melody will need composing, which will continue softly right until the end of the Act.

'In the second Act, the scene with the three sæter-girls, pages 57–60, is to be given musical treatment thought appropriate by the composer, but there must be some devilment in it! The monologue on pages 60–2 I imagined might be accompanied by chords, in the style of melodrama. The same applies to the scene between Peer and the Woman in Green, pages 63–6. There should also be some form of musical accompaniment to the scene in the Hall of the Dovre-Master, where, however, the speeches will be considerably shortened. The scene with the Boyg, which is also to be given in full, must also have musical accompaniment; the bird songs must be sung; there must be the sound of bell-ringing and psalm-singing in the distance.

'In Act III I need some chords, but not many, for the scene between Peer, the Woman and the Troll Child, pages 96–100. Similarly I imagine soft accompaniment from page 109 at the top to the bottom of page 112.

'More or less the whole of Act Four is to be omitted in performance. In its place I imagined a substantial musical tone-picture to represent Peer Gynt's wanderings about the world, in which American, English and French melodies might be heard as themes varying and fading. The chorus of Anitra and the girls, pages 144–5, are to be heard behind the curtain along with the orchestra. In the course of this, the curtain will go up and one will see like a distant dream-picture the tableau described at the bottom of page 164, where Solveig, now a middle-aged woman, sits singing in the sunlight outside her house. After her song the curtain slowly falls again, the orchestra continues the music which goes over to depict the storm at sea with which the fifth Act begins. The fifth Act, which in performance will be called the fourth or an epilogue, must be considerably abbreviated. Musical accompaniment is needed for pages 195–9. The scenes on the upturned boat and in the churchyard will be left out. Solveig sings on page 221, and the music continues to accompany Peer Gynt's following remarks, whereupon it then changes to the choruses on pages 222–5. The scenes with the Button-moulder and with the Dovre-Master are to be shortened. On page 254 the churchgoers sing on the path through the forest; the ringing of bells and the distant singing of psalms must be suggested by the music during what then follows until Solveig's song concludes the play, whereupon the curtain falls and the singing of psalms is once more heard closer and louder.

'This is roughly how I thought the whole work might be, and I beg to inquire whether you are willing to undertake the work?'

Grieg accepted the challenge; and on 8 February Ibsen wrote again:

'Dear Mr. Grieg

I am delighted to learn from your kind letter that you accept my proposal. How much music you wish to compose, and to which scenes, is of course entirely up to you; a composer's hands in this matter must be entirely free. Nor is there any objection to your postponing work on it until the summer; for the thing could not in any case be performed before next season. . . . '

The delay was, however, somewhat longer than expected. On 27 August 1874 Grieg wrote to his friend Frantz Beyer:

'... Things are going very slowly with "Peer Gynt", and there can be no thought of finishing this autumn. It is a frightfully intractable theme, apart from certain parts, for example where Solveig sings and where I have done it all. I've also done something of the Hall of the Dovre-Master which I literally can't bear to listen to—so full is it of cow platters, Norwegiomania and self-complacency! But I also expect that people will be able to sense the irony. Especially when Peer Gynt says afterwards, against his will: "I swear the dancing and music were both—quite good, or the cat can have me." '

Nor was the music ready by the following spring. On 3 March 1875 Ibsen wrote to Grieg: 'I can assure you that *Peer Gynt* cannot reckon with being performed within this season. You will therefore have the whole of the spring and the greater part of the summer at your disposal. I beg you most sincerely not to make any concessions on account of the poor level of the orchestra. Orchestrate your music by ideal standards, and let them up there worry about performing it.' Finally Grieg was able in the August of that year to report to Ibsen the completion of the score.

SELECT BIBLIOGRAPHY

(a) bibliographies
(b) biographies
(c) translations
(d) works of criticism

(a) BIBLIOGRAPHIES

Extensive bibliographical information is to be found in J. B. Halvorsen, *Norsk Forfatter–Lexikon 1814–1880*, vol. 3 (Christiania, 1892), pp. 1–89; Hjalmar Pettersen, *Henrik Ibsen 1828–1928, bedømt af Samtid og Eftertid* (Oslo, 1928); Reidar Øksnevad, *Norsk litteraturhistorisk bibliografi 1900–1945* (Oslo, 1951), pp. 163–222, and *Norsk litteraturhistorisk bibliografi 1946–1955* (Oslo, 1958), pp. 51–59; Ingrid Tedford, *Ibsen Bibliography 1928–57, Norsk bibliografisk bibliotek*, vol. 20 (Oslo, Bergen, 1961); and in the annual bibliographies of the *Ibsen-Årbok*, 1952 ff. Other bibliographical data, with particular emphasis on Ibsen's reception and standing in the English-speaking world, may be found in: Miriam A. Franc, *Ibsen in England* (Boston, U.S.A., 1919); Carl Burchardt, *Norwegian Life and Literature* (London, 1920), pp. 208–11; I. T. E. Firkins, *Henrik Ibsen: a bibliography of criticism and biography* (New York, 1921); Annette Andersen, 'Ibsen in America', in *Scandinavian Studies and Notes*, 14 (1937), pp. 65–109 and 115–55; and Brian W. Downs, 'Anglo-Norwegian literary relations 1867–1900', in *Modern Language Review*, xlvii, 4, Oct. 1952, pp. 449–94. For his reception in other countries, see: W. H. Eller, *Ibsen in Germany 1870–1900* (Boston, U.S.A., 1918); F. Meyen, *Ibsen-Bibliographie* (Brunswick, 1928); Wictor Hahn, *Henryk Ibsen w Polsce* (Lublin, 1929); B. A. Meuleman, *Ibsen en Nederland* (The Hague, 1931); H. Gregersen, *Ibsen and Spain* (Cambridge, Mass., 1936); Olav K. Lundeberg, 'Ibsen in France', *Scandinavian Studies and Notes*, 8 (1924–5), pp. 93–107; Kela Nyholm, 'Henrik Ibsen paa den franske Scene', in *Ibsen-Årbok 1957–59* (Skien, 1959), pp. 7–78; K. K. T. Wais, *Henrik Ibsens Wirkung in Spanien, Frankreich, Italien* (Brunswick, 1933); and N. Å. Nilsson, *Ibsen in Russland* (Stockholm, 1958).

(b) BIOGRAPHIES

Biographies available in English are: Henrik Jæger, *The Life of Henrik Ibsen*, tr. Clara Bell, with the verse done into English . . . by Edmund Gosse (London, 1890); Edmund Gosse, *Ibsen* (London, 1907); Adolf E. Zucker, *Ibsen the*

Master Builder (London, 1929); Theodore Jorgenson, *Henrik Ibsen: a study in art and personality* (Northfield, Minn., 1945); Bergliot Ibsen, *The Three Ibsens: memories of Henrik, Suzannah and Sigurd Ibsen*, tr. G. Schjelderup (London, 1951); Michael Meyer, *Henrik Ibsen*, 3 vols. (London, 1967–71); Hans Heiberg, *Ibsen: A Portrait of the Artist*, trans. Joan Tate (London, 1969); Halvdan Koht, *Life of Ibsen* (New York, 1971).

(c) TRANSLATIONS

(i) collected editions

The Pillars of Society, and other plays. [*The Pillars of Society*, tr. William Archer; *Ghosts*, tr. William Archer; *An Enemy of Society*, tr. Mrs. Eleanor Marx-Aveling.] Introduction by Havelock Ellis. (The Camelot Classics, London, 1888.)

Ibsen's Prose Dramas, ed. William Archer. Authorized English editions, 5 vols. (Walter Scott, London, 1890–1.) Vol. 1: *The League of Youth*, tr. William Archer; *The Pillars of Society*, tr. William Archer; *A Doll's House*, tr. William Archer. Vol. 2: *Ghosts*, tr. William Archer; *An Enemy of the People*, tr. Mrs. E. Marx-Aveling; *The Wild Duck*, tr. Mrs. F. E. Archer. Vol. 3: *Lady Inger of Ostråt*, tr. Charles Archer; *The Vikings at Helgeland*, tr. William Archer; *The Pretenders*, tr. William Archer. Vol. 4: *Emperor and Galilean*, tr. William Archer (based on an earlier translation by Catherine Ray). Vol. 5: *Rosmersholm*, tr. Charles Archer; *The Lady from the Sea*, tr. Mrs. F. E. Archer; *Hedda Gabler*, tr. William Archer.

The Prose Dramas of Henrik Ibsen, ed. Edmund Gosse. Lovell's Series of Foreign Literature. 3 vols. (New York and London, 1890.) Vol. 1: *A Doll's House, Pillars of Society, Ghosts*, all tr. William Archer; *Rosmersholm*, tr. M. Carmichael. Vol. 2: *The Lady from the Sea*, tr. Clara Bell; *An Enemy of Society*, tr. William Archer; *The Wild Duck*, tr. Mrs. E. Marx-Aveling; *The Young Men's League*, tr. Henry Carstarphen. Vol. 3: *Hedda Gabler*, tr. William Archer, with Preface by Edmund Gosse.

The Collected Works of Henrik Ibsen. Copyright edition. Revised and edited by William Archer. 12 vols. (Heinemann, London, 1906 ff.) Vol. 1 (1908): *Lady Inger of Ostråt*, tr. Charles Archer; *The Feast at Solhoug*, tr. William Archer and Mary Morison; *Love's Comedy*, tr. C. H. Herford. Vol. 2 (1906): *The Vikings at Helgeland*, tr. William Archer; *The Pretenders*, tr. William Archer. Vol. 3 (1906): *Brand*, tr. C. H. Herford. Vol. 4 (1907): *Peer Gynt*, tr. William and Charles Archer. Vol. 5 (1907): *Emperor and Galilean*, tr. William Archer. Vol. 6 (1906): *The League of Youth*, tr. William Archer; *Pillars of Society*, tr. William Archer. Vol. 7 (1907): *A Doll's House*, tr. William Archer; *Ghosts*, tr. William Archer. Vol. 8 (1907): *An Enemy of the People*, tr. Mrs. E. Marx-Aveling; *The Wild Duck*, tr. Mrs. F. E. Archer. Vol. 9 (1907): *Rosmersholm*, tr. Charles Archer; *The Lady from the Sea*, tr. Mrs. F. E. Archer. Vol. 10 (1907): *Hedda Gabler*, tr. Edmund Gosse and William Archer;

The Master Builder, tr. Edmund Gosse and William Archer. Vol. 11 (1907): *Little Eyolf*, tr. William Archer; *John Gabriel Borkman*, tr. William Archer; *When We Dead Awaken*, tr. William Archer. Vol. 12 (1912): *From Ibsen's Workshop*. Notes, scenarios, and drafts of modern plays, tr. A. G. Chater.

Early Plays, tr. Anders Orbeck (Amer.-Scand. Foundation, New York, 1921, and O.U.P., London, 1922): *Catiline; The Warrior's Barrow; Olaf Liljekrans*.

Everyman's Library (1910 ff.): *Lady Inger of Ostraat, Love's Comedy*, [and] *Rosmersholm*, tr. R. Farquharson Sharp (1915); *Brand*, tr. F. E. Garrett, with an introduction by P. H. Wicksteed (1915), re-issued with a new introduction by Brian W. Downs (1961); *Peer Gynt*, tr. R. Farquharson Sharp (1921); *The Pretenders, Pillars of Society*, [and] *Rosmersholm*, tr. R. Farquharson Sharp (1913); *A Doll's House, The Wild Duck*, [and] *The Lady from the Sea*, tr. R. Farquharson Sharp and Mrs. E. Marx-Aveling (1910); *Ghosts, The Warriors at Helgeland*, [and] *An Enemy of the People*, tr. R. Farquharson Sharp (1911); *Hedda Gabler, The Master Builder, John Gabriel Borkman*, tr. Eva Le Gallienne and Norman Ginsburg, intr. Brian W. Downs (1966).

Penguin volumes (1950 ff.): *Peer Gynt*, tr. Peter Watts; *A Doll's House, and other plays* [*The League of Youth, The Lady from the Sea*], tr. Peter Watts; *Ghosts, and other plays* [*A Public Enemy, When We Dead Wake*], tr. Peter Watts; *The Master Builder, and other plays* [*Rosmersholm, Little Eyolf, John Gabriel Borkman*], tr. Una Ellis-Fermor; *Hedda Gabler, and other plays* [*Pillars of the Community, The Wild Duck*], tr. Una Ellis-Fermor.

The Plays of Ibsen, tr. Michael Meyer (Rupert Hart-Davis, London, 1960 ff.): *The Pretenders; Brand; Peer Gynt; Pillars of Society; A Doll's House; Ghosts; An Enemy of the People; The Wild Duck; Rosmersholm; The Lady from the Sea; Hedda Gabler; The Master Builder; Little Eyolf; John Gabriel Borkman; When We Dead Awaken.*

Six Plays by Henrik Ibsen, tr. Eva Le Gallienne (Modern Library, New York, 1957): *A Doll's House; Ghosts; An Enemy of the People; Rosmersholm; Hedda Gabler; The Master Builder.*

Signet Classics: *Peer Gynt*, tr. Rolf Fjelde (New York, 1965); *Four Major Plays*, vols. 1 and 2, trans. Rolf Fjelde (New York, 1965 and 1970)—Vol. 1: *A Doll's House, The Wild Duck, Hedda Gabler, The Master Builder*; Vol. 2: *Ghosts, An Enemy of the People, The Lady from the Sea, John Gabriel Borkman.*

Bantam Classics: *Last plays of Henrik Ibsen*, tr. Arvid Paulson (New York, 1962) [*Rosmersholm; Hedda Gabler; The Master Builder; John Gabriel Borkman; When We Dead Awaken*].

Letters, articles, and speeches:
The Correspondence of Henrik Ibsen, ed. Mary Morison (London, 1905).
Speeches and New Letters, tr. Arne Kildal, with bibliographical index (Boston, 1910, and London, 1911).
Ibsen: Letters and Speeches, ed. Evert Sprinchorn (New York, 1964, and London, 1965).

*

The standard German edition of the works is: *Henrik Ibsens sämtliche Werke in deutscher Sprache*. Durchgesehen und eingeleitet von Georg Brandes, Julius Elias, Paul Schlenther, 10 vols. (Berlin, 1898 ff.)

The standard French edition of the works is: *Œuvres complètes*, traduits par P. G. la Chesnais, 16 vols. (Paris, 1914–45.)

(ii) individual translations into English of the works in this volume:

'The epic Brand': translated by Theodore Jorgenson, in *In the Mountain Wilderness and other works by Henrik Ibsen* (Northfield, Minn., 1957), pp. 65–110; and selected extracts by G. M. Gathorne-Hardy, in *Brand* (Oslo and London, 1966).

Brand: translated by C. H. Herford, F. E. Garrett, Michael Meyer, as above (Herford and Garrett originally published in 1894); and additionally by William Wilson (i.e. More Adey) into prose in 1891, by James Forsyth (very freely, as a stage version) in 1960, by Theodore Jorgenson in 1962, and by G. M. Gathorne-Hardy in 1966.

Peer Gynt: by William and Charles Archer (first published 1892), by R. Farquharson Sharp, Peter Watts, Michael Meyer and Rolf Fjelde, as above; and additionally by R. Ellis Roberts in 1912, by G. Hult in 1933, by Norman Ginsbury in 1946, by Paul Green in 1952, by H. M. Finney in 1955, and by Kay Jurgensen and Robert Schenkkan in 1967 (the last three all published in the USA).

(d) WORKS OF CRITICISM

(i) general studies, in English, arranged chronologically

Edmund Gosse, *Studies in the Literature of Northern Europe* (London, 1879), pp. 35–69.

Georg Brandes, *Eminent authors of the Nineteenth Century*, tr. Rasmus B. Anderson (New York, 1886), pp. 405–60.

Havelock Ellis, *The New Spirit* (London, 1890), pp. 133–73.

George Bernard Shaw, *The Quintessence of Ibsenism* (London, 1891)—second edition 'completed to the death of Ibsen', London, 1913.

Philip H. Wicksteed, *Four lectures on Henrik Ibsen dealing chiefly with his metrical works* (London, 1892).

F. Anstey [i.e. Thomas Anstey Guthrie], *Mr. Punch's Pocket Ibsen*. A collection of some of the master's best-known dramas. Condensed, revised, and slightly rearranged for the benefit of the earnest student (London, 1893).

'Zanoni' [pseud.], *Ibsen and the Drama* (London, [? 1894]).

H. H. Boyesen, *A Commentary on the Works of Henrik Ibsen* (London, 1894).

Edward Russell, *Ibsen*. A lecture delivered at University College, Liverpool, 26 Jan. 1894 (Liverpool, 1894).

George Bernard Shaw, *Our Theatres in the Nineties*. 3 vols. (London, 1932)—being dramatic criticisms contributed week by week to *The Saturday Review* from Jan. 1895 to May 1898.

Henry James, *The Scenic Art*, ed. Allan Wade (London, 1949), pp. 243–60, 286–94—including: 'On the occasion of Hedda Gabler', *New Review*, June 1891; 'The Master Builder', *Pall Mall Gazette*, 17 Feb. 1893; 'Little Eyolf', 'John Gabriel Borkman', *Harper's Weekly*, 23 Jan., 6 Feb., 1897.

Edward Russell and Percy Cross Standing, *Ibsen on his merits* (London, 1897).

Georg Brandes, *Henrik Ibsen, Bjørnstjerne Bjørnson.* Critical studies (London, 1899.)

Max Beerbohm, *Around Theatres* (London, 1953)—being dramatic criticisms May 1898–April 1910, including: 'An hypocrisy in play-going' [on *Hedda Gabler* played in Italian, Oct. 1903], pp. 277–81; 'Ibsen' [an obituary, May 1906], pp. 432–6; 'A memorable performance' [on *Rosmersholm*, Feb. 1908], pp. 497–501.

James Joyce, 'Ibsen's new drama' [i.e. *When We Dead Awaken*], *Fortnightly Review*, 73, 1900, pp. 575–90.

James Huneker, *Iconoclasts: a book of dramatists* (London, 1905), pp. 1–138.

Arthur Symons, *Figures of Several Centuries* (London, 1916), pp. 222–67. 'Henrik Ibsen', written 1906.

Jeanette Lee, *The Ibsen Secret*. A key to the prose dramas of Henrik Ibsen (London, 1907).

Haldane Macfall, *Ibsen: the man, his art and his significance* (London, 1907).

G. Saintsbury, *The Later Nineteenth Century* (London, 1907), pp. 307–26.

G. A. Mounsey, *The Life Work of Hendrik Ibsen from the Russian of Merejkowski* (n.d. [? 1908]).

J. Moses Montrose, *Henrik Ibsen: the man and his plays* (New York, 1908).

James Huneker, *Egoists: a book of supermen* (London, 1909), pp. 317–39.

Edward Dowden, *Essays, modern and Elizabethan* (London, 1910), pp. 26–60.

Archibald Henderson, *Interpreters of life and the modern spirit* (London, 1911), pp. 157–283.

Otto Heller, *Henrik Ibsen: plays and problems* (New York, 1912).

R. Ellis Roberts, *Henrik Ibsen: a critical study* (London, 1912).

Henry Rose, *Henrik Ibsen: poet, mystic and moralist* (London, 1913).

William Archer, 'The true greatness of Ibsen', a lecture delivered at University College, London. *Edda*, xii, 1919, pp. 175–91.

Carl Burchardt, *Norwegian life and literature* (London, 1920).

Storm Jameson, *Modern Drama in Europe* (London, 1920).

Janko Lavrin, *Ibsen and his creation*. A psycho-critical study (London, 1921).

T. M. Campbell, *Hebbel, Ibsen and the analytical exposition* (Heidelberg, 1922).

Illit Grøndahl and Ola Raknes, *Chapters in Norwegian Literature* (London, 1923), pp. 186–215.

Basil King, 'Ibsen and Emilie Bardach', *Century Magazine* (New York), 1923: Oct. pp. 803–15, Nov. pp. 83–92.

Benedetto Croce, *European Literature in the Nineteenth Century* (London, 1924), pp. 326–43.

Hermann J. Weigand, *The modern Ibsen: a reconsideration* (New York, 1925).

Paul Henry Grumman, *Henrik Ibsen: an introduction to his life and works* (New York, 1928).

Elizabeth Robins, *Ibsen and the actress* (London, 1928).

Bonamy Dobrée, *The Lamp and the Lute* (Oxford, 1929), pp. 1–20.

Harley Granville-Barker, 'The coming of Ibsen', in *The Eighteen Eighties*, Essays by Fellows of the Royal Society of Literature, ed. Walter de la Mare (Cambridge, 1930), pp. 159–96.

J. G. Robertson, *Essays and addresses on literature* (London, 1935), pp. 147–226.

A. Anstensen, *The Proverb in Ibsen* (Columbia U.P. and London, 1935).

E. M. Forster, *Abinger Harvest* (London, 1936), including chapter on 'Ibsen the Romantic'.

Theodore Jorgenson, *Henrik Ibsen: a study in art and personality* (Northfield, Minn., 1945).

Ronald Peacock, *The Poet in the Theatre* (London, 1946), pp. 65–71.

Brian W. Downs, *Ibsen: the intellectual background* (Cambridge, 1946).

Barrett H. Clark and George Freedley, *A History of Modern Drama* (New York and London, 1947), pp. 1–20—chapter by Alrik Gustafson.

Eric Bentley, *The Modern Theatre* (London, 1948), pp. 64–90 and *passim*.

M. C. Bradbrook, *Ibsen the Norwegian* (London, 1948).

P. F. D. Tennant, *Ibsen's Dramatic Technique* (Cambridge, 1948).

Alan Reynolds Thompson, *The Dry Mock* (Berkeley, Cal., 1948), pp. 197–244: 'Ibsen'.

Francis Fergusson, *The Idea of a Theatre* (Princeton U.P. and London, 1949)— with special reference to *Ghosts*.

Brian W. Downs, *A study of six plays by Ibsen* (Cambridge, 1950).

Janko Lavrin, *Ibsen: an approach* (London, 1950).

Raymond Williams, *Drama from Ibsen to Eliot* (London, 1952); 2nd rev. ed. *Drama from Ibsen to Brecht* (London, 1969).

John Northam, *Ibsen's Dramatic Method: a study of the prose dramas* (London, 1953).

G. K. Chesterton, *A Handful of Authors* (London, 1953), pp. 134–58: 'Henrik Ibsen', articles written in 1906 and 1928.

J. T. Farrell, *Reflections at Fifty, and other essays* (New York, 1954), pp. 66–96: 'Joyce and Ibsen'.

Francis Bull, *Ibsen: the man and the dramatist*. Taylorian Lecture (Oxford, 1954).

Eric Bentley, *In search of theatre* (London, 1954), pp. 365–80.

Eva Le Gallienne, *Hedda Gabler*, A preface . . . with a new translation (London, 1955), and *The Master Builder*, a translation . . . with a prefatory study (London, 1955).

T. R. Henn, *The Harvest of Tragedy* (London, 1956), pp. 172–88: 'A Note on Ibsen'.

J. W. McFarlane, *Ibsen and the Temper of Norwegian Literature* (London, 1960).

Una Ellis-Fermor, *Shakespeare the Dramatist* (London, 1961): chap. on 'Ibsen and Shakespeare as dramatic artists'.

J. Setterquist, *Ibsen and the beginnings of Anglo-Irish drama* (Harvard U.P., 1961).

Kenneth Muir, *Last Periods of Shakespeare, Racine and Ibsen* (Liverpool U.P., 1962).

F. L. Lucas, *The Drama of Ibsen and Strindberg* (London, 1962).

G. Wilson Knight, *Ibsen* (Edinburgh, 1962).

J. W. McFarlane (ed.), *Discussions of Ibsen* (Boston, U.S.A., 1962)—essays by various hands.

M. J. Valency, *The flower and the castle* (New York, 1964).

R. Brustein, *The Theatre of Revolt* (New York, 1964, and London, 1965), pp. 35–84: 'Henrik Ibsen'.

Rolf Fjelde (ed.), *Twentieth-century views on Ibsen* (New York, 1965)—essays by various hands.

John Northam, *Dividing Worlds* [on *The Tempest* and *Rosmersholm*] (Kristiansand, 1965).

Daniel Haakonsen (ed.), *Contemporary Approaches to Ibsen*, no. 1, Ibsen Yearbook, vol. 8 (Oslo, 1966).

B. W. Downs, *Modern Norwegian Literature 1860–1918* (Cambridge U.P., 1966), pp. 43–64 and 116–32.

Raymond Williams, *Modern Tragedy* (London, 1966).

Bernard de B. Nicol, *Varieties of dramatic experience* (London, 1969), pp. 153–72.

J. W. McFarlane (ed.), *Henrik Ibsen*. Penguin critical anthology (London, 1970).

Orley J. Holtan, *Mythic patterns in Ibsen's last plays* (Minneapolis, 1970).

Daniel Haakonsen (ed.), *Contemporary Approaches to Ibsen*, no. 2, Ibsen Yearbook, vol. 11 (Oslo, 1971).

(ii) other studies in English of the plays in this volume—extra to those items mentioned in the Appendices, pp. 447–8 and 500–1—include:

(*a*) BRAND: W. H. Auden, *The Dyer's Hand* (London, 1963), pp. 433–55: 'Genius and Apostle'; Harald Beyer, 'Ibsen's *Brand*', in *The Norseman*, viii, Jan./Feb. 1950, pp. 65–70; C. E. W. L. Dahlstrøm, 'Brand—Ibsen's bigot', in *Scandinavian Studies and Notes*, xxii, 1950, pp. 1–13; Irving Deer, 'Ibsen's *Brand*: Paradox and the Symbolic Hero', in *Ibsen. A collection of critical essays*, ed. Rolf Fjelde (Englewood Cliffs, N.J., 1965), pp. 52–62; Richard Findlater, 'Two Brands of Ibsen', in *Twentieth Century*, clxviii, 1960, pp. 337–42; G. M. Gathorne-Hardy, 'A stage version of *Brand*', in *The Norseman*, viii, Mar./Apr. 1950, pp. 122–9; John Hems, 'Abraham and Brand' [on Kierkegaard and Ibsen], in *Philosophy*, xxxix, 1964, pp. 137–44; F. W. Kaufmann, 'Ibsen's conception of truth', in *Germanic Review*, xxxii, 2, Apr. 1957, pp. 83–92; Edward McInnes, 'Ibsen and Poetic Drama', in *Forum for Modern Language Studies*, ii, 1966, pp. 141–9; Julius E. Olson, 'Gerd, the hawk, and the ice-church in Ibsen's *Brand'*, in *Scandinavian Studies and Notes*, vi, 1920/21, pp. 127–33; Martin B. Ruud, 'The story of the publication of Ibsen's *Brand'*, in *Scandinavian Studies and Notes*, v, 1918/19, pp. 91–5; H. A. Smith, 'Dipsychus among the shadows', in *Contemporary Theatre* (Stratford upon Avon Studies, no. 4, 1962), pp. 139–62; Miguel Unamuno, *Perplexities and Paradoxes* (New York, 1945), pp. 51–7: 'Ibsen and Kierkegaard'; A. E. Zucker, 'Ibsen – Hettner – Coriolanus – Brand', in *Modern Language Notes*, li, 2, 1936, pp. 99–106.

(b) PEER GYNT: Odd-Stein Anderssen, 'Before the century of *Peer Gynt'*, in *World Theatre* (Brussels), xii, 4, 1963–64, pp. 281–300; A. le Roy Andrews, 'Ibsen's *Peer Gynt* and Goethe's *Faust'*, in *Journal of English and Germanic Philology*, xiii, 1914, pp. 238–46; and 'Further influences upon Ibsen's *Peer Gynt'*, ibid., xv, 1915, pp. 51–5; A. Anstensen, 'Notes on the text of Ibsen's *Peer Gynt'*, in *Journal of English and Germanic Philology*, xxix, Jan. 1930, pp. 53–73; Sverre Arestad, 'Peer Gynt and the Idea of Self', in *Modern Drama*, iii, 2, Sept. 1960, pp. 103–22; W. H. Auden, see (a) above; Harry Bergholz, 'Peer Gynt's Redemption', in *Edda*, lxix, 1969, pp. 10–20; S. Bishop, 'Ibsen's *Peer Gynt:* a philosophy of life', in *Sewanee Review*, xvii, Oct. 1909, pp. 475–87; Ivor Brown, 'Peer Gynt', in *Saturday Review*, lxxxix, Feb. 1925, pp. 156–7; Trevor H. Davies, *Spiritual voices in modern literature* (New York, 1919), pp. 39–69: 'The ignominy of half-heartedness: Peer Gynt'; G. P. Dilla, 'Peer Gynt', in *English Journal* (Chicago), xi, Feb. 1922, pp. 108–10; Lee Rosenblum Edwards, 'A structural analysis of *Peer Gynt'*, in *Modern Drama*, viii, 1966, pp. 28–39; Rolf Fjelde, 'Peer Gynt, Naturalism, and the Dissolving Self', in *Drama Review*, xiii, 2, 1968, pp. 28–43; Rolf Fjelde and Sverre Arestad, 'Translating *Peer Gynt'*, in *Modern Drama*, x, 1967, pp. 104–10; Ronald Gaskell, 'Symbol and Reality in *Peer Gynt'*, in *Drama Survey*, iv, 1965, pp. 57–64; Georg Groddeck, 'Peer Gynt', in *Ibsen. A collection of critical essays*, ed. Rolf Fjelde (Englewood Cliffs, N.J., 1965), pp. 63–79; Einar Haugen, 'On translating *Peer Gynt'*, in *Scandinavian Studies*, xiv, 8, 1937, pp. 187–98; John Horten, 'Ibsen, Grieg and *Peer Gynt'*, in *Music and Letters*, Apr. 1945, pp. 66–77; James R. Hurt, 'Fantastic scenes in *Peer Gynt'*, in *Modern Drama*, v, 5, 1962, pp. 37–41; Harold Jeffreys, 'Ibsen's *Peer Gynt:* a psychoanalytical study', in *Psychoanalytical Review*, xi, 1924, pp. 361–402; and 'Some points in the interpretation of *Peer Gynt'*, in *Scandinavica*, iii, 1964, pp. 56–8; F. W. Kaufmann, 'Ibsen's search for the Authentic Self', in *Monatshefte*, xlv, 1953, pp. 232–9; H. Logeman, *A commentary, critical and explanatory, on the Norwegian text of Henrik Ibsen's 'Peer Gynt', its language, literary associations and folklore* (The Hague, 1917); and 'The "caprices" in Henrik Ibsen's *Peer Gynt'*, in *Edda*, vii, 1917, pp. 258–85; R. K. Nitschke, 'Peer Gynt in Poland', in *Edda*, lxviii, 1968, pp. 138–9; Julius E. Olson, 'Phases of Ibsen's authorship. I. Subconscious elements in the composition of *Peer Gynt*. II. The hiatus between

Ibsen's dramatic poems and the social dramas', in *Scandinavian Studies and Notes*, vii, 1921/23, pp. 65–80; Robert R. Reed, 'Boss Mangan, Peer Gynt and *Heartbreak House*', in *Shaw Review*, ii, 7, Jan. 1959, pp. 6–12; Jacob W. Richardson, '*Peer Gynt*: study and exposition', in *Holborn Review*, July 1928, pp. 306–16; Viva Schatia, '*Peer Gynt*: a study of insecurity', in *Psychoanalytical Review*, xxv, 1938, pp. 49–52; Denzell Smith, 'The relationship of setting and idea in *Peer Gynt*', in *Modern Drama*, xiii, 1970, pp. 169–73; H. Steinhauer, '*Faust* and *Peer Gynt*', in *Queen's Quarterly*, xxxv, Apr. 1928, pp. 364–9; Wilhelm Stekel, 'Analytical comments on Ibsen's *Peer Gynt*', in *Psyche and Eros*, i, 1920, pp. 152–6; A. M. Sturtevant, 'Ibsen's *Peer Gynt* and *Paa Vidderne*', in *Journal of English and Germanic Philology*, ix, 1910, pp. 43–8; and 'Three notes on Ibsen's *Peer Gynt*', in *Publications of the Society for the Advancement of Scandinavian Studies*, i, 1912/14, pp. 27–37; and 'Some phases of Ibsen's symbolism', ibid., ii, 1914/15, pp. 25–49; and 'Regarding "Subconscious elements in the composition of *Peer Gynt*" ' [see J. E. Olson, above], in *Scandinavian Studies and Notes*, vii, 1921/23, pp. 201–7; A. H. Winsnes, 'Some notes on the historical background of *Peer Gynt*' in *Ibsen's Peer Gynt* (London, 1944)—a Souvenir of the Old Vic production of 1944; Jules Zentner, '*Peer Gynt*—the quest for shine and the giving way of a loop', in *Scandinavica*, ix, 1970, pp. 116–26; A. E. Zucker, 'Heine's Uncle and *Peer Gynt*', in *Germanic Review*, xviii, 1933, pp. 40–3; and 'Goethe and Ibsen's Button Moulder', in *PMLA*, lvii, 4, pp. 1101–7.

(iii) secondary literature in other languages (especially Scandinavian) bearing generally or specifically on the plays in this volume is very extensive; the following selected items may be found useful:

(a) GENERAL: Emil Reich, *Henrik Ibsens Dramen* (Berlin, 1894, 14th ed. 1925); Roman Woerner, *Ibsen* (Munich, 1900, 3rd ed. 1922), 2 vols.; Henning Kehler, 'Studier i det ibsenske Drama', in *Edda*, 1915–16, iv, pp. 169–217 and v, pp. 40–98, 258–308; Erik Kihlman, *Ur Ibsen-dramatikens Idéhistoria* (Helsingfors, 1921); Arne Duve, *Symbolikken i Henrik Ibsens Skuespill* (Oslo, 1945), and *Ibsen—bak kulissene* (Oslo, 1971); C. Stuyver, *Ibsens dramatische Gestalten. Psychologie und Symbolik* (Amsterdam, 1952); Peter Szondi, *Theorie des modernen Dramas* (Frankfurt a. M., 1956); Harald Beyer, *Nietzsche og Norden* (Bergen, 1959), vol. ii.

(b) IBSEN IN ITALY: Øyvind Anker, 'Ibsen og Den skandinaviske Forening i Roma', in *Edda*, lvi, 1956, pp. 161–77; Vilhelm Bergsøe, *Henrik Ibsen paa Ischia og 'Fra Piazzo del Popolo'. Erindringer fra Aarene 1863–69* (Copenhagen, 1907); Francis Bull, 'Le premier séjour à Rome d'Ibsen et de Bjørnson', in *Revue de la littérature comparée*, ix, Jan. 1929, pp. 105–16, reprinted as 'Bjørnsons og Ibsens første romerophold', in *Essays i utvalg* (Oslo, 1964); Lorentz Dietrichson, *Svundne Tider I–IV* (Christiania, 1896–1917); Einar Østvedt, *Henrik Ibsen og la bella Italia* (Oslo, 1956).

(c) VERSIFICATION: André Bjerke, *Rim og rytme* (Oslo, 1956), pp. 21–35 [on *Brand* and *Peer Gynt*]; Leif Mæhle, *Ibsens rimteknikk* (Oslo, 1955).

(d) BRAND: Karl Bäschlin, 'Gefahren des Idealismus, veranschaulicht an Ibsens *Brand*' in *Gegenwart* (Bern), xix, 2, May 1957, pp. 83–90; E. Berggrav and F. Bull, *Ibsens sjelelige krise* (Oslo, 1937); H. Beyer, *Norsk og fremmed* (Oslo, 1961), pp. 103–18: 'Dunkle symboler i *Brand*'; Just Bing, *Henrik Ibsens Brand. En kritisk studie* (Christiania, 1919); Erik Bollerup, 'Om Ibsens *Brand* og Rydbergs *Prometheus og Ahasverus*', in *Nordisk tidskrift*, xliii, 1967, pp. 269–80; Pavel Frænkl, 'Ibsens *Brand* og europeisk titanisme', in *Edda*, lvi, 1956, pp. 324–37; H. W. Freihow, *Henrik Ibsens 'Brand'* (Oslo, 1936); D. Haakonsen, 'Henrik Ibsens *Brand*', in *Edda*, xli, 1941, pp. 350–78; Arild Haaland, 'Barnemorderen fra Betlehem', in *Samtiden*, lxxviii, 1969, pp. 311–22; Victor Hellern, '*Brand*: symboler og tolkninger', in *Edda*, lvi, 1956, pp. 91–110; Else Høst, 'Ibsens lyriske dramaer', in *Edda*, xli, 1941, pp. 379–406; Assar Janzén, 'Ibsens *Brand*: En självuppgörelse', in *Göteborgsstudier i litteraturhistorie tillägnade Sverker Ek* (Gothenburg, 1954), pp. 105–24; B. M. Kinck, 'Dramaet *Brand*', in *Edda*, xxx, 1930, pp. 81–94; P. G. La Chesnais, *Brand d'Ibsen. Étude et analyse* (Paris, 1933); Åse H. Lervik, *Ibsens verskunst i 'Brand'* (Oslo, 1969); Einar Molland, 'Ibsens *Brand* som religiøs idédiktning', in *Nordisk teologi: Festskrift til Ragnar Bring* (Lund, 1955), pp. 1–23; John Nome, *Dikternes verden* (Oslo, 1969), pp. 16–36; E. Skard, 'Slutreplikkene i Ibsens *Brand*', in *Edda*, lxiv, 1964, pp. 154–6; S. Svensson, '*Brand* och den svenska göticismen', in *Edda*, xxx, 1930, pp. 316–98.

(e) PEER GYNT: Karl Bäschlin, 'Zeitbetrachtungen an Hand von Ibsens *Peer Gynt*', in *Gegenwart*, xviii, 12, March 1957, pp. 475–83; H. Beyer, *Henrik Ibsens 'Peer Gynt'* (Oslo, 1928, 3rd ed. 1967); Milada Blekastad, 'Speculum og analogi i *Peer Gynt*', in *Tradisjon og fornyelse: Festskrift til A. H. Winsnes* (Oslo, 1960), pp. 239–59; Francis Bull, *Henrik Ibsens Peer Gynt* (Oslo, 1947, 2nd ed. 1956); Chr. Collin, *Det geniale menneske* (Christiania, 1914), pp. 33–55 and 101–13; Franz Fischer, *Der abendländische Mensch in der Entscheidung* (Vienna, 1954), pp. 49–69; D. Haakonsen, *Henrik Ibsens 'Peer Gynt'* (Oslo, 1967); Otto Hageberg, *Omkring 'Peer Gynt'* (Oslo, 1967), including essays by Arne Garborg, Hans Larsson, Hans Jacob Nilsen, Egil Wyller, Edvard Beyer, et al.; Gunnar Høst, 'Le conte de Per Gynt point de départ du *Peer Gynt* d'Ibsen', in *Revue de la littérature comparée*, xi, 1931, pp. 262–8; Werner Kohlschmidt, *Die entzweite Welt* (Gladbeck, 1953), pp. 50–68: 'Das Motiv der Entscheidung in Ibsens *Peer Gynt*'; R. Koskimies, *Der nordische Faust* (Helsinki, 1965); Arne Lidén, 'Peer Gynt i Egypten', in *Edda*, xl, 1940, pp. 237–64; H. Noreng, 'Litt om dyresymbolikken i *Peer Gynt*' in *Norsk litterær årbok* (Oslo, 1968), pp. 33–53; Gunhild Ramm, 'Solveigskikkelsen i *Peer Gynt*' in *Ibsen-Årbok 1967* (Oslo, 1967), pp. 32–47; F. J. Schöningh,

'Der unbekannte Ibsen: Bemerkungen zu *Peer Gynt*', in *Hochland* (Munich), xliv, 1950/51, pp. 116–37; Finn Thorn, *Henrik Ibsens 'Peer Gynt'* (Oslo, 1971); Leif Tjersland, ' "Den fremmede passager" i *Peer Gynt*' in *Ibsen–Årbok 1953* (Skien, 1953), pp. 72–81; Harald Tveterås, 'Botten Hansens *Huldrebryl-luppet* og Ibsens *Peer Gynt*', in *Edda*, lxvii, 1967, pp. 247–62.